The Value of Empathy

The Value of Empathy explores various approaches to understanding empathy and investigates its moral and practical role.

The central role of empathy in understanding others, and the need for it in our social and inter-personal encounters, is widely acknowledged by philosophers, social scientists and psychologists alike. Discussions of empathy abound, not only in more specialised academic publications, but also in traditional and social media. Yet neither a clear understanding, nor a uniform definition of this relatively new term is available. Indeed, one difficulty in discussing empathy, in philosophy and beyond, is the profusion of definitions; the difficulty is compounded by a lack of clarity in the distinction between empathy and cognate concepts such as sympathy and compassion.

This book has two aims: Chapters 1–5 seek to address the dual concerns of the lack of clarity and profusion of interpretations by suggesting new ways of approaching the topic. The second aim of the book is to connect the more abstract discussions of empathy with its normative functions. Chapters 6–8 engage with the theoretical concerns relevant to the ethics of empathy and raise interesting points about its significance in ethical thought and action. The final four chapters focus on the practical normative significance of empathy by examining the connections between empathy, vulnerability and care in circumstances of ill health.

The chapters in this book were originally published in the *International Journal of Philosophical Studies*.

Maria Baghramian is Full Professor of American Philosophy in the School of Philosophy at University College Dublin (UCD) and the Co-founder and Co-director of the Cognitive Science Programme at UCD. She is also a Member of the Royal Irish Academy. Currently she coordinates the Horizon 2020 project Policy, Expertise and Trust in Action (PEriTiA).

Meliné Papazian is completing a PhD in Cognitive Science on Empathy at University College Dublin. She has given conference papers and conducted workshops in France, Italy, Netherlands, Armenia and Ireland. She was also one of the editors of *Perspectives, International Postgraduate Journal of Philosophy*. In a previous life, she counselled victims of domestic violence in Los Angeles.

Rowland Stout is Professor of Philosophy at University College Dublin, a Member of the Royal Irish Academy and Editor of the *International Journal of Philosophical Studies*. He is Director of the UCD Centre for Ethics in Public Life and Team Leader for the Work Package on the Ethics of Trust within the EU Horizon 2020 project PEriTiA (Policy, Expertise and Trust in Action).

The Value of Empathy

Edited by
Maria Baghramian, Meliné Papazian and Rowland Stout

LONDON AND NEW YORK

First published 2021
by Routledge
2 Park Square, Milton Park, Abingdon, Oxon OX14 4RN

and by Routledge
52 Vanderbilt Avenue, New York, NY 10017

Routledge is an imprint of the Taylor & Francis Group, an informa business

© 2021 Taylor & Francis

All rights reserved. No part of this book may be reprinted or reproduced or utilised in any form or by any electronic, mechanical, or other means, now known or hereafter invented, including photocopying and recording, or in any information storage or retrieval system, without permission in writing from the publishers.

Trademark notice: Product or corporate names may be trademarks or registered trademarks, and are used only for identification and explanation without intent to infringe.

British Library Cataloguing in Publication Data
A catalogue record for this book is available from the British Library

ISBN 13: 978-0-367-47818-6

Typeset in MinionPro
by Newgen Publishing UK

Publisher's Note
The publisher accepts responsibility for any inconsistencies that may have arisen during the conversion of this book from journal articles to book chapters, namely the inclusion of journal terminology.

Disclaimer
Every effort has been made to contact copyright holders for their permission to reprint material in this book. The publishers would be grateful to hear from any copyright holder who is not here acknowledged and will undertake to rectify any errors or omissions in future editions of this book.

Contents

Citation Information	vii
Notes on Contributors	x
Introduction: The Value of Empathy *Maria Baghramian, Meliné Papazian and Rowland Stout*	1
1 The Relational Value of Empathy *Monika Betzler*	15
2 Relational Empathy *Mark Fagiano*	41
3 Language, Behaviour, and Empathy. G.H. Mead's and W.V.O. Quine's Naturalized Theories of Meaning *Guido Baggio*	59
4 No Empathy for Empathy: An Existential Reading of Husserl's Forgotten Question *Iraklis Ioannidis*	80
5 Finding Empathy: How Neuroscientific Measures, Evidence and Conceptualizations Interact *Riana J. Betzler*	103
6 The Contribution of Empathy to Ethics *Sarah Songhorian*	123
7 The Empathetic Soldier *Kevin Cutright*	144
8 Sentimentalist Practical Reason and Self-Sacrifice *Michael Slote*	165

9	Pathophobia, Vices, and Illness *Ian James Kidd*	183
10	Beyond Empathy: Vulnerability, Relationality and Dementia *Danielle Petherbridge*	204
11	Empathy, Respect, and Vulnerability *Elisa Magrì*	224
12	Empathy, Vulnerability and Anxiety *Rowland Stout*	244
	Index	255

Citation Information

The following chapters, except Chapter 8, were originally published in the *International Journal of Philosophical Studies*, volume 27, issue 2 (2019). Chapter 8 was originally published in the *International Journal of Philosophical Studies*, volume 26, issue 3 (2018). When citing this material, please use the original page numbering for each article, as follows:

Chapter 1
The Relational Value of Empathy
Monika Betzler
International Journal of Philosophical Studies, volume 27, issue 2 (2019), pp. 136–161

Chapter 2
Relational Empathy
Mark Fagiano
International Journal of Philosophical Studies, volume 27, issue 2 (2019), pp. 162–179

Chapter 3
Language, Behaviour, and Empathy. G.H. Mead's and W.V.O. Quine's Naturalized Theories of Meaning
Guido Baggio
International Journal of Philosophical Studies, volume 27, issue 2 (2019), pp. 180–200

Chapter 4
No Empathy for Empathy: An Existential Reading of Husserl's Forgotten Question
Iraklis Ioannidis
International Journal of Philosophical Studies, volume 27, issue 2 (2019), pp. 201–223

Chapter 5
Finding Empathy: How Neuroscientific Measures, Evidence and Conceptualizations Interact
Riana J. Betzler
International Journal of Philosophical Studies, volume 27, issue 2 (2019), pp. 224–243

Chapter 6
The Contribution of Empathy to Ethics
Sarah Songhorian
International Journal of Philosophical Studies, volume 27, issue 2 (2019), pp. 244–264

Chapter 7
The Empathetic Soldier
Kevin Cutright
International Journal of Philosophical Studies, volume 27, issue 2 (2019), pp. 265–285

Chapter 8
Sentimentalist Practical Reason and Self-Sacrifice
Michael Slote
International Journal of Philosophical Studies, volume 26, issue 3 (2018), pp. 419–436

Chapter 9
Pathophobia, Vices, and Illness
Ian James Kidd
International Journal of Philosophical Studies, volume 27, issue 2 (2019), pp. 286–306

Chapter 10
Beyond Empathy: Vulnerability, Relationality and Dementia
Danielle Petherbridge
International Journal of Philosophical Studies, volume 27, issue 2 (2019), pp. 307–326

Chapter 11
Empathy, Respect, and Vulnerability
Elisa Magrì
International Journal of Philosophical Studies, volume 27, issue 2 (2019), pp. 327–346

Chapter 12
Empathy, Vulnerability and Anxiety
Rowland Stout
International Journal of Philosophical Studies, volume 27, issue 2 (2019), pp. 347–357

For any permission-related enquiries please visit:
www.tandfonline.com/page/help/permissions

Notes on Contributors

Guido Baggio is Research Associate in Theoretical Philosophy in the Department of Philosophy, Communication and Performing Arts at Roma Tre University, Rome. His main research interests concern American philosophy, pragmatism, historical–conceptual and methodological interactions between philosophy, psychology and cognitive science. He has published a volume on *The Philosophy of Psychology of G. H. Mead* (2015) and various articles and essays in international journals and collected volumes.

Maria Baghramian is Full Professor of American Philosophy in the School of Philosophy, University College Dublin (UCD) and the Co-founder and Co-director of the Cognitive Science Programme in UCD. She is also a Member of the Royal Irish Academy. Currently she coordinates the Horizon 2020 project Policy, Expertise and Trust in Action (PEriTiA). Her most recent publications include *Relativism: The New Problems of Philosophy* (with Annalisa Coliva) and *From Trust to Trustworthiness* (both published in 2019 by Routledge).

Monika Betzler holds the Chair for Practical Philosophy and Ethics at Ludwig Maximilian University (LMU), Munich. She is the Director of the Munich Graduate School "Ethics in Practice", an elected Member of the Swiss Federal Ethics Committee on Non-Human Biotechnology and the current Director of the Munich Center of Ethics. She has published extensively on themes in moral psychology, theories of practical reason and normative ethics. Her recent work centres on normative dimensions of empathy, inverse akrasia, the value of close relationships, the particular significance of personal projects and autonomy.

Riana J. Betzler is currently McDonnell Postdoctoral Research Fellow in Philosophy, Neuroscience and Psychology at Washington University in St. Louis. She completed her PhD in History and Philosophy of Science at the University of Cambridge, where she also taught for two years. Her main research project investigates how scientific research on empathy bears on questions about its value in moral psychology, medicine and law.

Kevin Cutright is Lieutenant Colonel in the United States Army and an Academy Professor in the Department of English and Philosophy at the U.S. Military Academy at West Point. In between field assignments, the Army sent him to Vanderbilt University for an MA in Philosophy and to Saint Louis University for a PhD. His operational experiences have driven his scholarly interest in the ethics of military planning and conduct, as well as in the moral psychology of soldiers.

Mark Fagiano did his MA and PhD in Philosophy at Emory University, Atlanta. He also has an MA in the Anthropological Study of Religion from Graduate Theological Union (GTU) at University of California, Berkeley. His areas of specialisation are pragmatism, ethics and social-political philosophy. As a pragmatist, Dr Fagiano's research, publications and lectures are inspired by the relational and pluralistic approach of William James, which has contributed to the structure of his forthcoming book *Relational Empathy*. He is currently working on two other books, *The White Supremacy of Science and Philosophy* and *Why We Don't Know What Happiness Is*.

Iraklis Ioannidis is Affiliated Researcher at the University of Glasgow and a Member of the Existential Network Scotland. He studied Communication Studies at the National and Kapodestrian University of Athens (Ptyhion) and at Illinois State University (MA) and received a MLitt and a PhD in Analytic and in Critical-Continental Philosophy from University of Glasgow. He has published in *The Oxford Encyclopedia of Communication* and in *Sofia Philosophical Review*.

Ian James Kidd is Assistant Professor at the Department of Philosophy at the University of Nottingham. His current work uses feminist and phenomenological work to explore the ways that individual and collective vices contribute to the suffering of chronically somatically ill persons. Some recent publications include a set of papers on epistemic injustice and illness with Havi Carel and *The Routledge Handbook to Epistemic Injustice* (co-authored with José Medina and Gaile Pohlhaus, Jr., 2017). He also works to improve the intellectual and demographic diversity of academic philosophy.

Elisa Magrì is Assistant Professor of Philosophy at Boston College and an Honorary Associate Member of the Centre for Philosophy, University of Lisbon. Her current research centres on the affective and epistemic architecture of social sensitivity. Previously, she was a Humboldt Research Fellow at the University of Cologne and an Irish Research Council Post-doctoral Research Fellow at University College Dublin. Her publications include *Self-Reference, Memory, and Embodiment* (2017) and the co-edited books *Empathy, Sociality, and Personhood: Essays on Edith Stein's Phenomenological Investigations* (2018) and *Hegel and Phenomenology* (2019).

Meliné Papazian is completing a PhD in Cognitive Science on Empathy at University College Dublin. She has given conference papers and conducted workshops in France, Italy, Netherlands, Armenia and Ireland. She has published on empathy and related topics in various venues, including in the *International Journal of Philosophical Studies*. She was also one of the editors of *Perspectives, International Postgraduate Journal of Philosophy*. In a previous life, she counselled victims of domestic violence in Los Angeles.

Danielle Petherbridge is Assistant Professor in Philosophy at University College Dublin (UCD) and Deputy-Director of the UCD Centre for Ethics in Public Life. Her primary research projects include theories of intersubjectivity in phenomenology and social philosophy and theories of vulnerability and recognition. She also works in the area of medical humanities, specifically on embodied cognitive accounts of illness and is Principle Investigator of the research project BodyDementia, funded by the Irish Research Council and undertaken in partnership with the Alzheimer Society of Ireland. She is creator of the Irish Young Philosopher Awards.

Michael Slote is UST Professor of Ethics at the University of Miami. A Member of the Royal Irish Academy and former Tanner Lecturer, he is the author of many books and articles on ethics, epistemology, philosophy of mind and political philosophy. In recent years, he has argued in books and articles that Chinese thought can provide a much-needed corrective to some basic assumptions of Western philosophy. His book *The Philosophy of Yin and Yang: A Contemporary Approach* was published in Beijing in 2018 with side-by-side English and Chinese language texts.

Sarah Songhorian is Research Fellow in Moral Philosophy at the Vita-Salute San Raffaele University in Milan. She received her PhD in Cognitive Neuroscience and Philosophy of Mind in 2015 with a dissertation entitled *Empathy, Sympathy, and Morality. An Interdisciplinary Approach*. Her research focuses on empathy and sympathy with particular attention to the contribution that ethical theory, metaethics, moral psychology and neuroethics can provide to their understanding.

Rowland Stout is Professor of Philosophy at University College Dublin (UCD), a Member of the Royal Irish Academy and the Editor of the *International Journal of Philosophical Studies*. He is the author of three books on the philosophy of action and the philosophy of mind. Currently he is completing another book on the philosophy of emotions. He is Director of the UCD Centre for Ethics in Public Life and Team Leader for the Work Package on the Ethics of Trust within the EU Horizon 2020 project PEriTiA (Policy, Expertise and Trust in Action).

Introduction: The Value of Empathy

Maria Baghramian, Meliné Papazian and Rowland Stout

This collection brings together articles on the topic of empathy first published in the *International Journal of Philosophical Studies* (volume 27, issue 2, 2019 and volume 26, issue 3, 2018). Chapters 1–7 are the winning and short-listed articles from the 2018 Robert Papazian Essay Prize in Ethics and Political Philosophy, where the focus was on the moral and social roles and significance of empathy. The overall winner of the 2018 competition was "The Relational Value of Empathy" by Monika Betzler (LMU Munich). The paper was judged to be original, insightful with good use of textual evidence from various sources. The winner of the 2018 early career Robert Papazian Essay Prize was Mark Fagiano (University of Central Florida, Orlando), with the essay "Relational Empathy". The next five articles were short-listed for the Robert Papazian Prize and were commended for a variety of reasons. The last four articles in this book, by Ian Kidd, Danielle Petherbridge, Elisa Magri, and Rowland Stout, are the proceedings of a symposium held at the UCD Centre for Ethics in Public Life on the topic of "Empathy, Vulnerability and Illness". Connecting the two sets of entries is "Sentimentalist Practical Reason and Self-Sacrifice" by Michael Slote (University of Miami), originally published in *IJPS* 2018, vol. 26, issue 3.

A major difficulty in discussions of empathy, in philosophy and beyond, is the profusion of definitions and a lack of clarity in our understanding of the concept, its range and applications. Every article published in this volume, in different ways, engages with this difficulty. We will introduce the articles later in this introduction but an initial brief overview of current discussions of empathy, in so far as they bear on the themes picked out by the articles in this collection, may help to set the scene.

The usage of the word 'empathy' may be traced to the beginning of the 20th century with the translation of the term *Einfühlung*, which had currency in aesthetics and phenomenology in the late 19th century. Current discussions of the topic are also influenced by earlier debates on the cognate notion of sympathy, discussed by David Hume (1739) and Adam Smith (1759), among others, as well as by more recent empirical studies by psychologists and cognitive scientists.

The last decade has seen an explosion of books, articles and scholarly studies on empathy in fields as diverse as cognitive science, psychology, neuroscience, arts and aesthetics, politics, management theory, philosophy, education and the social and health sciences. Within philosophy, discussions of empathy are most common in the philosophy of mind, philosophy of cognitive sciences, phenomenology and moral philosophy. Calls for greater empathy have also become common in our social discourse and references to it abound in both the traditional and social media.

No doubt the abundance of research on empathy has enriched our understanding of the topic, but it has done little to give precision to the underlying concept. Indeed, neither a uniform definition, nor an uncontested account of the role, implications and range of applications of empathy seems to be available. The difficulty is compounded by a lack of clarity in the distinction between the concept of empathy and those of sympathy and compassion.

While the articles included in this collection were not initially written on a narrowly specified theme, there are common threads connecting them which reflect the current state of play in discussions of empathy. They address the lack of clarity in the concept of empathy, suggest new ways of approaching the topic, and connect abstract discussions of empathy with its applications to the moral domain and to the practical issue of care for vulnerable people. The collection fulfils two functions: it offers philosophical *accounts of empathy* that illuminate some of its defining characteristics, shedding light on some of its roles and applications; it also examines the moral significance of empathy by teasing out its normative features and its place in our moral life. By giving the collection the title *The Value of Empathy*, we are alluding to both of these functions simultaneously: to understand not just the value of empathy itself, but also the value of the concept of empathy.

Because empathy is taken to play a role in so many different aspects of human life, it is likely that a number of different ideas are covered by the term 'empathy'. Many see this diversity as an indication of confusion in the concept. Some argue that to overcome the confusion we should either come up with a better, more precise definition, abandon the talk of empathy altogether, or replace it with closely related terms, such as 'sympathy' or 'compassion'. Also, there are a variety of concepts in the neighbourhood of *empathy*, such as emotional sharing or emotional contagion, which are at times used interchangeably with empathy and at other times used as distinct notions. Further distinctions are made regarding types of empathy (e.g., emotional or affective vs cognitive empathy) and between contextual or functional variants of empathy (e.g., empathic concern, empathic caring, empathic perception, empathic understanding, empathic distress, empathic accuracy, among others), without any apparent consensus about their scope, connections, or differences. What everyone seems to agree on, however, is that the discussion about empathy, while high in volume, is low on agreement.

Attempts to distil some common features of empathy to facilitate a consensus and reconcile opposing views have neither proved very informative nor very helpful. For example, Derek Matravers suggests a broad definition: "using our imagination as a tool so as to adopt a different perspective in order to grasp how things appear (or feel) from there" (2017, 1–2). But he admits that even this definition cannot resolve controversies in the discourse on empathy, since many of the descriptions in this discourse are incompatible with one another. Compare, for instance, Dan Zahavi's (2011) direct perceptual account of empathy, where empathy is a precondition of any kind of intersubjectivity or social cognition, with Coplan's (2011) view of it as a complex imaginative process of simulating another person's states, or Goldie's view that empathy is "a process by which a person centrally imagines the narrative (the thoughts, feelings and emotions) of another person" (2000, 195), or with de Vignemont and Jacob's (2012) view which introduces the element of care to their multiple conditions of empathy.

Given the difficulties with the conceptualization of empathy, might avoiding the use of the term, a strategy suggested by Noel Carroll (2011) among others, be a reasonable option? The strategy promises to allow us to sidestep some of the more troublesome conceptual and definitional debates. However, it would also result in substituting for empathy a variety of narrower technical concepts, which, while convenient for researchers, might make a much used and presumably important notion less accessible to the wider public. Replacing 'empathy' with a similar concept such as sympathy does not seem to resolve the conceptualization problems either, since similar discussions and disagreements will arise for the replacement concept.

Many other concepts central to our social and psychological lives – 'love', 'happiness', 'friendship' come to mind – are equally messy, yet continue to be used in academic studies and in our daily lives. Despite some dissonance between the technical and daily use of such terms, we neither stop using them in everyday language nor do we stop investigating the concepts in theoretical or empirical research. Admittedly there are disanalogies between 'empathy' and 'love' and 'friendship'. The term 'empathy' is rather new in English, and has only approximate translations in different languages, while those other terms have close equivalents.[1] But, considering the widespread common use of 'empathy' and the extensive theoretical and empirical research on the topic, we shouldn't give up the term without a fight.

An empirical approach to our understanding of empathy might be a unifying strategy. There has been a lot of empirical research on its role in psychotherapy and social behaviour. Various tools, including scales to measure empathy, its individual and cultural variations, and its role in social relations have been widely used by psychologists. Since the 1990s, an important contribution to the empirical research on empathy has come from the neurosciences. The discovery of mirror neurons – a class of neurons first identified in the brains of macaque monkeys, which are activated not only when an action is performed but also when that action is observed – has presented a way of explaining the physical source of empathy (Iacoboni, 2009). Empirical studies have been aided by technological advances in areas of research such as the neuropsychological basis of empathy (Preston et al 2007; Decety, 2011), differences in empathy among children and adults (Eisenberg and Fabes 1990) and in relation to both personality disorders and autism spectrum disorder (Nichols 2004; Baron-Cohen, 2009; Marsh, 2014), as well as the growing area of social neuroscience (Decety and Lamm, 2006; Singer and Lamm, 2009). This research, however, has not been free of controversy. Critics, such as Lamm et al (2017), question the results of empirical studies that focus on empathic abilities or lack of empathy in people with ASD or those with psychopathic tendencies. They argue that such studies overlook the fact that empathy is a result of a complex process involving multiple intermediate steps. In this collection, Riana Betzler (Chapter 5) addresses some of the complexities and the advantages of empirical studies of empathy.

Arguing about the correct definition of empathy risks descending into a merely terminological dispute. But not defining the term and assuming a common understanding can lead to what Dan Zahavi (2014) portrays as different discussions passing by one another, because they are dealing with different phenomena. A productive approach in research on empathy would be to present a working definition of the term, based on the parameters of a specific topic under investigation, and occasionally supplementing this with further theoretical and empirical studies or accounts of empathy. In recent years, this approach is increasingly becoming common practice, especially in empirical research on empathy.

Some general points of agreement about key features of empathy are also beginning to emerge. Empathy does not happen in a void but in encounters with another, even if those encounters are not face to face or occur only in imagination. Empathy is elicited by another person's real or imagined experience, behaviour and psychological states rather than one's own. In Hoffman's (2000, 2001) words, empathic emotions are more appropriate to another person's situation and states than those of the person experiencing them. Empathy is *about* that other, and goes back to the *other*, or what sometimes is called, rather inelegantly, the 'target of empathy'. But it seems that even this characteristic of empathy is not accepted by all. There are views that count phenomena such as emotional contagion, personal distress, or sharing thoughts and emotions as empathy (Eisenberg and Fabes, 1990; Darwall, 1998; Preston and de Waal, 2002; de Waal, 2009). If we accept that the initiator of empathy is another's situation and experience and not one's own and that empathy is directed towards the other and is about the other, and that the empathizer is more or less aware of the distinction between the situation of oneself and the other person, none of these cases would be considered empathic. Researchers on the topic, including most contributors to this collection, agree that empathy is prompted from and directed towards the other. But even if this is a common feature of empathy, it is not sufficient for defining empathy. Moreover, accepting that empathic experience is about another person's emotional experience does not in itself rule out the possibility of an empathizer having abusive, manipulative, or simply unfavourable motives towards the other. For instance, the accounts that see empathy as a precondition of all other kinds of social understanding do not discount the possibility of this sort of abusive empathy. On the other hand, those who are inclined to see empathy as a positive prosocial attitude and consider self-interest or other manipulative and negative motives as the antithesis of empathy would reject it. Thus, the debate continues.

Many of the entries in this collection, including the two winning essays, address either directly or indirectly the question of how to define and understand empathy. Monika Betzler (Chapter 1) argues that adopting a relational understanding of empathy could overcome many of the problems encountered in empathy-related discussions, Mark Fagiano (Chapter 2) proposes a pluralist view of empathy characterized as a relation "between things, between activities, or between a thing and activity". Some suggest more specific definitions; Kevin Cutright (Chapter 7) provides a working definition of empathy as "grasping the felt characteristic of another person's experience" including their feelings, desires, intentions, commitment and worries. Rowland Stout (Chapter 12) describes empathy as being open to and adopting the emotional perspective of another person.

One of the most crucial and yet controversial roles assigned to empathy is in the moral domain. The question, put simply, is what, if anything, is the connection between empathy and morality? The answers, not surprisingly in the light of what has been discussed, are varied and at times conflicting.

Some deny that empathy is either a causal or a constitutive element of moral judgements and actions at all. They view empathy as a capacity which may have positive, negative, or neutral outcomes depending on the circumstances (Decety and Lamm, 2006, 2009). Zahavi (2014) sees empathy as a morally neutral precondition for any intersubjective understanding. Prinz (2011a, 2011b) argues that empathy is not necessary for moral judgement, moral motivation, moral development, or improving moral sensibility. And empathy is sometimes criticized for being biased and partial towards those close to us, not motivating us to help those in need but instead being prone to favouring the members of our in-group. From this perspective, empathy is regarded as potentially immoral, while sympathy and rational compassion are the morally superior capacities (Bloom, 2016).

On the other hand, empathy is viewed by many as a moral virtue, the very basis of our moral judgement and motivation. Empathy is described as "the spark of human concern for others" (Hoffman, 2000, 3) with a crucial role in moral development, prosocial and altruistic behaviour (Eisenberg, 2005, Eisenberg et al., 2010; Batson, 2011). Michael Slote, in particular (2010, 2017 and in this volume), takes empathy to be not only a primary moral motivator, a mechanism for care, benevolence and compassion, but also epistemically central in our moral life. He argues that cognitive empathy, which typically involves understanding the thoughts, emotions, intentions, beliefs or desires of others, enables us to recognize those in need of help. If this is right then cognitive empathy provides moral insight and moral intuition, and those who have rational capacities but lack empathic skills may have difficulties in making appropriate moral choices and judgements. With this in view, there are ongoing debates as to whether the autism spectrum involves a deficiency in some aspect of empathy and to what extent this is reflected in one's capacity to make moral judgements. Also, starting from the assumption that psychopathic personality disorder involves immoral behaviour and attitudes, it is important to ask whether this is associated with a reduced ability to empathize with people.

Even if there is a connection between a lack of empathy and a diminished capacity to make moral judgements, the question remains as to whether this is due to an inability to take another's perspective, an inability to feel certain things, or just an inability to work out what other people are feeling.[2]

Contributors to this collection agree that empathy, at the very least, plays an indirect role in our moral life. According to Monika Betzler (Chapter 1), giving and receiving empathy can lead to developing meaningful relationships and cultivating trust, attachment, or recognition. Elisa Magri (Chapter 11) suggests that empathy may enable moral behaviour and Rowland Stout (Chapter 12) argues that it may be necessary for moral development. For Sarah Songhorian (Chapter 6), empathy, although not necessary for morality, enables the development of sympathy, which in turn enables moral behaviour. For Kevin Cutright (Chapter 7), empathy improves moral judgements among soldiers at war. Some of the more concrete features of an empathetic engagement are investigated in Chapters 9 and 10 where Ian Kidd and Danielle Petherbridge explore the connections between empathy and vulnerability in experiences of illness and dementia.

In the remainder of this introduction we briefly introduce each article.

In "The Relational Value of Empathy" (Chapter 1), Monika Betzler argues that empathy is not best understood as something happening in an individual's mind. Rather, both the nature of empathy and its value depend on the relationship between the empathizer and the person being empathized with. Empathy is directed not only towards another person but also towards the relation with that person. This relational property is valuable for its own sake, both intrinsically and extrinsically, because of the kind of meaningful relationships it creates and the positive experiences, such as self-esteem, trust and self-trust, attachment, affection and recognition, it fosters. Understanding why someone feels a certain way is an important feature of moral judgement and is made possible through the relational value of empathy. It explains why we are at times morally required to empathize and at other times to abstain from it; we have only 'defeasible' moral reasons to empathize.

In "Relational Empathy", Mark Fagiano (Chapter 2), instead of looking for a single answer to the question of what is the nature of empathy, argues for a pluralistic understanding of it. Empathy, he argues, is a social construct, so there is no need for a full consensus on its conceptualization. Each approach serves a different purpose and the value of each study depends not so much on being right but on what it achieves, how it explains the experience and how it tries to change the quality of our experiences. Fagiano characterizes empathy not as a thing or an activity, but as a set of three conceptually distinct, though experientially overlapping, relations: the relations of *feeling into*, *feeling with*, and *feeling for*. He traces all three uses of empathy, and the closely related concept of sympathy, in texts dating from the late 18th century to the present and claims that his version of 'relational empathy' not only avoids but also potentially resolves the conflicting conceptualizations of the term. Finally, using this broad pluralistic and pragmatic approach, Fagiano proposes a conceptual framework which can be applied to problems in the US healthcare system.

"Language, Behavior, and Empathy. G.H. Mead's and W.V.O. Quine's Naturalized Theories of Meaning" by Guido Baggio (Chapter 3) provides a scholarly account of empathy in the context of the behavioural/behaviouristic theories of meaning and language of Mead and Quine. The article examines the similarities and differences between Mead's notion of sympathy and Quine's notion of empathy, and their roles in interpreting and using language. Baggio finds parallels between Mead's less ambiguous notion of sympathy as a natural capacity to depict others' beliefs, attitudes and intentions, and recent neuroscientific and neurophenomenological research on empathy, which similarly sees empathy in terms of pre-reflexive mechanisms that ascribe meaning to facial expressions and bodily attitudes. According to Baggio, for both Quine and Mead empathic identification is at the core of social interaction and the emergence of the linguistic from pre-linguistic communication. The article concludes with a description of the various stages of the formation of the mind of a child in terms of an interaction between neurological processes and interpersonal relations based on notions of 'gesture' and 'behavior'.

Iraklis Ioannidis in "No Empathy for Empathy: An Existential Reading of Husserl's Forgotten Question" (Chapter 4) challenges the idea that empathy should be characterized in terms of knowing another person's feelings. In particular, the working of biological or neurological mechanisms such as mirroring could not provide such knowledge. Empathy, understood as knowing what the other feels, is impossible, because we cannot appropriate someone else's experience and deliver it as our own. At best, we can only think or imagine that we know what another person thinks or feels. To substantiate his claim, Ioannidis looks back at Husserl's use of the term 'empathy' in some of his key texts. He maintains that, contrary to mainstream interpretations, for Husserl, any understanding of others through empathy is epistemically only partial. To understand how knowing another person is possible, Ioannidis argues, we need to look at the social and communal dimensions of empathy where knowing another person's feelings and intentions involves creating a community with them. He concludes that to know another is to co-create with them, to project ourselves in 'reciprocal creation', or in co-constitution, which would allow us to create what Ioannidis calls a 'sympathy of feelings' or the 'blending or attunement with the other'.

In "Finding Empathy: How Neuroscientific Measures, Evidence, and Conceptualizations Interact" (Chapter 5), Riana Betzler examines some remedies for the conceptual confusion in discussions of empathy in both philosophy and psychology, and challenges the idea that we can 'find empathy', i.e., achieve conceptual clarity and better understanding of the processes underlying it, by doing more neuroscientific research. She attempts to unpack the relationship between conceptual diversity and neuroscientific evidence by looking at how social neuroscientists use the concept of empathy in the development of their measures at the outset of their studies and in the interpretations of their data. She argues that within the same research community, researchers can communicate better despite the absence of consensus on definitions, but that conceptual diversity and disagreements create difficulties when it comes to interdisciplinary and applied research on empathy. These obstacles, however, are not insurmountable. Betzler argues that researchers need to pay attention to the definitions of empathy employed in their area of investigation as well as to the definitions used by investigators in other research groups that they refer to. This can be done by examining how the measures are conceptualized, developed and used in those other research areas. She suggests this model can be used to detect areas of convergence, as well as divergences, within communities of researchers. She concludes that while we cannot 'find' empathy through neuroscience, we can learn about *empathic* processes. Using established measures, she concludes, leads to continuity and stability in research, and progress comes from the expansion of these measures along with the increased flexibility of the concepts.

In "The Contribution of Empathy to Ethics" (Chapter 6), Sarah Songhorian investigates the extent to which moral behaviour should be understood in terms of empathy. She resists any attempt to reduce the notion of morality to that of empathic response, pointing out that empathy involves biases and other ethical limitations; empathy does not always lead to helping others or caring for them. She takes emotional attunement to be the minimal and non-reducible feature of the ordinary ways we talk about empathy, and argues that this minimal notion can explain behaviours such as partiality, sadism and psychopathy. This minimal notion is related to cognitive empathy and perspective-taking, which have a central role in understanding others' behaviour and developing moral capacities, but neither are strictly necessary for empathy. On the other hand, attuning with another's emotional states may have an enabling role in developing sympathy. While empathy is neither normative nor imaginative, according to Songhorian, sympathy is both. She concludes that while empathy is neither necessary nor sufficient for moral behaviour, it does have an affective route to morality through its role in developing a sympathetic engagement by the impartial spectator.

"The Empathetic Soldier" (Chapter 7) by Kevin Cutright deals with the important but neglected topic of the role of empathy in relation to the conduct of war. Cutright aims to show the relevance of empathy and its various benefits to the tactical and ethical demands of war. To do so, he starts with a survey of contemporary theories of empathy: theory-theory, simulation theory, direct perception, narrative theory and theories of low-level and high-level empathy. He thinks that empathy offers an *experiential* understanding of others, in the sense of enabling one to grasp the 'felt characteristic' of others' experiences, including their emotions, beliefs, perspectives, intentions, worries, or commitments. Having empathy does not mean agreeing with others' perspectives or adopting them as our own; *understanding* another's experience is distinct from *identifying* with it. Empathy is not only a sort of understanding of others from 'inside', but it also has corresponding moral benefits in that it expresses recognition and respect, and reinforces the humanity of others. Applying his views to the army, Cutright concludes that empathy bolsters the attitudes and moral judgements of soldiers, improving their understanding of human actors in the war environment.

Michael Slote, in "Sentimentalist Practical Reason and Self-Sacrifice" (Chapter 8), seeks to show that the moral objectivity defended in his 2010 book, *Moral Sentimentalism*, allows for full moral normativity along sentimentalist lines. He defends what he calls 'sentimentalism' about practical reasons, according to which all reasons for action, whether prudential or moral, are grounded in emotional states. The role of empathy in this model is not only as a mechanism for the transmission of emotions but also as a mechanism for the transmission of reasons for action. If someone, through their well-grounded fear, has a reason to escape a burning building and someone else empathizes with this fear, the second person now has a reason to help the person escape the burning building. It is a reason grounded in their own emotional state, derived through empathy from the frightened person's emotional state. In this way, empathy is taken to be the basis of altruistic behaviour. Slote claims that this model explains why we have stronger reason to help others in need who are closer to us in one way or another than we have to help very distant people in need. We empathize and sympathize more with family members and have more reasons to react to their needs compared to strangers with similar problems. He adds that psychopaths lack the moral reasons to help others because they lack associative empathy. These are things that Slote argues cannot be explained in rationalist/cognitivist approaches, such as Nagel's in *The Possibility of Altruism* (1970).

In "Pathophobia, Vices, and Illness" (Chapter 9), Ian Kidd introduces the concept of 'pathophobia' as a morally objectionable attitude towards somatically ill people. Kidd sees 'vice ethics' (by analogy and contrast with virtue ethics) as the way to frame pathophobia and suggests that instead of imposing an artificial moral framework, it is vital for philosophical analysis to be based on narrative descriptions of the lived experiences of somatically ill people. Using testimonies, narratives and the literature related to ill people's experiences, he describes five clusters of pathophobia that are shaped by the character of the illness itself and social factors such as identity, gender, race, and class, as well as cultural norms, behaviours and stereotypes. These are aversion to and avoidance of illness, trivialization of illness through banality, callousness towards ill people, insensitivity to the ill person's experience and untruthfulness about illness. This taxonomy, he contends, may guide our practices of moral appraisals based on testimonies of ill people's experience of how they are treated. He argues that the failure to empathize with people who are ill is bound up with these pathophobic vices. Certain types of illnesses or identities elicit more empathy, credibility, sympathy and trust than others, while certain vices, such as individual and structural callousness in healthcare, are opposed to compassion and kindness and thereby lead to increased failure of empathy, compassion and care.

In "Beyond Empathy: Vulnerability, Relationality and Dementia", Danielle Petherbridge (Chapter 10) challenges the traditional view of dementia according to which people with dementia have lost their personhood and the capacity for subjective experience and meaningful interactions. She argues against the conventional view that personhood is associated with a conception of autonomy in which persons must be seen as rational and independent decision makers. She defends instead a relational view, where personhood and selfhood are based on intersubjectivity and intercorporeality, i.e., the dynamic interconnection between embodied creatures to one another, which begins in infancy. Petherbridge argues that this view of vulnerability extends 'beyond or behind' empathy, providing a primary form of openness towards others upon which empathic responses are built. In this sense, vulnerability as openness to the other is a precondition of empathy, but not sufficient for it. In the case of dementia, mutual empathy is not possible due to the asymmetrical nature of the interaction. Yet mutual vulnerability is possible, creating reciprocal openness, and forming the basis of a relationship that involves empathic responsiveness and supports full recognition of the other as a person and the locus of respect.

Elisa Magri starts her treatment in "Empathy, Respect, and Vulnerability" (Chapter 11) with a consideration of the relationship between empathy and moral motivation. She agrees with Heather Battaly's (2011) view that empathy is not itself a moral virtue, but rather should be seen as a capacity that is fundamental for moral behaviour. But while Battaly argues that empathy must be driven by *care* to have this role in moral motivation, Magri argues that it is respect and not care that is the main moral feeling that is distinctive of empathy. Empathy can exist without care but not without respect. The feeling of respect for another person's experience in the situation they face grants what Magri calls 'epistemic dignity', which amounts to the recognition of the significance of their subjective experience. This involves recognizing an individual's affective experiences as worthy of attention and discernment, even when one disagrees with them. For Magri, empathy is a second-person relation that opens up the realm of interpersonal relatedness, whether one intends to act for another's good or not. It attends to another person's specific horizon, informed by respect towards their autonomy. She concludes that even when someone's personal agency seems inhibited, as in the case of having OCD and being driven to repetitive behaviour in response to a lack of trust in their world, empathy, as understood in this way as driven by respect, is still possible as a way of vindicating the autonomy of their subjective experience.

Rowland Stout in "Empathy, Vulnerability and Anxiety" (Chapter 12) holds that empathy is openness towards the emotional perspective of another person, an openness to their *way* of seeing, thinking and feeling about things. He argues that empathizing is not about *what* others feel but about *how* things are for them in that situation; in empathy, one looks outwards to another person's emotional world and not into their mind. Stout calls this phenomenon *adopting* someone's perspective, but distinguishes this from accepting or sharing that perspective, which Stout takes to be characteristic of what he terms sympathy. In empathy, someone else's perspective is adopted for the sake of the encounter only. This means that while empathizing one holds two emotional perspectives in mind simultaneously, one's own as well as the adopted perspective in a kind of dialogue with each other. Being *open* towards another's perspective is being vulnerable to it, and this is why adopting another's emotional perspective may be difficult, according to Stout – posing a challenge to one's own perspective and identity. For example, if one is insecure about one's own identity, empathizing may become threatening.

The articles published in this volume, in different ways, engage with problems of defining and understanding empathy. They also raise new questions about the range of its roles and applications, and in the process engage directly with the ethical concerns related to empathy and raise interesting points about its moral dimension. We therefore hope that this collection will go some way towards addressing these widely recognized concerns.

Maria Baghramian and Rowland Stout's work on this volume was supported by funding from the European Union's Horizon 2020 research and innovation programme under grant agreement **No 870883.**

The symposium on "Empathy, Vulnerability and Illness" was jointly organized by University College Dublin and the University of Nottingham and was sponsored by Universitas 21 and UCD Centre for Ethics in Public Life.

Notes

1. In recent years, the term 'empathy' itself, rather than its translations, is increasingly being used in different languages.
2. For further discussions regarding the causal and constitutive roles of empathy in moral judgments, if any, see Kauppinen (2017) and Maibom (2014, 2017).

References

Baron-Cohen, S. 2009. Autism: The Empathizing-Systemizing (ES) Theory. *Annals of the New York Academy of Science*, 1156, 68–80.

Batson, C. D. 2011. *Altruism in Humans*. New York: Oxford University Press.

Battaly, H. D. 2011. Is Empathy a Virtue? In: A. Coplan & P. Goldie (Eds.) *Empathy: Philosophical and Psychological Perspectives*. Oxford: Oxford University Press, 277–301.

Bloom, P. 2016. *Against Empathy: The Case for Rational Compassion*. London: HarperCollins.

Carroll, N. 2011. On Some Affective Relations Between Audiences and the Characters in Popular Fiction. In: A. Coplan & P. Goldie (Eds.) *Empathy: Philosophical and Psychological Approaches*. New York: Oxford University Press, 162–184.

Coplan, A. 2011. Understanding Empathy: Its Features and Effects. In: A. Coplan & P. Goldie (Eds.) *Empathy: Philosophical and Psychological Approaches*. New York: Oxford University Press, 3–18.

Darwall, S. 1998. Empathy, Sympathy, Care. *Philosophical Studies*, 89, 261–282.

de Vignemont, F., & Jacob, P. 2012. What Is It Like to Feel Another's Pain? *Philosophy of Science*, 79, 295–316.

de Waal, F. B. M. 2009. *The Age of Empathy: Nature's Lessons for a Kinder Society*. New York: Harmony Books.

Decety, J. 2011. Dissecting the Neural Mechanisms Mediating Empathy. *Emotion Review*, 3, 92–108.

Decety, J., & Lamm, C. 2006. Human Empathy Through the Lens of Social Neuroscience. *Scientific World Journal*, 6, 1146–1163.

Decety, J., & Lamm, C. 2009. Empathy Versus Personal Distress: Recent Evidence from Social Neuroscience. In: J. Decety & W. Ickes (Eds.) *The Social Neuroscience of Empathy*. Cambridge, MA: MIT Press, 199–214.

Eisenberg, N. 2005. The Development of Empathy-Related Responding. In: G. Carlo & C. P. Edwards (Eds.) *Moral Development through the Lifespan: Theory, Research, and Application*, The 51st Nebraska on Motivation. Lincoln, NE: University of Nebraska Press, 73–117.

Eisenberg, N., & Fabes, R. 1990. Empathy: Conceptualization, Measurement, and Relation to Prosocial Behavior. *Motivation and Emotion*, 14, 131–149.

Eisenberg, N., Eggum, N. D., & Di Giunta, L. 2010. Empathy-Related Responding: Associations with Prosocial Behavior, Aggression, and Intergroup Relations. *Social Issues and Policy Review*, 4(1), 143–180.

Goldie, P. 2000. *The Emotions: A Philosophical Exploration*. Oxford: Oxford University Press.

Hoffman, M. L. 2000. *Empathy and Moral Development*. New York: Cambridge University Press.

Hoffman, M. L. 2001. A Comprehensive Theory of Prosocial Moral Development. In: D. Stipek & A. Bohart (Eds.) *Constructive and Destructive Behavior*. Washington, DC: American Psychology Association, 61–86.

Hume, D. 1739 (1978 edition). *A Treatise of Human Nature*. L. A. Selby-Bigge (Ed.), 2nd rev. ed., P. H. Nidditch. Oxford: Clarendon Press.

Iacoboni, M. 2009. Imitation, Empathy and Mirror Neurons. *Annual Review of Psychology*, 60, 1–19.

Kauppinen, A. 2017. Empathy and Moral Judgement. In: H. Maibom (Ed.) *Routledge Handbook of Philosophy of Empathy*. New York: Routledge, 215–225.

Lamm, C, Coll, M. P., Viding, E., Rutgen, M., Silani, G., Cutmur, C., & Bird. G. (2017) Are We Really Measuring Empathy? Proposal for a New Measurement Framework. *Neuroscience and Biobehavioral Reviews*, 83, 132–139.

Maibom, H. 2014. Introduction: (Almost) Everything You Ever Wanted to Know about Empathy. In: H. Maibom (Ed.) *Empathy and Morality*. Oxford: Oxford University Press, 1–40.

Maibom, H. 2017. (Ed.) *Routledge Handbook of Philosophy of Empathy*. New York: Routledge.

Marsh, A., 2014. Empathy and Moral Deficit in Psychopathy. In: H. Maibom (Ed.) *Empathy and Morality*. Oxford: Oxford University Press.

Matravers, D. 2017. *Empathy*. Cambridge: Polity Press.

Nagel, T. 1970. *The Possibility of Altruism*. Oxford: Oxford University Press.

Nichols, S. 2004. *Sentimental Rules: On the Natural Foundations of Moral Judgment*. New York: Oxford University Press.

Preston, S. D., & de Waal, F. 2002. Empathy: Its Ultimate and Proximate Bases. *Behavioral and Brain Sciences*, 25, 1–72.

Preston, S. D. et al. 2007. The Neural Substrates of Cognitive Empathy. *Social Neuroscience*, 2(3–4), 254–275.

Prinz, J. 2011a. Is Empathy Necessary for Morality? In: A. Coplan & P. Goldie (Eds.) *Empathy: Philosophical and Psychological Approaches*. New York: Oxford University Press, 211–229.

Prinz, J. 2011b. Against Empathy. *Southern Journal of Philosophy*, 49, 214–233.
Singer, T., & Lamm, C. 2009. The Social Neuroscience of Empathy. *Annals of the New York Academy of Sciences*, 1156, 81–96.
Slote, M. 2010. *Moral Sentimentalism*. Oxford: Oxford University Press.
Slote, M. 2017. The Many Faces of Empathy. *Philosophia*, 45, 843–855.
Smith, A. 1759 (1976 edition). *The Theory of Moral Sentiments*. Oxford: Oxford University Press.
Zahavi, D. 2011. Empathy and Direct Social Perception: A Phenomenological Proposal. *Review of Philosophy and Psychology*, 2(3), 541–558.
Zahavi, D. 2014. *Self and Other*. Oxford: Oxford University.

The Relational Value of Empathy

Monika Betzler

ABSTRACT
Philosophers and scholars from other disciplines have long discussed the role of empathy in our moral lives. The distinct relational value of empathy, however, has been largely overlooked. This article aims to specify empathy's distinct relational value: Empathy is both intrinsically and extrinsically valuable in virtue of the pleasant experiences we share with others, the harmony and meaning that empathy provides, the recognition, self-esteem, and self-trust it enhances, as well as trust in others, attachment, and affection it fosters. Once we better understand in what ways empathy is a uniquely relational phenomenon, we can unveil its relevance to morality, which avoids the strictures of both partiality and impartiality. On the one hand, it is the relational value of empathy that grounds defeasible reasons to empathize insofar as empathy is morally called for by a particular relationship (or if we have defeasible reasons to establish a relationship by empathy). On the other hand, it is precisely empathy's relational value that allows us to show that it can be kept within bounds. To realize empathy's relational value, we are not constantly required to empathize. Instead, once we properly appreciate empathy's distinct relational value, we can show that this leaves us room to respond to impartialist concerns.

1. Introduction

Philosophers and scholars of other disciplines have long discussed the role of empathy in our moral lives. Upon first inspection, one may think that those who are able to empathize with others care more about their well-being, are more attentive to their needs, and have more respect for their autonomy. As a result, they seem more likely either to do more for others than they otherwise would (Sober and Wilson 1998, 236f.), or to behave morally by being empathic (Slote 2007). One may therefore conclude that there exists either a causal or a conceptual link between empathy and morality.

After careful consideration, however, the link between empathy and morality turns out to be more complicated. There are many cases in which empathy does not lead to moral motivation. Taking delight in the joy of another person, for example, is not simply an instance that calls for additional other-regarding action; one might be motivated by the aim of ensuring that another person's joy lasts as long as possible, although it is not clear that this can be regarded as a genuine moral motivation.[1] Hence, there are counterexamples to the claim that empathy leads to moral action.

One might also take issue with the alleged conceptual link. As has been repeatedly pointed out in the literature, empathy involves partiality, which implies favoritism (Snow 2000; Prinz 2011; Bloom 2016). By contrast, it is a widespread assumption that the moral point of view is impartial and does not differentiate between specific others. These concerns substantiate the view that empathy and morality are two different and potentially conflicting concepts. Empathy is neither necessary nor sufficient to bring about moral behavior. It can even lead to immoral actions through the neglect of others. We can empathize too little or too much, and we can empathize with immoral people with whom we should not empathize. There are other problems that cast doubt on the alleged link between empathy and morality, but these preliminary remarks should suffice to make us question this link.

This skepticism, however, has inspired proponents of an empathy-based morality to introduce more sophisticated proposals to the debate. They are meant to convince us that empathy is, in *some qualified sense*, necessary and sufficient for, or, at the very least, 'essential' to, morality. Broadly, we can identify three sets of approaches that have been put forward in support of the case for empathy's qualified role in morality.

According to one set of proposals, although the unrestricted practice of empathy may not be morally significant, it can be restricted in the way it is exercised so as to pass moral muster. At least two strategies have been devised to regulate the *practice* of empathy in this manner.[2] One is to limit what a person should empathize with: the process of empathy can only be said to have been properly practiced when it has been based on a person's concern for another's basic well-being (Simmons 2014, 101ff.; Masto 2015, 90). Another strategy is to broaden the perspective of the person who is empathizing[3]: empathy should be felt and expressed in the way of an impartial and benevolent spectator. According to both strategies, it is this qualified practice of empathy – carried out on a target that meets particular conditions or executed under idealized conditions – that is regarded as both necessary and sufficient to bring about moral behavior.

However, to limit the object of one's empathy to the basic well-being of others does not lend support to the argument that empathy is essential to morality; it is simply an *ad hoc* strategy. It also remains doubtful whether an ideally regulated and thus 'impartial' empathy is a psychologically realistic option that can be of normative import to non-idealized agents. After all, it asks us to refocus our attention on what things look like from the perspective of each of those affected by an action and to detach ourselves from our own personal ideals and goals. It is unclear, however, whether we can develop and sustain empathy if we are to empathize with possibly conflicting perspectives – and do so independently of our own perspective. This strategy seems to rob empathy of its essentially perspectival nature. After all, we empathize from our particular perspective with particular others. And even if such impartial empathy were possible, it is questionable whether it provides non-ideal agents like us with normative reasons to act on behalf of others (Ramirez 2017, 515ff).

A second set of proposals may be more promising. It contains suggestions for employing empathy in moral decision-making and states that empathy should be recognized for what it is – namely as partial or biased – but that, in principle at least, can be balanced against moral principles, such as impartiality, justice, and self-respect (Carse 2005, 176). The problem with this view is that it is unclear how and on what basis an agent should navigate between her empathy and her moral principles. As a result, both sets of proposals – either regulating the practice of empathy, or balancing its unregulated practice against moral principles – largely fail to explain *why* we should and *how* we can accord empathy, however cautiously, its proper place in the moral domain.[4]

More recently, a third set of proposals has been mooted that promises to explain more fully why empathy should feature in our moral decision-making: empathy is considered to have a particular epistemic significance.[5] Experiencing how another person feels is believed to be irreducibly valuable as it provides us with a shortcut to gaining unique insights and helps us to understand *why* another person feels the way she does. Thus, it is the information about other people's emotions provided by empathy that can be taken to be a basis for defeasible moral reasons, which can then be balanced against other moral reasons. The problem with this proposal is not so much that it is wrong, but that it is incomplete. Understanding why another person feels the way she does is an important input for moral deliberation. But as I will set out below, there is a yet deeper explanation as to why that is the case. The explanation is provided by empathy's distinct *relational value*, which I hope to pin down and illuminate in this article, and that has, so far, been largely overlooked in the literature.

To date, only a few philosophers have touched on the *relational* significance of empathy (Halpern 2001, 111ff.; Carse 2005; Herrmann 2013; Song 2015). Here I take up their suggestions and demonstrate, in more detail, that empathy has a distinct relational value that helps us to establish, maintain and deepen relationships with others. What makes empathy unique is not so much that we gain access to a certain kind of knowledge or understanding by engaging in it, but rather that we enter into and maintain a distinct kind of relationship with another person. Once we better understand this relational value, it will be easier for us to establish the basis for restricting empathy, both internally and externally, and to informatively explain its particular role in the moral domain. I will thus argue the case for a novel normative connection between empathy and morality. To the extent that empathy has relational value, it generates morally relevant, yet defeasible, reasons. They are morally relevant to the extent that they help fulfill empathy's relational, and thus (in part, at least) other-regarding, value. They are defeasible insofar as empathy's relational value can be balanced against other values.[6]

The article is structured as follows: After providing an account of empathy, I will specify what I mean by 'relational value'. I will follow this by demonstrating that empathy is both intrinsically and extrinsically valuable because of various evaluative dimensions, such as the pleasant experiences we share with others, the harmony and meaning that empathy provides, the recognition, self-esteem, and self-trust it enhances, as well as the trust in others, attachment, and affection it fosters. To conclude, I will examine the relevance of empathy's relational value to morality, which avoids the strictures of both partiality and impartiality.

2. Conceptualizing empathy

While the moral relevance of empathy is a well-established object of enquiry, an independent debate exists on the nature or concept of empathy. The term 'empathy', however, is not only used to cover a variety of different phenomena; it is also employed differently in different disciplines.[7] A conceptual analysis therefore seems hard to come by and requires a paper in its own right.

Despite the blurriness that surrounds the analysis of the concept, many philosophers have come to subscribe to what I call the *Standard Account* of empathy. Accordingly, empathy is a 'process or activity, where to empathize with a person, A, is to vicariously experience A's internal experience' (Song 2015, 438; Coplan 2011, 5). Somewhat more precisely, the Standard Account takes the following conditions to be at least characteristic or prototypical of an instance of empathy: for a person P (the subject) to empathize with person Q (the target), (i) P is aware of and apprehends Q's internal experience E (awareness condition); and (ii) P experiences E*, with E* being sufficiently similar to E, because Q is undergoing E (re-enactment condition).[8]

Hence, the conceptual analysis that is widely shared among philosophers – various quarrels notwithstanding[9] – has thus far been primarily concerned with empathy as an individualist, unidirectional, and static phenomenon. A key feature of this analysis is that empathy is instantiated in an individual's mental state that is directed at another person's mental state. This is not surprising given that this analysis played an important role in an earlier debate on what it takes to read other minds (Carruthers and Smith 1996; Stueber 2010). What is striking, however, is that the debate about the connection between empathy and morality has tacitly maintained that conceptualization. While it is valuable for the purpose of understanding other minds, I question whether it is fully apt to capture what is at issue when we think about the role empathy might play in our moral and thus normative practices. After all, we make moral demands with regard to other's empathy. We blame others for not being empathic enough, we criticize others for not allowing us to empathize with them, and we think that some people over-empathize or misuse their empathy. What underlies this moral practice is that empathy is thought to have some proper function, and that it is therefore thought to be good for something. Whenever we blame others with regard to their empathy or lack thereof, we take it that what empathy is good for has not been realized.

But only once we understand what empathy is good for are we able to assess its potential connection with morality. If empathy can be good for something, certain conditions must hold that go beyond what it means for one person to empathize with another person.

Instead of framing the debate exclusively in terms of what it means for one person to empathize with another person, we should also examine what it takes for empathy to arise and persist between two or more people. This will help us to see that empathy is (at least also) a relational property, and not just the property of an individual's state of mind. Important insights from empirical research, such as social psychology and linguistics, serve to underscore the point that empathy is a feature of the particular relation between the persons involved.

'Relational models theory,' as advocated in social psychology, shows, for example, that the function of empathy is not primarily to get to know how others feel, but rather to shape one's relationships by encouraging mutual adjustments to be made in the minds and behavior of the subjects and the targets.[10] Empathy thus caters to relational needs, and it is the latter that help to explain why people are motivated to empathize: they hope to achieve 'dynamic complementarity.'[11]

The dynamics of interpersonal exchange are also corroborated by the empirical research undertaken in other disciplines. Conversation analysis in linguistics substantiates the claim that empathy is an interpersonally achieved and sequentially developed phenomenon: it results from expressions of the subject's emotions, which the target either confirms, by demonstrating that she understands them, or questions and investigates further in order to understand them more clearly.[12] Empathy does not reveal itself so much in a particular exchange, but instead arises on account of 'the sequential contingencies in the telling of an experience' (Kupetz 2014, 22).

These insights provide support for my claim that empathy is not only an *intra*personal, but also an *inter*personal phenomenon that is dynamic in nature and manifest in two or more persons relating to each other in particular ways.

To illustrate these ways of interpersonal relating, let us consider an example. Let us imagine a woman, Olga, who has, quite unexpectedly, been informed by her husband Mario that he is romantically involved with twenty-year-old Carla and has decided to leave her. The scenario is depicted by Elena Ferrante in her novel *The Days of Abandonment*. Ferrante vividly illustrates the train of thoughts, emotions, and feelings that Olga subsequently experiences:

> I couldn't calm down. Was it possible that Mario should leave me like this, without warning? It seemed to me incredible that all of a sudden he had become uninterested in my life, like a plant watered for years that is abruptly allowed to die of drought. I couldn't conceive that he had unilaterally decided that he no longer owed me any attention (Ferrante 2005, 21).

> I began to change. In the course of a month I lost the habit of putting on makeup carefully, I went from using a refined language, attentive to the feelings of others, to a sarcastic way of expressing myself, punctuated by coarse laughter (Ferrante 2005, 26).

> In parallel there began to grow inside me a permanent sense of danger. The weight of the two children – the responsibility but also the physical requirements of their lives – became a constant worry (Ferrante 2005, 27).

> [...] the nights, nearly sleepless already, became a torment. Where was I coming from, what was I becoming (Ferrante 2005, 30).

We learn from these passages that Olga feels let down and rejected by her husband, that she is angry with him, and that she is also in a state of disbelief about his change of commitment. She becomes unable to carry on with her daily tasks and instead constantly ruminates about what she has done wrong.

Let us now imagine that Lea, Olga's friend, empathizes with Olga. What are the conditions for empathy to arise? How do the two women need to relate for empathy to be good for something? The Intrapersonal Account only specifies the success conditions of empathy for the person doing the empathizing. As a result, for Lea to empathize with Olga she would need to vicariously experience what Olga is going through. But the Intrapersonal Account remains mute as to what it takes for empathy to arise and persist. It is only the Interpersonal Account that can explain how Olga and Lea have to relate to each other for empathy to come about and be good for something.

Only when Olga is ready to express herself and to communicate her particular situation of abandonment and is confident in the way she relates it to Lea, and only when Lea is ready to listen and to show the concern and open-mindedness necessary to pick up on that information, can empathy occur. A basic relation between a subject and a target – that is, one in which the subject and the target express themselves and are open to what is being expressed – is thus an important condition of empathy. Empathy proves to be a relational phenomenon as it presupposes that there is such a basic relation between the subject and the target. The process of empathy is also more dynamic than the Standard Account would have it. The use of information-seeking, feedback, dialogue, and adjustment between a subject and its target is what enables empathy to fulfill its role by correctly assessing the target's situation, which is causing the latter's emotional responses.[13] Lea will inquire whether she has understood everything correctly, and Olga will portray her situation in vivid detail so that Lea is able to understand Olga's perspective. That empathy manifests itself in individual mental states is not being questioned in this kind of interpersonal account. However, for empathy to occur, it must be based on a dynamic interpersonal relationship between the subject and the target. Hence, it takes two to empathize.[14]

It is the interpersonal and thus relational and dynamic conditions of empathy that are better suited to make sense of our moral practices and to explain what empathy is good for. If Olga blames Lea for not empathizing enough, for not empathizing satisfactorily, or for lacking empathy, she criticizes her for not relating properly to her.[15] It thus takes a *proper relation* between two people for empathy to arise. Such a relation has two defining features. It is a relation in which there is a shared understanding about particular situations, events, and personal backgrounds. And it is a relationship in which there is a shared concern for the other.

After all, we can only empathize with a target, and thus on the target's behalf, if we share her concerns. And it is these features that are at stake in our normative practices. To be sure, much more needs to be said to fully conceptualize empathy, but for my purposes it should suffice to observe that empathy is also a relational property, and that the Standard Account at least should be supplemented. Given what it takes for empathy to arise, I will now examine in more detail what exactly is valuable about empathy. This will demonstrate that relating properly entails that empathy's distinct relational value is being realized.

3. Empathy as a source of relational value

A few axiological considerations are needed to understand more fully what is meant by empathy's 'relational value.' That it takes two to empathize is a condition of the existence of empathy's value. However, this condition is not what makes empathy ultimately valuable.[16] What makes empathy a good thing is the kind of *relationship* that is forged between two or more people.[17] 'Relational value' in this sense is the notion of a *source of value*, and not a particular kind of value. The relationship that develops between two people as a result of their specific ways of responding to each other is an important source of empathy's value, and my primary interest lies in examining in detail the good qualities of such relationships.[18]

My aim here is first to explain intuitively why relating empathically to others is a source of value. To this end, I will consider instances where empathy with another person failed. What missing elements could account for these failures? I also hope to show how failures in empathy can be corrected.

Let us return to Lea and suppose that she is unable or unwilling to empathize with Olga. There are at least three different kinds of cases that could be regarded as instances of failed empathy. First, Lea could look at Mario's abandonment in the same way as Olga but fail to experience vicariously what Olga is going through. Second, Lea could be indifferent to Olga's situation, which would mean that she is not likely to have any vicarious experiences. Third, Lea could come to a different value judgment about Olga's situation and not share the same feelings as Olga. She could react angrily to Olga's reactions and blame her for having the emotions she does, given that they do not make sense to her.

In all three cases Lea does not vicariously experience what Olga is feeling. Hence, they are all instances of failed or missed empathy. In the first case, Lea could still be regarded as being empathic in a cognitive sense: she may judge Olga's pain and sorrow to be acute, even though she does not experience the same emotions as Olga. She may also be inclined to help Olga in a number of ways and show sympathy for her plight. Epistemic discussions on the difference between propositional knowledge and understanding *why* can help to explain the difference between judging what is good and feeling an emotion. By not feeling the same way about the situation, Lea cannot possibly understand *why* Olga considers her situation to be so threatening. Although she knows about Olga's hurt feelings and judges them to be bad, Lea can only acknowledge them in a generalized sense, based on the inferences she can draw from the behavior of other people in similar situations or from her generalized knowledge about Olga. Unfortunately, her inferences are likely to be highly erroneous, since Lea cannot reliably track what is precisely troubling Olga, given the specific way she feels about her particular situation. What is more, by not feeling what Olga is going through, Lea is unable to justify Olga's response. However, by helping Olga and by judging her situation to be bad, Lea can still be regarded, to some extent at least, as having acted on Olga's behalf.

As for the second case, Olga will feel that the way she perceives her situation has not been validated and, as a result, she will feel that she, as a person, has not been validated. Given that her husband's rejection already undermines her sense of self, Lea's neutral assessment and lack of empathy are likely to add to these negative emotions. If one makes use of the study of epistemic injustice, it becomes clear that in disregarding and not acknowledging Olga's particular way of responding to what has happened to her,[19] Lea is behaving unjustly in an evaluative sense. By remaining indifferent, Lea fails to give credibility to Olga's evaluative perspective and thus undermines (possibly inadvertently) Olga's status as a good judge of what is good or bad for her.

In the third case, if Lea feels differently about the situation, she is more likely to dismiss Olga's feelings and banish them from her mind. The idea behind Lea's non-empathizing strategy is then to convey to Olga that the object of her painful experience does not merit empathy: she may try to belittle Olga's feelings. By doing so, she is not only behaving unjustly in an evaluative sense, she is also being condescending by undermining the justificatory basis for Olga's way of apprehending her own situation (provided Olga has interpreted her situation correctly).

What effect will Lea's lack of empathy and her alternative strategies have on Olga? Depending on the particular case of failed empathy, Olga may feel unsupported and her pain unacknowledged. Since her experiences have been called into question, Olga will feel even more rejected and she will start to question herself even more. Thus, by not experiencing vicariously what Olga is feeling, Lea is much more likely to increase rather than alleviate Olga's pain. This can hardly be regarded as a close connection between the two women; rather it betokens distance and separation. Furthermore, if she does not sense any empathy from Lea, Olga is likely to shut off her emotions in order to protect herself. As a consequence, it is thus very possible that the women's relationship will be damaged.

Even if Lea may still try to help Olga, it seems clear that cases of failed empathy are characterized by the absence of a valuable connection. This connection is meaningful as it affords Lea ways of communicating to Olga that she is right about how she regards her particular situation and about who she is. Similarly, it provides Lea with the opportunity to open up to Olga and to allow her to get close to her. By empathizing, Lea is thus much more likely to do something good for Olga, given her particular situation.

The scenarios of failed empathy thus substantiate the intuitive conviction that empathy establishes a valuable relationship between two people and that this relationship is absent when empathy does not occur. The evaluative justice and recognition provided by empathy make the relationship valuable. The relationship is thus manifested in an intimate bond between the subject and the target. By contrast, without empathy the other person feels alone and separated from the perspectives of others, which can lead to her questioning her viewpoint.

Not every case of empathy, however, is a condition of empathy's value. So, even if failed empathy implies the absence of a valuable connection between two people in the aforementioned ways, this does not imply that empathy always creates valuable relationships. Indeed, the following cases illustrate that there are a number of instances when empathy can fail to do just that.

First, a relationship is not valuable when empathic powers are used in a manipulative or abusive way. For example, Lea may suffer from helper syndrome and may cultivate her empathy in order to make herself feel good. She thus risks paternalizing and overwhelming Olga with her vicarious feelings, since she is likely to empathize too much and too often.

Second, and not unrelatedly, Lea may not empathize with Olga to the right degree. For example, she may over-empathize with Olga, even if what has happened to Olga does not matter that much to her. Perhaps Olga stopped loving Mario long ago and had expected him to leave her. In such a scenario, the empathy shown by Lea would not lead to a meaningful relationship.

Third, it is possible to empathize so inaccurately that a meaningful relationship is not created. It is easy to underestimate cultural, social, and personal contingencies that account for the different ways in which people perceive their environment. Even if Olga tells Lea how she feels, empathy is prone to be inaccurate (Ickes and Hodges 1997). Lea may, for example, come to feel sorrow, while Olga feels anger.

Fourth, empathy may simply be unsuccessful because it is not welcomed by the target: Olga may not want any empathy, at least not from Lea, and as such she may be unwilling to forge an empathic relationship.

These four cases in which empathy fails to establish a meaningful relationship tell us something about the criteria that empathy has to meet. For empathy to result in a meaningful relationship, it must: (a) be realized on behalf of the target; (b) be sufficiently accurate; (c) resonate sufficiently with an experience that is relevant and meaningful to the target; and (d) be accepted by the target. These conditions, however, are not what make empathy ultimately valuable: rather, they are the conditions of the existence of empathy's value and thus pertain to the relational nature of empathy. But they do guarantee that empathy can lead to valuable relationships being formed.

As a result, I hope to have succeeded in arguing the case for empathy's relational value. So far, however, my examination of that value has been relatively superficial. Now I shall analyze in more detail the precise source of empathy's relational value.

4. Empathy as relational value for its own sake

There are both intrinsic and extrinsic qualities that make empathy relationally valuable for its own sake, so that some of empathy's value comes from its internal features and some from the value of other things.[20] Its value is thus based on the more specific ways in which the subject and the target relate to each other.

Regarding empathy's intrinsic value, it is the mental states involved in empathy that comprise the source of relational value, which is thus intrinsic or internal to these mental states. If the experiences of the target are positive, experiencing them oneself will result in pleasant feelings for both the subject and the target. The subject experiences positive emotions, while the target feels that she is receiving empathy, is being taken seriously, and is worthy of such attention, all of which add to the pleasurable quality of her experiences. This will, in turn, make the subject feel that she has had a positive effect on the other person, which will enhance her own positive experience. Thus, empathy is valuable insofar as it means that we relate to each other through the sharing of experiences, which results in both parties being in harmony. By contrast, when the other person's experiences are negative, then experiencing them oneself will not in itself be pleasant, although to respond appropriately to what another person is experiencing is, in itself, a source of value. There are two reasons for this. First, it is valuable to have appropriate responses, since this helps us to get things right. Second, if Lea takes a negative stance toward Olga's predicament through experiencing vicariously the feelings of sorrow herself, she then makes a normative case for Olga's unfortunate situation. She thereby conveys to Olga that her feelings are warranted. This explains the meaningful connection between Lea and Olga: Lea appraises Olga's situation appropriately and Olga sees that Lea takes her interpretation of the situation to be justified.[21] Hence, empathy can be said to be relationally valuable for its own sake when a person responds appropriately to another person's situation. There is value, too, in responding appropriately on the basis that it creates meaning.[22] The source of empathy's value is intrinsic to the experiential character of empathy, and it can be described as *pleasantness, harmony,* and *meaning* for the subject and the target.

As a 'fitting attitude,' empathy additionally provides justification, which gives it a normative dimension that is relationally valuable. This value is extrinsic in that it is based not on empathy's experiential qualities, but rather on what it does, in a justifiable sense, to another person. That is, empathy is valuable for its own sake because of the kind of relationship that is created between two people. This can be clarified if we look more closely at what empathy realizes by virtue of its relationship to the person who is empathized with. Olga, for example, will regard her viewpoint as being affirmed, since, by empathizing, Lea affirms that Olga's emotional perspective on her situation is justified.[23] She conveys to Olga that it is appropriate to feel the way she does, given the reality of her situation. Ultimately, because Olga's emotional perspective is what matters to her, Lea's affirmation will extend to Olga as a person (Herrmann 2013). Olga will feel accepted and recognized as the person she is because of Lea's affirmation of her evaluative perspective. Empathy is thus a response to the value of an individual person, which is a consequence of experiencing vicariously the evaluative perspective of that person's experiences.[24]

By contrast, if Olga's husband had reproached her for overreacting, Lea's empathy would provide justification that this is not the case, and that Olga's reading of the situation is intelligible and correct. Olga's experiences are thus justified not only by the circumstances of her experiences, but also by Lea's empathy.[25] Empathy is thus relationally valuable for its own sake by virtue of the recognition that it gives to the person receiving the empathy. Since recognition implies that one regards someone as having intrinsic worth, Lea's expression of empathy recognizes Olga as having intrinsic worth by affirming Olga's emotional perspective on a situation that matters to her. Lea thus conveys to Olga that she is not alone in how she views her situation. Her empathy can provide this recognition because of its normative function, that is, by affirming that Olga's emotions are justified.[26]

That empathy's value is extrinsically based on recognition can be clarified further if we return to the cases of failed empathy mentioned earlier. Suppose Lea cannot bring herself to empathize with Olga. She expresses that she would feel rather differently in such a situation; she may even say that Olga's feelings are unjustified. Olga's situation is, after all, hardly unique, and one should not make such a fuss about it. Such a non-empathic reaction would seem to suggest a degree of disapproval, on her part, of Olga's emotional outlook on things. Thus, by dismissing Olga's emotional outlook, Lea withholds her recognition of Olga.

Lea's empathy thus affects how Olga regards her own evaluative perspective and, ultimately, herself. As a result, Lea's empathy also enhances Olga's self-esteem and self-trust. If Olga sees that her evaluative perspective is being regarded as justified, then she is more likely to have confidence in her ability to assess things correctly. Empathy is thus a way of providing testimonial justice to the target by affirming her evaluative perspective, as well as conveying to the target that she matters to the subject. Lea considers Olga's evaluative perspective to be worthy of attention and, by experiencing vicariously what Olga is going through, she provides Olga with her own valuation of the situation. Lea's empathy is thus relationally valuable because it gives further justification to Olga's assessment of her situation.[27]

There remains one concern pertaining to my claim that empathy has relational value in this sense: What makes empathy a source of justification? The person giving empathy may get things just as wrong as the person receiving empathy. As a result, the very fact that the subject is empathizing can make the target's perspective appear more unjustified. Let us suppose that Olga overreacted to her husband's announcement, owing to her own experiences of abandonment as a child. Her husband had, in fact, informed her early on in their marriage how ill at ease he felt with her. However, Olga ignored his concerns, shut herself off, and showed no willingness to work on their marriage. Against this backdrop, it seems that her reaction to his request for a divorce is less justified. If Lea were to agree with Olga's perception of her situation, how could she provide further justification to Olga's feelings? Instead, it seems that Lea should point out to Olga that she should have heeded her husband's concerns all along.

In response to this concern, let me highlight the fact that the justification given by empathy is not an all-things-considered justification of Olga's perspective. Nor does it imply that Olga and Lea's viewpoints are true. Rather, Lea's perspective adds a further testimonial justification to Olga's. This does not rule out the fact that Lea may have been misinformed about Mario's behavior, or that she may have shared similar childhood experiences to Olga, which would complicate an appropriate evaluation of the situation. However, the fact that another person can come to hold a similar viewpoint increases the likelihood that that perspective is well-founded. This seems to be sufficient to give further justification to Olga's perspective, although the justification remains perspectivist, not objectivist.[28]

To the extent that *recognition* is a source of value as it enhances *self-esteem* and *self-trust*, and bearing in mind that empathy is valuable by virtue of the recognition it gives, empathy is extrinsically valuable for its own sake. That is, it is valuable because of the relationship it forges between people by way of recognition and testimonial or evaluative justice.

Provided that empathy is a relational value that is valuable for its own sake, it also has a constitutive value: because it is valuable for its own sake, it is also of value to other values.

5. Empathy as constitutive value

Since empathy is valuable for its own sake by virtue of its intrinsic and extrinsic qualities, it is also an important building block of close relationships. Close relationships are those that include enduring, substantive, and mutually affirmed interactions between two or more people over time (Seglow 2013, chap. 2). Empathy is thus not only directed at another individual and at what she conveys about her situation; it is also targeted at the relationship with that individual, however basic it may be, since the relationship involves the exchange of emotional perspectives (Bohl 2015, 684). Thus, Lea also shapes her ongoing relationship with Olga by empathizing.[29]

What seems to intuitively support the claim that empathy has constitutive value, insofar as it helps to establish and maintain close relationships, is that those who apply evaluative or testimonial justice to how we value things are the kind of people who we tend to regard as being good-willed towards us. We thus seek out their attention and company, and are also more likely to like them and be more willing to reciprocate favors.

That empathy is an important building block of close relationships can also be further substantiated if we look at cases where empathy is expressed and yet the empathizing person shows little or no interest in developing the relationship any further. If we are enjoying genuine empathy, if we are not particularly concerned about protecting our privacy, and in the absence, more often than not, of confounding factors,[30] we typically raise our normative expectations with regard to our relationship with that person. Particularly if we receive empathy on a number of occasions, we are likely to infer that the subject is concerned about our well-being and our value as a person. If we welcome this concern, we typically yearn to have more contact with that person in order to develop a closer relationship. However, if the empathizing person is not inclined to do so, we usually become frustrated and feel somewhat manipulated. It seems that genuine empathy is an offer of intimacy; if further intimacy is not forthcoming, feelings of rejection can result. Thus, the intimate bond that empathy creates helps us to develop close relationships over longer periods of time with specific others.[31]

This intimate bond can also be seen if we consider the instances in which empathy is unwelcome. If we find intimacy inappropriate – and we all have a legitimate claim to privacy – we will find empathy to be uncalled for, even if the person giving empathy empathizes appropriately. This may occur when we do not welcome the intimate bond that empathy can foster, either because of the timing or because of the empathizer. But again, this does not mean that empathy does not have important relational value. It merely illustrates that we do not seek to realize that value with just anyone.

In addition to these intuitive ways of supporting the claim that empathy is constitutively valuable for close relationships, I will now show in more detail how empathy can be said to constitute, in part at least, the value of close relationships. To this end, I will make use of the so-called 'relationship goods' theory.

Relationships can be said to be valuable for their own sake on account of the relationship goods that the parties generate and that forge a particular type of relationship. These goods include intimacy, mutual concern and care, common purposes, shared experiences, trust, assistance, and favor (Seglow 2013, chap. 2; Brighouse and Swift 2014; Pettit 2015, chap. 1). The idea behind such a relationship goods theory is that participants in relationships can generally be regarded as generating relationship goods through their 'mutually oriented interactions' (Seglow 2013, 30). Each participant must, therefore, be both an agent and a beneficiary for relationship goods to be conferred, and these goods can be conferred only if each agent engages in activities directed towards the other over time. These goods are partly constitutive of the kind of relationship that is being fostered.[32] The list of goods is not finite, and some goods may consist of the more concrete parts of more comprehensive goods.

Empathy can thus be regarded as a part of the more comprehensive good of intimacy and as encompassing shared experiences, both of which appear on the list of relationship goods that proponents of the viewpoint typically provide. Ultimately, it is up to the parties involved to decide whether they are successful in generating the goods. However, if they are not, their relationship will deteriorate. The goods, of course, vary according to the particular type of relationship. Unsurprisingly, intimacy is not a good that teachers and students typically generate, although it is a good that involves partners, friends, and family members. Hence, the goods that parties in a particular relationship generate are based, in part at least, on the kind of relationship that is being fostered, which is largely governed by social norms.

To generate these relationship goods, however, the parties involved need to value each other and their relationship in a non-instrumental way. This entails that they regard themselves as partners in a particular relationship and that for the sake of their relationship they generate such goods. In other words, the value of a particular relationship depends on the goods of a specific relationship being delivered. Furthermore, these goods should be provided reliably or in a 'robust' way.[33] For example, if Lea and Olga are friends, they cannot only show mutual concern on one occasion and when they feel like it; they must also be prepared to show concern when they feel disinclined to do so or when one of them seems less deserving.

If I am on the right track, then it would be helpful to focus on empathy as being part of a particular relationship good and to tease out how it contributes to the value, in part at least, of the friendship between Lea and Olga. What is it about empathy's relational value that helps explain both its contribution to friendship and its role in maintaining that friendship? Let us recall that empathy is intrinsically and extrinsically valuable on account of the pleasant experiences, harmony, and meaning it provides, and the recognition, self-esteem, and self-trust it enhances. Against this backdrop, we can propose three more concrete ways in which empathy can be seen to contribute to developing the women's friendship.

First, empathy enhances trust in the goodwill of the other by making the target feel recognized and singled out on account of the testimonial justice she receives. By trusting in Lea's goodwill, Olga opens up to Lea and feels that she has reason to continue seeking out the latter's company. Olga thus develops an interest in generating additional goods with Lea. It is these goods that characterize their particular friendship.

A second way in which empathy can be thought to contribute to the value of a particular relationship is that it creates attachment. If Lea empathizes with Olga, and Olga feels empathized with, then their sense of closeness and belonging will be nurtured and they will come to feel relaxed in each other's company. This is thanks to empathy's intrinsic and extrinsic qualities. Lea will start to matter to Olga (and vice versa) in ways that strengthen Olga's need for Lea and their relationship.[34]

Since we typically have a deeply entrenched need to belong, and empathy caters to that need, we will find reasons to seek and give empathy not just once but on a regular basis.[35] As it is usually not only empathy *per se* that is appreciated but also the giving and receiving of empathy, the parties will seek to engage with each other on a more ongoing basis.

Finally, empathy enhances loving attitudes and affection. If Lea affirms Olga's interpretation of her situation, she will respond to what Olga values or disvalues, and ultimately to Olga. Since Olga appreciates having been singled out, she is more likely to develop a positive attitude towards Lea. A person who receives empathy will feel liked or loved, which, in turn, may intensify the target's own positive attitudes towards the subject.

Trust in the goodwill of the other, *attachment*, and *affection* constitute the most important relationship goods that are generated in close relationships such as friendships. Insofar as empathy fosters these goods, it can indeed be considered to have important constitutive value.

To be sure, my claim that empathy is constitutively valuable for good close relationships does not imply that empathy is necessary or sufficient for such relationships. My claim is compatible with the idea that not all close relationships involve empathy. After all, some friends generate other goods, such as common purposes and mutual aid, and still qualify as having a friendship, even if they never empathize with each other. However, even if there are friendships that make do without empathy, they must surely lack a particular good, and it will be hard to qualify them as being close and intimate. All I mean to say is that empathy is a building block of intimate relationships.

In addition, my claim does not imply that all instances of empathy will necessarily help us to develop a good relationship: we can have an empathic exchange with a complete stranger. All I try to show is that empathy, by virtue of its relational value, *also* has constitutive value. Having constitutive value simply implies that empathy's intrinsic and extrinsic qualities help us to establish relationships. It does not suggest that relationships will always ensue. But one might even worry that empathy actually lowers the value of a particular relationship. As it can reinforce a state of helplessness and thereby undermine the receiver's autonomy, it could be argued that empathy may not always be beneficial to the people involved, and thus not foster good relationships. It is important to note in this connection that the various relationship goods as well as the other goods that participants in relationships may seek, independent of their particular relationship, are plural and sometimes incommensurable, and that they need to be balanced. These properties do not minimize empathy's constitutive value, but they do show that empathy sometimes has to be weighed against autonomy and other values.

Also, some relationships are unhealthy, such as abusive relationships and relationships with bad endings, although they could still be said to involve empathy. How can we then think about empathy having constitutive value if it contributes to something bad? It is important to bear in mind that empathy's relational value is not unconditional. Rather, as I emphasized above, it depends on other conditions for its existence. One such condition is that empathy is neither directed at people whose evaluative perspective does not merit it, nor is it directed at people who fail to express empathy's relational value and end up hurting someone instead. Hence, we do not have a list of all-things-considered reasons for the occurrence of empathy in every possibly context. In addition, empathy is only, *pro tanto*, of relational value: it can lose its value if it is connected with things that are negative. An example of such a case could be an empathic relationship with immoral ends. However, the relational value of empathy can also be enhanced thanks to other goods, such as the benefits provided to the target person. Finally empathy can sometimes lead to relationships being irreparably damaged. For example, if too many negative emotions are shared and empathized with, empathy may well be enhanced, even though the relationship will ultimately suffer, since it is unlikely that anyone will want to share negative emotions over a long period of time. So how can my claim about the constitutive value of empathy be sustained?

This worry does not show that empathy can undermine close relationships. Rather, it reveals that parties to a close relationship can misuse one another. For example, the person receiving empathy can take advantage of the person giving empathy by using the close relationship simply as an opportunity to vent their negative feelings. Such an instance teaches us that empathy is only valuable when it ultimately leads to a meaningful relationship. If we empathize or demand too much, the relational value of empathy will not be realized.

Empirical research offers further support to my claim that empathy is constitutively valuable, and serves as an important building block for close relationships. Various psychological studies provide additional evidence that there is a close connection between a flourishing close relationship and a high level of empathy, and between a malfunctioning close relationship and a lack of empathy. Studies in social psychology, for example, confirm that emotional intelligence, empathy, and reports on relationship satisfaction are intimately linked: couples with high levels of empathy tend to have more positive relationship outcomes than couples with low levels of empathy. Conversely, divorce and separation, which are experienced as negative life events with severe effects on self-esteem, are correlated with deficiencies in empathy.[36]

In a similar vein, patients with certain psychiatric illnesses, who have trouble empathizing with others and with whom it is extremely hard to empathize, find it difficult to form and maintain satisfying close relationships. People with disorders on the autistic spectrum, for example, are reported to have difficulty feeling and expressing emotion. This deficit, it is hypothesized, prevents them from engaging in social interaction, let alone from forming close relationships. Even though the aspect of empathy that is dysfunctional in autism spectrum disorder remains disputed, there is clear evidence of a link between lack of empathy and poor relationships (Decety and Moriguchi 2007, 15f; Hobson 2002).

These observations add further support to my claim that there is a connection between empathy and close relationships, one that, I maintain, exists because of empathy's relational value.

6. Back to morality

I have tried to spell out the different ways in which empathy can be considered to have relational value, that is, value it has due to the specific kind of relationship it forges between subject and target. However, one could still reflect on what this tells us about the link between empathy and morality.

There are at least two interesting moral implications to consider. It is empathy's relational value that ultimately explains both why the practice of empathy should be restricted and how to navigate between empathy and moral principles in moral decision-making. As a result, it is the relational value of empathy that explains why we are sometimes morally required to empathize and why sometimes we should morally abstain from giving empathy. Let me explain.

As to the first implication, we have defeasible moral reasons to empathize if this is what a close relationship calls for. Hence, if Lea failed to show any empathy towards Olga, Olga would be justified in accusing Lea of not being a good friend. It is empathy's relational value that can justify partiality. But even if it does, how can it help us navigate between partial and impartial demands? After all, it is empathy's partiality that has generated skepticism concerning empathy's link with morality. As recent research in social psychology convincingly shows, while we show empathy with in-group members, we display apathy, if not antipathy, towards out-group members (Cikara et al. 2014). Does an emphasis on the relational value of empathy thus strengthen these psychological yet immoral tendencies to exclude, disregard, or even look down on others?

This skepticism brings me to the second moral implication of empathy's relational value. It would be a mistake to conclude that empathy's relational value gives us reasons to empathize all of the time and always to the fullest extent. If we are selective about when, how, and to whom we give empathy, we will undermine neither the value of a particular relationship nor the relational value of empathy. It is the relational value of empathy that helps us to understand that when no empathy is needed, we have no reason to empathize, such as when the people with whom we have relationships do not need our help, are not suffering, or do not find themselves in difficult situations that they do not care about. In these kinds of cases, empathy does not fulfill any particular relational value. Therefore, we can realize the relational value of empathy and still take impartial concerns into consideration.[37]

So, although it remains difficult to accommodate partialist and impartialist demands in theory, it is far from impossible in practice. In fact, we do it all the time. Again, it is the relational value of empathy that provides further guidance as to how to balance these demands. We are only required to realize the relational value of empathy, which means that we are left with a number of ways of taking impartial demands into account, and thereby restricting empathy externally.

As a result, the link between empathy and morality is twofold. On the one hand, we have defeasible reasons to empathize insofar as empathy is morally called for by a particular relationship (or if we have defeasible moral reasons to establish a relationship by empathy). On the other, it is precisely empathy's relational value that allows us to show that it can be kept within bounds. We are not always and constantly required to realize the relational value of empathy. The link between empathy and morality is, therefore, normative. We sometimes have moral reasons to empathize, while other times we have moral reasons to refrain from empathizing and take up an impartialist perspective; our normative capacities will enable us to decide how to respond to particular cases. Empathy as such is an interpersonal and thus relational phenomenon. It relates us to others, and this can, but need not, be what morality demands.[38]

In this article, I have tried to clarify the essential features of the relational value of empathy. Moreover, I hope to have contributed to the debate on how empathy and morality are linked: it is the relational value that makes empathy unique, and that provides a basis for the moral demands placed on us; empathy's relational value also helps to limit our practice of empathy and open up room for impartial concerns. Although my claim is modest in that the relational value of empathy only gives rise to defeasible moral reasons, it is also potentially far-reaching in that it might finally put to rest the perennial debate on the link between empathy and morality.

Notes

1. Similarly, it is difficult to imagine what kind of other-regarding motivations could be drawn from empathizing with someone who is angry: going after the cause of the person's anger will hardly count as moral action.
2. Many of the authors of this set of proposals make use of both strategies, but fail to distinguish clearly between them.
3. See Kauppinen (2014, 97ff). Idealizing strategies were proposed as far back as the eighteenth century. See Smith ([1759] 2002). Cf. Carse (2005, 171), who argues for 'morally contoured empathy' as a 'reflective notion.' See Masto (2015, 92).
4. In this vein, Song (2015, 440), claims that the debate about empathy 'in its proper form' invokes different normative standards, so that the concept of what constitutes empathy in its proper form remains ambiguous. See Carse (2005, 188); Simmons (2014, 97); Masto (2015, 92).
5. See Oxley (2011, chap. 3); Steinberg (2014); Song (2015); Masto (2015, 84f.); Hamington (2017, 264ff.); Smith (2017, 711ff.). However, the precise role of the epistemic significance of empathy with regard to moral behavior remains unclear. Oxley (2011, chap., 3), thinks that empathy is a means to morality; Masto (2015, 92), claims that it is 'often necessary for doing the right thing for the right reason.'
6. For the purposes of this article, I remain silent on the precise connection between values and reasons.
7. Batson (2009, 3–15), distinguishes between eight distinct concepts of empathy. See also Michael (2014). Cuff et al. (2016), claim there are forty-three definitions in the literature!
8. See, e.g. Deonna (2007); Steinberg (2014, 49f.); Smith (2017, 713). Cf. Vignemont and Jacob (2012), who add a caring condition to what they call the affectivity condition, the interpersonal similarity condition, the causal path condition, and the ascription condition; Snow (2000). Cf. Michael (2014, 157ff). Furthermore, a certain degree of cognitive representation of the target's situation and experiences as well as a clear self-other distinction are necessary to differentiate empathy from emotional contagion or some automatic 'mirrored understanding.' See Debes (2010, 232). It also needs to be emphasized that empathy differs from mere empathic understanding or imagination, neither of which requires any affective response. Cf. Debes (2010, 221); Maibom (2017, 1ff.); Matravers (2017, 1f).
9. The condition of affective matching or emotional congruence, for example, has recently been met with a certain degree of skepticism. Patients with psychiatric illnesses are cases in point. See Ratcliffe (2017a, 2017b). But Wondra and Ellsworth (2015, 418ff.), convincingly show that the so-called 'appraisal theory' of empathy explains more effectively why empathy arises from what they call 'matching emotions,' while 'non-matching emotions' qualify as a different kind of appraisal of the situation in which a target finds herself. See also Cuff et al. (2016).
10. See Fiske and Haslam (1996). Cf. Fiske (2012). Conversely, a lack of empathy can harm relationships. E.g. patients suffering from psychiatric illnesses, who have a tendency to attribute, without basis, malevolent thoughts and emotions to others, put their relationships at risk.

11. Bohl (2015, 689). Smith (2017, 713), maintains that empathy's aim is to relate to specific others and thereby to achieve a 'social purpose'.
12. See Wynn and Wynn (2006, 1388). Cf. Kupetz (2014, 9ff.), who explores the resources that can be used to show empathy in response to affect displays.
13. See Main et al. (2017, 5), for an interesting development of this idea of empathy involving 'continuous emotional attunement.' Cf. Kupetz (2014), who employs conversation analysis in his study of empathy as a temporal process. Wynn and Wynn (2006) draw on conversation analysis to show how empathy occurs in the actual interactions between therapists and their patients.
14. See Zaki, Bolger, and Ochsner (2008, 400), who conclude, from their data, that empathy is a 'fundamentally interpersonal process.' See Halpern (2001, 88).
15. Bohl (2015, 683ff.), draws from research in social psychology to defend the view that the role of empathy is normative. We can monitor and shape our social relationships through practicing empathy. That empathy has a normative dimension is also supported by recent psychological research that shows how empathy is based on our evaluation of the target's situation and not merely on the target's emotion. See Wondra and Ellsworth (2015). This stance has an important historical precedent in the viewpoint of Adam Smith. See Smith ([1759] 2002, 14f.), who claimed that 'sympathy [...] does not arise so much from the view of the passion, as from that of the situation which excites it.'
16. Tannenbaum (2010) describes this distinction between the condition of the existence of a value, and the source of a value.
17. Animals are not taken into account in this article.
18. This notion of a source of value pertaining to relational value needs to be distinguished from claims about the *relational nature of value*. One could assume that debate on the relational value of empathy implies that value is essentially relational: things can only be good because there are sentient beings *for* whom things can be good. By asking in what way empathy is good, I am not supporting any particular viewpoint about the nature of value; I am only trying to ascertain the source of empathy's goodness. Korsgaard (2013, 4f.), e.g. defends this view. See Rosati (2009, 225f.).
19. Here, I have drawn on Fricker's work on epistemic injustice. See Fricker (2009).
20. I have benefitted from the work of Rabinowicz and Rønnow-Rasmussen (2000), who distinguish between 'intrinsic' and 'extrinsic' qualities. See also Tannenbaum (2010, 273ff.), for a lucid analysis of value categorization. Cf. Korsgaard 1983, 169–195.
21. See Wolf (2010). Bohl (2015, 683), points out, with reference to relational models theory, that social connection is generally perceived as desirable, meaningful, and rewarding in itself.
22. See Wolf (2010), who believes that meaning in life arises when we value something of objective value subjectively.
23. See Debes (2010, 222). Cf. Darwall (1998, 268), who asserts that we are unable to empathize if we are unaware of the details of the target's situation, which help to explain the latter's emotions.
24. See Aaltola (2014), who emphasizes that empathy is directed at the value of individuals.

25. See Debes (2010, 223f.), who points out that when one empathizes, one 'accepts' the other's emotion in light of the 'why.'
26. Ikäheimo and Laitinen (2007), define recognition along these lines. See Brandom (2007, 136), who writes that recognition is a normative attitude. Insofar as I analyze empathy as a recognitional attitude, my aim is to understand more fully the distinct normative role of empathy.
27. This is why Ikäheimo and Laitinen (2007), refer to a dialogical conception of recognition.
28. One may question whether a perspectivist justification is a proper justification at all. Indeed, empathy may reinforce an ill-founded perspective. But in lending warrant to another person's perspective, thus coming to a similar evaluation than her, provides at least additional evidence that there is something to be said for the perspective of the person empathized with. I am grateful to an anonymous reviewer for pressing me on this issue.
29. This is substantiated by studies in social psychology. Cf. Fiske and Haslam (1996).
30. These could include the fact that we meet that person by happenstance and only on a single occasion.
31. There are clearly different kinds of relationships. What links these relationships is the amount of depth they have with regard to how people connect with each other. It is the degree of empathy that provides, in part at least, this depth.
32. I draw from Seglow (2013, 30f.), who gives a detailed analysis of the relationship goods theory.
33. Pettit (2015, 34f.), helpfully characterizes relationships as requiring the provision of 'robust' goods, and that for these goods to be delivered the parties need to conduct themselves appropriately in actual circumstances and in variations of these circumstances.
34. See Wonderly (2016, 232), for an illuminating analysis of 'security-based' attachment. By becoming attached, the attached party has a relatively enduring desire to engage with a non-substitutable particular, and she will suffer from a reduced sense of security if separated from the object of attachment.
35. This is substantiated by recent studies in psychology. According to Zaki (2014, 1629), people seek empathy even if it is painful, provided that empathy allows them to establish and maintain a relationship.
36. There is a great deal of literature on this topic, which I cannot survey here *in toto*. See, e.g. Schutte et al. (2001, 52ff.), and Malouff, Schutte, and Thorsteinsson (2014, 523ff).
37. Cikara et al. (2014, 120ff.), suggest that reducing the perceived in-group and out-group 'entitativity' by engaging in cooperation can significantly attenuate counter-empathic responses. Hence, impartial concerns may require us to recategorize those with whom we do not have close relationships.
38. I am grateful for feedback I received from audiences at the University of Belgrade in May 2018, from the University of Lucerne in October 2017 on presented earlier versions of this paper. I am also indebted to Alexander Bagattini, Christian Budnik, André Grahle, Jörg Löschke, Hannah Read, Anna Wehofsits and two anonymous reviewers for helpful suggestions.

Disclosure statement

No potential conflict of interest was reported by the author.

References

Aaltola, E. 2014. "Affective Empathy as Core Moral Agency: Psychopathy, Autism and Reason Revisited." *Philosophical Explorations* 17: 76–92. doi:10.1080/13869795.2013.825004.
Batson, C. D. 2009. "These Things Called Empathy: Eight Related but Distinct Phenomena." In *The Social Neuroscience of Empathy*, edited by J. Decety and W. Ickes, 3–15. Cambridge, MA: MIT Press.
Bloom, P. 2016. *Against Empathy: The Case for Rational Compassion*. London: Penguin.
Bohl, V. 2015. "We Read Minds to Shape Relationships." *Philosophical Psychology* 28: 674–694. doi:10.1080/09515089.2014.893607.
Brandom, R. 2007. "The Structure of Desire and Recognition. Self-Consciousness and Self-Constitution." *Philosophy & Social Criticism* 33: 127–150. doi:10.1177/0191453707071389.
Brighouse, H., and A. Swift. 2014. *Family Values: The Ethics of Parent-Child Relationships*. Princeton: Princeton University Press.
Carruthers, P., and P. K. Smith, eds. 1996. *Theories of Theories of Mind*. Cambridge: Cambridge University Press.
Carse, A. L. 2005. "The Moral Contours of Empathy." *Ethical Theory and Moral Practice* 8: 169–195. doi:10.1007/s10677-005-3291-7.
Cikara, M., E. Bruneau, J. Van Bavel, and R. Saxe. 2014. "Their Pain Gives Us Pleasure: How Intergroup Dynamics Shape Empathic Failures and Counter-Empathic Responses." *Journal of Experimental Social Psychology* 55: 110–125. doi:10.1016/j.jesp.2014.06.007.
Coplan, A. 2011. "Understanding Empathy: Its Features and Effects." In *Empathy: Philosophical and Psychological Perspectives*, edited by A. Coplan and P. Goldie, 3–18. Oxford: Oxford University Press.
Cuff, B. M., S. J. Brown, L. Taylor, and D. J. Howat. 2016. "Empathy: A Review of the Concept." *Emotion Review* 8: 144–153. doi:10.1177/1754073914558466.
Darwall, S. 1998. "Empathy, Sympathy, Care." *Philosophical Studies* 89: 261–282. doi:10.1023/A:1004289113917.
Debes, R. 2010. "Which Empathy? Limitations in the Mirrored 'Understanding' of Emotion." *Synthese* 175: 219–239. doi:10.1007/s11229-009-9499-7.
Decety, J., and Y. Moriguchi. 2007. "The Empathic Brain and Its Dysfunction in Psychiatric Populations: Implications for Intervention across Different Clinical Conditions." *BioPsychoSocial Medicine* 1: 1–21. doi:10.1186/1751-0759-1-22.
Deonna, J. 2007. "The Structure of Empathy." *Journal of Moral Philosophy* 4: 99–116. doi:10.1177/1740468107077385.
Ferrante, E. 2005. *The Days of Abandonment*. Translated by Ann Goldstein. New York: Europa Editions.
Fiske, A. 2012. "Metarelational Models: Configurations of Social Relationships." *European Journal of Social Psychology* 42: 2–18. doi:10.1002/ejsp.847.
Fiske, A., and N. Haslam. 1996. "Social Cognition Is Thinking about Relationships." *Current Directions in Psychological Science* 5: 143–148. doi:10.1111/1467-8721.ep11512349.

Fricker, M. 2009. *Epistemic Injustice: Power and the Ethics of Knowing*. Oxford: Oxford University Press.

Halpern, J. 2001. *From Detached Concern to Empathy*. Oxford: Oxford University Press.

Hamington, M. 2017. "Empathy and Care Ethics." In *The Routledge Handbook of the Philosophy of Empathy*, edited by H. L. Maibom, 264–272. London: Routledge.

Herrmann, M. 2013. "Empathie in Beziehungen zwischen Personen." In *Person. Anthropologische, phänomenologische und analytische Perspektiven*, edited by I. Römer and M. Wunsch, 363–382. Münster: mentis Verlag.

Hobson, R. P. 2002. *The Cradle of Thought*. London: Macmillan.

Ickes, W., and S. D. Hodges. 1997. "Empathic Accuracy in Close Relationships." In *Empathic Accuracy*, edited by W. Ickes, 218–250. New York: Guilford Press.

Ikäheimo, H., and A. Laitinen. 2007. "Analyzing Recognition: Identification, Acknowledgment and Recognitive Attitudes Towards Persons." In *Recognition and Power: Axel Honneth and the Tradition of Critical Social Theory*, edited by B. van Den Brink and D. Owen, 33–56. Cambridge: Cambridge University Press.

Kauppinen, A. 2014. "Empathy, Emotion Regulation, and Moral Judgment." In *Empathy and Morality*, edited by H. L. Maibom, 87–121. Oxford: Oxford University Press.

Korsgaard, C. 1983. "Two Distinctions in Goodness." *The Philosophical Review* 92: 169–195. doi:10.2307/2184924.

Korsgaard, C. 2013. "The Relational Nature of the Good." In *Oxford Studies in Metaethics 8*, edited by R. Shafer-Landau, 1–26. Oxford: Oxford University Press.

Kupetz, M. 2014. "Empathy Displays as Interactional Achievements – Multimodal and Sequential Aspects." *Journal of Pragmatics* 61: 4–34. doi:10.1016/j.pragma.2013.11.006.

Maibom, H. L. 2017. "Introduction: Everything You Ever Wanted to Know about Empathy." In *Empathy and Morality*, edited by H. L. Maibom, 1–40. Oxford: Oxford University Press.

Main, A., E. A. Walle, C. Kho, and J. Halpern. 2017. "The Interpersonal Functions of Empathy. A Relational Perspective." *Emotion Review* 9: 358–366. doi:10.1177/1754073916669440.

Malouff, J. M., N. S. Schutte, and E. B. Thorsteinsson. 2014. "Trait Emotional Intelligence and Romantic Relationship Satisfaction: A Meta-Analysis." *The American Journal of Family Therapy* 42: 53–66. doi:10.1080/01926187.2012.748549.

Masto, M. 2015. "Empathy and Its Role in Morality." *The Southern Journal of Philosophy* 53: 74–96. doi:10.1111/sjp.12097.

Matravers, D. 2017. *Empathy*. Cambridge: Polity Press.

Michael, J. 2014. "Towards a Consensus about the Role of Empathy in Interpersonal Understanding." *Topoi* 33: 157–172. doi:10.1007/s11245-013-9204-9.

Oxley, J. C. 2011. *The Moral Dimensions of Empathy: Limits and Applications in Ethical Theory and Practice*. Basingstoke: Palgrave Macmillan.

Pettit, P. 2015. *The Robust Demands of the Good: Ethics with Attachment, Virtue, and Respect*. Oxford: Oxford University Press.

Prinz, J. 2011. "Is Empathy Necessary for Morality?" In *Empathy: Philosophical and Psychological Perspectives*, edited by A. Coplan and P. Goldie, 211–229. Oxford: Oxford University Press.

Rabinowicz, W., and T. Rønnow-Rasmussen. 2000. "A Distinction in Value: Intrinsic and for Its Own Sake." *Proceedings of the Aristotelian Society* 100: 33–51. doi:10.1111/j.0066-7372.2003.00002.x.

Ramirez, E. 2017. "Empathy and the Limits of Thought Experiments." *Metaphilosophy* 48: 504–526. doi:10.1111/meta.12249.

Ratcliffe, M. 2017a. "Empathy and Psychiatric Illness." In *The Routledge Handbook of Philosophy of Empathy*, edited by H. L. Maibom, 190–200. London: Routledge.

Ratcliffe, M. 2017b. "Empathy without Simulation." In *Imagination and Social Perspectives: Approaches from Phenomenology and Psychopathology*, edited by Michela Summa, Thomas Fuchs, and Luca Vanzago. 274–306. London: Routledge.

Rosati, C. 2009. "Relational Good and the Multiplicity Problem." *Philosophical Issues* 19: 205–234. doi:10.1111/j.1533-6077.2009.00167.x.

Schutte, N. S., J. M. Malouff, C. Bobik, T. D. Coston, C. Greeson, C. Jedlicka, E. Rhodes, and G. Wendorf. 2001. "Emotional Intelligence and Interpersonal Relations." *The Journal of Social Psychology* 141: 523–536. doi:10.1080/00224540109600569.

Seglow, J. 2013. *Defending Associative Duties*. London: Routledge.

Simmons, A. 2014. "In Defense of the Moral Significance of Empathy." *Ethical Theory and Moral Practice* 17: 97–111. doi:10.1007/s10677-013-9417-4.

Slote, M. 2007. *The Ethics of Care and Empathy*. London: Routledge.

Smith, A. [1759] 2002. *The Theory of Moral Sentiments*. New York: Cambridge University Press.

Smith, J. 2017. "What Is Empathy For?" *Synthese* 194: 709–722. doi:10.1007/s11229-015-0771-8.

Snow, N. 2000. "Empathy." *American Philosophical Quarterly* 37: 65–78. http://www-1jstor-1org-1wqr0dbos01f7.emedia1.bsb-muenchen.de/stable/20009985

Sober, E., and D. S. Wilson. 1998. *Unto Others: The Evolution and Psychology of Unselfish Behavior*. Cambridge, MA: Harvard University Press.

Song, Y. 2015. "How to Be a Proponent of Empathy?" *Ethical Theory and Moral Practice* 18: 437–451. doi:10.1007/s10677-014-9525-9.

Steinberg, J. 2014. "An Epistemic Case for Empathy." *Pacific Philosophical Quarterly* 95: 47–71. doi:10.1111/papq.12016.

Stueber, K. R. 2010. *Rediscovering Empathy. Agency, Folk Psychology, and the Human Sciences*. Cambridge: MIT Press.

Tannenbaum, J. 2010. "Categorizing Goods." In *Oxford Studies in Metaethics 5*, edited by R. Shafer-Landau, 257–294. Oxford: Oxford University Press.

Vignemont, F., and P. Jacob. 2012. "What Is It like to Feel Another's Pain?" *Philosophy of Science* 79: 295–316. doi:10.1086/664742.

Wolf, S. 2010. *Meaning in Life and Why It Matters*. Princeton: Princeton University Press.

Wonderly, M. L. 2016. "On Being Attached." *Philosophical Studies* 173: 223–242. doi:10.1007/s11098-015-0487-0.

Wondra, J., and P. Ellsworth. 2015. "An Appraisal Theory of Empathy and Other Vicarious Emotional Experiences." *Psychological Review* 122: 411–428. doi:10.1037/a0039252.

Wynn, R., and M. Wynn. 2006. "Empathy as an Interactionally Achieved Phenomenon in Psychotherapy. Characteristics of Some Conversational Resources." *Journal of Pragmatics* 38: 1385–1397. doi:10.1016/j.pragma.2005.09.008.

Zaki, J. 2014. "Empathy: A Motivated Account." *Psychological Bulletin* 140: 1608–1647. doi:10.1037/a0037679.

Zaki, J., N. Bolger, and K. Ochsner. 2008. "It Takes Two: The Interpersonal Nature of Empathic Accuracy." *Psychological Science* 19: 399–404. doi:10.1111/j.1467-9280.2008.02099.x.

Relational Empathy

Mark Fagiano

ABSTRACT
This work explains the practical benefits of a new and pluralistic notion of empathy that I call *relational empathy*. Rather than defining empathy as a thing or an activity, as most scholars have done, I define empathy as a set of three conceptually distinct though experientially overlapping relations: the relations of feeling into, feeling with, and feeling for. I then turn to historical discourses about empathy from the late 1700s to the present to demonstrate how different conceptualizations and definitions of empathy during this time span are descriptions of one, two or all three of these relations. I then explain how relational empathy has the potential both to dissolve mere verbal disputes about what empathy is and to shift our attention away from narrowly conceived theories about the 'nature' of empathy and toward more practical concerns. Finally, I explain how my theory of relational empathy can help to resolve a number of problems throughout the healthcare system.

1. Empathy and Pluralism

Peering into the wilderness of research that has shaped the study of empathy, one might experience a sense of bewilderment. Conflicting definitions of the word 'empathy' abound, and this often causes confusion. Quite aware of this, contemporary scholars will often begin a work on the subject of empathy by noting this ambiguity and stipulating precisely what they mean by the word 'empathy'. Definition in hand and theoretical framework in mind, they then demonstrate how their understanding of empathy addresses an important problem. This is a useful and strategic approach, but it hasn't helped us reach a consensus about the meaning of empathy.[1] Since empathy is a social construct, there is no reason a consensus needs to be reached. Different definitions and theories of empathy serve different purposes, and their value should be judged by what they do – that is, by how they explain experience, guide our actions or help create a framework for a scientific inquiry.

Empathy has been and still is often thought to be primarily either a thing or an activity. As a thing, empathy has been defined as a *condition* of possible knowledge of the outside world (Stein 1964 [1917], 63); a natural *capacity* to share, understand and respond with care (Decety 2012, vii); an *ability* to identify and to respond (Baron-Cohen 2012, 16); a shared affective *state* (de Vignemont and Singer 2006, 435); or a complex *form* of psychological inference (Ickes 1997; Danzinger, Prkachin, and Willer 2006). As an activity, empathy has been defined as *perceiving* the internal frame of reference within another (Rogers 1957); *recognizing* what another may be feeling or thinking (Baron-Cohen 2005, 2012); *imagining* the narrative of another (Goldie 2002, 195); or *responding* to another with affect or emotion (Batson and Oleson 1991, 63; Eisenberg and Fabes 1998, 702; Hoffman 2000, 4). Given this tangle of dissenting voices in which even experts disagree, might it be possible to weave together these and other conflicting perspectives about empathy into a pluralistic, inclusive and pragmatic theory? In consideration of this question, I put forth here a new theory of empathy – what I will call relational empathy. I define relational empathy as the convergence of three relations between things and/or activities, rather than as a given activity or thing, though each of these relations has been referred to as a type of 'empathy'.

I refer to three distinct though experientially overlapping relations of experience as the relations of (1) feeling into, (2) feeling with and (3) feeling for. By 'feeling', I signify the general and broad meaning of the Greek understanding of *pathos* as *anything experienced* (Graver 2002, 79; Munteanu 2012, 50; Cayuela 2016, 4).[2]

A *relation* is the mode or manner by which two or more things are interrelated within experience. The term 'relation' is nothing new in the language games of philosophy, but the philosopher William James's articulation and use of it was revolutionary. Relations, for James, are not simply the mode or manner by which things are connected. They are these, but they are also the *fundamentum of experience* itself or James called 'pure experience'.[3] Noticing the myriad relations that connect our thoughts, words and experiences draws out the multiplicity and complexity of experience itself and directs our attentions toward the functionality of our descriptions. James's turn to relations was pragmatic because it helped him dissolve a number of unnecessary philosophical debates. In the same spirit, turning to relations for the purpose of reconstructing empathy provides an opportunity to include conflicting definitions rather than exclude them. It also allows us to reject a number of unhelpful historically prominent dualisms that have influenced contemporary empathy research.

1.1. The Relation of 'feeling into'

We experience this first relation whenever we *feel into* an object of perception or reflection. The object can be anything – another person's thoughts, a beautiful sunset, a Kandinsky painting. It might sound odd to suggest that a characteristic feature of any theory of empathy includes acts of feeling into inanimate objects. After all, isn't it the case that empathy only refers to interpersonal relationships? That might be the case today, but it wasn't before the twentieth century. The word 'empathy' is an historically young word; it was coined in 1909 by the psychologist Edward Titchener (1867–1927) based on the German word *Einfühlung*, which means feeling into – or feeling one's way into – an object (see Titchener 1909). Before Titchener, the German verb *sich einfühlen* was employed variously to signify an experience of 'feeling into' among the romanticists of the late eighteenth century, medical doctors and aestheticians in the mid- to late nineteenth century and, more familiarly perhaps, psychologists during the late nineteenth and early twentieth centuries.

During the late eighteenth century, a number of philosophers, romanticists and Counter-Enlightenment thinkers believed that feeling one's way into things could help combat the misgivings and assumptions of overly systematic and rationalistic interpretations of nature. For example, the poet Novalis (1772–1801) lamented excessively rigid scientific interpretations of nature and how they deaden our poetic and spiritual sense of the world. However, by feeling ourselves into the beauty and magnificence of nature, we can overcome our feelings of separateness from nature that have arisen from rigid scientific portrayals of it and instead feel 'one with nature'. Johann Gottfried Herder (1744–1803) widened our understanding of this first relation by defining it as our ability to feel into *everything* in order to *feel with* all things outside of ourselves, including but not limited to feeling with and understanding others (Herder 1964 [1774], 7–8). Feeling into certain objects, such as the different ideals, goals and ways of life expressed within cultures and histories other than our own, enhances our ability to feel with both similar and dissimilar lived experiences of other people (see Herder 1877–1937, 5: 502–503, 506).[4] Herder's larger aim for thinking this way was to convince the historians of his time that empathic projection (i.e. feeling oneself into an object) ought to be central to the historian's craft. Hermann Lotze (1817–1881) adopted Herder and Novalis's pluralistic view by thinking of what was later termed 'empathy' as an act of feeling into any object. In Lotze's (1856, I, 584) words, there is 'no shape so coy that our fancy cannot ... enter into it'.

By the middle of nineteenth century, the act of feeling into was seen as both an object of scientific inquiry and as a technique for perceiving and understanding aesthetic objects. Friedrich Theodor Vischer (1807–1887) argued that the so-called essential properties of objects in nature are in truth the projections of our own bodily perceptions. Feeling into inanimate objects, on his account, animates matter by infusing it with 'buoyant life' through the linear and planar suspension of its parts (Vischer (1922–1923

[1857], 3: 229 [section 559]). Friedrich's son Robert Vischer (1847–1933), in his 1873 dissertation, coined the term *Einfühlung* to signify a process in which the body and soul are unconsciously projected into the form of an object, especially those objects we call works of art.[5] Based on changes in scientific disciplines, Robert Vischer noted that the act of feeling into objects gives rise to a number of internal bodily processes.

These conceptualizations of empathy gave rise to the notion of empathy as an interpersonal phenomenon. Karl Groos (1861–1946) and Theodor Lipps (1851–1914) offered an important contribution to this historical shift. Each argued that *Einfühlung* is made possible by our natural ability to *internally mimic or imitate* the form, structure and dynamism of external objects. In addition to this, Lipps argued that *Einfühlung* is useful for facilitating aesthetic contemplation as well as to gain knowledge of other people's minds. These conceptual shifts that focus on the physical process of the observer's body – especially the mental states of the observer – were one reason psychologists of the late nineteenth and early twentieth centuries either adopted or rejected *Einfühlung* as a method of psychoanalysis.

1.2. The Relation of 'feeling with'

We experience this second relation whenever we have a sense of being united, in concord or in sync with another person or thing. In contemporary discourses, this relation of *feeling with* is often described as an interpersonal phenomenon, but we can also experience it as a feeling of unity or connection with objects, such as when we have a feeling of oneness with a piece of music. As an interpersonal experience, this relation is noted, most commonly, when we perceive that we grasp, feel or have adopted the perspective of another person. This is generally called 'empathic perspective-taking', but there are two types of perspective-taking, and these are sometimes conflated. For example, you can imagine how you would personally feel if you held the other person's perspective about a given situation, or you can imagine how the other person actually perceives the situation. C. Daniel Batson refers to this first option as 'imagine-self perspective' and the second as 'imagine-other perspective' (see Batson 2009).[6]

Depending upon the context, this relation, and sometimes the relation of feeling into, is experienced in various ways – e.g. feeling an emotional connection with another person or thing; believing we understand another's point of view; mentally simulating the experience of another person; 'catching' another person's mood; co-experiencing another's emotional experiences; mimicking the body language of another; and reading another person's thoughts. Despite the differences between these experiences, they all involve, in one way or another, both the relation of feeling with and the relation of feeling into.

Returning to my historical narrative, Groos's focus on imitation and Lipps's emphasis on reading other people's minds engendered a major paradigmatic shift from thinking of empathy *centrally* as a technique to feel one's way into any object to thinking of empathy as a skill for feeling with or grasping the experiences of other human beings. Nevertheless, it is evident among the theories I have explored thus far that the final goal of the act of feeling into was to feel *with* some object of perception or reflection. For instance, feeling one's way into objects was aimed toward feeling with them in order to experience a form of sympathetic understanding (Herder), a feeling of unity with nature (Novalis), an internal resonance with or an inward mental tracing of aesthetic objects (Lotze, the Vischers), or a process of inner imitation, mimicry, or aesthetic sympathy (Groos and Lipps). These all denote some type of fusion or identification with one's object of perception or reflection. This is important because it shows that the relation of feeling into and the relation of feeling with were never conceived as being independent of one other.

After Lipps, psychologists and sociologists began to explore the usefulness of empathy in psychotherapy and social psychology. In his analysis of humor, Freud (1960 [1905], 186) states that *Einfühlung* signifies not the act of feeling into aesthetic inanimate objects but rather an act in which 'we take the producing person's psychical state into consideration, put ourselves into it and try to understand it by comparing it with our own'. We see a similar stipulation of the word 'empathy' in the works of pragmatist George Herbert Mead, who wrote that social meaning arises through the individual simulating himself to take the attitude of the other in his reaction toward the object (Mead 1938, 545). Mead considered the ability to 'take the role of the other' to be both a biological and a social process within which one perceives the internal frame of reference of another with accuracy.[7] The habit of thinking about empathy as a was reintroduced in the discipline of psychology in the middle of the twentieth century with the works of Carl Rogers. Rogers defined empathy also as the accurate understanding of or feeling with the other, specifically in situations in which the therapist is completely at home in the universe of the patient (Rogers et al. 1967). This understanding, sense and feeling with the perspective of the patient was also central to the approach of Heinz Kohut, who interpreted empathy as a manifestation of the relation of feeling with, which served as a method of therapy offered by the psychologist to the patient (Kohut 1981).

Toward the end of the twentieth century and into the beginning of the twenty-first century, we find a number of attempts to find the biological mechanisms of the relation of feeling with, most notably with the discovery of mirror neurons. These neurons are specialized cells in the brain that are purported to 'fire' not only when one performs a particular action but also when one watches or hears another perform the same action. The theory of mirror neurons was birthed, quite accidentally, during a study of a macaque monkey in Parma, Italy (see di Pellegrino et al. 1992; Gallese et al. 1996; Rizzolatti et al. 1996).[8] In other investigations of mirror neurons following this study, scientists found that a number of auditory neurons also fire in the F5 region upon hearing the sound of an action. Theorists and practitioners interested in empathy should continue to follow these and other exciting developments concerning mirror neurons, as well as all other types of mirroring processes.[9]

1.3. The Relation of 'feeling for'

The third relation occurs whenever we *feel for* other persons or things by caring for them and acting primarily for their benefit. Understanding empathy as consisting simply of the relation of feeling into and/or the relation of feeling with excludes not only how a number of scholars have operationalized empathy as feeling *for* other persons, but also how empathy is used colloquially as a term denoting *one's response to and concern for another*. The validity of defining empathy simply as empathic projection (feeling into) or empathic perspective-taking (feeling with) begins to break down when we examine the different contexts of our experiences and our usages of the word 'empathy' to describe them. Is it possible for a psychologist to feel with patients without feeling for them – that is, without caring? Certainly it is possible, but I suspect that most people within this profession would think that this way of relating to a patient is lacking something vital.

Roughly a century after Lipps's contribution, we find that the concept of empathy is increasingly conjoined with – and even defined as – this relation of feeling for. This seems to have been encouraged by acts of linking the notion of empathy not only with the experience of feeling with another but also with the act of responding or reacting to another's state or condition. The social psychologist C. Daniel Batson also facilitated this historical transition from the relation of feeling with (what he calls 'feeling as') to the relation of feeling for. Quite differently from others, Batson is more philosophically careful, in that he is aware of the multiple and different meanings ascribed to the term 'empathy'. For instance, in one of his many famous works, Batson (2011, 4–8) lists eight different experiences that have been called empathy:

(1) Knowledge of another's internal state, including his or her thoughts and feelings
(2) Adopting the posture or matching the neural response of an observed other

(3) Coming to feel as another person feels
(4) Intuiting or projecting oneself into another's situation
(5) Imagining how another is thinking and feeling
(6) Imagining how one would think and feel in the other's place
(7) Feeling distress at witnessing another person's suffering
(8) Feeling for another person who is suffering

Number 4 here clearly denotes a concrete experience of the relation of feeling into; numbers 1–3 and 5–6 signify both the relation of feeling into and the relation of feeling with; and numbers 7 and 8 might incorporate, in certain circumstances, all three of these relations I have been outlining. Batson employs the notion of empathy and empathic concern to indicate the relation of feeling for in order to analyze both egoism and altruism. Empathic concern, as 'an other-oriented emotional response elicited by and congruent with the perceived welfare of a person in need' (Batson 2011, 11), often produces the motivation to act for the benefit of others rather than ourselves. Yet helping others can also produce a number of consequences that benefit us or boost our ego. For instance, by responding to the needs of another, we may relieve ourselves of the distress we feel at seeing him/her in need, avoid feelings of guilt and shame and/or receive praise from others and gain a sense of pride from acting on another's behalf. Batson's empirical investigations have demonstrated that these three ego-based reactions to helping a person in need do not generate the same kind of motivation as do one's feelings of empathic concern. Empathic concern for another, according to Batson's empathy-altruism hypothesis (Batson 1991, 2011; Batson and Oleson 1991), produces *altruistic* motivation.

A significant number of neuroscientists of the early twenty-first century have incorporated the relation of feeling for into the relation of feeling with. For example, in relational terms, Jean Decety's (2012, vii) definition of empathy as 'the natural capacity to share, understand, and respond with care to the affective states of others' signifies that one is capable of *feeling with* (i.e. sharing and understanding) another's state, and able to *feel for* (i.e. responding with care) the affective states of others. And to do these things well requires that one correctly observes and identifies these states – in other words, that one *feels into* them with perceptual acuity, so that one's sharing and understanding of another's state informs the manner in which one responds with care.

2. Putting Relational Empathy to Work

Relational empathy and all other conceptualizations of empathy are identical to one another in one important way: they are all social constructs that aim not only to describe experience but to change the quality of our lived experiences. The value of any given notion of empathy, then, lies not in its 'being right' in some silo of truth apart from and unrelated to our lived experiences, but rather in *what the notion does* – the manner in which, for example, it shapes habits, decreases the suffering of sentient beings or contributes to the flourishing of our lives. Relational empathy does at least three important things. First, it includes and embraces conflicting definitions of empathy, and consequently, it has the potential to dissolve mere verbal disputes about what empathy is. Second, it directs recurring questions about empathy (e.g. Can empathy be developed? Is empathy moral?) away from abstract speculations about the 'nature' of empathy and toward the variety, contexts and consequences of different experiences. Lastly, it serves as a conceptual framework for recognizing specific experiences of these general relations, and for collecting and analyzing data for the purpose of improving the structure and functionality of organizations. Let us look at these three claims in turn.

2.1. Dissolving Verbal Disputes about What Empathy Is

How might the theory of relational empathy include rather than exclude conflicting definitions of empathy? It seems to me that the value of any given concept or definition of empathy lies in its ability to both illuminate experience and stimulate satisfactory behavioral change. Although exclusionary definitions and narrow conceptualizations of empathy serve a number of purposes, they limit our ability to conceive empathic experiences as they have been described historically. The words 'exclusionary' and 'narrow' are not pejorative here; rather, they signify a pragmatic move in which one's stipulation of the meaning of empathy aims to delineate the parameters of an experience, bring to light particular truths of experience, and ground inquiry toward some end(s). Narrowing the meaning of empathy is clearly worthwhile when it produces insight; nevertheless, narrow approaches necessarily exclude what people have meant or could mean by empathy.

Consider, for instance, three contemporary definitions of 'empathy' today. Returning to Frederique de Vignemont and Tania Singer's work mentioned at the start of this investigation, empathy is defined as a *thing* (i.e. a state) in which 'there is empathy if (i) one is in an affective state, (ii) this state is isomorphic to another person's affective state, (iii) this state is elicited by the observation or imagination of another's person's affective state, (iv) one knows that the other person is the source of one's own affective state' (de Vignemont and Singer 2006, 435). This conceptualization and definition of empathy greatly limits what others have meant and what one could mean by 'empathy' despite the fact that it might serve to help us eradicate a number of problems within certain contexts of experience. In other words, this definition states that empathy exists only when one person observes another and experiences an affective state that is similar to that person's, while noting that the other person is the source of her/his affective state. Conceived relationally, this definition utilizes the relation of *feeling into* and the relation of *feeling with* by asserting that the state that is isomorphic to another person's affective state arises only after observing or imagining the other's affective state (feeling into), but there is no mention of the relation of *feeling for*. Or think about the definition Derek Matravers (2017, 1–2) provides: 'Empathy involves using our imaginations as a tool so as to adopt a different perspective in order to grasp how things appear (or feel) from there.' If we interpret this conceptualization and definition of empathy in relational terms, then the use of our imagination is a manifestation of the relation of *feeling into*, while the adoption of our ability to grasp a different perspective is a demonstration of one way that we *feel with* others (i.e. by grasping an experience other than our own). Again, here the relation of *feeling for* is absent. But if we turn again to Decety's (2012, vii) definition of empathy as 'the natural capacity to share, understand, and respond with care to the affective states of others', we find an explanation of our capacity to experience all three relations.

The theory of relational empathy avoids – and also has the potential to resolve – the conflicts between seemingly irreconcilable definitions and conceptualizations of empathy. It does this by thinking of empathy as a relation between things, between activities, or between a thing and an activity, rather than thinking of it as a discrete thing or activity. With the definitions provided above by de Vignemont and Singer, Matravers, and Decety, we find two understandings of empathy that define empathy primarily as a *thing* and a third that defines it as an *act*. If we were to adopt one of the above definitions of empathy as either a thing or activity – or other similar descriptions of empathy – what purpose would such an understanding serve? If we were to think of empathy as a state, as de Vignemont and Singer do, or as a capacity (Decety) or as activities of the imagination and grasping the experiences of others (Matravers), what would happen in the world? The adoption of relational empathy – conceived as an experience of the intersection of the relations of *feeling into*, *feeling with* and *feeling for* – could provide a conceptual framework for thinking about the value of a number of diverse contextualized experiences relevant to these and other articulations of empathy as a thing or an activity.

Looking at a pluralistic definition of empathy other than my own, we find that there is room for including all three of the relations I have delineated here. For instance, Stephanie Preston and Frans de Waal define empathy as 'any process where the *attended perception* of the object's state generates a *state in the subject* that is more applicable to the *object's state or situation* than to the subject's own prior state or situation' (Preston and de Waal 2002, 4; emphasis added). With this pluralistic, broad and general definition, the 'attended perception of the object' incorporates the relation of feeling into, while the 'state in the subject' could be applied to any specific experience of the subject, that is, to *feeling for* and/or *feeling with* the 'object's state or situation'. Some argue that these and other broad approaches for understanding empathy are too vague to be helpful.[10] Conceived relationally, however, it is clear that these terms serve as particular general notions, each of which can refer to a number of nuanced and contextualized empathic experiences. Appropriately broad definitions of empathy, then, offer a great deal of conceptual and semantic flexibility in relation both to the historical dissimilarities about the nature of empathy and to the plurality of conflicting voices about the meaning of empathic experiences.

2.2. Directing Questions about Empathy toward the Contexts of Different Experiences

In addition to its ability to resolve the conflict between rival notions of empathy, how might relational empathy help us concretize abstract questions about empathy (e.g. Can empathy be developed? Is empathy moral?)? First, I think it is crucial to explain what we mean by 'empathy', and second, I think it is essential to unveil the situational experiences to which answers to these questions point.

Michael Slote and Jesse Prinz (and many others) have addressed this question in light of what they conceive empathy to be. Empathy, says Slote (2010, 15), involves having the 'feelings of another (involuntarily) aroused in ourselves, as when we see another person in pain'; it is the 'cement of the moral universe' because it helps create something like moral approval and disapproval, which he contends are crucial for understanding what moral claims, utterances and judgments mean. Following Hume's account of sympathy but moving beyond it, Slote sees empathy as a mechanism that allows our moral approval and disapproval to focus on moral agents rather than on the consequences of their actions. But is empathy itself moral? Is it fundamentally moral? Is it ever necessary for morality? Answers to each of these questions depend on how one conceives and defines empathy as well as our approach to morality. The philosopher Jesse Prinz, although inspired by the same tradition of philosophy that Slote adopts (i.e. Humean moral sentimentalism), defines empathy slightly differently and thus offers a different answer to the question: Is empathy moral? For Prinz (2012, 212), empathy is primarily

> a kind of vicarious emotion: it's feeling what one takes another person to be feeling. And the 'taking' here can be a matter of automatic contagion or the result of a complicated exercise of the imagination

Defining empathy in this way, Prinz is skeptical about Slote's claims that empathy serves as the cement of the moral universe. A number of studies, Prinz notes, have shown that, as a vicarious emotion, empathy does not substantially motivate us to act on behalf of those in need. It is also highly selective, prone to in-group biases and in some cases results in preferential treatment for those who are spatially close to us. Even when empathy serves as a moral guide, our acts of empathizing are often biased and partial, and we often have more empathy for the suffering and pain of those who are similar to us (Xu et al. 2009; Gutsell and Inzlicht 2010) than for those whom we perceive as different. Conclusively for Prinz, empathy is not necessary for the capacities that make up basic moral competence, and one can acquire moral values, make moral judgments and act morally without empathy (Prinz 2011, 2012).

Conceptualizing empathy relationally offers a radically different approach for answering this main question about empathy. If we were to accept the definition of empathy that Slote provides, then the morality of empathy would be measured only by those instances in which the feelings of others are involuntarily aroused in us, and by how such feelings help us make sense of moral language. But since empathy is then defined so narrowly, there is no room for assessing the variety of empathic experiences that may also act as a 'cement' (or a solvent) of moral experience. And if we were to accept the definition of empathy that Prinz provides, then empathy is not necessary in order to acquire any dimension of moral competence. But if empathy were to be defined more broadly and pluralistically, then the question of its moral significance would have to address the ways in which a variety of our capacities and actions function within different circumstance and situations to produce moral ends – however those moral ends are defined. Adopting the pragmatic notion of relational empathy therefore provides a pluralistic framework for interpreting deeds, action or behavior as moral, immoral, non-
moral or amoral in the contexts and situations in which they are experienced. Narrow conceptualizations, on the contrary, limit discourses about morality because they do not offer the breadth of hermeneutical possibilities that relational empathy can offer. Slote defines empathy as having the feelings of another (involuntarily) aroused in ourselves, so that empathy is the 'cement of the moral universe' and necessary for morality. Prinz defines empathy as feeling what one takes another person to be feeling, and hence as unnecessary for morality. If nothing happens as a consequence of this verbal disagreement, then it is a moot debate, for what work is there to be done? With relational empathy, however, the question is not whether or not the act or activity of empathy is moral in and of itself, but instead: How do contextualized experiences of one, two, or all three of these relations of feeling into, feeling with and feeling for produce moral satisfaction?

2.3. Relational Empathy as a Conceptual Framework

How might the conceptual framework of relational empathy be helpful for collecting and analyzing data for the purpose of improving the structure and functionality of organizations? In the United States, I believe this new theory of empathy will find an important application in healthcare. One of the biggest problems in healthcare is that patients don't feel cared for.[11] Unless we are already inclined to note what exactly is at stake here, this may seem unimportant for many of us who do not grasp the consequences of this problem. Gone are the days when successful medical outcomes were the only criteria used to measure effective treatment in healthcare. Today, patient perception of care matters – patient satisfaction matters, both financially and medically.[12]

After 2008, administrative focus on patient perception of care and patient satisfaction greatly increased with the introduction of the Hospital Consumer Assessment of Healthcare Providers and Systems (HCAHPS), a government-mandated survey that is used as a tool to measure a patient's perception of care. Although the majority of leaders in healthcare provide additional, more thorough measures of patient satisfaction, the results of this survey greatly affect a healthcare organization's ability to exceed its bottom-line goals, which subsequently influences its overall ability to provide the best healthcare for its community. The Center of Medicare and Medicaid Services (CMS), which requires hospitals to report their inpatients' perceptions of care, withholds up to 3% of a hospital's total costs based on these interpretations of caregiving. CMS also reduces its payments to hospitals that have excess readmissions, which are a sign of inadequate care coordination and follow-up care in the community.[13] In addition to these, there are other financial losses that works against an organization's ability to function and flourish. Compared to physicians with the top satisfaction survey ratings, physicians in the middle tertile have malpractice lawsuit rates that are 26% higher, while physicians in the bottom tertile have malpractice lawsuit rates that are 110% higher (see Stelfox, Gandhi, and Orav et al. 2015; Jones and Gates 2007).[14]

Interestingly, the majority of non-demographic questions on the HCAHPS survey are easy to analyze if one applies relational empathy to them; however, they are quite difficult to access if one adopts a narrow approach for defining empathy. For example, questions 1–3 and 5–7 on this survey ask patients whether their nurses and doctors treated them with respect, listened to them carefully and explained things to them in a way they could understand. If chief nursing officers (CNOs), chief medical officers (CMOs) and other leaders in healthcare were to adopt an exclusionary and narrow approach to understanding empathy, their ability to analyze patients' answers to these questions would be severely limited. If empathy were to be defined narrowly as a particular instance of only *one* of the first two relations – such as taking another's perspective (feeling with) or empathic projection (feeling into) – it is unlikely that discussions about caregiving would be very practical with such an exclusion of the historical traditions that have stipulated empathy to be a manifestation of the relation of *feeling for*. If we think of the acts of treating others with respect, listening carefully to others and explaining things carefully to others, each of these requires us to perceive acutely (feeling into), to grasp accurately (feeling with) and to care passionately about (feeling for) the well-being of another person or situation.

Adopting relational empathy as a conceptual framework for our current healthcare system will help leaders reflect upon and analyze a host of different relationships that either fuel or foil their attempts to provide compassionate healthcare. Take, for instance, the following situation: Imagine a doctor perceiving and observing (feeling into) the condition of a patient in order to understand accurately (feel with) this patient's health condition, but doing so without observing and grasping the safety conditions in the room. Narrow theories of empathy employed only to analyze interpersonal relationships would exclude thinking about empathy as between a person and an object (in this case the safety of the room). Or think about another situation: A small child has broken her arm and is reticent to speak about it. If we were to think of empathy narrowly (e.g. as involuntarily catching the emotions of others or as taking the perspective of another), then we would be limited as interpreters and would miss seeing that empathic mimicry – *acting out* the child's condition – could elicit the child's explanation and assist her in describing her situation.

As Press Ganey's CMO Thomas Lee notes, to drive sustained improvement in healthcare throughout the United States, 'we need measures, we need data, and we need wisdom about how to use them'; moreover, Lee states that in order to increase empathic care throughout the healthcare industry, 'we also need a new language' (Lee 2016, 85, 7). In addition to Lee's insights, the healthcare industry needs to tap into new technologies that will allow patient-centered care coordinators to collect data of the perceptions of both patients and healthcare professionals. A number of emerging technologies will serve as valuable tools for maximizing patient-centered care and engendering organizational efficiency, but perhaps the most relevant current technology useful for driving sustained development in healthcare is virtual reality. In addition to applying the methodologies of biometrics, data science and social network science, virtual reality will become very instrumental for future training and development departments of healthcare organizations. Eventually, healthcare professionals will be faced with a choice: They can either adopt a narrow conceptualization of empathy that will limit both the content of their VR simulations and the scope of their investigations, or they can embrace and implement the historically rich interpretive framework of relational empathy that will expand such content and broaden their empirical approaches.

One can locate the presence of these intersecting relations throughout different historical traditions, notice how they are manifested within a variety of experiences and find novel ways of employing them in circumstances other than those mentioned here. We can give the co-existence of these three relations in experience any name we wish. Here, I have chosen the term 'relational empathy' in the hope that this neologism and the pluralistic, pragmatic approach upon which it is based will help us develop an individual and social *ethos* and eradicate pressing philosophical and organizational problems.

Notes

1. I think it is important not only to be clear about what one means by empathy but also to be informed about – and try to include what – others have meant by this term historically. In light of this, I have adopted a pluralistic, philosophical and relational perspective on the subject of empathy (Fagiano 2016).
2. See the OED's definition of *pathos*, 2a: 'To have experience of; to meet with; to feel or undergo.' Margaret Graver describes the ancient Greek understanding of this general and neutral sense of *pathos* as 'a broad and colorless term, roughly equivalent to "experience" in English' (Graver, trans and comm 2002, 79). In Plato's *Gorgias*, we find one such example of using pathos to signify a general experience: 'Well, Callicles, if human beings didn't share common experiences [*pathos*], some sharing one, others sharing another, but one of us had some unique experience [*pathos*] not shared by others, it wouldn't be easy for him to communicate what he experienced [*pathema*] to the other' (Plato, 481c-d; Cooper 1997, 826). Historically, the Latin term *sensus* has been used in a similar fashion, signifying anything sensed without signifying any sort of ontologically rigid dualism.
3. For a lucid explanation of James's notion of pure experience, see James 1996 [1912], 93–95, and Gavin 2013, 44–65.
4. As Isaiah Berlin (1997, 253) notes, Herder 'believed that to understand anything was to understand it in its individuality and development, and that this required the capacity of *Einfühlung* ("feeling into") the outlook, the individual character of artistic tradition, a literature, a social organization, a people, a culture, a period of history. To understand the "organic structure" of the society in terms of which alone the minds and activities and habits of its members can be understood.'
5. R. Vischer states that the body 'unconsciously projects its own ... form – and with this also the soul – into the form of the object. From this I derived the notion of what I call *Einfühlung*' (Vischer 1994 [1873], 92).
6. See also Batson's earlier collaborative work on this distinction: Batson, Early, and Salvarini (1997).
7. The twofold process of feeling into for the purpose of feeling with is often described today as an act of inferring (feeling into) for the purpose of

understanding or feeling with another accurately. The social psychologist William Ickes has conducted a number of studies of empathic inference and its relation to empathic accuracy (i.e. 'mindreading'), defining the latter as the measure of one's ability to infer accurately the specific content of other people's thought and feeling: see Ickes (1997, 2–6). For earlier accounts, see Rogers 1957 and Malcolm 1963, 130–140.
8. During this study, Italian scientists noted that certain neurons in the F5 region of the premotor cortex of the monkey fired both when it picked a piece of food with its own hand and when it observed another monkey pick up a piece of food.
9. For a good start on the ongoing discourse surrounding the concepts of mirror neurons and/or mirroring processes, see Iacoboni 2008; Iacoboni and Dapretto 2006; Keysers 2011. It is important to note that although explorations of mirror neurons are attempts to find evidence for the biological foundations of a notion of empathy as the relation of feeling with, they are not examining the perceptual processes (feeling into) and/or the compassionate feelings and actions (feeling for) that are connected to the mirror neuron activity. What would it look like if we were to conduct a neuroscientific exploration of all three of these relations within a particular experience?
10. Amy Coplan (2013, 5 n. 19), for example, claims that 'we need more specificity, not more generality' to grasp what empathy 'really' is.
11. In a 2011 national survey, when hospitalized patients were asked if compassionate care is essential for successful medical care, 80% of these patients said yes, while only 53% of these patients professed that contemporary healthcare in the US provides such care. See Lowen, Rosen, and Marttila 2011.
12. Discourses about patient-centered care and patient satisfaction in the US began in the 1980s and were centered on the goal of providing better 'service' for patients. This turn among healthcare professionals was stimulated initially by a number of shared goals, for instance, to avoid gaining a bad reputation, to reduce the number of medical malpractice lawsuits leveled against them, and to avoid losing market share. Also in the 1980s, it was discovered that if patients believed they were adequately cared for during their stay in a hospital, then they were less likely to file a lawsuit, independent of the technical quality of the medical care they received. See Lee 2016, 86–92.
13. For more on this, see Orszag and Emanuel 2010; see also Hines et al. 2014.
14. Beyond these financial losses, hospitals in the top quartile of HCAHPS's ratings are noted to have better performance on quality metrics for all four clinical conditions examined: acute myocardial infarction, congestive heart failure, pneumonia, and prevention of surgical complications (Lee 2016, 101).

Disclosure statement

No potential conflict of interest was reported by the author.

References

Baron-Cohen, S. 2005. "The Male Condition." *The New York Times*, August 8, p. A15.
Baron-Cohen, S. 2012. *The Science of Evil: On Empathy and the Origins of Cruelty*. New York: Basic Books.
Batson, C. D., S. Early, and G. Salvarini. 1997. "Perspective Taking: Imagining How Another Feels Versus Imagining How You Would Feel." *Personality and Social Personality Bulletin* 23: 751–781. doi:10.1177/0146167297237008.
Batson, C. D., and K. C. Oleson. 1991. "Current Status of the Empathy-Altruism Hypothesis." In *Review of Personality and Social Psychology*, Vol. 2, edited by M. S. Clark, 62–85. Newbury Park, CA: Sage Publications
Batson, C. D. 1991. *The Altruism Question: Toward a Social Psychological Answer*. Hillsdale, NJ: Lawrence Erlbaum.
Batson, C. D. 2009. "Two Forms of Perspective Taking: Imagining How Another Feels and Imagining How You Would Feel." In *Handbook of Imagination and Mental Simulation*, edited by K. S. Markman, W. M. P. Klein, and J. A. Juhr, 267–279. New York: Psychology Press.
Batson, C. D. 2011. *Altruism in Humans*. Oxford: Oxford University Press.
Berlin, I. 1997. "The Counter-Enlightenment." In *The Proper Study of Mankind: An Anthology of Essays*, edited by I. Berlin, 243–68. New York: Farrar, Strauss and Giroux.
Cayuela, A. 2016. "Vulnerable: To Be between Life and Death." In *Human Dignity of the Vulnerable in the Age of Rights: Interdisciplinary Perspectives*, edited by A. Mansferrer and E. Garcia-Sanchez, 63–79. New York: Springer International Publishing.
Cooper, J. M., ed. 1997. *Plato's Works*. Indianapolis, IN: Hackett Publishing Company.
Coplan, A. 2013. "Understanding Empathy: Its Features and Effects." In *Empathy: Philosophical and Psychological Perspectives*, edited by A. Coplan and P. Goldie, 3–18. Oxford: Oxford University Press.
Danzinger, N., K. M. Prkachin, and J. C. Willer. 2006. "The Perception of Others' Pain in Patients with Congenital Insensitivity to Pain." *Brain* 129 (9): 2494–2507. doi:10.1093/brain/awl063.
de Vignemont, F., and T. Singer. 2006. "The Empathic Brain: How, When, and Why?" *Trends in Cognitive Sciences* 10: 435–441. doi:10.1016/j.tics.2006.08.008.
Decety, J., ed. 2012. *Empathy: From Bench to Bedside*. Cambridge, MA: MIT Press.
di Pellegrino, G. L., L. F. Fadiga, V. Gallese, and G. Rizzolatti. 1992. "Understanding Motor Events, A Neurophysiological Study." *Experimental Brain Research* 91: 176–180. doi:10.1007/BF00230027.
Eisenberg, N., and R. A. Fabes. 1998. "Prosocial Development." In *Handbook of Child Psychology, Vol. 3: Social, Emotional and Personality Development*, edited by W. Damon and R. M. Lerner, 701–78 . New York: John Wiley & Sons.
Fagiano, M. 2016. "Pluralistic Conceptualizations of Empathy." *Journal of Speculative Philosophy* 30 (1): 27–44. doi:10.5325/jspecphil.30.1.0027.
Favre, D. 2011. "The Measure of Empathy, Emotional Contagion, and Emotional Cut-Off as an Indirect Indicator of the Efficiency of Teacher Training for Preventing Violent Behavior and Social Failure." In *Psychology of Empathy*, edited by D. J. Scapaletti. Hauppauge, NY: Nova Science Publishers.

Freud, S. 1960 [1905]. *Jokes and Their Relation to the Unconscious.* New York: W. W. Norton & Company.
Gallese, V., L. Fadiga, L. Fogassi, and G. Rizzolatti. 1996. "Action Recognition in the Premotor Cortex." *Brain* 119: 593–609.
Gavin, W. J. 2013. *William James in Focus.* Bloomington: Indiana University Press.
Goldie, P. 2002. *The Emotions.* Oxford: Oxford University Press.
Graver, Margaret, trans. and comm. 2002. *Cicero and the Emotions: Tusculan Disputations 3 and 4.* Chicago: University of Chicago Press.
Gutsell, J. N., and M. Inzlicht. 2010. "Empathy Constrained: Prejudice Predicts Reduced Mental Simulation of Actions during Observations of Outgroups." *Journal of Experimental Social Psychology* 46: 841–845. doi:10.1016/j.jesp.2010.03.011.
Herder, J. 1877–1937. *Sämmtliche Werke.* Vol. 5. edited by B. Suphan. Berlin: Weidmann.
Herder, J. 1964 [1774]. "Vom Erkennen und Empfinden der Menschlichen Seele." In *Herders Werke*, edited by J. Herder, 7–69. Vol. 3. Berlin: Aufbau Verlag.
Hines, A. L., M. L. Barrett, H. J. Jiang, and C. A. Steiner. 2014. "Conditions with the Largest Number of Adult Hospital Readmissions by Payer, 2011." *HCUP Statistical Brief #172.* Rockville, MD: April Agency for Healthcare Research and Quality.
Hoffman, M. 2000. *Empathy and Moral Development: Implications for Caring and Justice.* Cambridge: Cambridge University Press.
Iacoboni, M. 2008. *Mirroring People: The New Science of How We Connect with Others.* New York: Farrar: Straus and Giroux.
Iacoboni, M., and M. Dapretto. 2006. "The Mirror Neuron System and the Consequences of Its Dysfunction." *Nature* 7: 942–951.
Ickes, W. 1997. *Empathic Accuracy.* New York: Guilford Press.
James, W. 1996 [1912]. *Essays in Radical Empiricism.* Lincoln: University of Nebraska Press.
Jones, C. B., and M. Gates. 2007. "The Costs and Benefits of Nurse Turnover: A Business Case for Nurse Retention." *The Online Journal of Issues in Nursing* 12 (3): 5.
Keysers, C. 2011. *The Empathic Brain: How the Discovery of Mirror Neurons Changes Our Understanding of Human Nature.* Social Brain Press.
Kohut, H. 1981. "On Empathy." *International Journal of Psychoanalytic Self Psychology* 5 (2): 122–131.
Lee, T. H. 2016. *An Epidemic of Empathy in Healthcare: How to Deliver Compassionate, Connected Patient Care that Creates a Competitive Advantage.* New York: McGraw Hill Education.
Lotze, H. 1856. *Microcosmus: An Essay Concerning Man and His Relation to the World.* Vol. 1. 4th ed. Edinburgh: T. & T. Clark, 1894.
Lowen, B. A., J. Rosen, and J. Marttila. 2011. "An Agenda for Improving Compassionate Care: A Survey Shows about Half of Patients Say Such Care Is Missing." *Health Affairs* 30: 1772–1778. doi:10.1377/hlthaff.2011.0539.
Malcolm, N. 1963. *Knowledge and Certainty: Essays and Lectures.* Englewood Cliffs, NJ: Prentice-Hall.
Matravers, D. 2017. *Empathy.* Malden, MA: Polity Press.
Mead, G. H. 1938. *The Philosophy of the Act*, edited by C. W. Morris in Collaboration With, J. M. Brewster, A. M. Dunham, and D. L. Miller. Chicago: University of Chicago Press.

Munteanu, D. L. 2012. *Tragic Pathos: Pity and Fear in Greek Philosophy and Tragedy*. Cambridge: Cambridge University Press.
Orszag, P. R., and E. J. Emanuel. 2010. "Health Care Reform and Cost Control." *New England Journal of Medicine* 363 (7): 601–603. doi:10.1056/NEJMoa1011205.
Preston, S. D., B. M. F. de Waal. 2002. "Empathy: Its Ultimate and Proximate Bases." *Behavioral Brain Sciences* 25 (1): 1–20.
Prinz, J. 2011. "Against Empathy." *The Southern Journal of Philosophy* 49: 214–233. doi:10.1111/sjp.2011.49.issue-s1.
Prinz, J. 2012. "Is Empathy Necessary for Morality?." In *Empathy: Philosophical and Psychological Perspectives*, edited by A. Coplan and P. Goldie, 221–29. New York: Oxford University Press.
Rizzolatti, G., L. Fadiga, V. Gallese, and L. Fogassi. 1996. "Premotor Cortex and the Recognition of Motor Actions." *Cognitive Brain Research* 3: 131–141. doi:10.1016/0926-6410(95)00038-0.
Rogers, C. 1957. "The Necessary and Sufficient Conditions of Personality Change." *Journal of Consulting Psychology* 21: 95–103. doi:10.1037/h0045357.
Rogers, C. R., E. T. Gendlin, D. J. Kiesler, and C. B. Truax, ed. 1967. *The Therapeutic Relationship and Its Impact: A Study of Psychotherapy with Schizophrenics*. Madison: University of Wisconsin Press.
Slote, M. 2010. *Moral Sentimentalism*. Oxford: Oxford University Press.
Stein, E. 1964 [1917]. *On the Problem of Empathy*, translated by W. Stein. The Hague: Martinus Nijhoff.
Stelfox, H. T., T. K. Gandhi, E. J. Orav, M. L. Gustafson. 2015. "The Relation of Patient Satisfaction with Complaints against Physicians and Malpractice Lawsuits". *American Journal of Medicine* 118: 1126–1133. doi:10.1016/j.amjmed.2005.01.060.
Titchener, E. B. 1909. *Lectures on the Experimental Psychology of the Thought-Processes*. New York: MacMillan Company.
Vischer, F. T. 1922–1923 [1857]. *Ästhetik oder Wissenschaft des Schönen*. 2nd ed. edited by R. Vischer. Munich: Meyer & Jessen.
Vischer, R. 1994 [1873]. *Empathy, Form and Space: Problems in German Aesthetics, 1873–1893*, edited by H. Mallgrave and E. Ikonomou. Santa Monica, CA: Getty Center for the History of Art and the Humanities.
Xu, X., X. Zuo, X. Wang, and S. Han. 2009. "Do You Feel My Pain? Racial Group Membership Modulates Empathic Neural Responses". *Journal of Neuroscience* 29: 8525–8529. doi:10.1523/JNEUROSCI.2418-09.2009.

Language, Behaviour, and Empathy. G.H. Mead's and W.V.O. Quine's Naturalized Theories of Meaning

Guido Baggio

ABSTRACT
The paper compares Mead's and Quine's behaviouristic theories of meaning and language, focusing in particular on Mead's notion of sympathy and Quine's notion of empathy. On the one hand, Quine seems to resort to an explanation similar to Mead's notion of sympathy, referring to 'empathy' in order to justify the human ability to *project ourselves into the witness's position*; on the other hand, Quine's reference to the notion of empathy paves the way to a more insightful comparison between Mead's behaviourism and an explanation of the emergence of the linguistic from pre-linguistic communication based on empathic identification processes. However, Mead is less ambiguous than Quine in his use of the notion of sympathy finds a fecund parallel in the current neuroscientific and neuro-phenomenological hypothesis on 'empathy'. The article contends that the ambiguity in Quine's account of empathy is due to the exigency of trying to elucidate the link between the rules of language in a cultural context and the natural, that is 'instinctive', basis of the process of learning a language. This is the reason why his epistemological behaviourism is particularly close to the non-reductionist naturalism of Mead. The working hypothesis proposed in the conclusion deals with the core notions of 'gesture' and 'behaviour'.

1. Introduction

The behavioural theory of meaning that Mead sketched in the 1920s (Mead 1922, 1925, [1934] 2015), and which Dewey integrated into his *Experience and Nature* (1929) presents many analogies with Quine's behaviouristic account of meaning and the process of learning language. More specifically, Quine (1969) refers to Dewey's *Experience and Nature* to argue that the meaning of a word or linguistic expression is determined by the linguistic and behavioural situations of individuals. He also argues (Quine 1969, 81, 1987, 5, 1992, 37–38) that individuals learn words and propositions through listening and using them in the presence of the environmental stimuli which act both on the learner as well as on the speaker from whom she is learning. The use of language is therefore socially determined and dependent on fitting the statements to shared stimulation, which is possible only, as Quine argues, by 'projecting ourselves into the witness's position' (Quine 1992, 43). Now, Quine's expression sounds very similar to Mead's 'taking the role of the other' (Mead [1934] 2015), which lies at the basis of the emergence of meaning. Both for Mead and for Quine the triangulation between subject, sensory stimulus and others' reactions to such a stimulus is rooted in a natural dimension which expresses the social character of survival instincts at the roots of the consciousness of meanings. Though Mead seems to be more explicit than Quine in pointing to the strict interconnection between physical events and psychosocial processes, Quine's reference to the notion of empathy paved the way to a more insightful comparison between Mead's behaviourism and an explanation of the emergence of the linguistic from prelinguistic communication based on empathic mechanism.

In this paper, I aim to show how close Mead and Quine are in their behavioural explanations of meaning and language, and also that Quine's epistemological behaviourism is particularly close to the non-reductionist naturalism of Mead and Dewey. In the first part, I describe Mead's (and Dewey's) behaviouristic theory of meaning. Then, I introduce Quine's behaviouristic account of meaning and the process of learning a language, highlighting some similarities with Mead's theory. Mead's use of the notion of sympathy is then addressed by sketching some parallels with current hypotheses on 'empathy' related to recent studies in cognitive science. The similarities between Mead's notion of sympathy and Quine's notion of empathy are displayed before focusing on Baghramian's and Picardi's interpretations of Quine's references to empathy. These authors highlight Quine's controversial use of the notion of empathy and the ambiguity in his reliance on it. I contend that this ambiguity is due to his exigency of trying to elucidate the relationship between the rules of language in a cultural context and the natural, that is, 'instinctive' basis of the process of learning a language. This is the reason why his epistemological behaviourism is particularly close to the non-reductionist naturalism of Mead (*via* Dewey). In conclusion, I propose a working hypothesis in the field of cognitive science, referring to the notions of 'gesture' and 'behaviour' as core notions of an account of empathy, to overcome the dichotomy between the descriptive and the normative levels in which Quine's theory seems to be trapped.

2. Mead's bio-social theory of meaning

Mead's elucidation of the term 'behaviour' was at the basis of a non-reductive naturalistic conception of the emergence of meaning, and (in the phylogenetic and ontogenetic perspectives on human language), of the learning of symbolic language in the non-mentalistic terms of social interaction. In particular, in his works he raised the problem of the transition from the vocal gesture to abstract language,[1] and this question was strictly intertwined with that of the emergence of human consciousness. The solution Mead proposed uncovered the condition of possibility of the existence of consciousness as rooted in the internalization by the organism of the conversations of vocal gestures through visual and auditory perception, which allows the internalization of gestural conversation.

His behavioural theory of language and mind dates back to his early contributions to Dewey's theory of emotion (Mead 1895, 2001), in which Mead hypothesized that it was possible to find the passage from sensorial to symbolic stimulus in the qualitative differentiation of emotional tones expressed in the different instinctive attitudes.[2] In particular, together with Dewey, Mead pointed out in the emotional attitude expressed in inhibited acts the first phases of the rise of meaning from the gestural interaction between organism and environment, and the mutual adaptation between social stimulus, individual response and activities at which these processes eventually arrive. The mere reference to the original situation of social interaction would not otherwise have allowed the bodily and vocal gestures to become meaningful. It was firstly the reference to the change in the expression of other individuals involved in the act from a mere outcome of the nervous excitement in meaning, which allowed the development of communication, shared understanding, and mutual recognition within the field of social interaction. More specifically, according to Mead the elements of coordination of social behaviour and communication are already present in the evolution of the initial phases of instinctive acts and their physiological correlates, characterized by emotional content and its expression, even before the communication of symbols is expressed in signs. As Mead writes:

> Before conscious communication by symbols arises in gestures, signs, and articulate sounds there exists in these earliest stages of acts and their physiological fringes, the means of co-ordinating social conduct, the means of unconscious communication. And conscious communication has made use of these very expressions of the emotion to build up its signs. They were already signs. They had been already naturally selected and preserved as signs in unreflective social conduct before they were specialized as symbols. (Mead 2001, 3)

What Mead calls 'unconscious communication' is a kind of 'preconscious', and then prelinguistic, communication that uses emotional attitudes to build its signs, referring to a pre-reflexive process as a prerequisite for the emotional transposition that characterizes the possibility of interpretation of the movements of others. The result is a possible explanation of the genesis of propositional language through the conditioning of bio-social canons and structures that have their roots in pre-linguistic behavioural attitudes. As Mead writes: 'What we see in the faces and attitudes of others is not the face or the body. It is the indication of certain sorts of conduct, and the evidence of the feeling that conduct involves. We see the coming acts and feel the values which express themselves in those actions.' (Mead 2001, 4)

Meaning has, therefore, a *bio-social* nature, which is expressed in gestures that show a *functional identity* of the responses of individuals to the same stimulus, an identity that is rooted in the *cooperative* behavioural attitude of individuals as the manifestation of the social character of natural instincts.[3] And the interpretation of gestures is not a process of the mind, but a process that is fully implemented in the field of social experience. The articulated sounds – the vocal gestures – that the body emits are heard by the individual in the same way they are heard by the recipient of vocal gestures, revealing themselves to her in the same way they reveal themselves to others. In the most evolved phase, gestures include, following Mead, the recognized attitude that stimulates response, and the inner attitude, that is, the possession of a precise idea in the experience of the individual. The significant vocal gesture then becomes a symbolic gesture when it has the same effect on the agent and on the recipient of the gesture.

Meaning arises 'through the individual stimulating himself *to take the attitude of the other* in his reaction toward the object', that is toward similar sensory stimuli. Meaning, Mead argues, 'is that which can be indicated to others while it is by the same process indicated to the indicating individual' (Mead [1934] 2015, 89. Italics added).[4] Taking on the role of the other on the part of an individual corresponds to anticipating his response to the same sensitive stimulus, thus allowing the meaning to arise from the relationship of mutual adaptation between the sensory stimulation and the social response, and the activities in which these processes eventually issue.

To sum up, there are three conditions necessary for meaning to arise: a social situation in which the act of an organism connected to a sensory stimulus is identified; the awareness that one's gesture provokes a change in the consciousness of another individual; and the environmental conditions under which this relationship emerges into consciousness.

In this perspective, meaning can be described, explained or defined in terms of symbols in its highest and most complex phase of development (the phase that it reaches in human experience), but the symbolic language does nothing but identify through the social process a situation that already exists in it logically. Symbolic language is merely a significant or conscious gesture. As Mead says, against the mentalist theory of meaning, the language 'is not an affair of the individual soul, and its laws are frequently generalizations which would not have the slightest meaning if read into terms of the experience of the individual soul'. The individual may be responsible for 'the changes and the growth and development of language, but the product lies outside of the experience of the souls whose mechanisms are responsible for it' (Mead [1934] 2015, 377–8). In other words, the phenomena of language are those that appear within a set of social interactions (Mead [1934] 2015, 184).

This thesis was later taken up by Dewey, who in *Experience and Nature* argued in a Meadian 'mood':

> Take speech as behavioristically as you will, including the elimination of all private mental states, and it remains true that it is markedly distinguished from the signaling acts of animals. Meaning is not indeed a psychic existence; it is primarily a property of behavior, and secondarily a property of objects. But the behavior of which it is a quality is a distinctive behavior; *cooperative*, in that response to another's act involves contemporaneous response to a thing as entering into the other's behavior, and this upon both sides. (Dewey 1929, 137. Italics added.)

It has to be noticed, by the way, that Mead was not really clear on the passage from vocal gesture to significant symbol. In this regard, one can agree with Habermas' observation that Mead 'paid no attention to the propositional structure of language', analysing instead from the standpoint of the psychology of perception 'the cognitive structure of experience underlying the formation of propositions' (Habermas 1987, 28). Though Mead did not give explicit attention to propositional language as such, we can find in his behavioural theory of meaning, *via* Dewey, at least some analogies with Quine's theory of language. In fact, it is from Dewey's *Experience and Nature*, and in particular from the passage just quoted above, that Quine developed his behavioural theory of meaning and language.

3. Language and empathy. Quine's behaviouristic theory of meaning

Referring to Dewey's behavioural doctrine of meaning, Quine argued that the meaning of a word or statement is determined in principle by the linguistic dispositions of individuals and that 'there are no meanings, nor likenesses nor distinctions of meaning, beyond what are implicit in people's dispositions to overt behavior' (Quine 1969, 29). Language, thence, is 'a social art which we all acquire on the evidence solely of other people's overt behaviour under publicly recognizable circumstances. Meanings, therefore, those very models of mental entities, end up as grist for the behaviourist's mill' (Quine 1969, 26).

In particular, Quine has distinguished three levels of alleged explanation of 'meaning': the mental, the behavioural, and the physiological levels. If Quine dismisses the first as 'superficial', the second and the last are in his opinion the only possible levels of explanation, the physiological level being the most ambitious and, we will see later, also the most problematic. The behavioural level, instead, which is the intermediate level between mental and physiological, is what we can access in order to obtain an explanation that is at least more satisfactory than mental theory (Quine 1975, 87).

In *Epistemology Naturalized* Quine has also exposed a behavioural theory of propositional language learning, arguing that the learning of words and sentences takes place through listening and using them in the presence of environmental stimuli that act on both the learner and the speaker from whom she is learning. The use of language is therefore socially controlled and is dependent on the matching of the sentences to shared stimulation (Quine 1969, 81). Also, in *Pursuit of Truth* he explicitly claims:

> Each of us learns his language by observing other people's verbal behavior and having his own faltering verbal behavior observed and reinforced or corrected by others. We depend strictly on overt behavior in observable situations. As long as the command of our language fits all external checkpoints, where our utterance or our reaction to someone's utterance can be appraised in the light of some shared situation, so long all is well. Our mental life between checkpoints is indifferent to our rating as a master of the language. There is nothing in linguistic meaning beyond what is to be gleaned from overt behavior in observable circumstances. (Quine 1992, 37–8)[5]

The sentences that are connected to the observable circumstances are the 'occasion sentences'. According to Quine's definition, occasion sentences are sentences that have a meaning with regard to similar sensory stimuli for all individuals belonging to a community of speakers. They include within them 'observation sentences', that is, sentences that the speaker uses in the presence of sensory stimuli which are high on scale of 'observationality'; what makes an occasion sentence low on observationality scale is, by definition, 'wide intersubjective variability of stimulus meaning' (Quine 1960, 44).[6]

The recognition of an occasion sentence by a community of speakers occurs when each member of the community agrees to assent or dissent on the witness of the occurrence of the sentence, which is possible, according to Quine, *'by projecting ourselves into the witness's position'* (Quine 1992, 43).

Now, this expression, that Quine first used in 1953 (Quine 1953), sounds similar to Mead's expression 'take the attitude of the other' which, as seen above, indicates in Mead's theory the condition of possibility of the arising of meaning. The meaning is therefore shown for Quine, as for Mead (and, naturally, for Dewey), as the product of the interaction between organisms.[7] For both Mead and Quine, the triangulation between subject, sensitive stimulus and reaction of others to this stimulus is embedded in a natural dimension that expresses the social character of the instincts at the origin of the rise of the consciousness of meanings. Similarly to Mead, in fact, Quine claims the need for a 'substantial agreement, however *unconscious*, as to what counts as similar' if people 'are to succeed in learning, one person from another, when next to assent to a given observation sentence' (Quine 1984, 294). The active involvement of the individual in a social act, that is, her active selection of sensory stimuli which introduces a triangulation between the individual, the environment, and the responses of other individuals to the same stimuli, highlights the crucial role that behaviour plays in constructing shared meanings; that is, behaviour always has practical consequences.

Quine, then, refers to 'empathy' in order to justify the human ability to *'project [...] ourselves into the witness's position'*. In particular, since 1990 he explicitly refers to the notion of empathy as a necessary condition for the learning of language. As he writes:

> Empathy dominates the learning of language, both by child and by field linguist. In the child's case it is the parent's empathy. The parent assesses the appropriateness of the child's observation sentence by noting the child's orientation and how the scene would look from there. In the field linguist's case it is empathy on his own part when he makes his first conjecture about 'Gavagai' on the strength of the native's utterance and orientation, and again when he queries 'Gavagai' for the native's assent in a promising subsequent situation. We all have an uncanny knack for empathizing another's perceptual situation, however ignorant of the physiological or optical mechanism of his perception. The knack is comparable, almost, to our ability to recognize faces while unable to sketch or describe them.
>
> Empathy guides the linguist still as he rises above observation sentences through his analytical hypotheses, though there he *is trying to project into the native's associations and grammatical trends rather than his perceptions.* And much the same must be true of the growing child. (Quine 1992, 42-3)

This long passage is illuminating of Quine's naturalized account of language and the fundamental role and nature of empathy in it. In 1995 Quine further developed his references to empathy, defining it as an 'instinctive' element at the basis of the child's acquisition of her first observation sentences. He argued that the child does not just associate the sentence with the reported object or event, but she 'also notes the speaker's orientation, gesture, and facial expression'. In other words, she 'perceives that the speaker perceives the object or event' even in her as yet inarticulate way. Thus, when the child puts the sentence to use, the perceiving is reversed: the listener takes note of the child's orientation and facial expression (Quine 1995, 89). Empathy is also at work in the 'radical' translator, to whom empathy is the method of his 'practical psychology' through which 'he imagines himself in the native's situation as best he can' (Quine 1969, 46). Moreover, empathy also works with animals. It is the medium through which we ascribe propositional attitudes such as 'perceives that' both to human and non-human animals (Quine 1995, 89). Empathy is thence the element that humans have in common with animals; it helps us to associate gestures to propositional language. As Mead would have said, symbolic language-learning presupposes a social situation which is logically there already and refers to significant gestures, that is, to gestures which have at least an indexical meaning – they implicitly indicate some object or event. The child, as well as the radical translator, are then involved in an external, overt, physical, or physiological process going on in the actual field of social experience.

4. Mead's sympathy, Quine's empathy, and cognitive science

Quine's notion of empathy as instinct, which is at the basis of a child's noting of the 'gestures' of the speaker, resorts to an explanation similar to Mead's notion of sympathy, that is, with the idea of a natural basis of ontogeny and phylogeny of vocal from gestural communication.[8] Similarly to Quine, in fact, also Mead highlights the pivotal role that gestural communication plays in the early stages of communication.[9] He discovers a non-reductive naturalistic explanation of the passage from gestural (behavioural) to symbolic (propositional) language based on a *'sympathetic'* identification. As he argues:

> If the gesture simply indicates the object to another, it has no meaning to the individual who makes it, nor does the response which the other individual carries out become a meaning to him, unless he assumes the attitude of having his attention directed by an individual to whom it has a meaning. Then he takes his own response to be the meaning of the indication. *Through this sympathetic placing of themselves in each other's roles*, and finding thus in their own experiences the response of the others, what would otherwise be an unintelligent gesture, acquires just the value which is connoted by signification, both in its specific applications and in its universality.' (Mead 1964, 246. Italic added).

Sympathy consists, according to Mead's definition, in adopting another's 'attitude toward, and his role in, the given social situation, and by thus responding to that situation implicitly as he does or is about to do explicitly' (Mead [1934] 2015, 300). Sympathetic identification is depicted as a natural process presenting both cognitive and affective aspects, since it refers to both the capacity to represent the other's intentions and beliefs (attitudes) and to share her feelings. The identification has to be understood in the sense of an individual who, in an entirely natural way, stimulates a certain response in herself since her gesture works on her as well as working on another.

Although Mead's notion of sympathy has its philosophical basis in David Hume's *Treatise of human nature* and in Adam Smith's *Theory of moral sentiments*,[10] a more fecund parallel with Mead's notion of sympathy can be nowadays found in the current neuroscientific and neurophenomenological hypothesis on 'empathy' related to the recent studies on embodied cognition and the rise of human mind and language. It is worth noting, in fact, that nowadays Mead's theory of gestural conversation as the expression of an innate social dimension of human beings is undergoing a revival among neuroscientists. Rizzolatti and Sinigaglia (Rizzolatti and Sinigaglia 2006, 48–49, 148–149), for instance, explicitly refer to the work of Mead as supporting the hypothesis according to which the rise of human language would have had at its basis a gestural attitude linked to a pre-conscious mechanism for understanding the gestural attitudes of others. Moreover, McNeill (2005, 30–31) refers to what he has called 'Mead's loop theory' as 'a capacity, not present in other primate brains, for the mirror neuron circuit to respond to one's own gestures as if they belonged to someone else'. Mead himself argued that all that is innate 'in connection with minds and selves is the physiological mechanism of the human central nervous system, by means of which the genesis of minds and selves out of the human social process of experience and behavior – out of the human matrix of social relations and interactions – is made biologically possible in human individuals' (Mead [1934] 2015, 237n).

In line with Mead, in neurosciences, empathy is generally depicted as a pre-reflexive embodied mechanism that plays a role in understanding the intentional actions of others, by ascribing meaning to their unreflective facial expressions and being able to 'read' their emotionally laden bodily attitudes. Like Mead's reference to sympathetic identification, the concept of empathetic identification depicts 'an individual who perfectly naturally arouses a certain response in himself because his gesture operates on himself as it does on the other' (Mead [1934] 2015, 300). Thanks to the empathetic identification, an individual can comprehend the other's behavioural and expressive attitudes and interact with him through a so-to-speak *natural social-enlargement* in which the affective and cognitive dimensions are closely related, without ceasing to be able to separate which beliefs and feelings belong to which self.[11] This process has its *conditio sine qua non* in the social interaction through which individuals introject others' behavioural attitudes, and its biological support in the simulation function of mirror neurons.

Now, also Quine's notion of empathy as instinct, which seems akin to Mead's idea of sympathy, partly anticipates current hypothesis on 'empathy' related to the recent studies on cognitive science. However, Quine allows little room for an explanation of the nature of empathy, preferring to leave the notion vague. He defines empathy as an *'uncanny knack'*, a mysterious skill (or talent), which has both an affective and a cognitive character, put to the test by intersubjective communication; he compares it to the human ability to recognize the expressions of others despite the inability to describe them. Eva Picardi highlighted the ambiguity in Quine's reliance on empathy, arguing that such ambiguity is due to a shift of emphasis from a conception of language as a 'social art' to a conception of language as a vehicle of information contiguous with non-human animals. In particular, Picardi pointed out that the close link between perception, empathy, and the stimulus-meaning of observation sentences goes hand in hand with Quine's 'Darwinian turn' after 1990. As she writes: 'In Quine's latest writings empathy is both a heuristic principle in the radical translator's methodology *and* a psychological capacity of which he avails himself for framing his guesses as to what might have prompted a native's utterance' (Picardi 2000, 129). So, Quine's appeal to 'empathy' seems to suggest his interest in psychological reality, but it is unclear if this is the perspective he positively suggests or if it is that of the field-linguist. In other words, Quine seems to answer the question about the basis for our ability to engage in explaining and predicting behaviour, by appealing to a notion of empathy based on two apparently irreconcilable readings, namely the naturalistic and normative readings.[12] Such an ambiguity raises serious questions regarding the extent of his commitment both to behaviourism and to naturalism, undermining, in particular, the first.[13] Picardi tried to find out a solution by relying on a 'quasi-normative interpretation of empathy', referring to Quine's subscription to Davidson's anomalous monism and to the idea that *intentional* idiom is built into the very fabric of radical translation (Picardi 2000, 130). She also referred to a naturalistic reading of 'empathy', recalling the debate between simulation approach and theory-theory approach in philosophy of mind, but maintaining the ambiguity in Quine's account of empathy.

More recently, Maria Baghramian noted that Quine's use of empathy is controversial for he extends the scope of our reliance on perceptual empathy beyond the basic projection of observational states 'to more complex propositional attitudes such as belief', thus going 'beyond the sort of states that we might also ascribe to non-human animals' (Baghramian 2016, 33). Quine's linguistic naturalism seems then to be controversial because 'it leads to the highly counter-intuitive doctrines of the indeterminacy of translation and inscrutability of reference. Its two defining features are the rejection of the very idea of meaning and a commitment to a behaviourist view of language acquisition' (Baghramian 2016, 26). She then proposes an account of the connection between Quine's linguistic naturalism and the normative features of empathy, referring to the distinction between low level (or primary) and high level (more complex), instances of empathy, arguing that Quine encompasses both levels. She claims that Quine's description encompasses the low-level, by appealing to the discovery of mirror neurons which enable the mental 'mimicry' or mirroring experienced by humans, as well as some animals, at a subconscious level. She then argues that Quine's views 'seem to be in line with, if not a precursor to, the mirroring route to empathy' (Baghramian 2016, 35). To make the point, she refers in particular to the notion of 'instinctive' empathy at the basis of the perception of another's unspoken thought, as 'older' than language; as can be seen in a newborn infant's responses to an adult's facial expression, even to the imitation of it by the unlearned flexing of appropriate muscles (Quine 1995, 89), as well as to the 'uncanny knack' at the basis of the empathizing with another's perceptual situation. She also argues that this view of empathy, seen as an innate ability for mimicry, is not normative for it operates 'at a preconscious level and is a nonlinguistic or pre-linguistic stratum of cognition' (Baghramian 2016, 35). However, she continues, low-level empathy is not sufficient to Quine, for learning or translating a language. On the contrary, Quine seems to be defending different versions of high-level empathy. In particular, the reiteration of the high-level empathy is needed when the radical translator goes beyond the perceptual level and attempts to attribute beliefs and desires to the subject. She then refers to Goldman's Simulation Theory (1995, 1998, 2011, 2013) to claim that Quine seems to be thinking of empathy as something similar to Goldman's 'perspective-taking' rather than automatic mirroring. And she refers to Batson's (2011) distinction between three types of high-level empathy, to try to overcome the ambiguity highlighted by Picardi in Quine's account of empathy, arguing that all three variants of high-level empathy, unlike automatic mirroring, explicitly or implicitly rely on normative judgements.[14]

However, it seems to me that Baghramian does not solve the problem of the connection between the two levels of empathy. Even if she is right in pointing to the strict link between the natural and the normative levels in Quine's explanation of the role of empathy in language learning and translation, I think that Quine's description cannot be clarified by just referring to a functional distinction between low and high levels of empathy, without trying to find out the continuity between the two. It seems that the ambiguity in Quine's account is due, instead, to the exigency of trying to string together both a naturalistic perspective and the interpretation of language as a social art; that is, the problem lies in trying to elucidate the link between the rules of language in a cultural context and the natural, that is 'instinctive' basis of the process of learning a language. This is the reason that Quine refers to Dewey's behavioural theory of meaning, while his epistemological behaviourism is particularly close to the non-reductionist naturalism of Mead (*via* Dewey).

5. Overcoming the descriptive/normative dichotomy

As Baghramian also admits, the normative features of empathy are not another version of the instrumental norms that Quine allows into his naturalized account of knowledge. The normative judgments involved in empathic interpretation cannot be seen as mere tools for achieving specified epistemic goals; instead they are the starting points of the very endeavour to understand and learn a language, an endeavour that marks us off from other animal species (though not in the sense that our normative grounding is detached entirely from a natural ground). A possible clarifying solution has therefore to refer to the notions of 'gesture' and 'behaviour' which must enter as the core notions of a possible account in order to overcome the dichotomy between the descriptive and the normative levels in which Quine's theory seems to be trapped. More specifically, such an account would aim at pointing out the strict link between the innate ability to understand another's perceptional orientation, gesture, and facial expression from inarticulate prelinguistic to linguistic levels, and empathetic identification. Indeed, references to the epistemic prerogative of the neuro-socio-psychological to the linguistic level are needed.[15] As already claimed, in fact, Quine's notion of empathy as instinct is in line with Mead's idea of sympathy, for both notions are considered to have a social character and to be at the basis of the ontogenetic and phylogenetic explanation of symbolic/propositional language arising from gestural communication. From this perspective, human language is considered as the extension of some prelinguistic communicative behaviours at the basis of the neuro-socio-psychological empathetic identification.[16] It is important to notice, however, that to identify with the attitudes of others means to refer to higher cognitive abilities in which automatic mirroring have a functional role. People's ability to understand the intentions and preferences of others is not identical to people's brain activation of the neural mimetic mechanism. There would be, otherwise, a specular identification, a mere imitative mirroring. It is necessary to presuppose a process of cooperation since only within a theory of social stimulus and response, and the social situations that create these stimuli and responses, does imitation find its proper place.[17]

After all, also the notion of 'simulation', which is often used in reference to imitation, has not been given a uniform, invariable definition in neuroscience. Some neuroscientists use the concept of neural mechanism through which to understand the mind's activity exclusively (Gallese and Goldman 1998), whereas others consider simulation as a conscious process depending on a deliberate re-activating of some actions accomplished beforehand (Decety and Ingvar 1990). Thus, a distinction should be made between a *simulation mechanism* referred to as an embedded 'proto-intentional' structure of recognition of the attitudes of others (namely, a neural recognition of a conspecific's intentions),[18] and a *simulation process* which refers to interpersonal interactions in which the individual's higher cognitive and affective abilities, that have simulation mechanism as their material causal condition but are not reducible to it, are involved in the process of identification with the attitudes and intentions of others. It is also possible to see the distinction made by Baghramian between low-level and high-level empathy in Quine as analogous to that between the simulation mechanism referred to as the embedded 'proto-intentional' recognition of the attitudes of others, and the simulation process in which the individual's higher cognitive and affective abilities have a simulation mechanism as their material causal condition but are not reducible to it (and which can be included in Bateson's three types of high-level empathy).

A working hypothesis would then assume, as Mead does and Quine seems implicitly to accept, that the mind of the child is formed in the interaction between neurobiological processes and interpersonal relations.[19] It would be possible then to distinguish various phases of child development, in the first of which the perceptual and interactional capacities reinforced and generally employed to recognize increasingly others' movements, facial expressions and more general embodied behaviours, facilitating mimetic processes. In the first phase, a fully developed cognitive simulation process is not yet present; rather, an affective, instinctive, perception-based understanding emerges through face-to-face intersubjective experiences.[20] It can be supposed that these first stages of intersubjectivity are related to a child's identification with the other, that is what Zlatev (2008) called the *diadic mimesis*, which is the subject's capacity to place herself in the shoes of the other and understand what she is attending to. As the subject grows up, she learns to assume the gestural and language attitudes of others, and their responses to her gestures (Mead [1934] 2015, 154), gradually becoming a social being, learning social meanings, values and rules. Meanings are then the readiness to respond in certain ways to similar stimuli, as according to Quine's and Mead's views.[21] At this point, the first phases of the learning processes of children extend and expand on their embodied practical abilities and skills, including linguistic abilities, through what Zlatev called the *triadic mimesis*; that is, the understanding of the communicative use of one's bodily movement and objectivity, and the phenomenon of 'the same meaning for the addressee as for the sender'. Having the same meaning implies a development of a third order mentality and a third high-level of empathy. A partial understanding of others' minds is therefore rooted in an instinctive 'residue in the form of a natural human relationship with respect to which human language is an extension and sophistication. As seen above, through the sympathetic placing of themselves in each other's roles, 'and finding thus in their own experiences the response of the others, what would otherwise be an unintelligent gesture, acquires just the value which is connoted by signification, both in its specific applications and in its universality' (Mead 1964, 246).[22] In this case, the empathetic identification seems to have a crucial role in the passage from triadic mimesis to the acquisition of language (in the sense of conventional signs) as well as in learning more and more about the complexity of the experienced relations. It is here that the reference to Quine supports the idea of learning language by observing other people's verbal behaviour and having one's first faltering verbal behaviour observed and reinforced or corrected by others, based on the uncanny knack for empathizing another's perceptual situation, however ignorant we are of the physiological or optical mechanism of this perception.

This allows us to consider empathetic identification as a function of the anticipation of the behaviours of others, and so to place it at the core of social interaction in the same social environment.[23] The theoretical framework sketched above supports Quine's idea that the same contextual social values pertaining to the empathetic interpretation of behaviour hold also for the situation of the 'radical translator'.[24]

Notes

1. Mead, 'Untitled essay on social consciousness and social science', Box X Folder 24, Regenstein Library, [p. 6].
2. I refer here to what can be considered Dewey's and Mead's 'theory of emotion' (Dewey [1894] 1971, [1895] 1971; Mead 1895, 2001), according to which the expression of an emotional attitude is the mark of the passing over of emotional attitude into *a communicative gesture*. As Dewey wrote: 'Emotion in its entirety is a mode of behaviour which is purposive or has an intellectual content, and which also reflects itself into feeling or Affects, as the subjective valuation of that which is objectively expressed in the idea or purpose' (Dewey [1895] 1971, 170–1). Behaviour is then the centre of the condensation of organic activities in which emotional attitude creates a tension between some behavioural habits and ideal situations. A two-page abstract of a paper Mead presented at the third annual meeting of the American Psychological Association of 1894 (Mead 1895), and other

fragments on the relation between evolution, the development of intelligence, and the control of emotion, passion, or reflex action testify of Mead's contribution to Dewey's theory (Mead 1895, 2001). See also: Mead, *Untitled Fragment on Sense of Perception and Behavior (Typescript, Not Necessarily Continuous)*. Box X, Folder 35, and *Untitled Essay on Social Consciousness and Social Science*, Box X Folder 24, both present at Regenstein Library of the University of Chicago.

3. According to Mead, it is necessary to presuppose a process of cooperation to imitation because only within a theory of social stimulus and response and of the social situations that create these stimuli and responses does imitation find its proper place. As he writes: imitation 'gives no solution for the origin of language. We have to come back to some situation out of which we can reach some symbol that will have an identical meaning, and we cannot get it out of a mere instinct of imitation, as such. There is no evidence that the gesture generally tends to call out the same gesture in the other organism. [...] as soon as you recognize in the organism a set of acts which carry out the processes which are essential to the life of the form, and undertake to put the sensitive or sensory experience into that scheme, the sensitive experience, as stimulus we will say to the response, cannot be a stimulus simply to reproduce what is seen and heard; it is rather a stimulus for the carrying out of the organic process'. (Mead [1934] 2015, 59–60).

4. And he continues: 'In so far as the individual indicates it to himself in the role of the other, he is occupying his perspective, and as he is indicating it to the other from his own perspective, and as that which is so indicated is identical, it must be that which can be in different perspectives. It must therefore be a universal, at least in the identity which belongs to the different perspectives which are organized in the single perspective, and in so far as the principle of organization is one which admits of other perspectives than those actually present, the universality may be logically indefinitely extended' (Mead [1934] 2015, 89).

5. See also Quine (1987, 5), Quine (1976, 56–58).

6. On this point see Gibson (2004, 186–88).

7. 'We must indicate to ourselves not only the object but also the readiness to respond in certain ways to the object, and this indication must be made in the attitude or role of the other individual to whom it is pointed out or to whom it may be pointed out. If this is not the case it has not the common property which is involved in significance. It is through the ability to be the other at the same time that he is himself that the symbol becomes significant.' (Mead 1964, 244).

8. As it is well known, sympathy and empathy are two terms that have different historical roots, and have been involved in different kinds of theorizing. Though for long time theorists have often been trying to define the terms by supposing one as merely a type of the other, they mainly refer to two distinct and complex psychological capacities that have quite distinct meaning (for a recognition see Switankowsky 2000; Wispé 1986). But this distinction still does not guarantee univocal definitions for the terms 'sympathy' and 'empathy'. For instance, Aring (1958) distinguishes between 'sympathy' as the act or capacity of entering into or sharing the feelings of another, and 'empathy' as an identification of sorts also connoting an awareness of one's separateness from the observed. Switankowsky defines instead 'sympathy' as

pre-reflective emotional identification between two individuals, whereas 'empathy' consists of *'understanding* another person's situation, which presupposes reflexivity' (Switankowsky 2000, 86). According to Corradi-Fiumara (2009), 'sympathy' refers to a process of affection for the same feeling of another, namely an identification with the other, while 'empathy' is conceived as a capacity to take the role of the other and understand what is inherently foreign in others in distinction from our self. If empathy tends to expand our relational field, whereas sympathy could be considered as an egoistic natural mechanism of identification with those who are like us. From this perspective, sympathizing with another's feelings and beliefs refers to a total identification of her feelings and beliefs with ours. On the contrary, to empathize with other's intentions and beliefs is to put ourselves in his/her situation, that is, to take his/her attitude. A similar elaboration of the notion of 'empathy' in psychology can be found in Rogers (1975). For two elaborations of the notion of 'empathy' see Gieser (2008) and Gordon (1995).

9. See Miller (1973, 146).
10. According to Hume (1739, Bk II, Part II, sec. V), sympathy is a disposition to share sentiments, to participate in the emotional life of others and to form general rules to pursue. Smith, who further elaborated Hume's use of sympathy, considers sympathy as individual's 'fellow-feeling with any passion whatever' which may arise from 'the view of a certain emotion in another person', but not 'from the view of the passion, as from that of the situation which excites it' through the imagination (Smith 1759, I, I, 1, §10). This is due to the fact that people have *learned from experience* the ways to approve or disapprove of the opinions of others (I, I, 3, §§ 3 and 4), as well as their own (III, 1, §§ 4 and 5). According to Smith, sympathy is a complex imaginative process that presents an emotive content and that helps the individual to evaluate the complex situation to approve or disapprove. Sympathy is thence strictly intertwined with moral evaluations which interest also self-evaluations.
11. See Bower (1983). Although recently both cognitive and affective components have been seen as crucial factors of empathy (see Vreeke and Van der Mark 2003), Giusti and Locatelli (Giusti and Locatelli 2007) have pointed out that Mead has been among the first authors to introduce the cognitive element in the affective meaning of 'empathy'. See among others Borghi and Cimatti (2009); Gallese (2009a, 2009b); Gallese and Goldman (1998).
12. Picardi (2000, 130): 'The ambiguity consists in the conflation of a notion of empathy belonging to a normative domain (where principles of rationality, humanity, benefit of doubts etc. have their home) and a notion of "empathy" belonging to a naturalistic domain'.
13. According to George (2000, 21–2), the introduction of empathy undermines Quine's behaviourism.
14. As Baghramian puts it: '[Quine's] account of empathy moves from low level, automatic, mirroring or mimicry to complex acts of ascribing cultural and contextually informed beliefs and other propositional attitudes resulting in full-blown psychological interpretations of others. Empathising, at the more complex level, is a normative act, while low level automatic empathy arguably is not. [...] In Quine's account, the translator, through empathy 1, engages in psychological conjectures as to what the native is likely to believe in specific circumstances, or alternatively, through empathy 2, imagines what the native

would believe or feel, given her psychological states and, finally, in empathy 3, the empathiser project herself or reads herself "into the minds of others" (Quine 1987, 28–29). Norms are involved in these acts of imagination and counter-factual thinking because empathic understanding is achieved not just within the context of a physical environment but also within the culturally informed web of beliefs, which have a cultural context and would follow norm infused conventions.' (Baghramian 2016, 37).

15. As Keskinen argues, psychological research has shown that empirical work on social-cognitive development supports Quine's attribution of empathy to the child, and many studies converge on the general view that infants have some understanding of others' perceptions in their prelinguistic phase of development.

16. The hypothesis, anticipated by Mead and Quine, has recently been taken into account by Cozolino 2006; Franks 2010; Goldman (2013). According to Franks (2010), the human brain is organized for sociality but 'What is needed is an interactional environment of mutual responsiveness which involves the active participation of both the baby and the caregiver. Without any environmental supports for this sociality (most of which is emotional), we do not develop the foundations for anything else' (Franks 2010: 55). Zlatev (2008) speaks about proto-mimesis indicating an embodied, emotional, sensorimotor and non-conceptual practice. According to this perspective, through gestures and facial expression interactions referring in the first phases to emotive and affective expressions, the individual affectively reacts to their physical environment and to co-specifics' non-mental behavioural attitudes as social objects (see Bowlby 1979; Panksepp 1998).

17. See Mead (1964, 98–102). Recently, Hickok (Hickok 2014) has argued against the 'myth' of the neuron mirrors mechanism of imitation (that we mimic because we are social), and rather that social situations guide imitation.

18. See Gallese (2009b). The concept of 'proto-intention' refers to Damasio's concept of 'proto-self'- a biological preconscious function, which pre-exists the feeling of self (Damasio 1999). Like the proto-self, 'proto-intention' is a function arising from the interaction between neural signals and social and natural environmental stimuli.

19. Siegel (1999). See also Baggio (2016, 195–203).

20. As recently Trevarthen (2011) suggested, the development of cultural intelligence in an infant is motivated by the innate intersubjective sympathy that an alert infant can show shortly after birth in sharing meanings with adults. See also Gallagher and Hutto (2008); Reddy (2008) and Rochat (2009).

21. According to Meltzoff and Brooks (2001), the infant apprehends cooperative actions in the way that they are able to re-enact the goal-directed behaviour that someone else fails to complete. It is possible to refer also to Stern's (1985) idea of the 'tuning of affection' in action: that is, the working of complex non-verbal processes expressed either in consequential behaviour, single acts, or vocal gestures through which the social act is realized (Stern refers, in particular, to the affective participation between a mother and an infant).

22. We can also suppose that in the secondary stage of interaction an infant would apprehend the cooperative actions in the way that they can re-enact the goal-directed behaviour that someone else fails to complete (Meltzoff and Brooks 2001).

23. Cf. Turner (2007).
24. As he writes: «But [the translator] will not cultivate these values at the cost of unduly complicating the structure to be ascribed to the native's grammar and semantics, for this again would be bad psychology; the language must have been simple enough for acquisition by the natives, whose minds, failing evidence to the contrary, are presumed to be pretty much like our own» (Quine 1992, 46).

Disclosure statement

No potential conflict of interest was reported by the author.

References

Aring, C. D. 1958. "Sympathy and Empathy." *JAMA* 167 (44): 448–452. doi:10.1001/jama.1958.02990210034008.
Baggio, G. 2016. "Sympathy and Empathy: G. H. Mead and the Pragmatist Basis of (Neuro)Economics." In *Pragmatism and Embodied Cognitive Science*, edited by R. Madzia and M. Jung, 185–210. Berlin/Boston: de Gruyter.
Baghramian, M. 2016. "Quine, Naturalised Meaning and Empathy." *Argumenta* 2 (1): 25–41.
Batson, C. D. 2011. *Altruism in Humans*. New York: Oxford University Press.
Borghi, A., and F. Cimatti. 2009. "Embodied Cognition and Beyond: Acting and Sensing the Body." *Neuropsychologia* 5: 763–773.
Bower, G. H. 1983. "Affect and Cognition." *Philosophical Transaction of the Royal Society of London, Series B* 302: 387–402. doi:10.1098/rstb.1983.0062.
Bowlby, J. 1979. *The Making and Breaking of Affectional Bonds*. London: Tavistock.
Corradi-Fiumara, G. 2009. *Spontaneity. A Psychoanalytic Inquiry*. London and New York: Routledge.
Cozolino, L. J. 2006. *The Neuroscience of Human Relationship: Attachment and the Developing Social Brain*. New York: Norton.
Damasio, A. R. 1999. *The Feeling of What Happens. Body and Emotion in the Making of Consciousness*. Boston, MA: Harcourt.
Decety, J., and D. H. Ingvar. 1990. "Brain Structures Participating in Mental Simulation of Motor Behavior: A Neuropsychological Interpretation." *Acta Psychologica* 73: 13–24. doi:10.1016/0001-6918(90)90056-L.
Dewey, J. [1894] 1971. "The Theory of Emotion. I. Emotional Attitudes". In *John Dewey: The Early Works*, edited by J. A. Boydston. Vol. 4, 152–169. Carbondale IL: Southern Illinois University Press.
Dewey, J. [1895] 1971. "The Theory of Emotion. II. The Significance of Emotions". In *John Dewey: The Early Works*, edited by J. A. Boydston and I. L. Carbondale, Vol. 4, 169–188. Southern Illinois University Press.
Dewey, J. 1929. "Experience and Nature." 1981. In *The Later Works*. edited by J. A. Boydston. Vol. 1. Carbondale IL: Southern Illinois University Press.
Franks, D. D. 2010. *Neurosociology. The Nexus between Neuroscience and Social Psychology*. New York: Springer.
Gallagher, S., and D. Hutto. 2008. "Understanding Others through Primary Interaction and Narrative Practice." In *The Shared Mind. Perspectives on*

Intersubjectivity, edited by J. Zlatev, T. P. Racine, C. Sinha, E. Itkonen, 17–38. Amsterdam: John Benjamins.

Gallese, V. 2009a. "Motor Abstraction: A Neuroscientific Account of How Action Goals and Intentions are Mapped and Understood." *Psychological Research* 73 (2009): 486–498. doi:10.1007/s00426-009-0232-4.

Gallese, V. 2009b. "Mirror Neurons, Embodied Simulation, and the Neural Basis of Social Identification." *Psychoanalytic Dialogues* 19: 519–536. doi:10.1080/10481880903231910.

Gallese, V., and A. I. Goldman. 1998. "Mirror Neurons and the Simulation Theory." *Trends in Cognitive Science* 2: 493–501. doi:10.1016/S1364-6613(98)01262-5.

George, A. 2000. "Quine and Observation." In *Knowledge, Language and Logic: Questions for Quine*, edited by A. Orenstein and P. Kotatko, 21–47. Dordrecht: Kluwer.

Gibson, R. F., Jr. 2004. "Quine's Behaviourism Cum Empiricism." In *The Cambridge Companion to Quine*, edited by R. F. Gibson Jr., 181–199. New York: Cambridge University Press.

Gieser, T. 2008. "Embodiment, Emotion and Empathy: A Phenomenological Approach to Apprenticeship Learning." *Anthropological Theory* 8: 299–318. doi:10.1177/1463499608093816.

Giusti, E., and M. Locatelli. 2007. *L'empatia integrata. Analisi umanistica del comportamento motivazionale nella clinica e nella formazione*. Roma: Soveria Multimedia.

Goldman, A. 2011. "Two Routes to Empathy: Insights from Cognitive Neuroscience." In *Empathy: Philosophical and Psychological Perspectives*, edited by A. Coplan and P. Goldie, 31–44. Oxford: Oxford University Press.

Goldman, A. 2013. *Joint Ventures. Mindreading, Mirroring, and Embodied Cognition*. New York: Oxford University Press.

Goldman, A. I. 1995. "Simulation and Interpersonal Utility." *Ethics* 105 (4): 709–726. doi:10.1086/293749.

Gordon, R. M. 1995. "Sympathy, Simulation, and the Impartial Spectator." *Ethics* 105 (4): 727–742. doi:10.1086/293750.

Habermas, J. 1987. *The Theory of Communicative Action. Volume 2: Lifeworld and System: A Critique of Functionalist Reason*. Boston MA: Beacon Press.

Hickok, G. 2014. *The Myth of Mirror Neurons. The Real Neuroscience of Communication and Cognition*. New York/London: W. W. Norton & Company.

Hume, D. 1739. *A Treatise of Human Nature*, Ed. by L. A. Selby-Bigge. Oxford, MA: Clarendon Press, 1896.

Keskinen, A. T. "Epistemology and empathy: A Quinean perspective." Draft paper https://www.academia.edu/1522967/Epistemology_and_Empathy_A_Quinean_Perspective

McNeill, D. 2005. *Gesture and Thought*. Chicago: Chicago University Press.

Mead, G. H. *Untitled Essay on Social Consciousness and Social Science*, Box X Folder 24. Chicago: Regenstein Library.

Mead, G. H. *Untitled Fragment on Sense of Perception and Behavior (Typescript, Not Necessarily Continuous)*. Box X, Folder 35. Chicago: Regenstein Library.

Mead, G. H. [1934] 2015. *Mind, Self, and Society*. C. W. Morris (ed.). Annoted Edition by D. R. Huebner and H. Joas. Chicago: University of Chicago Press.

Mead, G. H. 1895. "A Theory of Emotions from the Physiological Standpoint (Abstract of A Paper Read to the Third Annual Meeting of the American Psychological Association, 1894)." *Psychological Review* 2: 162-164.

Mead, G. H. 1922. "A Behavioristic Account of the Significant Symbol." *Journal of Philosophy* 19: 157-163. in Mead (1964). doi:10.2307/2939827.

Mead, G. H. 1925. "The Genesis of the Self and Social Control." *International Journal of Ethics* 35 (1925): 251-277. in Mead (1964). doi:10.1086/intejethi.35.3.2377274.

Mead, G. H. 1964. *Selected Writings*. edited by.A. J. Reck. Chicago: Chicago University Press.

Mead, G. H. 2001. "The Social Character of Instincts." In *Essays on Social Psychology*, edited by M. J. Deegan, 3-8. New Brunswick, NJ: Transaction Publishers.

Meltzoff, A. N., and R. Brooks. 2001. "'Like Me' as a Building Block for Understanding Other Minds: Bodily Acts, Attention, and Intention." In *Intentions and Intentionality: Foundations of Social Cognition*, edited by B. Malle, L. J. Moses, and D. A. Baldwin, 171-191. Cambridge, MA: MIT Press.

Miller, D. L. 1973. *George Herbert Mead. Self, Language and the World*. Chicago & London: University of Chicago Press.

Panksepp, J. 1998. *Affective Neuroscience: The Foundation of Human and Animal Emotions*. Oxford: Oxford University Press.

Picardi, E. 2000. "Empathy and Charity." In *Quine: Naturalized Epistemology, Perceptual Knowledge and Ontology*, edited by L. Decock and L. Horsten, 121-134. Amsterdam-Atlanta: Rodopi.

Quine, W. V. O. 1953. "The Problem of Meaning in Linguistics." In *From a Logical Point of View*, 47-64. New York: Harper & Row Publishers.

Quine, W. V. O. 1960. *Word and Object*. Cambridge Mass: MIT Press.

Quine, W. V. O. 1969. *Ontological Relativity and Other Essays*. New York: Columbia University Press.

Quine, W. V. O. 1975. "Mind and Verbal Dispositions." In *Mind and Language*, edited by S. Guttenplan, 80-91. Oxford: Clarendon Press.

Quine, W. V. O. 1976. "Linguistics and Philosophy." In *The Ways of Paradox and Other Essays*, 56-58. Cambridge Mass: Harvard University Press.

Quine, W. V. O. 1984. "Relativism and Absolutism." *The Monist* 67: 293-296. doi:10.5840/monist198467318.

Quine, W. V. O. 1987. "Indeterminacy of Translation Again." *Journal of Philosophy* 84: 5. doi:10.2307/2027132.

Quine, W. V. O. 1992. *Pursuit of Truth*. Cambridge Mass: Harvard University Press.

Quine, W. V. O. 1995. *From Stimulus to Science*. Cambridge Mass.: Harvard University Press.

Reddy, V. 2008. *How Infants Know Minds*. Cambridge, MA: Harvard University Press.

Rizzolatti, G., and C. Sinigaglia. 2006. *So quel che fai*. Milano: Raffaello Cortina.

Rochat, P. 2009. *The Infant's World*. Cambridge, MA: Harvard University Press.

Rogers, C. 1975. "Empathic: An Unappreciated Way of Being." *The Counseling Psychologist* 5 (2): 2-10. doi:10.1177/001100007500500202.

Siegel, D. 1999. *The Developing Mind. How Relationships and the Brain Interact to Shape Who We Are*. New York: Guilford Press.

Smith, A. 1759. *The Theory of Moral Sentiments.* edited by D.D. Raphael and A.L. Macfie. Oxford: Oxford University Press, 1976.
Stern, D. 1985. *The Interpersonal World of the Infant.* New York: Basic Books.
Switankowsky, I. 2000. "Sympathy and Empathy." *Philosophy Today* 44 (1): 86–92. doi:10.5840/philtoday200044156.
Trevarthen, C. 2011. "What Is It like to Be a Person Who Knows Nothing? Defining the Active Intersubjective Mind of a Newborn Human Being." *Infant and Child Development* 20: 119–135. doi:10.1002/icd.v20.1.
Turner, S. 2007. *Human Emotions: A Sociological Theory.* New York: Routledge.
Vreeke, G., and I. Van der Mark. 2003. "Empathy, an Integrative Model." *New Ideas in Psychology* 21 (3): 177–207. doi:10.1016/j.newideapsych.2003.09.003.
Wispé, L. 1986. "The Distinction between Sympathy and Empathy. To Call Forth a Concept, a Word Is Needed." *Journal of Personality and Social Psychology* 50 (2): 314–321. doi:10.1037/0022-3514.50.2.314.
Zlatev, J. 2008. "The Co-Evolution of Intersubjectivity and Bodily Mimesis." In *The Shared Mind. Perspectives on Intersubjectivity*, edited by J. Zlatev et al., 214–244. Amsterdam: John Benjamins.

No Empathy for Empathy: An Existential Reading of Husserl's Forgotten Question

Iraklis Ioannidis

ABSTRACT
Empathy is a term used to denote our experience of connecting or feeling with an Other. The term has been used both by psychologists and phenomenologists as a supplement for our biological capacity to understand an Other. In this paper I would like to challenge the possibility of such empathy. If empathy is employed to mean that *we know* another person's feelings, then I argue that this is impossible. I argue that there is an equivocation in the use of the term 'empathy' which conditions the appropriation of the Other *as we think that we know* how the Other feels. To claim that we do know an Other's feelings – or any kind of their intentional experience – means to appropriate their experience through our own. I will first reveal the equivocal use of the term 'empathy' and, then, I will explore Husserl's use of the term. In Husserl, the understanding of an Other as empathy is only partial. I shall conclude by reiterating a thesis from philosophy of existence and feminist theory according to which to know another person comes from creating a community with them and not because we have a biological structure that can mirror each other's feelings.

Introduction[1]

Phenomenology and Psychology have contributed considerably in shaping up the contemporary discourse of empathy.[2] Psychologists use empathy to denote how neural systems, such as the discovery of so-called mirror neurons, make possible the understanding of an Other's actions – 'action understanding'[3] – or their feelings – 'the capacity to understand others' feelings.'[4] Despite some skepticism on the matter,[5] they also go so far as to claim that such neural mechanisms have as '*primary role*' *of the meaning of others*.'[6] Phenomenologists, on the other hand, have been following Husserl who used the term 'empathy' in order to explore both how we know that an Other, as an embodied consciousness like us, exists, and how we can understand them. Recent phenomenological analyses side with the latest developments in cognitive psychology and neuroscience in order to provide proof for both of these two claims.

In this paper I would like to challenge the possibility of such empathy. If empathy is employed to mean that *we know* another person's feelings because they can be possibly mirrored in our brain – or somewhere in us for that matter – then, I argue that this is impossible. To be clear, I am not arguing that mirror neurons, (or however the biological structure is named) do not exist. Nor am I trying to claim that some kind of mirroring is not taking place. Rather, I am arguing that there is an equivocation in the use of the term 'empathy' which conditions the appropriation of the Other *as we think that we know* how the Other feels. To claim that we do know an Other's feelings – or any kind of their intentional experience – means to appropriate their experience through our own.

To this end, I shall first start with raising our awareness to an equivocation in the use of the term 'empathy.' Then, I shall go back to Husserl's key writings who used the term empathy to denote the phenomenon by which we can come to know that another person, as embodied consciousness, exists. Contrary to mainstream readings, I will try to show that Husserl's empathy, as the possibility of the knowledge of the existence of another person,[7] is *partially* accomplished epistemically. Inspired by philosophy of existence and feminist theory, I shall conclude by reiterating the thesis that knowing another person, in all senses, comes from creating a community with them and not because we have a biological structure that can mirror each other's feelings.

Which empathy?

When empathy is used to denote the sharing of another person's feelings, it refers to both positive and negative feeling.[8] This fact immediately creates a conceptual mist which allows 'empathy' to be used as a supplement to 'understanding.' For instance, pain is usually associated as a negative affect and it is linked to suffering. Yet, what I register as positive affect may not be positive for another person. Precisely because *'registering an experience as...'* means attributing a valance to it, such attributions imply some sort of reflection. Arguably, by extending what, in the philosophy of mind, has been referred to as the multiple realizablity problem,[9] we can say the following: We can all have the same brain states activated, but one of us could register that activation as positive and another as negative. The reverse holds as well. We might have different brain states or even different physical make up altogether but we may still agree on how to describe a particular experience – and we could still come to (an) understanding with each other. Biological structure may be a necessary but not a sufficient condition for understanding.

At times, empathy as a term is used to (1) denote just the fact that different brains are similarly activated; and at times (2) to include the congruent or matching evaluations of the activations of the brain areas of objects/subjects of study. The case of one is done involuntarily/non-consciously/passively. Obviously, one may claim with (1) that we are connected biologically, but it raises serious questions of the sort of the connection that takes place if with (2) we evaluate our similar biological experience differently. This happens because (2) involves some kind of reflection and evaluation.[10] The case of (2) is not passive or non-conscious.

One of the claims of this paper is that knowing another's personal feelings or any kind of their intentional experience implies reflection and, thus, the 'biological' connection as a passive connection is not enough to condition it. To arrive at this claim we shall go back to Husserl who explored the possibility of the knowledge of the possibility of knowledge. Following Husserl, we must 'make a new beginning, each for himself and in himself, with the decision of philosophers who begin radically.'[11]

Husserl's other

As we know, Husserl, following Descartes' suggestion advances what he called the epistemic or phenomenological reduction. Phenomenological reduction is doubting everything in a radical way. We refuse to 'accept anything as existent unless it is secured against every conceivable possibility of becoming doubtful.'[12] We will accept something as existing only if it is furnished with absolute apodictic certainty which is 'a mental seeing of something itself.'[13] Apodicticity relies on how things themselves affect us in the how of their appearing to us. Yet, the givenness of things themselves, for Husserl, should not be conflated with the empiricist theory of 'feeling of evidence' as he tells in the *Ideas I*.[14] However, according to Husserl in *Ideas II*,[15] each mental seeing, each cogito is a sort of affection, a coming into contact with. This apodicticity, this mental seeing, is the principle of principles for the possibility of knowledge. It feels like intuitive touching. Such touching is an affection which runs two ways at the same time. It is like putting one's hand on a physical thing where the hand is touching-touched. This affection, this a-logical touching is integral to mental seeing because Husserl asks us to doubt even logic since 'like every other already given science, logic is deprived of acceptance by the universal overthrow'[16] – deprived by the thorough-going doubt.

'In short, not just corporeal nature but the whole concrete surrounding life-world is for me, from now on, only a phenomenon of being, instead of something that is.'[17] With the phenomenological reduction then, everything is reduced with respect to its being. That does not mean that nothingness emerges. Quite the contrary, everything that was given before, in its particularity or generality, is now given as *a phenomenon of being which claims being*. The self doubts; the self reduces everything, including itself, to a phenomenon. This allows everything to be received anew. But, according to Husserl, during this reduction, while the being of things is doubted, their givenness is phenomenally the same. Even if I doubt that this cup exists and it is just an illusion, it is still the same phenomenal thing that I used to call a cup. With the doubting, I call into question its being by accepting its phenomenal givenness and bracketing, the process of phenomenological ἐποχή, all its 'existential positions.'[18] By doubting all existential positions, all previous ontological predications are forcibly suspended, they are concomitantly bracketed. Things silently appear themselves, ontically, in their being themselves.

This process reveals an interesting phenomenon in the case of the one who performs the reduction. The self, the ego as Husserl likes to call it, is a part of a world which the ego itself reduces and is itself being reduced as part of the world, thus, the ego is the one that initiates this process of reduction and is itself also reduced. Yet, as is the case with everything being reduced, the givenness of the ego to itself will be phenomenally the 'same.' But since I, as the ego that reduces, bracket my existential position, that which will receive the reduced self, the phenomenal ego, cannot be the ego that initiates the reduction and which will now appear in its pure phenomenality. By the phenomenological reduction the ego is given to that, to _(something)_, which has its ontology suspended, which cannot be itself in its previous empirical being as the former is now bracketed as part of the world. That means that the self 'transcends'[19] itself to be given to itself in its pure givenness. 'That which' conditions this transcendence, the coming back to the ego which conditions the bracketing, can only be a transcendental ego.

> If this "transcendence," which consists in being non-really included, is part of the intrinsic sense of the world, then, by way of contrast, the Ego himself, who bears within him the world as an accepted sense and who, in turn, is necessarily presupposed by this sense, is legitimately called transcendental, in the phenomenological sense.[20]

Let us look more deeply into this process. Through the phenomenological reduction, which is a form of a reflection as we crudely adumbrated earlier, I transcend myself to be given to myself anew as a phenomenon – part of an equally phenomenalised world. This process reveals an ego which is part of the world and its transcendental *onlooker*[21] who receives the reduced ego as a phenomenon, as part of a phenomenalised world. This is an 'alter ego,' an ego 'not as "I myself," but as mirrored in my own ego.'[22] This Other, this alter-ego, this onlooker receives the ego as part of the world which is also given phenomenologically. This alter-ego is the condition based on which everything can be reduced. But this reduction does not mean being at an Archimedian point outside of the ego. It is the very ego that transcends itself to be given transcendentally to itself and not transcendently. Let us explore this with an example. This cup that I perceive becomes a something, something that affects me in a particular way through the ways that I can be (so) affected by it. But in terms of my ego and the cup, after the reduction, I do not perceive an additional thing, myself as from afar and a thing that I called a cup before the *ἐποχή*. The splitting of the ego that Husserl refers to is taking place in immanence and not in exteriority as if I were a new metaphysical ego looking back at my empirical ego from *a physical* distance. It is an immanent transcendence and this is justified by the fact that Husserl insists on the sameness of the 'phenomenally experiential result' before and after the *ἐποχή*. However, this alter-ego as onlooker, cannot be found as a phenomenon in the reduced world precisely because it is the condition of the phenomenological reduction. It is revealed as the condition of the everyday ego which performs the reduction. Only if there is such an unworldly transcendental ego can the ego perform such a *cogitatum*, a transcendence of the world and its parts, of which one is the empirical everyday self. And since such an ego is immanent it amounts to acquiring 'myself as the pure ego with the pure stream of my *cogitationes*.'[23]

Because of the *ἐποχή*, where I have abstracted everything even the everyday intersubjective predications which I used before the reduction to convey my experience in the world, what I find is an ego 'the only Object "in" which I "rule and govern" immediately.... As perceptively active, I experience (or can experience) all of Nature, including my own animate organism, which therefore in the process is reflexively related to itself.'[24] Sinply, I am given myself to myself objectively in its purest form. I am an-Other to myself. I come into contact with (my) transcendental *subjectivity* – I am self-given to myself.

In this exercise, Husserl is absolutely right to point out that were I to abstract everything from what is given to me in the stream of consciousness and, all the more so, if I abstain from all the use of language which is the manifestation of an intersubjective yet empirical enterprise in the world of experience prior to the *ἐποχή*, then I am left with '"*my animate organism*" and "*my psyche*," or myself as a psychophysical unity.'[25] Indeed, I am given to myself as an-Other, but not as another subject because that would mean another version of the empirically intentional subject. If the reduction is properly undertaken, and this is the point where Husserl parts with the Cartesian reduction which he considers incomplete, then the transcendental ego is pure subjectivity which conditions the experience in the world. And the world is given to subjectivity in its pure form. But as a condition, transcendental subjectivity not only receives a phenomenological plenum but also projects this plenum into being a world; it gives it being, it constitutes it by 'means of acts of perception, imagination, and categorical observation.'[26] It is itself intentional in its pure form and, hence, Husserl arrives at the conclusion that the task of transcendental phenomenology is the 'systematic disclosure of constituting intentionality.'[27]

So far the reduction has revealed to us a transcendental subjectivity, which Husserl seems to be identifying with constituting intentionality, and an ego given to the latter as a psychophysical unity.[28] We follow Husserl's syllogisms to understand how Husserl can claim that we can know whether another person as an embodied consciousness, a psychophysical unity, exists. As we shall see, it is precisely this issue of transcendentality that blocks the knowledge of the possibility of knowledge of an other person.

The ego which is received by the primordial self is a phenomenon and, as part of the world, it is a phenomenon among all other phenomena. To be precise, however, after the reduction there should only be phenomenalising rather than phenomena. Phenomena come after the phenomenalising is being itself thematised – when the horizon of what is phenomalised is being given contours or boundaries, that is, definitions. For Husserl, however, we have the phenomenon of the 'cup,' and, most importantly, other entities which before the reduction and the ἐποχή I called other persons. That is to say, it is as if the revelation of my primordial self as transcendental 'makes constitutionally possible a new infinite domain of what is "other:" *an Objective Nature* and a whole Objective world, to which all other Egos and I myself belong.'[29] Following this line of thought, as I am given to myself, all others whom I used to experience as egos before the ἐποχή are now also given to me as phenomena, since all egos are part(s) of the world. Once again, these are all given to me in the same objective way as I have been given to myself. Thus, if all other persons are like me before the reduction, then, *simpliciter*, these other egos must also be given to me and to themselves in the same manner as I am given to myself after the reduction.[30] The apodictic revelation of the Other then, if there is one, must be revealed as an other subjectivity – which has been revealed in my reduction. What we are looking for, then, is what Husserl calls transcendental intersubjectivity, that is, how transcendental egos or pure subjectivities relate. We are looking for an affection of blending, where our *'perspectives blend,'*[31] to use Maurice Merleau-Ponty's expression. It is this 'blending' or this 'communication,' while being 'immediately in touch with the world'[32] in which we will find the Other.

We have to remember that Husserl's starting point is not to answer the question of the existential basis of the Other; his aim is to discover the methodological principles which will always allow us to arrive at an Objective view of the world, the ultimate foundation for a philosophy as science, for absolute true knowledge. The quest to find the other as Other becomes shortlisted in his philosophical agenda due to the criticisms of phenomenology resulting in solipsism; solipsism will never allow an objective world to be revealed when objective means being given to me as to all other fellow human beings. The quest to find the Other becomes a need to find where we converge; an objective world in an other sense of objective – the world as an object to all.

We need to elaborate on this convergence – sometimes also called a transcendental principle of justification.[33] The constitution of an object has as its ultimate condition (a point of) unity. This unity is what remains identical throughout all the possible ways of its appearing to an ego. This objective sense as 'that which remains identical throughout the variations of sense'[34] is the new Husserlian conceptualization of the Kantian schema, 'a rule-governing schema.'[35] Something repeats itself in its various appearings and Husserl admits that the Other, who can also receive the schema of the world or the world as schema is important for saving me from a possible solipsistic pathology. If I constitute the world alone and myself and 'everything is in harmony,'[36] then it could be the case that 'I become for them an interesting *pathological* Object, and they call my actuality, so beautifully manifest to me, the hallucination of someone who up to this point has been mentally ill.'[37] My verification principle *is* the Other. This convergence, this blending, or the recognition of what is common to all, a 'mutual understanding'[38] is a fundamental condition for knowledge and sanity. This convergence, sometimes also referred to as co-constitution, is fundamental precisely because it neutralises the possibility of illusory or abnormal uncovering of the world at the same time of uncovering *the* world itself. '"The true thing" is then the object that maintains its identity within the manifolds of appearances belonging to a multiplicity of subjects,' it is an intuited object for all 'related to a community of normal subjects.'[39] Therefore, if a transcendental subjectivity refers to the way the appearing world appears, that is, the phenomenalising is constituted into phenomena, then, a transcendental intersubjectivity is the condition for the objectivity of the object, 'the appearing of the true thing.'[40] But apart from the true thing, what the Other also secures, at the same time, is my normality, the negation of my being an *interesting pathological Object*.

Husserl attempts to prove the Other as an Other with the following transcendental schematic analysis. The Other in their being, if they are to be like me, which in this case is another consciousness, must experience the same phenomenon of Other-ness of self – if they were to perform the reduction. But this, as mentioned, cannot be accessible to me from here as an objectivating ego or to the ego that is given to me in that process. And this is only logical since, 'if what belongs to the other's own essence were directly accessible, it would be merely a moment of my own essence, and ultimately he himself and I myself would be the same.'[41] So, the only way remaining to uncover other empirical persons as transcendental subjectivities in the reduced world, is by, what Husserl calls, analogising apperception through appresentation.

'Appresentation' is a thought of Husserl's which we first find in the *Logical Investigations*. To use his example, suppose we experience a box. We perceive the box from a particular perceptual angle but never as a whole. To perceive all of it we need to turn it over or change our angle, but we will then be 'losing' the perceptual content we had before. What we 'lose' we appresent. What we call a box is an apperception,[42] an object as 'a web of partial intentions fused together in the unity of a single total intention.'[43] Appresenting reveals how consciousness, as an intentional act, transcends itself becoming something that it is not. And by this transcendence, the intentional act is constituting consciousness. For instance, when I see the front side of a box and I am appresenting the rest so as to talk of an experience of a 'box,' the latter becomes something that I reach as a consciousness beyond that which I am actually experiencing. But to appresent something I must have had a prior experience of it (or something similar) and apperceived or apprehended it as such.[44] If I experience a box now, I apperceive it as box based on a '*"primal instituting*," in which an object with a similar sense became constituted [as a box] for the first time.'[45] Put simply, I analogise my current apperception with that apperception which was primally instituted as 'box.'[46]

But this process of analogical apperception through appresentation cannot be (of) the same regional *eidos* as that used when we apperceive the transcendental subjectivity of the Other within the reduction. The analogising apprehension must be conditioned on a primal instituting if we are to claim an experience as an *experience of*. Without our analogising apprehension there is no possibility to claim an *experience of* which is built up through the relevant appresentations. The reason for this is that the primal instituting becomes a blueprint, if we can use such an expression, the rule-governing schema, by which a verification of what the consciousness transcends in the process of appresentation can be achieved through a corresponding fulfilling (empirical) presentation of what is transcended. Put simply, the primal instituting conditions the criterion of verification of the analogical apperception. For instance, if I am faced with the front part of a car, I have a perceptual horizon of the front part which I apperceive as the front part of a car. But to arrive at the conclusion that I am indeed having an experience of the front part of a car I need to experience the whole car out of which my experience of the front can be validated as such. By changing perspectives and perceiving the rest of the object I can receive the corresponding fulfilling presentations of what I appresented and thus validate my experience when these appresentations are *adequate* (or not – it might turn out to be a replica of the front of a car). However, the possibility of such appresentation after the phenomenological reduction with respect to the Other as Other like me, that is, a consciousness, is, as Husserl emphatically mentions, 'excluded a priori.'[47]

After the reduction, I am given to myself as a psychophysical unity which Husserl calls an animate organism. The Other is given to me firstly as a body. I cannot as of yet claim that this body *there* (of the Other) which I can appresent analogically with the body of my animate organism is equally another animate organism. To do that it would mean that I could have the possibility of a corresponding fulfilling presentation of the Other as a psyche in order to complete the appresentation which is impossible. What Husserl must have in mind is not the problem of epistemic access to the Other's mental experience as framed by Descartes, for example. Rather, the issue must be the very possibility of that body there having epistemic access to itself, that is, to be conscious and, also, the possibility of my knowing that the how of my accessing myself is structurally/essentially the same yet not identical with the way that the body there can have access to itself. In simplified terms, whether there is another mind like mine, discovering its mind in the way I discover mine. *Simpliciter*, if the Other can perform a phenomenological reduction.

Husserl attempts to resolve this difficulty and to explain the analogising apperception at a transcendental level through the phenomenon of pairing. Pairing is defined as the phenomenological unity of similarity of distinct data that are given with the same prominence in consciousness. It is a form of association but this association is marked by a passivity in the sense that things are given in themselves and, though distinct, they are nevertheless given uncontrollably and synchronously in the unity of consciousness. The distinct data constitute a pair, a phenomenological unity, by being given 'into' consciousness together, in essence simultaneously, and with the same prominence even though there are distinct; or, as Husserl maintains, in coincidence. Their mutual givenness in the unity of consciousness associates them and constitutes them as a pair. That also means that, as a pair, an apperception of the one can be possible through the other by 'a mutual transfer of sense.'[48]

Pairing is the first step towards apprehending the Other as a transcendental subjectivity, like when I apprehend my self as I am given to myself after the reduction. And this starts with the body. We shall quote Husserl's explication extensively to make manifest a second sense of pairing that is presupposed in his exposition. Husserl writes:

> Now in case there presents itself, as outstanding in my primordial sphere, a body "similar" to mine – that is to say, a body with determinations such that it must enter into a phenomenal *pairing* with mine – it *seems* clear and without more ado that, with the transfer of sense, this body must forthwith appropriate from mine the sense: animate organism.[49]

In the margin of this passage we can see that Husserl is oscillating between two types of association which are at work indeterminately. Let's follow the reduction carefully. After the reduction and the ἐποχή of all predications,

I am given to myself as an animate organism, a psychophysical unity. This is the first pairing that I must be experiencing. My body and my psyche are given to me as a unity. Their prominence is equal and their distinctness as data (not as objects) are given simultaneously in the objectified ego, my ego as phenomenon. My transcendental subjectivity is then revealed to me by and through reduction simultaneously with the psycho-physical unity, an original pairing. The reference point for this pairing is my transcendental subjectivity, whilst 'its data' is the unity of the psyche and the body. So, the first otherness is located in a new way within me in immanence: I am a psychophysical unity; better, I experience myself as a psychophysical unity, or, even better, I apprehend myself as a psychophysical unity.

The pairing that the previous quotation suggests is a different one. This pairing may have the same reference point, my transcendental subjectivity (or so it seems because Husserl is never clear on this), but its data is different. The body of mine and the body of the Other need to be first paired so that I can experience the Other as Other, as another psychophysical unity which could enable a transfer of sense to their transcendental subjectivity. The likeness now will refer to my body and the body of the Other. It seems that, by the body of another organism which I apprehend like mine, there must be a pairing, the same psychophysical unity of a body and a psyche hence the other is an other like me. But 'is the apperception actually so transparent?'[50] This is indeed the second pairing that I must apperceive but since I apperceive it, I cannot arrive at it inferentially as we just did. I must be given it somehow. But how? It is at this point that Husserl's intersubjectivity gets its transcendental flavor.

With the reduction, my body is given to me objectively but this objectivity cannot mean perspectival wholeness. As already mentioned, the transcendence that the reduction offers implies a stepping out of the world so it can be looked at from a distance, but this distance is not of a physical nature where one actually stands outside the physical like a metaphysical entity, able, from such a distance, to take an objective view. That implies that though objectively given, it is given from the reference point of the 'I' – or better yet, the mental eye since Husserl talks about mental seeing. Phenomenally, though, this means one possible appearing, and this appearing is always present though not always prominent to the transcendental ego. Now, the presence of another's body is first given as another body that enters my intentional horizon much like my own body. It is just a body not an Other's body. To be precise it is not even a body, it is a phenomenon first and foremost much like my body as a phenomenon. The modality of givenness of the objectified body here must be the same with those in a phenomenological reduction. Both phenomenal entities are phenomenally given in the same modality to my primordial objectivating, constituting ego, and thus their difference becomes a difference of spatial presentation, and only that.[51] The only difference that reveals itself in the appearing is spatial, here versus there. This difference in spatial presentation suggests that as the modality of my body is given to me in its spatial exteriority from here, the givenness of the other bodily presence presents an analogue of the spatial modes that my body would have if it were there.

The phenomenal likeness of these two thematised phenomenalisations, given simultaneously in one act of consciousness, is what suggests a pairing but a pairing of a different kind and one very much close to an analogising apperception. To use the scissors example that Husserl mentions, when I apprehend scissors as scissors the primal instituting which guides the analogising is not present in my perceptual act. However, in the case of the other body and my body, both phenomena are simultaneously present and are analogised with and through each other due to their perceived likeness. Husserl is very clear about this from the start of §51 in the *Meditations*: 'the *primally institutive original* is always *livingly present*, and the primal instituting itself is therefore always going on in a livingly effective manner.'[52] It may well be that my body as a phenomenon from here becomes the primal constituting based on which the other phenomenon becomes a body as my body would look from there. But since both are present, the analogising apperception of that phenomenon over there as body like mine is of a different kind. It has the form of inter-x, where 'x' is a placeholder. I can constitute my body-phenomenon as a body only through appresenting it with another body which has become a body after being analogised as another (possible) appearing of my body-phenomenon. This pairing conditions how I am given my body in its fullest since, as mentioned earlier 'in primordinal viewing, I can never represent my body to myself as a whole.'[53] In other words, in primordial givenness I cannot arrive at the noema of my body without there being another body. This pairing becomes the possibility of completing the rest of the possible appearings of my body here through the similarity of the body over there. If we allow ourselves the terminology of the *Investigations*, there can be no schema of my body without an Other's body. The other body comes also to fill up the rest of the possible appearings that are missing from the way I am given my body. I appresent my body as an object in the transcendental field through the other body that is found in my intentional horizon. In the case of my body, the Other's body allows *both* for the schematisation of 'body' and the limit of what will constitute its adequate intention. We could say that the reduction that has phenomenalised 'my' 'psycho-physical unity' and the appearing of the Other's body, manifests a pairing which, in turn, allows for the constitution of 'my body.' Only such an interpretation can make sense of why Husserl ends up asking 'What makes this organism another's, rather than a second organism of my own?'[54]

This very question is what makes our reading radically different compared to orthodox readings of Husserl. I shall mention only two which are relevant in the point that I am trying to make concerning empathy. For instance, Theunissen[55] reads Husserl as having proved the other body as an organic non-thing and then goes on to look at how Husserl will answer the belongingness question of that body. Yet Husserl excludes the experience of the Other inferentially, and though Theunissen does indeed appreciate the non-inferential aspect of Husserl's analysis, he continues to prioritise the apprehension of the Other as an animate organism before it is available to me as not being my body. In this way he cannot show how the Other is given as an Other through the governing of their body which reveals both that they are not me and that they are like me who governs my own body. Now this reading becomes of crucial importance because it relates to what we saw earlier: the issue of mine-ness.[56]

This problematic surfaces again in Thompson's attempt to link Husserl's account to neuroscience. Thompson attempts to show that when neuroscience tries to account for the recognition of the Other through the so-called mirror-neurons it echoes Husserl's account of pairing. With mirror-neurons we witness the display of activity of goal directed bodily movements whether the movements are of the object of study (monkey) or an object of the object of study. Yet, if they are the 'same,' and the stipulation of non-inferential recognition of the Other is kept, Husserl's question '*What makes this organism another's, rather than a second organism of my own?*'[57] remains unanswered. Either there is a mineness that will characterise this activity as mine and the other's as an other, or, a difference between the activities must exist for the non-inferential pairing to occur as (felt) immediate pairing.

Let us look at it differently with an example. I move my arm up and down. With the phenomenological reduction I can describe this movement in the following ways.

R1: I am moving my arm
R2: My arm is moving
R3: An arm is moving

The discourse of mirror-neurons can only capture R3 but cannot capture the feeling of mineness that is implied in R2 or R1. Thompson's reading of pairing as empathy seems to imply that all three are of equal phenomenological import which is clearly not what Husserl implies with the question above.

Husserl's question explores why we are left with the question of belongingness. In the phenomenological reduction, the modality of objectified givenness is the same for all parts of the phenomenally reduced world. That is, the phenomenal sameness of a body here with the body there are each two parts that together constitute a primal instituting of 'body.' Treating that appearance here as another appearing of the 'there' which together constitute a whole, could leave us with the impression of a split of my body here and there. It is precisely when the other side of my body *is not given* as mine[58] that the Other as an animate organism will reveal themselves, thus leading to the original pairing that I transcendentally experience the Other as an Other like me. Yet, once again this revealing will be carried out appresentatively.

As a psychophysical unity, I experience the giveness of myself in the way I behave. I govern my body. It is me who moves there, turns here, and operates my body. The other body there, through which I appresent my own, is not, however, governed by me. But the way I apprehend myself governing my body in a reflective act is manifold. Moving my arm, for instance as we saw earlier, is a three-fold givenness in the plane of consciousness: (my) arm is moving, the movement of (my) arm, my moving my arm. The Other who moves their arm in a like manner *suggests* their being an animate organism like me. My behavior and the way my behavior is given phenomenally to me, becomes the analogue based on which I can arrive at the Other as a pairing; as a psychophysical unity which has been given in the mode of pairing for me in the reduction. As already mentioned, I cannot appresent their psyche. I can only appresent the unity as a pair. I apprehend the Other's body as body because it is through that body that I claim my living body. But that organism having a body like mine does not necessarily mean that it is an animate organism like me. The analogizing apprehension will have to occur by revelation of the Other's psyche.

This apprehension will be carried out appresentatively in the following manner. It will be done through the Other's behavior which reveals the governing of the Other's body which in turn will reveal their being an Other like me. When the other body is revealed as not being governed by me it reveals its being an animate organism, *simpliciter*. That organism is appresented as an Other inasmuch as their behavior, the governance of that body, finds its analogue in mine in the way I have experienced my body being governed by me. In this way, the appresentation of the Other proceeds by a *continuous* fulfilment of analogizing apprehensions of the Other's behavior with mine. There is a 'fulfilling verifying *continuation*' of the Other's behavior which appertains to mine as it has been given in my own experience of my ego. This is why Husserl calls it a harmonious behavior 'as having a physical side that indicates something psychic appresentatively.'[59] The possibility of coming to that knowledge is thus not secured but constantly indicated; never verified. Also, the reference point for this process of appresentation is always me. This empathy is one-directional only. I empathize the Other based on my own criteria.[60]

Husserl's attempt to find and found the Other in oneself through the phenomenological reduction has been challenged by existential philosophers as one sided. Briefly, Heidegger first objects to what we can refer to as the chronological order of the encountering-the-Other. The Other is not 'encountered by a primary act of looking at oneself in such a way that the opposite pole of distinction first gets ascertained.'[61] For Heidegger, the self, or *Dasein*, is structurally connected in being with the others in the world, and this connection is manifested through the everyday concerns of the self. Clearly, Heidegger's point of departure is our everyday life, what we can call the plainly empirical. But Husserl's avenue, according to Heidegger, thwarts this possibility. A transcendental phenomenology starts with the ontological manifestation of the self's being related back to itself through transcendence and equates the otherness of the self with itself as a phenomenon of otherness in general. It becomes an issue of commutative praxis between the transcendental and the empirical levels. It becomes 'a Projection of one's own Being-toward-oneself "into something else." The Other would be a duplicate of the Self.'[62] Now this projection, even if one takes it in the psychological sense that it might suggest (but clearly not the psychoanalytical), it is not necessarily problematic. For instance, if by projection we include the appresentation of my body through the body of the Other in exteriority, no issues seem to spring up. Briefly, I might experience embarrassment when someone points out to me that there is a big stain on the back of my outfit. This being, that I would be, cannot *but be conditioned* on a primal instituting of my having been the observer of such an occurrence in another. I cannot be embarrassed about something that is not happening to me. But this happening to me – on my outfit – is not happening in me, it is happening there, in the exteriority of my body the access to which can be gained only through the Other.

Yet Heidegger insists by suggesting that all these cases which reveal an empathy among Daseins cannot hold based only on a presupposition that 'Dasein's Being towards an Other is its Being towards itself.'[63] If Dasein's being toward an Other is its being toward itself how is the relationship of itself to be made manifest to the Other as Other? Heidegger's single line challenge is indeed insurmountable. Husserl does not resolve the problem of the Other but transposes it. Transcendent egos reveal the primordial egos through and in a community of objectified embodied egos, but in this transcendence the transcendental subjectivities remain incommunicable. If the absolute certainty of the phenomenological reduction, as absolute bare givenness, is secured in the transcendental level, then the gap between the transcendental subjectivities that Husserl opens up renders his 'transcendental intersubjectivity' a formal concept only. The givenness of the Other as a transcendental subjectivity can never be achieved not only because of its unworldliness, as Theunissen says, but also because the givenness of Other is always mediated by its phenomenological counterpart. The *inter-* in Husserl is between constituted subjects or, at best, between a constituting subjectivity and a constituted subjectivity but not between constituting subjectivities.[64] The real problem is not because there is an observable distance between self and Other.[65] We accepted that distance in the phenomenological reduction. The problem is that of the *asymmetry* of constituting intentionalities (i.e. empathy)[66] and a misguided presupposition of the 'reflective self-understanding of an isolated first-person subject.'[67] This phenomenon as empathy is *intersubjection* rather than intersubjectivity.[68] It seems, so far, as Sartre claimed, that 'the true problem is that of the connection of transcendental subjects who are beyond experience.'[69]

Trying to find a biological, i.e. material, basis for this connection does not help either. Sartre has shown the problems of any theory which attempts to link consciousness to 'cerebral impressions'[70] thus anticipating the discourse of mirror neurons. We shall use an existential graph to clarify his fine point. The experiments of mirror neurons work with a mediating factor, that is, the machine that records the electrical or biochemical alterations in the brain. Notice has to be given to the fact that all the experiments are done in controlled environments and not in real life – and we shall come back to the importance of this issue. Just like in the original experiments of Rizzolatti, the following schematic analysis applies to all mirror-neuron experiments:

The feeling or thought of subject 1, represented in their brain as a particular stimulation, is matched and recognized as the same or analogous to that of subject 2 by the mediating device (the scan) which is interpreted by the researcher; the third term. S1 and S2 by themselves might claim *that they think* that they know that they are feeling the same thing, but they can never ultimately justify it. The principle of justification of what they think they now is not included in what is impressed on them. It is the device or interpreter as third term that mediates between the two – or makes the matching. And it is precisely the principle of justification which does not allow us to claim from our own perspective that we indeed can have empathy for the Other.

What the experiments on mirror neurons suggest is that if, for example, S1 moved their hand, then a particular area of their brain would light up. This movement would also light up in the analogous area of the brain of S2. Even if indeed it is the case that we have analogies between the brain stimulations – the evidence of which is not conclusive[71] – the issue becomes

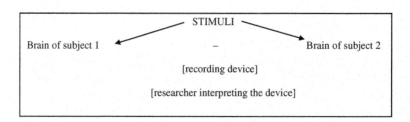

STIMULI		STIMULI
Brain of subject 1 in T1	–	Brain of subject 1 in T2
	[stream of consciousness]	
	[transcendental subjectivity]	

of matching that particular stimulation with one's own. Even if one wants to claim that this pairing – we can see that we fall back to Husserl's questions – is the same and is done non-consciously or unreflectively or passively, all of which amount to the same, then how does one know it by themselves? We fall back to Husserl's predicament. We can analogize the above schema from the first person perspective with the help of time – especially since to reflect means to see oneself as an other in time.

From this perspective, if it is possible for me to analogize that stimulation in T1 is the same or analogous to stimulation in T2, then I am still lacking the principle of verifying that this is the case. As we saw earlier, Husserl himself recognized that a transcendental subjectivity could not function as a principle of epistemic verification.

I mentioned earlier that all experiments in neuroscience are undertaken in controlled environments. That means that the focus is on very particular stimulations. In actual life, we always experience a plethora of stimulations coming from all over. Accepting that all stimulations are mirrored in our brains, how are they differentiated so that we know which one is which in our attributions? Suppose I am talking with two people and both of them raise their arms like in our previous example. Now suppose that one is voluntary raising her arm while the other has his armed propped without my knowing about it. Now suppose that both raise their arms and from my visual horizon I can tell that one has their arm raised by a mechanical prop and the other does not. If neuroscientists and neuro-phenomenologists were correct I would have to say that all these arm movements would have the 'same' impact on my brain which is clearly false. The fact that all these movements may light up the same area in my brain is of little significance epistemically.

What these examples 'show,' *without actually showing it in the scan*, is that there is something that is never mirrored in one's brain and that is their intention – as a feeling of mineness, discussed previously. And the intention is always about the future – that to which *I* transcend or aspire.[72] Empathy mutes the intention of the Other. As Irigaray has claimed, with empathy we take the Other as an other of the Same – which means that we imagine that we know what the Other's intention is based on what has or would have occurred in us if it had happened to us.

Conclusion: back to sym-pathy

If empathy means *to know* what the Other thinks or feels, then empathy is impossible. In this paper I tried to show how empathy as knowing what another person is thinking or feeling is ultimately impossible. To claim that we do is to appropriate the Other and deliver their experience in our own terms. We can only think or imagine that we know. To use Theunissen's expression we can never achieve 'the certification of the character of the Other as transcendent transcendence.'[73] Even if a biological connection as mirroring is a fact, such happening is not adequate to advance a proposition that we can empathize the Other as if we knew what they thought or felt. Each person as subjectivity, transcendental or otherwise, can never be adequately analogised. In the *Logical Investigations*, Husserl tells us that in reality 'adequate perception represents an ideal.'[74] But that does not mean that the Other remains an ideal and can never be touched.

The only way we can know the Other is by creating something together. We need time apart from a biological connection. Projecting ourselves together in reciprocal creation, in co-constitution, is what allows to create a sympathy of feeling. Peirce called it a pure communication of feeling which happens when we rejoice with the Other.[75] Another term used for this communication is the blending or attunement with the Other in creating something new rather than relying on already uttered words.[76] But that is not empathy, which by the way in ancient terms means partial affection,[77] but sympathy, a com-passionate affection.[78]

Notes

1. Part of the original version of this paper was presented in the SEP-FEP Conference in 2015. I would like to thank Susan A. J. Stuart and Olivier Salazar-Ferrer for their valuable help in shaping up the final version of this paper. A special acknowledgement to Ryan John Anderson Gemmell whose comments have been a source of inspiration marked all over this paper. Finally, I would like to thank the two anonymous reviewers whose comments allowed me to clarify certain challenging points.
2. See Zahavi for a comprehensive account of the semantic trajectory of the term (2014).
3. (Rizzolatti and Craighero 2004).
4. (Klimecki et al. 2014, 873).
5. See Edith Stein (1989). For a recent critique see Bloom (2016).
6. (Rizzolatti and Sinigaglia 2008, 124; emphasis in original).
7. As Lee Hardy prefaces Husserl's *The Idea of Phenomenology*, Husserl tries to secure "the possibility of the knowledge of the possibility of knowledge, not the possibility of knowledge in general (1999, 3). As I will show, the Other is required for Husserl for such an epistemic possibility.
8. See Pfaff (2015) and Rakel for a summary (2018).

9. (Putnam 1988). As suggested to me by an anonymous reviewer, multiple realizability might not be an issue for the relevant neurological claims. For instance, what the discourse of mirror neurons suggests is that if A observes B performing an action x, A's neurons are then activated in a way that B's neurons would, were A to perform the action (let us call it pattern Z). For multiple realizability to be a challenging issue for the mirror neuron discourse, that would mean that Z would be observed in A for, let us say, action x or y or a completely different action for B. If that were the case, then it would not be clear as to why pattern Z would be (also) activated in A when they observed B doing x. This question, however, presupposes a one-to-one correspondence between activation and action. As we shall later see, we could never have such direct correspondence between activation and object to which a causal agency is attributed for such an activation. But even if it were possible to prove a one-to-one correspondence, ie. that one state corresponds exclusively to one event which is supposed to be its cause, then multiple realizability would still be a challenge with respect to the material basis where the states obtain.
10. Recent neuroscientific studies try to tackle this issue by claiming that empathy as an overall connection of feeling happens in different areas of the brain if it is positive i.e. compassion and when it is negative i.e. empathic distress (cf. Klimecki et al. 2014). That means that there is a differential pattern in the brain which one may think that it overcomes the issue of the multiple realizability. However, it does not. Suffice it to say that in order for such differentiation to happen in the experiment, the participants required relevant 'training' (871).
11. (Husserl 1960, 7).
12. (Husserl 1960, 3).
13. (Husserl 1960, 12).
14. (Husserl 1983, 40, 1999, 66).
15. (Husserl 1996, 370). A 'a pure act of seeing' as givenness 'insofar as I reflect on them' (Husserl 1999, 24).
16. (Husserl 1960, 13).
17. (Husserl 1960, 19).
18. (Husserl 1960, 20).
19. We should make a note here that the use of the term transcendence is still in a sense constitution by a detour of an overcoming, a surpassing of the ego. Conscious ego surpasses the ego to be given as consciousness.
20. (Husserl 1960, 26).
21. In the Second Meditation of the *Cartesian Meditations* Husserl refers to this onlooker as 'disinterested' (35), or 'non-participant' (37), or the primordial self in order to make explicit the purity of the givenness of the experience in the transcendental level. Whilst acknowledging reception of Derrida's reading of the phenomological reduction revealing the Other in Me, that is, that I am always already intersubjective, we cannot at this point follow this path. *Stricto sensu*, Husserl is first motivated toward the possibility of revealing the Other as an embodied consciousness with epistemic certainty. The Other here is meant as an other individual person not as Otherness in the Stoic sense which, arguably, Derrida's point could lead us to. (1973).
22. (Husserl 1960, 94).
23. (Husserl 1960, 21; original emphasis).

24. (Husserl 1960, 97).
25. (Husserl 1960)
26. (Strasser 1967, 338).
27. (Husserl 1960, 86).
28. Reading Husserl, Donn Welton (1999) claims that Husserl moves us from a mind-body dualism to a body-body dualism, the conscious body as the psychophysical body. The lived body is the conscious body without consciousness being localised in a particular area of the body, for example the brain. While this is true, phenomenologically speaking, there is never a dualism as Husserl talks about two poles and a connecting dash. The phenomenological reduction as 'first reduction' (*Ideas I*, 138–141) reveals the psychophysical unity and a transcendental something; but, then, Husserl advances *a transcendental reduction* to penetrate descriptively deeper into what constitutes the 'transcendental.' Here a 'genuine μετάβασις' [transition] (139) is required. Yet, the phenomenological/eidetic or epistemological reduction is itself a 'μετάβασις εἰς ἄλλο γένος' (1999, 30). Different reductions correspond to the difference between *epoche* and ἐποχή and also the ἀποχή which is required in the transitions. Rather than a dualism, we read in Husserl consciousness as trialism where the connecting dash, the passing into, 'a surplus' (1999, 39) is as essential as the poles.
29. (Husserl 1960, 107).
30. 'The phenomenological-eidetic reduction places me on the footing of a possible monad in general' (Husserl 1998, 146).
31. (Merleau-Ponty 1962, xii).
32. (Merleau-Ponty 1962, xiii).
33. (Zahavi 2005, 2011, 2014).
34. (Steinbock 1999, 189).
35. (Steinbock 1999)
36. (Husserl 1996, 84).
37. (Husserl 1996, 85).
38. (Husserl 1996, 87).
39. (Husserl 1996, 87).
40. (Husserl 1996)
41. (Husserl 1996, 109). This is the first instance where pure mirroring of another person is not possible in Husserl because it raises the issue of time. What Husserl does here is to bring into the discussion the issue of time. Overtime, if mirroring were possible all the time, what would the difference of myself and an Other be? A possible answer could be that we differ physically, that is, through our bodies. But for Husserl we are always a psychophysical unity.
42. 'Apperception: a consciousness that is conscious of something individual that is not self-given in it' (Husserl 1998, 151).
43. (Husserl 1970, 211).
44. For Husserl, 'apperception' and 'apprehension' are identifying the same function. As Husserl himself states in the *Investigations*: 'The term "apperception" is unsuitable despite its historical provenance, on account of its misleading terminological opposition to "perception;" "apprehension" would be more usable' (1970, 243).
45. (Husserl 1960, 111).

46. There is clearly a tension here between constitution and institution. What I constitute for a first time as something can be a primal instituting for the next phenomenalising which will, by its phenomenological similarity, be constituted as the same something or something different. What this theorising opens up though, is the conditions of the first constitution – genesis – which counts as a primal institution. There is a great philosophical discussion as to whether this 'primal instituting' should be conceived in the way Husserl talked about it in the *Ideas*, that is, as a core sense or a schema which comes to be constituted through repetition, or as a genetic impression closer to a Humean conceptualization of an empirical datum impressed on consciousness and retained somehow (in memory), or as a *cogitatio* whose re-presentation in the analogising process becomes a riddle or non-conceptualizable (following Henry (2012; 2015) and Derrida (1973, 2003)). To analogise with an older similar phenomenalising/schema, the new datum must somehow be presented but it is not – yet it must somehow exist, to be analogised. Representation here reveals its full equivocality. The intentional act of consciousness as transcendence becomes either a re-presentation with a sense of simulation or a synthesis. The synthesis seems to make the notion of analogising redundant and the simulation demands another representation as synthesis with what is (synthesised?) as analogon. That is why some phenomenologists, following Merleau-Ponty and giving primacy on the embodied aspect of consciousness, will depart from this metaphysically atomistic notion of the primal instituting and theorise about the intentional act of consciousness as pure transcendence in the sense of an ongoing dialogical interaction between the body and the world in which both reveal themselves without prior institution/constitution (1968). (An example which makes the analogical relation redundant could be the person who engages in *parkour*).
47. (Husserl 1960, 109).
48. (Husserl 1960, 113).
49. (Husserl 1960, 113).
50. (Husserl 1960, 113).
51. It is very tempting at this point for sexual categories to deter us and wonder how this is possible. But if we perform the reduction following Husserl's instruction and keep those categories in parentheses, the appearing of the Other's body (which is not yet a body but phenomenalising) is phenomenally the same formally or schematically, a surface which is not sexed to use Judith Butler's expression (Butler 1989). Sex as a category requires constitution in the sense of directing one's consciousness to a particular horizon. Phenomenology cannot be charged with sexism if one is willing to follow Husserl's reduction as much as possible.
52. (Husserl 1960, 112; all emphases in original).
53. (Theunissen 1986, 66).
54. (Husserl 1960, 113).
55. (Theunissen 1986).
56. The same critique applies to Zahavi's latest readings where the transcendental 'I' takes the form of minimal self-consciousness (2014).
57. This problematic surfaces again in Thompson's attempt to link Husserl's account to neuroscience (Husserl 1960, 113; emphasis in original). As will shall see, it is precisely this question which has been not been problematised that disturbs the neuro- and neurophenomenological discourse of empathy as understanding (2001).

58. See Stuart's analysis of the necessity of transgression in the phenomenological pairing as intercorporeality (2017).
59. (Husserl 1960, 114; my emphasis).
60. From the subjective perspective there is only indication of knowing, that is, *partial understanding*. Empathy from the subjective standpoint is only partial. Zahavi explores how Husserl uses the term iterative empathy in order to explain the possibility of reciprocal understanding (See also Zahavi and Overgaard 2013; Zahavi 2014). It will go beyond the scope of this paper to explore whether iterative empathy can be authentic reciprocal knowing.
61. (Heidegger 1962, 155).
62. (Heidegger 1962, 162).
63. (Heidegger 1962, 155).
64. Zahavi tries to solve this problem in his later work with Husserl's concept of 'iterative empathy.' It would take us far away from the main purpose of this paper to explore how Zahavi's solution does not alleviate the Heideggerian worries. Suffice it to say that iterative empathy is a concept used to refer to our everyday interactions but cannot be applied satisfactorily to resolve the difficulties that such concept poses to the possibility of transcendental intersubjectivity (2014).
65. (cf. Crossley 1996).
66. (cf. Depraz 2004).
67. (Apel 1998, 131).
68. (cf. Ioannidis 2017).
69. (Sartre 1993, 234, 324).
70. (Sartre 1993, 108).
71. See Rizzolatti and Craighero (2004).
72. To clarify, 'intention' here is used in the phenomenological sense which, as we saw earlier with Husserl, implies primarily a feeling of mineness not just the colloquial meaning of intention in the sense of an end or aim. Intention in the colloquial sense is included in the phenomenological sense but not the reverse. In the neuroscientific discourse the term is used in both senses which is precisely what is challenged in this paper. For instance, when Rizzolatti and Sinigaglia write that the intentions of an Other are mirrored in our brain they do not see intention in the scans, or in whatever methodology being used. *They infer it* by analogizing what is tracked in their scanners. But this inference, though with some charity warranted, can never be justified. Just because the 'same' brain areas are activated with the 'same' intensities and, possibly duration, in actors and observers, it does not follow that such 'identity' relations reveal matching intentions. If that were the case, how could phenomena such as bluffing, deceiving, dissimulating and the like, take place? An actor may be just that, an actor, who intends to give an impression to deceive.
73. (Theunissen 1986, 146).
74. (Husserl 1970, 238).
75. (Peirce 1931).
76. (Schutz 1945, 1951); (Irigaray 2008).
77. Empathy in ancient Greek always refers to a subjective or partial feeling. The ἐμπαθ-ής is a term used to signal the deep affection of a person from their own perspective (cf. Lidell, Scott and Jones entries http://stephanus.tlg.uci.edu/lsj/#eid=35259&context=lsj&action=from-search). As we saw earlier, Husserl's empathy does justice to this meaning.

78. To clarify, the communication of feeling as sym-pathy, as com-passion has very little, if anything, to do with Bloom's rational compassion (2016). While I share Bloom's arguments against empathy as moral compass, as I try to show in this paper, *feeling with* cannot be successful when it involves reflection.

Disclosure statement

No potential conflict of interest was reported by the author.

References

Apel, Karl-Otto. 1998. *From a Transcendental Semiotic Point of View*. Manchester: Manchester University Press.
Bloom, P. 2016. *Against Empathy: The Case for Rational Compassion*. New York, NY: Harper Collins.
Butler, J. 1989. "Foucault and the Paradox of Bodily Inscriptions." *The Journal of Philosophy* 86: 601–607. doi:10.5840/jphil198986117.
Crossley, N. 1996. *Intersubjectivity: The Fabric of Social Becoming*. London: Sage.
Depraz, N. 2004. "Autrui: Autrui et L'Atruisme." In *Dictionnaire d'éthique et de philosophie morale*, edited by M. Canto-Sperber, 123–127. Paris: PUF.
Derrida, J. 1973. *Speech and Phenomena*. Evanston: Northwestern University Press.
Derrida, J. 2003. *The Problem of Genesis in Husserl'S Phenomenology*. Chicago, IL: University of Chicago Press.
Heidegger, M. 1962. *Being and Time*. Oxford: Blackwell.
Henry, M. 2012. *Barbarism*. Paperback. London: Continuum International Publishing Group.
Henry, M. 2015. *Incarnation: A Philosophy of Flesh*. Chicago: Northwestern University Press.
Husserl, E. 1960. *Cartesian Meditations*. London: Kluwer.
Husserl, E. 1970. *Logical Investigations Vol.II*. London: Routledge & Kegan Paul.
Husserl, E. 1983. *Ideas Pertaining to a Pure Phenomenology and to a Phenomenologica Philosophy (First Book)*. Hingham, MA: Kluwer.
Husserl, E. 1996. *Ideas Pertaining to a Pure Phenomenology and to a Pure Philosophy (Second Book)*. Norwell, MA: Kluwer Academic Publishers.
Husserl, E. 1998. "Essay 2: On Static and Genetic Phenomenology." *Continental Philosophy Review* 31: 143–152.
Husserl, E. 1999. *The Idea of Phenomenology*. Leuven: Kluwer Academic Publishers.
Ioannidis, I. 2017. "Broaching the Difference between Intersubjectivity and Intersubjection Inspired by the Feminist Critique." *Sophia International Review* 10 (2): 38–68.
Irigaray, L. 2008. *Sharing the World*. London: Continuum.
Klimecki, O. M., S. Leiberg, M. Ricard, and T. Singer. 2014. "Differential Pattern of Functional Brain Plasticity after Compassion and Empathy Training." *Scan* 9: 873–879.
Merleau-Ponty, M. 1962. *Phenomenology of Perception*. New York, NY: Routledge.
Merleau-Ponty, M. 1968. *The Visible and the Invisible*. Evanston: Northwestern University Press.

Peirce, C. S. 1931. *Collected Papers of Charles Sanders Peirce: Vol. II.* Cambridge, MA: Harvard University Press.

Pfaff, D. W. 2015. *The Altruistic Brain: How We Are Naturally Good.* Oxford: Oxford University Press.

Putnam, H. 1988. *Representation and Reality.* Cambridge, MA: MIT Press.

Rakel, D. 2018. *The Compassionate Connection: The Healing Power of Empathy and Mindful Listening.* New York: Norton & Company.

Rizzolatti, G., and C. Sinigaglia. 2008. *Mirrors in Our Brains: How Our Minds Share Actions and Emotions.* Cambridge: Cambridge University Press.

Rizzolatti, G., and L. Craighero. 2004. "The Mirror-Neuron System." *Annual Review of Neuroscience* 27: 169–192. doi:10.1146/annurev.neuro.27.070203.144230.

Sartre, J.-P. 1993. *Being and Nothingness.* Reprint 1st ed. Washington: Washington Square Press.

Schutz, A. 1945. "The Homecomer." *American Journal of Sociology* 50 (5): 369–376. doi:10.1086/219654.

Schutz, A. 1951. "Making Music Together: A Study in Social Relationships." *Social Research* 18 (1): 76–97.

Stein, E. 1989. *On the Problem of Empathy.* Washington, DC: ICS.

Steinbock, A. A. J. 1999. "Saturated Intentionality." In *Body*, edited by D. Welton, 178–200. Malden, MA: Blackwell.

Strasser, S. 1967. "Phenomenologies and Psychologies." In *Readings in Existential Phenomenology*, edited by Nathaniel Lawrence and Daniel O'Connor, 331–352. Englewood Cliffs, NJ: Prentice-Hall, Inc.

Stuart, S. 2017. "Feeling Our Way: Enkinaesthetic Enquiry and Immanent Intercorporeality." In *Intercorporeality: Emerging Socialities in Interaction*, edited by C. Meyer, J. Streeck, and J. Scott, 104–140. Oxford: Oxford University Press.

Theunissen, M. 1986. *The Other: Studies in the Social Ontology of Husserl, Heidegger, Sartre, and Buber.* Cambridge, MA: MIT Press.

Thompson, E. 2001. "Empathy and Consciousness." *Journal of Consciousness Studies* 8 (5–7): 1–32.

Welton, D. 1999. "Soft, Smooth, Hands: Husserl'S Phenomenology of the Lived-Body." In *The Body*, edited by D. Welton, 38–56. Malden, MA: Blackwell.

Zahavi, D. 2005. *Subjectivity and Selfood: Exploring the First Person Perspective.* London: MIT Press.

Zahavi, D. 2011. "Intersubjectivity." In *Routledge Companion to Phenomenology*, edited by S. Luft and S. Overgaard, 180–189. London: Routledge.

Zahavi, D. 2014. *Self and Other: Exploring Subjectivity, Empathy, and Shame.* Oxford: Oxford University Press.

Zahavi, D., and S. Overgaard. 2013. "Intersubjectivity." *The International Encyclopedia of Ethics*, February 1. http://onlinelibrary.wiley.com/doi/10.1002/9781444367072.wbiee274/full

Finding Empathy: How Neuroscientific Measures, Evidence and Conceptualizations Interact

Riana J. Betzler

ABSTRACT
Questions about how empathy should be conceptualized have long been a preoccupation of the field of empathy research. There are numerous definitions of empathy that have been proposed and that often overlap with other concepts such as sympathy and compassion. This makes communication between research groups or across disciplines difficult. Many researchers seem to see the diversity of definitions as a problem rather than a form of benign pluralism. Within this debate about conceptualization, researchers sometimes suggest that more neuroscientific evidence will make the problem go away – that uncovering the processes underlying empathy will thereby also sort out conceptual difficulties. In this paper, I challenge this assumption by examining how neuroscientists studying empathy use concepts in practice – both in the development of their measures and in the interpretation of their data. I argue that this neuroscientific literature demonstrates that continuity and stability comes from the use of certain established measures, while progress comes from expansion upon those measures and the flexibility of stated concepts. We do not 'find' empathy through increased neuroscientific evidence but we do get closer to understanding empathic processes, flexibly understood.

Introduction

Conceptual diversity is widely acknowledged in empathy research. There are several definitions of empathy currently in circulation, as well as significant overlap between empathy and related concepts, such as sympathy, compassion, perspective-taking, and mind-reading. Many authors begin their papers by acknowledging this state of affairs. Reactions to this conceptual diversity vary but in general, people seem to see it as a problem that needs to be solved. Although researchers have attempted several different strategies for resolving this conceptual confusion – or at least

---

This article has been republished with minor changes. These changes do not impact the academic content of the article.

tidying up the literature – none of them have gained significant traction. Conceptual diversity, and confusion, persists.

Among the strategies for resolving confusion, researchers sometimes suggest that by doing more science – and in particular more neuroscience – we will better understand the processes underlying empathy. Once we better understand the processes, the suggestion goes, conceptual resolution will follow. In this paper, I target this particular idea, which I call the 'finding empathy' proposal. I unpack this suggestion and then turn to the literature on the social neuroscience of empathy to examine its plausibility. Does more neuroscience lead to more conceptual clarity? I argue that the simple answer is no, because neuroscientific measures and evidence are deeply intertwined with the ways in which empathy is conceptualized at the outset. There is no straight line between neuroscientific evidence and conceptual clarity. What role, then, does neuroscientific evidence play in furthering understanding of empathy? What impact does it have on conceptualization? I look to the practices of researchers operating within the field of the social neuroscience of empathy to investigate how evidence and concepts interact. I argue that while our current neuroscience does not allow us to 'find empathy', it does allow us to better understand the landscape of *empathic processes* and how they are modulated. I also demonstrate that while the space of stated empathy concepts remains messy, by following the measures and 'paradigms' that researchers use, we can trace fairly stable lines of thinking about what empathy is and pinpoint areas of convergence within the field.

That there are areas of stability and convergence indicates that conceptual diversity might not be such a big problem for the practice and progress of empirical research on empathy. Researchers working within a given tradition can communicate well with one another, build upon each other's measures, and pursue new investigations despite the lack of convergence among their stated definitions. Where the true conceptual problem might lie, then, is in interdisciplinary and applied pursuits. This is where researchers need to be especially careful about what exactly it is that they mean by empathy – what they want to investigate or intervene on. To do so – to achieve this level of care and use empathy research wisely – they must be sensitive to their own priors and to the priors of the groups whose work they intend to draw on. I point to some examples of both effective and detrimental attempts at collaboration across disciplines or within an applied domain. Once again, looking closely at the measures that investigators are using in these kinds of pursuits is the best way to uncover those priors.

In unpacking the relationship between conceptual diversity and neuroscientific evidence, I hope to contribute primarily to the literature on empathy, where worries about conceptualizations are widespread, and secondarily to wider debates in philosophy of science about pluralism, interdisciplinarity, measurement and scientific communication. Empathy research is highly interdisciplinary. Researchers approach empathy from various perspectives – anthropological, philosophical, psychological, ethological, developmental, and neuroscientific. Empirical investigations of empathy also interact with public, everyday understandings of it. My approach here provides a new take on the conceptual difficulties that empathy researchers have faced, one that I hope will make interdisciplinary research in this field run more smoothly. The problems and difficulties that empathy researchers face are potentially common to other interdisciplinary pursuits; thus, empathy research may provide a good case study, contributing to the growing body of literature on interdisciplinarity in philosophy of science. Finally, this paper sheds light on how measurement, evidence, and conceptualization interact – and why both scientists and philosophers should follow the measures and not the concepts when tracing the development of a field of research.

I begin by briefly outlining the longstanding conceptual problem and the standard solutions to it that have been proposed. I then turn to the idea that we will 'find empathy' by better understanding the neuroscientific processes or mechanisms underlying it. Finally, I draw on a detailed examination of the social neuroscience literature to explain my alternative view, in which concepts, measures, and evidence co-evolve with one another. I conclude by outlining the implications of this view for both research within a given domain and for interdisciplinary and applied pursuits.

The conceptual problem

Researchers have long debated the meaning of the term 'empathy.' Since its inception in English – which is usually credited to Edward Titchener's translation in 1909 from the German *Einfühlung* – the word has held several meanings. It was, at the time of translation, predominately used to refer to a form of aesthetic understanding whereby one comes to better understand a work of art by feeling oneself into it. It is rarely used in this way today. Gradually, the term took on increasingly interpersonal meanings, as well as many of the features of the older term 'sympathy'. As the historian Susan Lanzoni (2012, 2017) points out, there were multiple paths by which the concept of empathy entered into scientific psychology. Within contemporary scientific psychology, the term remains contentious. In this section, I provide an overview of the major points of contention and the ways in which scholars have tried to organize the field in response to this contention. Because this is such well-worn territory, I rely primarily on the work of others who have completed recent reviews of the literature and comment on the strategies that they have employed to distinguish among them and to try to overcome confusion.

In what is perhaps the most recent and up-to-date review of the empathy concept, Cuff, Brown, Taylor, and Howat (2016) identify 43 discrete definitions of empathy. They also identify eight themes or questions that organize debate about these empathy concepts: (1) Distinguish empathy from other concepts (especially sympathy and compassion); (2) Cognitive or affective? (3) Congruent or incongruent? (4) Subject to other stimuli? (5) Self/other distinction or merging? (6) Trait or state influences? (7) Has a behavioural outcome? (8) Automatic or controlled? (Cuff et al. 2016, 144). Cuff et al. (2016) argue that empathy concepts differ primarily along these eight dimensions – in terms of (1) the degree to which they contain a stark distinction from other concepts as well as (2) where they lie in their answers to each of the seven binary questions above.

It is worth saying a few words about Cuff and colleagues' approach – about how they identified the 43 different definitions. They use a snowballing procedure, which involves first identifying a set of articles on the basis of key words and then using the reference lists of those articles to identify further areas of interest. This procedure is by no means exhaustive. It does not allow us to identify every definition of 'empathy' that has been proposed by scholars, and we can expect that many more than 43 might really exist. What it does capture is the set of definitions at play within a given network of scholars or research community. The method depends on patterns of citation to pull out relevant definitions. This network-based approach provides a sense of what disciplines are interacting with one another, as well as what areas are being left out. For example, Cuff and colleagues' table of 43 definitions draws predominately from various areas of psychology (social, developmental, and clinical) and neuroscience. While it does include some definitions developed by philosophers, it only captures a small sliver of the extensive literature on empathy in philosophy; the definitions that make the cut are the ones developed by philosophers like Amy Coplan and Dan Zahavi, whose work interacts heavily with the empirical psychological literature. Likewise, there is minimal inclusion of the literature on empathy in other animals or in the context of psychoanalysis. While there are some historical definitions present in the list, these tend to be ones coined by authors who are constantly being cited in the potted histories found at the start of articles in the psychological and neurosciences. I point out the limited scope of this snowballing procedure not as a criticism; the limited nature of the analysis resulting from it is helpful insofar as it allows us to identify a particular research community, even when that research community is somewhat interdisciplinary – a point that I will return to later in the paper. It gives us a sense of which definitions are receiving significant 'airtime' within that research community which, in turn, paves the way for further analysis of the ways in which those definitions and approaches might interact with one another. Cuff et al. (2016) select only shorthand conceptualizations, or definitions, rather than fully fledged models of empathy, for inclusion in their analysis, but I argue that these discrete definitions are actually not the best indicators of the current state of the field. Focusing on measures and larger models of empathy provides a more apt representation of researchers' thinking at any given time.

There are, of course, other ways of carving up the space of empathy concepts. Cuff et al.'s (2016) paper provides only one example. Different researchers who attempt such projects come up with different numbers of concepts, as well as different dimensions along which they might be organized. Dan Batson (2009), a prominent empathy researcher famous for his work on the empathy-altruism hypothesis, for example, identifies eight different things called empathy; he argues that they are related but distinct phenomena. My aim here, then, is not to endorse Cuff and colleagues' approach as the right one for identifying and organizing the space of empathy concepts. Instead, my aim is to point out (1) that there is a large number of different empathy concepts, (2) that researchers seem to think that these empathy concepts refer to different psychological phenomena, and (3) that they organize them in different ways.

Researchers furthermore seem to think, in general, that conceptual diversity in the case of empathy is a problem. I pull out a couple of quotations to illustrate this attitude. Amy Coplan (2011, 4), a philosopher, writes:

> The number of competing conceptualizations circulating [in] the literature has created a serious problem with the study of empathy by making it difficult to keep track of which process or mental state the term is being used to refer to in any given discussion.

Cuff and colleagues (2016, 144) open their paper with the statement: 'The inconsistent definition of empathy has had a negative impact on both research and practice.' They, like other authors (e.g. Pedersen 2009), point out that definitional inconsistency poses problems when empathy concepts are applied within clinical education and practice. They also argue that definitional inconsistency poses problems for scientific research; it has led to issues such as incomparability between scales and study outcomes. It is this latter issue that I am interested here – what kinds of problems does definitional inconsistency pose for scientific research? Does it always pose such problems? To answer these questions, we need to go beyond simply identifying the various definitions present within the field, as Cuff and colleagues do, and take a closer look at how definitions shape empirical work and *vice versa*. There has been a little bit of work that attempts to undertake this task in social psychology, which I review in the next subsection, before moving on to outline the currently existing suggestions for how to handle the conceptual problem.

The conceptual problem in social psychology

There are two papers that make a serious effort to identify the relationship between empathy concepts and measures: Lauren Wispé's (1986) highly cited 1986 paper and Vanessa Lux's (2017) recent contribution to the edited collection, *Empathy: Epistemic Problems and Cultural-Historical Perspectives of a Cross-Disciplinary Concept*. Both deal primarily with methods used in social psychology and illustrate the depth of the conceptual problem.

Wispé's article primarily aims to distinguish empathy from sympathy. Like other authors, she begins by tracing the historical roots of the empathy concept and notes that there was a shift in the language of psychology, from sympathy to empathy. She then argues, following Allport, that language matters. As Allport (1968, 27) writes, 'psychological analysis depends to a considerable degree upon the categories of language available to the analyst'. This assumption, that language matters, forms a starting point for Wispé's investigation of the empathy concept.

One of Wispé's central concerns is about the construct validity of the empathy concept. Construct validity, as developed by Cronbach and Meehl in 1955, is about whether psychological tests truly measure what they purport to measure. Does the construct in question account for performance on the test? Or are there other factors at play? A psychological construct, as Cronbach and Meehl define it, is an attribute of people. It may be qualitative or quantitative. Questions about construct validity usually become important when, as the APA Committee on Test Standards put it in 1954, 'the tester has no definite criterion measure of the quality with which he is concerned, and must use indirect measures' (Technical Recommendations for Psychological Tests and Diagnostic Techniques1954, 14). It is of concern when there are no unquestionable criteria available to capture a given attribute and no stabilized operational definition for that construct. Cronbach and Meehl (1955, 284) write:

> An unquestionable criterion may be found in practical operation, or may be established as a consequence of an operational definition. Typically, however, the psychologist is unwilling to use the directly operational approach because he is interested in building a theory about a generalised construct. A theorist trying to relate behaviour to 'hunger' almost certainly invests that term with meanings of other than the operation 'elapsed time since feeding'.

The question of construct validity, then, becomes especially relevant when it is difficult to capture all of the relevant features of a psychological attribute using a single operationalized definition. When we are dealing with a very broad concept like empathy, we can see how the question of construct validity might arise.[1]

Wispé doubts the construct validity of empathy. On her view, construct validity would be present in the case of empathy if the various approaches and operational definitions provided ways of measuring the same underlying attribute or phenomenon. She is sceptical about the construct validity of empathy primarily because of the ambiguous, indefinite, and inconsistent way that the term 'empathy' has been defined. She writes:

> Because empathy may mean different things to different investigators, they investigate it in different ways. Many researchers who say they are studying *empathy* may be studying something else. As a result it is hard to know whether we have one concept treated differently, or two or more different concepts. (Wispé 1986, 317)

In other words, the different ways in which various research groups – all purportedly investigating *empathy* – define and operationalize it may mean that they are not all investigating the same thing. This casts doubt on the comparability of measures and results across studies – a problem that Cuff and colleagues raise in their paper as well. While this problem clearly applies to research that involves interaction among multiple research groups using different methods, it is not clear that it poses great risks for groups working with the same methods or constructs from the outset. I will explore this idea in more detail in the context of social neuroscience.

Wispé identifies another problem, stemming from the nature of situational measures, which necessitate the involvement of lay participants. Many social psychological measures involve inducing empathy, which involves finding some way of instructing subjects to empathize. Wispé (1986, 317) writes:

> Empathy researchers are in a dilemma. If they instruct subjects to empathise, the subjects do not know what empathy means ... so they do not know what to do. If the investigators use any of the various cognitive or affective terms putatively related to empathy, either alone or in conjunction with empathise, it becomes even more difficult to infer the subjects' mental states.

The problem, as identified by Wispé, is that the instruction to empathize is ambiguous. While she focuses on ambiguity in the ways in which researchers construct their measures, there is another, subtly different problem here, related to the lack of correspondence between researchers' and subjects' conceptualizations of empathy. Because empathy is both a popular, everyday term and a scientific term, this further complicates matters, especially in fields like social psychology, which depend on questionnaire and other methods that may directly use the term 'empathy'. Newer measures do not typically involve explicitly instructing subjects to empathize. Instead, they tend to use other manipulations, such as similarity information or imagination instructions, to manipulate participants' feelings of closeness to the victim. While these approaches get around some of the semantic issues with instructions to empathize, they remain indirect and do not entirely overcome the problem of dissociation between what the researchers think they are measuring and what the participants think they are doing.

Vanessa Lux (2017), in her recent paper, reconsiders the distinction between empathy and sympathy. Like Wispé, she begins with some historical background and then examines two strategies for measuring emotions in psychological research: (1) psychophysiological measurement, and (2) self-report. She focuses on how the unclear boundaries between sympathy and empathy are engrained in psychological measurements.

Psychophysiological measurements, on her view, make it difficult to distinguish between empathy and sympathy because they measure a general physiological reaction and cannot get at the specific experiential quality of emotions. Self-report, on the other hand, is better able to record the qualitative dimension of emotions but nonetheless encounters problems when distinguishing between sympathy and empathy, due to significant conceptual overlap between scales aimed at capturing the two concepts. This conceptual overlap is largely due to the wording of items and efforts to make them accessible to a general public. These kinds of scales are often used in conjunction with other methods in order to validate or corroborate findings. For example, cognitive neuroscientists often administer self-report scales alongside their scanning measures. Lux argues that the conceptual overlap present with these scales thereby affects neuroscientific efforts to distinguish neural circuits underlying different processes. Lux concludes by arguing that conceptual diffusion and overlap are deeply inscribed in the measurement techniques that empathy researchers use.

The work of both Wispé and Lux shows that the conceptual problem runs deep. It affects the way that researchers carry out their investigations in developing measures and communicating with research participants. Both Wispé and Lux also raise questions that will become important in my investigation of the social neuroscientific work on empathy, especially insofar as that work is integrated with work in the social psychological tradition. Can work on 'empathy' be considered a body of work on the same phenomenon? Do measures transfer across different contexts? Do the same kinds of conceptual problems arise when using different research methodologies or do some research methodologies manage to skirt around the conceptual difficulties? Before turning to these questions, I close my section on the conceptual problem by outlining the standard solutions to it that have been given in the field.

Standard solutions

As I have mentioned, the conceptual problem is widely acknowledged in empathy research. Researchers have taken a number of different approaches to it. In this sub-section, I identify four main strategies for dealing with conceptual confusion: (1) Create a taxonomy of empathy concepts; (2) Propose a new definition or stabilize existing definitions; (3) Just get on with it; and (4) Do more neuroscience. Researchers also sometimes combine these different strategies when approaching the conceptual problem.

Creating a taxonomy of empathy concepts – the first strategy – usually involves reviewing the literature on empathy, suggesting criteria upon which empathy concepts may be distinguished, and sometimes, explaining how different empathy concepts are related to one another and to concepts like sympathy and compassion. In this way, it looks like other kinds of taxonomizing or classifying efforts, most classically those of biological species. Dan Batson's (2009) paper, 'These Things Called Empathy: Eight Related but Distinct Phenomena' takes such a taxonomizing approach. Nancy Eisenberg, another prominent social psychologist, takes a similar taxonomizing approach, but instead of calling all the multiple phenomena she identifies 'empathy', she chooses to apply different names to them, such as 'sympathy' and 'distress'. Her taxonomizing efforts involve both separating out different phenomena and explaining how they relate to one another, building up a kind of model of empathy (e.g. Eisenberg and Fabes 1990). Martin Hoffman, a developmental psychologist, likewise provides a taxonomy of empathy concepts, driven by developmental stages. He calls the phenomena at all of these stages 'empathy' rather than giving them different names but tries to make it clear how they relate to one another (Hoffman 2008). Cuff et al.'s (2016) paper, by providing a review of the many empathy concepts that exist, likewise represents a systematizing or taxonomizing effort. Taxonomizing efforts can be useful for providing a sense of the landscape of empathy concepts existing at any given time – or at least, how a given researcher views that landscape. However, they have not been successful in providing any real resolution to the conceptual problem because they do not tend to converge with one another. We therefore end up with a plurality of taxonomies on top of the plurality of definitions such that taxonomizing efforts sometimes contribute to, rather than clear up, conceptual confusion.

Taxonomizing efforts often go hand-in-hand with the second strategy – propose a new definition or stabilize existing definitions. Within the taxonomy that a given researcher proposes, there is often a single empathy concept that researcher favours. In the case of Batson's taxonomy, for example, the final, eighth definition that he identifies is the one that corresponds most closely with that used in his own work: 'Feeling for another person who is suffering' (Batson 2009, 8). Eisenberg likewise seems to be aiming for stability in constructing her model of empathy, sympathy and distress. In these cases, the researcher may not be proposing an entirely new definition but is instead aiming to stabilize particular conceptualizations as 'the right ones'. Cuff et al. (2016) combine their initial taxonomizing with the proposal of a new definition. This new definition is supposed to capture many of the core elements of the other definitions they identify and to provide a 'more widely shared understanding of empathy' (2016, 150). Their new, consensus definition is as follows:

> Empathy is an emotional response (affective), dependent upon the interaction between trait capacities and state influences. Empathic processes are automatically elicited but are also shaped by top-down control processes. The resulting emotion is similar to one's perception (directly experienced or imagined) and understanding (cognitive empathy) of the stimulus emotion, with recognition that the source of the emotion is not one's own. (Cuff et al. 2016, 150)

The proposal of a new empathy definition can also occur in the absence of taxonomizing work. The difficulty with such proposals or top-down stabilization efforts is that they rarely seem to gain any traction across the field as a whole. They tend to simply add yet another definition to the pile. It is rare that one of these new definitions gets adopted by researchers working with an alternative one. They therefore do not stabilize the field.

The third strategy – to just get on with it – is more of an anti-strategy. It represents a certain kind of dismissiveness about the conceptual problem and whether it really deserves the attention it receives. Stephanie Preston and Frans de Waal (2002) express this dismissiveness to a certain degree, especially about efforts to draw distinctions among different concepts: 'These distinctions are empirically based and help to categorize behaviour ... . But they have been overemphasised to the point of distraction' (Preston and de Waal 2002, 2). Their dismissiveness in part comes from their own take on the conceptual difficulties, which is to provide a unified model of empathy, one that can function both developmentally and phylogenetically. Thus, while Preston and de Waal express some frustration with the conceptual debate – especially insofar as it tends toward splitting rather than lumping – they themselves have done considerable work on the conceptual problem. True dismissiveness about the conceptual problem can be more readily found at the start of empirical articles on empathy. These articles often begin by acknowledging the conceptual problem and then simply eliding past it, stating the definition that the particular study intends to use – often a definition recycled from other areas in the field – and carrying on with the research. This particular dismissive strategy is sometimes accompanied by the attitude that doing more research will make the conceptual problem go away – an attitude that ignores the theoretical and analytic work that must go in to that research at the start, even to simply come up with measures.

Similar to the dismissive attitude, but subtly different, is the idea that the conceptual problem will somehow go away if we simply do more research – and in particular, do more neuroscience. Lauren Wispé expresses something like this in her paper on distinguishing sympathy from empathy. She argues for more research directed toward understanding the *processes* underlying sympathy and empathy, using autonomic or neuromuscular responses. Although she identifies numerous ways in which the conceptual difficulties impact the formation of social psychological measures, she assumes that neuroscientific measures are more direct and that they will help us to pinpoint precisely what empathy is. This 'finding empathy' strategy is the one that I am interested in interrogating in this paper. In what sense can conceptual distinctions be 'empirically based' and what does the neuroscientific literature contribute to conceptual disputes?

Both the third and the fourth strategies fail to account for the role of theoretical work in constructing measures of empathy – especially psychometric ones. By 'theoretical work', I mean the initial articulation of a conceptualization of what it is that is being measured. While this theoretical work is sometimes expressed through stated definitions, it also enters into the details of test items. Dan Batson and his colleagues, for example, in developing an early measure of empathic concern, compiled a list of adjectives that seemed '*a priori* relevant to the emotional states of empathic concern and personal distress' (Coke, Batson, and McDavis 1978, 759). These were then used to construct their study questionnaires. It is not clear exactly what this process of coming up with *a priori* relevant adjectives involves, or whether there is a systematic process like conceptual analysis, but it is clear that there is some level of initial theorizing that directs the process of developing the measure. This theorizing can then be obscured or forgotten, however, through processes of experimental research. Writers on construct validity have made similar points about the uncomfortable relationship between theory and psychometric testing (see Alexandrova and Haybron 2016; Borsboom, Mellenbergh, and van Heerden 2004). The interaction between theorizing and empirical data may be slightly more complex in the case of neuroscience, a point that will occupy the background of my discussion in the rest of this paper.

Finding empathy

There are multiple ways of understanding the idea that doing more neuroscience will help us to somehow 'find empathy' and thereby resolve conceptual disputes. On the one hand, there is the idea, sometimes expressed simplistically in the popular press, that there is a brain area for empathy or an 'empathy cortex'. These kinds of claims are similar to those found in popular representations of genetics: the idea that there is a gene for empathy. While we can find abundant examples of these kinds of oversimplified statements in the popular literature, they are almost certainly not what most researchers actively investigating empathy have in mind. Thus, I will try to provide a more sophisticated reading of what the idea that 'finding empathy' might consist in. The kinds of claims that I will focus on are of the type that Preston and de Waal (2002) make – that certain conceptual distinctions are 'empirically based' – or that Paul Bloom makes in arguing against empathy and for rational compassion. Bloom (2016) argues that different networks in the brain support conceptual distinction: 'This distinction between empathy and compassion is critical for the argument I've been making throughout this book. And it is supported by neuroscience research' (2016, 138). Bloom's work – distinguishing empathy from compassion – has significant implications for the applied and moral domains. Thus, it is important that we better understand what he means when he says that the distinction – which he uses to argue *against* empathy and for compassion – is supported by neuroscience research. We also need to better understand how the neuroscientific literature proceeds, to see whether this really is the case.

Let's take Bloom's work in his 2016 book, *Against Empathy: The Case for Rational Compassion*, as an example to illustrate what some researchers might mean when they suggest that certain conceptual distinctions are empirically based or supported by neuroscience. Although this book is written for a popular audience, it has received a great deal of attention among academics as well, and represents the views of a very prominent Yale psychologist. A further advantage of taking Bloom's work as an example is that it relies heavily on the same body of social neuroscientific work that I will draw on in formulating my own view about how neuroscientific conceptualization, evidence and measures feedback on one another.

In 'The Anatomy of Empathy', Bloom begins by disparaging just the kind of naïve neuroscientific claims that I mention at the start of this section – the kind of claims that can often be found in the popular press. Bloom writes that the question that he dreads the most when he gives popular talks is 'Where does it happen in the brain?' – a question that reflects a desire for simple localization (Bloom 2016, 60). Bloom points out that underlying this question is often the idea – even sometimes endorsed by trained psychologists and neuroscientists – that localization proves that the phenomenon in question, in this case empathy, truly exists.[2] This assumption gets us into interesting territory about the realism of neuroscientific phenomena, which I will unfortunately have to leave aside in this paper. After disparaging simple localization efforts, however, Bloom (2016, 60) argues that 'the tools of neuroscience, properly applied, can give us considerable insight into how the mind works' and then delves into the field of social neuroscience. What these neuroscientific studies get right, in Bloom's view, is that they go beyond simple localization; they not only find out what parts of the brain are involved in particular activities but also 'compare and contrast the correlates of mental activity to tell us what aspects of mental life fall together and what influences what' (2016, 61). On this view, then, the neuroscientific literature does not allow us to 'find empathy' in the simplistic sense suggested by localization. Nonetheless, it allows us to untangle different networks operating in the brain when participants are completing different tasks. Some of these networks correspond to what Bloom designates 'empathy proper' – 'when someone feels the same thing as they believe the other person is feeling' – while others correspond to other phenomena (2016, 61-62). By untangling networks, the neuroscientific literature at very least shows where we should draw the lines between our different concepts – if not what words should be attached to those concepts. Bloom uses this basic strategy to draw a distinction between empathy and compassion – the conceptual distinction on which his whole argument hinges. In doing so, he cites several prominent papers by Tania Singer, Matthieu Ricard and Olga Klimecki.

In the following section, I provide a closer examination of this body of social neuroscientific literature to illustrate where I think Bloom is on the right track and where he still adopts an overly simplistic view of what the neuroscientific literature can tell us and whether it can support sharp distinctions of the kind he makes between empathy and compassion. In doing so, I also describe my own view about how conceptualization, evidence and measurement co-evolve.

The social neuroscience of empathy: how concepts, measures and evidence co-evolve

In 2004, Tania Singer and her colleagues (2004) published a paper in *Science* titled, 'Empathy for Pain Involves the Affective but Not Sensory Components of Pain'. This seminal work pioneered a new method for inducing empathy in the lab and provided one of the first fMRI demonstrations of the networks involved in empathic responses to pain. I focus on this paper as a starting point for a significant body of literature that seeks to delineate the processes involved in the phenomenon of 'empathy'. In this section of the paper, I focus on two facets of this body of literature: (1) formal statements defining the empathy concept and (2) specific measurement techniques taken to get at those concepts. I identify any discrepancies between these two things and how they interact with one another. How do empirical findings and methods influence stated concepts and *vice versa*?

Singer et al. (2004) begin their paper by stipulating a definition where the function of empathy is about succeeding within a social context. This includes both the ability to understand others' intentions and beliefs (mentalizing, theory of mind) and also the ability to understand what the other feels (empathy). Empathy, on their definition, applies both to feeling emotions (happiness, sadness) and feeling sensory states (pain, tickling, touch). Note that this is their stated definition – their starting point. It is interesting just how much is already embedded in this definition – how much is assumed at the outset. For example, while Singer et al. (2004) consider empathy to be the same whether applied to emotions or sensory states, this seems like an open question to me. It assumes a very broad category of 'feeling'. This question about what is assumed at the outset relates to my earlier points about the unacknowledged importance of initial theorizing.

To measure empathy, defined in this broad way, they develop a new experimental 'paradigm', which they call 'empathy in vivo'. Singer et al. (2004) identify this experimental work as building on previous social scientific work as well as Preston and de Waal's (2002) model, in which observing or imagining another person in a particular emotional state activates a representation of that state in the observer. It also builds upon previous neuroscientific studies that involve watching video clips or seeing pictures related to emotional expressions and disgust. The authors argue that while these studies get at emotional contagion, they do not necessarily capture *empathy*. This is because seeing the other individual's facial expression may trigger a simple form of emotional transmission that does not rely on any mentalizing efforts. Their 'in vivo' paradigm is supposed to go beyond emotional contagion to demonstrate 'that empathic responses can be elicited automatically in the absence of an emotional cue (such as facial emotional expressions) through mere presentation of an arbitrary cue that signals the feelings state of another person' (Singer et al. 2004, 1158). Note that already in the construction of their experimental protocol, they have begun to distinguish empathy from emotional contagion.

Their experimental procedure consists of inviting a couple into the lab. They then put the female member of the couple into the scanner and assess her brain activity while painful stimulation is being applied either to her hand or her partner's. Her partner is sitting next to her outside the scanner and she can see both of their hands through a mirror set up. She can also see a large board indicating whether she or her partner will get a low or high pain stimulation. The researchers then assess pain-related brain activity, using fMRI, in self versus other, targeting in particular the network of areas in the 'pain matrix', as established by previous neuroscientific studies. The researchers also administer questionnaire measures after scanning, to obtain subjective evidence for empathic experience during scanning and assess stable individual differences in empathy (Singer et al. 2004). One advantage of this kind of experimental protocol, as compared with the social psychological methods that I discussed earlier in this paper, is that manipulations can proceed without the participants knowing what the study is about – without the experimenters ever having to instruct the participants 'to empathize' in any way.

In the 2004 study, the investigators found that the pain matrix was activated in the 'self condition', when painful stimuli were applied. In the 'other condition', where somatosensory stimulation was absent, only some areas of the pain matrix were activated. From these observations, the authors conclude that 'only part of the network mediating pain experience is shared when empathizing with pain in others' (Singer et al. 2004, 1160). They argue that while regions of the pain matrix are highly interactive, their study suggests that we can segregate sensory-discriminative and autonomic-affective attributes of pain experience. In short, and as summed up in their title, empathy for pain involves the affective but not sensory elements of pain responding.

A large body of literature follows from this initial study, largely focusing on empathy for *pain* and using similar methodologies. For example, in another study, Singer and colleagues (2006) used the same basic experimental protocol to assess whether empathic preferences are modulated by learned preferences, especially fairness *versus* unfairness. The fairness manipulation was an iterated prisoners dilemma game. Using a similar fMRI protocol, the researchers found that in men in particular, empathy-related responses are reduced when observing an unfair person. This illustrates how researchers begin to build on research protocols to get at different features of a phenomenon. In this case, Singer's empathy-for-pain protocol was combined with methods from behavioural economics, such as the prisoners dilemma game (Singer et al. 2006).

In a review paper published in 2006, after their initial study of empathy for pain, they again explicitly state their definition of empathy:

> There is empathy if: (i) one is in an affective state, (ii) this state is isomorphic to another person's affective state, (iii) this state is elicited by the observation or imagination of another person's affective state; (iv) one knows that the other person is the source of one's own affective state. (De Vignemont and Singer 2006, 435)

They furthermore point out that this definition is motivated by their investigations into the neuronal basis of empathy:

> The narrow definition of empathy proposed above was partially motivated by the investigation of the neuronal basis of empathy. Recent functional magnetic resonance imaging (fMRI) studies have shown that observing another person's emotional state activates parts of the neuronal network involved in processing that same state in oneself, whether it is disgust, touch, or pain. (De Vignemont and Singer 2006, 435)

Note that this definition of empathy is already somewhat different from the one provided at the outset of the 2004 paper.

Even in these early studies we can begin to see how conceptualization shapes measurement and *vice versa*. Tania Singer and her colleagues began with a given idea about what empathy is – about what they sought to investigate – largely derived from previous research in social psychology and neuroscience. They then developed a new protocol for investigating this particular idea about what empathy is and found something out about how it operates. This particular experimental protocol could then be used to investigate other aspects of empathy as a phenomenon which in turn led to the narrowing down of the definition of empathy, as stated in their review paper. As Singer and colleagues explicitly state, this new definition is informed by their empirical findings.

Given the feedback between measurement and conceptualization, which often happens very rapidly – in the example above we can already see it beginning to happen within the span of two years – how do research groups keep track of definitions or conceptualizations, and which one is current at any given time? Keeping track of such quickly evolving definitions, both within a given research group's work and across the field as a whole, seems like an insurmountable task. When we look to how researchers work within a given field, however, it becomes clear that it is not really the stated definitions or conceptualizations that they are keeping track of. Instead, it is particular measures or experimental protocols that travel across the field and create continuity within a research tradition. To further illustrate this, researchers in psychology and neuroscience often refer to their experimental protocols as 'paradigms'. For example, in a 2008 paper, Singer and colleagues refer to the method that they pioneered in 2004 as the 'empathy-for-pain paradigm' (Singer et al. 2008, 783). They also refer to it as a 'classical empathy paradigm' (Singer et al. 2008, 786). The use of the term 'paradigm' is apt – and in pointing it out here, I mean to highlight its Kuhnian connotations as well (Kuhn 1996). Researchers working within a given tradition often use the same experimental protocols as other groups. They furthermore build on them and adapt measures from other research traditions to get at specific details about the operation of *empathic processes*, broadly construed. The conceptualizations and definitions in use are largely flexible enough to respond to new findings. Thus, in understanding how a given research tradition works, we should follow the measures and not the definitions.

What is the scope of a research tradition or a research group? While this question is sometimes difficult to answer, the picture that emerges here is of a research tradition or group as defined by the use of similar measures and the investigation of similar targets. One way of identifying such a group, as I have already suggested, is to follow the measures. Another way, however, is to follow the citation data – as Cuff et al. (2016) do by using a snowballing method. A given research group need not be defined by a given set of people working within a given laboratory or university.

Therefore, while empirical evidence clearly informs our conceptualizations of empathy, the process does not seem to be quite as straightforward as Bloom's characterization suggests. Social neuroscientists are indeed making good progress in better understanding how empathic processes operate but because of the flexible and subtle way in which evidence feeds in to conceptualization, this work does not support sharp distinctions of the sort that Bloom makes. It does not really tell us that empathy and compassion are completely separate processes. It also does not tell us whether effects that seem to show sharp distinctions between phenomena such as empathy and compassion, or empathy and emotional contagion, really are simply artefacts of the way in which those concepts have been defined at the outset. It is by allowing their definitions to remain flexible rather than sharp, that the field of empathy research in social psychology makes progress.

Conclusion

I have argued, thus far, that the widely acknowledged conceptual problem in empathy research need not be as much of a danger to progress in empirical work as it seems, on its face, to be. By focusing on the particular measures and techniques – including the concepts that go into those measures at the outset – researchers can attain some kind of stability or consensus on what it is that they are targeting when they conduct scientific studies.

Significant questions remain, however, when it comes to interdisciplinary and applied research. As I noted at the start of this paper, empathy is a target of investigation across a broad array of fields, both scientific and humanistic. It is also of immense concern in everyday discourse and applied contexts. Part of the motivation behind doing empirical research on the neural correlates of empathy is to enable us to intervene on our empathic capacities – whether those interventions are aimed at making us more empathic or better able to exert control our empathic tendencies. In these kinds of applied contexts, and in interdisciplinary pursuits, the conceptual problem – the diversity and disagreement about what it means to be empathic – has serious consequences and there are significant risks in ignoring it. These risks are especially clear in the case of medicine (Pedersen 2009). In interdisciplinary pursuits, understandings of empathy might be rooted in different traditions and have little in common with one another.

In closing, I would like to suggest that while the conceptual problem certainly becomes more intractable when we deal with increasingly divergent research traditions or increasingly complex applied problems, this does not mean it is insurmountable or that we should avoid doing such research altogether. Rather, the same principles that I have discussed in this paper – of following the measures and citation tendencies – can help us to understand both commonalities within a research tradition and where sharp boundaries or changes in concepts may have occurred. It might give us a sense of which groups are working within the same framework or 'paradigm' and which groups are working outside of that framework. This may help to circumvent the kinds of problems that occur when people use the wrong 'tool' – the wrong concept or measure – for the job. In the case of medicine, for example, measures that were co-opted from social psychology did not capture the qualities that people think of when they think about the 'empathic doctor' (Pedersen 2009). Realizing that those measures come from a very different tradition of thinking about empathy, before implementing them in a new context, might have circumvented those issues. Knowing the different concepts and measures stem from different research traditions might also help us to identify what kinds of research pursuits may be more difficult than others. It will also help us to understand how and why some research traditions have split off from one another – because it will point us towards the different aims and functions of those measures and concepts – and potentially what we might need to do to bring them back together. In short, following the measures and the research communities will help us to understand the lines of conceptual divergence and thereby provide better starting points for our efforts to apply research.

Notes

1. Recent work provides a more detailed analysis of what construct validity entails (see e.g. Borsboom, Mellenbergh, and van Heerden 2004; Alexandrova and Haybron 2016). While full discussion of construct validity in psychological research on empathy is outside the scope of this paper, this is an important area for future work to consider.
2. He reassures his reader on the next page that empathy does exist – that it 'really does light up the brain' (Bloom 2016, 61).

Acknowledgments

This paper was written while I was based at the Konrad Lorenz Institute for Evolution and Cognition Research in Klosterneuburg, Austria. I would like to thank my colleagues there – in particular Isabella Sarto-Jackson, Chia-Hua Lin, and Ivan Gonzalez Cabrera – for listening to multiple versions of this paper in talk format and providing incisive comments. I would also like to thank members of the Department of Psychology at the University of Vienna, especially Claus Lamm and Giorgia Silani, for welcoming me into their labs and helping me to better understand how they work.

Disclosure statement

No potential conflict of interest was reported by the author.

ORCID

Riana J. Betzler http://orcid.org/0000-0002-3971-6482

References

Alexandrova, A., and D. Haybron. 2016. "Is Construct Validation Valid?" *Philosophy of Science* 83: 1098–1109. doi:10.1086/687941.
Allport, G. W. 1968. "The Historical Background of Modern Social Psychology." In *Handbook of Social Psychology*, edited by G. Lindzey and E. Aronson, 1–80. Reading, MA: Addison-Wesley.
Batson, C. D. 2009. "These Things Called Empathy: Eight Related but Distinct Phenomena." In *The Social Neuroscience of Empathy*, edited by J. Decety and W. Ickes, 3–15. Cambridge, MA & London, England: MIT Press.
Bloom, P. 2016. *Against Empathy: The Case for Rational Compassion*. London: Penguin Random House.
Borsboom, D., G. J. Mellenbergh, and J. van Heerden. 2004. "The Concept of Validity." *Psychological Review* 111 (4): 1061–1071. doi:10.1037/0033-295X.111.4.1061.
Coke, J. S., C. D. Batson, and K. McDavis. 1978. "Empathic Mediation of Helping: A Two-Stage Model." *Journal of Personality and Social Psychology* 36 (7): 752–766. doi:10.1037/0022-3514.36.7.752.

Coplan, A. 2011. "Understanding Empathy: Its Features and Effects." In *Empathy: Philosophical and Psychological Perspectives*, edited by A. Coplan and P. Goldie, 3-18. Oxford: Oxford University Press.

Cronbach, L. J., and P. E. Meehl. 1955. "Construct Validity in Psychological Tests." *Psychological Bulletin* 52: 281-302. doi:10.1037/h0040957.

Cuff, B. M. P., S. J. Brown, L. Taylor, and D. J. Howat. 2016. "Empathy: A Review of the Concept." *Emotion Review*, 8 (2): 144-153. doi:10.1177/1754073914558466.

De Vignemont, F., and T. Singer. 2006. "The Empathic Brain: How, When and Why?" *Trends in Cognitive Sciences* 10 (10): 435-441. doi:10.1016/j.tics.2006.08.008.

Eisenberg, N., and R. A. Fabes. 1990. "Empathy: Conceptualization, Measurement, and Relation to Prosocial Behavior." *Motivation and Emotion* 14 (2): 131-149. doi:10.1007/BF00991640.

Hoffman, M. L. 2008. "Empathy and Prosocial Behavior." In *Handbook of Emotions, 3rd Edition*, edited by M. Lewis, J. M. Haviland Jones, and L. Feldman Barrett, 440-455. New York & London: Guilford Press.

Kuhn, T. 1996. *The Structure of Scientific Revolutions, 3rd Edition*. Chicago & London: University of Chicago Press.

Lanzoni, S. 2012. "Empathy in Translation: Movement and Image in the Psychological Laboratory." *Science in Context* 25 (3): 301-327. doi:10.1017/S0269889712000154.

Lanzoni, S. 2017. "Empathy's Translations: Three Paths from *Einfühlung* into Anglo-American Psychology." In *Empathy: Epistemic Problems and Cultural-Historical Perspectives of a Cross-Disciplinary Concept*, edited by V. Lux and S. Weigel, 297-315. London: Palgrave MacMillan.

Lux, V. 2017. "Measuring the Emotional Quality – Empathy and Sympathy in Empirical Psychology." In *Empathy: Epistemic Problems and Cultural-Historical Perspectives of a Cross-Disciplinary Concept*, edited by V. Lux and S. Weigel, 115-138. London: Palgrave MacMillan.

Pedersen, R. 2009. "Empirical Research on Empathy in medicine—A Critical Review." *Patient Education and Counseling* 76: 307-322. doi:10.1016/j.pec.2009.06.012.

Preston, S. D., and F. B. M. de Waal. 2002. "Empathy: Its Ultimate and Proximate Bases." *Behavioral and Brain Sciences* 25: 1-31.

Singer, T., B. Seymour, J. O'Doherty, H. Kaube, R. J. Dolan, and C. D. Frith. 2004. "Empathy for Pain Involves the Affective but Not Sensory Components of Pain." *Science* 303: 1157-1162. doi:10.1126/science.1093535.

Singer, T., B. Seymour, J. P. O'Doherty, K. E. Stephan, R. J. Dolan, and C. D. Frith. 2006. "Empathic Neural Responses are Modulated by the Perceived Fairness of Others." *Nature* 439 (7075): 466-469. doi:10.1038/nature04271.

Singer, T., R. Snozzi, G. Bird, P. Petrovic, G. Silani, and M. Heinrichs. 2008. "Effects of Oxytocin and Prosocial Behavior on Brain Responses to Direct and Vicariously Experienced Pain." *Emotion* 8 (6): 781-791. doi:10.1037/a0014195.

Technical Recommendations for Psychological Tests and Diagnostic Techniques. 1954. *Psychological Bulletin Supplement* 51 (2): Part 2:, 1-38.

Wispé, L. 1986. "The Distinction between Sympathy and Empathy: To Call Forth A Concept, A Word Is Needed." *Journal of Personality and Social Psychology* 50 (2): 314-321. doi:10.1037/0022-3514.50.2.314.

The Contribution of Empathy to Ethics

Sarah Songhorian

ABSTRACT
Empathy has been taken to play a crucial role in ethics at least since the Scottish Enlightenment. More recently, a revival of moral sentimentalism and empirical research on moral behavior has prompted a renewed interest in empathy and related concepts and on their contribution to moral reasoning and to moral behavior. Furthermore, empathy has recently entered our public discourse as having the power to ameliorate our social and political interactions with others.

The aim of this paper is to investigate the extent to which such a role can be actually granted. Before focusing on a positive assessment, I will delve into a few problems our ordinary concept of empathy and our commonsensical way of conceiving its connection to ethics will need to face. Specifically, I will show how an exaggerated reliance on the ordinary concept of empathy could lead to an underestimation of its biases and potential limitations (§ 2), how a naïve conception of its connection to morality can overlook relevant counterexamples (§ 3) and lead to forms of reductionism (§ 4). Overcoming this possible shortsightedness would pave the way for arguing in favor of an important – though not sufficient and possible neither necessary – role for empathy in ethics (§ 5).

1. Introduction

The concept of empathy and some of those related to it – as for instance the concept of sympathy – have been taken to play a crucial role in ethics at least since the Scottish Enlightenment (Hume [1739] 2000; Smith 1774). Despite their many differences, Hume and Smith conceive of sympathy as the principle allowing our moral judgment to emerge and as the source of our moral distinctions. More recently, a revival of moral sentimentalism (e.g. Kauppinen 2014; Slote 2010) on the one hand, and empirical research on moral behavior (Eisenberg, Zhou, and Koller 2001; Eisenberg 2000; Eisenberg and Fabes 1998; Eisenberg et al. 1989; Eisenberg and Strayer 1987) on the other, have prompted a renewed interest on these concepts and on their role in moral reasoning and in moral behavior. Furthermore, empathy has recently entered our public discourse, and it has been conceived as having the power to ameliorate our social and political interactions with others (see for instance Obama's talk of 'empathy deficit'; see also Rifkin 2009, 42; de Waal 2009; Oxley 2011, 3–4 for a similar account of empathy's role in the public discourse).

In the context of this extensive interest in empathy and in its contribution to moral, social, and political debates, the aim of this paper is to investigate the extent to which such a moral role can be actually granted. Before focusing on a positive assessment of empathy's actual contribution to ethics, I will delve into a few aspects that would show how prudence is recommended when dealing with this issue (similarly, Decety and Cowell 2014). More precisely, I will show how an exaggerated reliance on our ordinary concept of empathy could lead to an underestimation of its biases and potential limitations (§ 2), how a naïve conception of its connection to morality would render extremely complicated to account for specific cases that will function as counterexamples (§ 3), and how a too broad conceptualization of what empathy actually is runs the risk of entailing forms of reductionism (§ 4). Overcoming this possible shortsightedness can pave the way for arguing in favor of an important – though not sufficient and possibly neither necessary – role for empathy in ethics, once empathy is defined in a narrow and fine-grained way (§ 5).

2. The Limits of Empathy

Pretheoretically, if empathy is or implies the ability to understand others, to take care of them, and to share their emotions (e.g. Shamay-Tsoory 2011; Baron-Cohen 2011; Rifkin 2009; Preston and de Waal 2002), it is easy to see how it can be a 'moral good' (Bloom 2014; see also2017; Slote 2013, 25; Battaly 2011) and how it can be conceived of as, at the very least, entailing morally good behavior. While this understanding of empathy makes it a moral virtue and, subsequently, makes the connection between empathy and morality extremely easy to grasp, it does so in a philosophically unsatisfying manner (Battaly 2011, 282). As Battaly claims, we expect 'our theoretical concepts to improve on our ordinary concepts' (2011, 282). The ordinary concept of empathy neither improves nor fosters our knowledge. Even more importantly, when it is understood this way, empathy is unable to overcome its own limitations and biases. Hence, while this colloquial use of empathy would provide an extremely simple response to the inquiry into the role empathy can play in ethics – i.e. empathy is necessary and sufficient for moral behavior (see for instance Batson 2011; Slote 2007; Eisenberg et al. 1989) –, it is unable to account for some features of empathy. This section and the next ones (§ 2–4) are devoted to investigating the features such ordinary understanding of empathy cannot account for.

Humans – as well as other species – have long been shown to have a tendency to empathize better and more easily with those that are similar to them and with those that are, physically or emotionally, closer (Hoffman 2000, 197). We have a somewhat natural tendency to share more and better with our family members and with those belonging to our in-group (e.g. Xu et al. 2009; Kunstman and Plant 2008; Pratto and Glasford 2008; Saucer, Miller, and Doucet 2005; Gaertner, Dovidio, and Johnson 1982). Given this preferential attitude, if the relationship between empathy and morality is as direct and simple as our ordinary use implies – i.e. if by having the ability to empathize one is *ipso facto* a morally good agent – then one needs either to refute the evidence showing that humans are biased in their empathic engagement or to put forth an argument claiming that such biased responses are actually appropriate from a normative standpoint. In fact, while we can easily recognize evolutionary reasons for these biases to be there in the first place – as it might have been useful for our ancestors to have an instinctive access only to their kin or conspecifics' emotions – they are hardly justifiable from a moral standpoint. Why is it the case that I *should* empathize more with a family member of mine as opposed to a stranger? How can I *justify* behaving better toward the former as opposed to the latter, other things being equal? While in the context of scarce resources it is often claimed that one has special duties towards one's own family and, hence, is justified in allocating a greater amount of such resources to help a family member as opposed to a stranger when consequences are not disproportionate[1]; empathy and good moral behavior do not come, or at least they seldom do, as scarce resources. My behaving in an altruistic manner toward a certain person does not *per se* imply that the same kind of behavior could not be available to me afterward toward someone else. Analogously, my feeling bad for one's suffering does not *per se* imply that I would not be able to share someone else's emotions afterward.

Given that the empirical evidence on the impact similarity and proximity – together with other contextual factors – have on empathy is extensive, well replicated, and solid, the burden of proof lies upon those who want to claim that our ordinary concept of empathy is all we need to be morally good agents, and politically and socially responsible individuals. If that were the case, one would need to argue that the very same biases that seem to limit a justifiable role in ethics and in politics for empathy actually enable or entail such a role. Hence, the advocates of this direct and comprehensive role of empathy in ethics would need to argue for the moral justifiability of our biases. They would need to justify, for instance, our tendency to donate more when we are told the story of a single individual who is a victim of an earthquake than when we are exposed to the data on the number of people who suffered the negative consequences of that same earthquake. That can again be explained by our easiness to identify and share the feelings of an identifiable individual who is perceived as more similar and closer than statistics. And yet this *explanation* does not suffice as a *moral justification*.

On the contrary, I take the fact that similarity and proximity modulate empathy as a limitation our ability to empathize with others suffers from (agreeing with Bloom 2017; Fuchs 2017; Bloom 2014; Oakley 2011; Prinz 2011a, 2011b). We *should not* feel worse for the identifiable victim than what we feel when we learn of the statistics about the same tragic event. And yet, as a matter of fact, we *actually do*. As I will show in § 6, these features modulating empathy can be recognized as biases and limitations only insofar as one accepts that our ordinary concept of empathy is fallible and does not prove useful in research. A narrower definition of empathy and a more modest conception of its contribution to ethics are more suited to account for these features. By recognizing that empathy is an *amoral* ability from which we can develop either a moral or an immoral character one can account for its fallibility and for its biases. Empathy *by itself* can be easily biased by factors that are not morally relevant (skin color, gender, nationality and the like), and can lead to forms of unjustified preference towards some individuals because they are similar or close to the agent. Hence, empathy *per se* is not sufficient to act and to judge morally. Several other abilities – such as fairness and impartiality – are needed for morality.

3. Empathy's Alleged Direct Role in Ethics: Some Flaws

Some other risks of an excessive reliance on our ordinary concept of empathy and on the direct derivation of moral behaviors from it are: pathological altruism, the inability to explain or account for *Schadenfreude* or sadism, and the difficulty in accounting for moral agency in Autistic Spectrum Disorder (ASD) and in psychopathy. All of these risks depend on a too straightforward derivation of ethics from empathy. On the one hand, if such derivation was correct, we would not have to account for the fact that empathy can lead to behaviors that we would consider neither morally correct nor supererogatory as those driven by pathological altruism (Bloom 2014; Oakley 2011). On the other hand, we would not have instances of morally deviant behavior in individuals with typical empathic abilities. If empathy were all we need for morally good behavior, then all individuals with typical empathy would be good moral agents and those that behave badly would only be those with empathic deficits. Unfortunately (or not) that is not the case. In fact, all combinations are possible: individuals with typical empathy are free to behave morally or immorally and, at least given some conditions, those with atypical empathy or with empathic deficits can still behave morally.

As for the former possibility, let me briefly consider the case of *Schadenfreude* or sadism. Sadism has been excluded from the American Psychiatric Association's *Diagnostic and Statistical Manual of Mental Disorders* (DSM) since the Fourth Edition (APA 1980). Having excluded its pathological nature, sadism is an interesting conceptual counterexample to the thesis according to which having empathy is sufficient to be a morally decent agent. Sadism is the pattern of behavior of a person that 'is amused by, or takes pleasure in, the psychological or physical suffering of others' (Criterion 4 in DSM III-R). The hypothesis, which has to be verified, is that a sadist does not have a neural impairment in, or a reduced activation of, what can be called the 'empathic circuit', but that the disorder must be found at a different level. With regard to a pure description of the neural activity, a sadist will not be substantially different from everyone else with respect to the empathic circuit's volume, structure, connectivity, and activation. The level of the disorder is quite different from the one typically attributed to people within the ASD (Baron-Cohen 2011; against this view, see Smith 2009) or to psychopaths: a sadist understands other people's feelings, but she has a response opposite to the typical and desirable one – when she sees someone in pain, she rejoices. *Schadenfreude* can also be defined in a way similar to the definition of sadism reported above:

> *Schadenfreude* – derived from the German from *Schaden* (adversity, harm) and *Freude* (joy) – means taking enjoyment in another's pain or misfortune. Schadenfreude is the flip side of empathy: similar cognitive abilities are used (e.g. perspective taking, awareness of others' emotions), but the result is not sympathy or a desire to help another person but rather a sense of pleasure when another person experiences pain or distress. [...] Schadenfreude is related to envy; brain imaging studies show that when a person feels envy, brain regions associated with physical pain (i.e. the anterior cingulate cortex) are activated. When a person one envies experiences a misfortune, triggering feelings of Schadenfreude, the ventral striatum (a brain region associated with pleasure and reward) is activated (Takahashi et al. 2009). (Reevy, Ozer, and Ito 2010, 237, emphasis in original)

If these interpretations of *Schadenfreude* and sadism are correct, then it is clear that a subject can have typical empathy prompting what we would define as immoral behavior. Even more so, sadists 'logically could not engage in sadism *unless* they were capable of identifying what their victims are thinking or feeling' (Matthews 2014, 74, emphasis in original).

Conversely, even subjects with atypical empathy – in its ordinary meaning – can engage in moral behaviors and be moral agents. Example of this situation are high-functioning ASD individuals. Regardless of whether one accepts the claim that ASD is characterized by a lack of empathy (Baron-Cohen 2011) or that the empathic reactions towards others' emotional states are excessive and imbalanced in ASD (Smith 2009),[2] one has to admit that the empathic feelings of individuals with ASD seem to function differently from those of typically developed people. If that is the case, then either one has to claim that people with ASD are not capable of *any* moral action and moral agency or one needs to accept that at least some moral actions and some form of moral agency can be granted even in the absence of typical empathy. High-functioning ASD individuals are able to engage in moral actions even if they might have learned how they should behave in a more cognitive and rule-guided manner as opposed to the way in which typical children do. Something along the same lines can also be said for what concerns moral judgment. Patil et al. (2016) have shown that adults with high-functioning autism exhibit 'a normal pattern of moral judgment' (Patil et al. 2016, 1). Interestingly, Patil and colleagues tried to investigate how this can be related to their well-documented difficulties in 'social cognition and emotional processing' (Patil et al. 2016, 1). Their thesis is that the kind of deficits usually attributed to autism (as in Baron-Cohen 2011) actually depends on an alexithymic trait often, but not necessarily, associated with the autistic one (40–65% preponderance in ASD subjects), and that high-functioning autistic adults who have both autism and alexithymia compensate these two traits, thus exhibiting typical moral judgments. Hence,

> after accounting for co-occurring alexithymia, autism is no longer associated with aberrant neural activation while empathizing with others' pain, self-reported deficits on dispositional empathy, or deficits in interocepting on one's own emotional states. (Patil et al. 2016, 2)

A commonsensical and ordinary definition of empathy, however, would certainly incorporate the ability to identify and understand emotions (i.e. the negation of alexithymia); hence, advocates of this broad definition of empathy would be unable to assess how subjects with what in their view are empathy deficits can exhibit a normal pattern of moral judgment. A more fine-grained analysis of empathy (§ 5) would serve better this purpose.

Advocates of a direct relation between empathy and ethics often use the case of psychopathy as the paradigmatic case showing that lacking empathy hinders moral behavior. They do so because there is little debate on their lack of empathy – as opposed to what has been shown for ASD. The classical case of psychopathy are convicted criminals (on average 20% of prison inmates in the US according to Hare 1999, 87). When one focuses on this example, the connection between immoral behavior and lack of empathy seems rather obvious. And yet, 'not all psychopaths are criminals' (Hare 1999, 86). On the contrary, some of them can lead apparently normal lives (Hare 1999, 102–123), there is a sense in which they know the difference between right and wrong – even though they do not distinguish between a moral and a conventional sense of this dichotomy, thus treating all rules as conventional (Nichols 2004, 76–77) – and they perform just as any typical adult on standard perspective-taking tasks (Nichols 2004, 59; see also Blair et al. 1996). Hence, psychopaths are capable of some degree of perspective-taking which is itself a trait usually encompassed by our ordinary concept of empathy. Finally, even though they usually engage in some form of immoral behavior, that is not necessary. Agreeing with Hoffman (2000) and Oxley (2011, 10), while I take empathy to have an important role in ethics, I do not think that being unable of empathy necessarily 'doom one to manipulating or killing others' (Hoffman 2000, 36). If we are interested only in the outward behavior – and not in the authenticity or morality of the motivations for it – then it is at least conceptually possible that they would follow those rules just as much as they follow most conventional rules for self-interest. They might help someone in a specific context not out of altruism but because of the beneficial consequences they might enjoy, and yet the behavior itself might be the moral one – not genuinely so, but still a good one. Advocates of the ordinary concept of empathy and of its direct connection with ethics might need to explain why sometimes psychopaths perform good actions and how it is possible that they perform just as any typical adult on standard perspective-taking tasks. Either they have empathy – contrary to the typical claim made about psychopaths – or perspective-taking does not fall within the scope of a proper definition of empathy.

The aim of this section and of § 2 was to show that an exaggerated reliance on our ordinary concept of empathy is bound to underestimate or even to disregard empathy's intrinsic pitfalls as well as cases in which the connection between empathy and moral behavior or moral judgment is less direct than what may appear when one considers only positive evidence. Furthermore, if one is interested in moral behavior only as long as it produces good consequences, then psychopaths might be a counterexample of empathy's necessity for morality – again in its ordinary use. Hence, a more fine-grained analysis of what empathy stands for seems necessary to get an idea of its actual role in ethics, since up until now the only conclusion one might have reached is that it is not sufficient *per se* and, given certain circumstances, might also not be necessary.[3] Before moving to a more refined analysis (§ 5), I will briefly focus on another risk a broad and ordinary conception of the relationship between empathy and morality runs – i.e. the possibility that it may lead to reductionism (§ 4).

4. Leading to Reductionism

A further important risk the commonsensical idea of an immediate connection between empathy and morality runs is that of leading one to believe that it is possible to reduce the latter to the former (Churchland 2011). This idea has an obvious appeal. If, by conceiving of empathy in its colloquial sense, it appears as necessary and sufficient for our moral behavior and our moral reasoning, then, once the natural correlates of empathy are fully discovered, one could eliminate or reduce all of the problematic features of morality by appealing to its natural functioning. According to this naturalistic perspective, morality is the by-product (or the final aim) of our empathic and natural endowment. Once we know about the functioning of the neural or hormonal mechanisms, there is nothing else to be investigated, no further questions to be asked. Recent developments in moral cognition have identified the areas whose activation correlates with empathic engagement – such as, Anterior Cingulate Cortex (ACC) and Anterior Insula (AI) (Singer et al. 2004; Lamm, Decety, and Singer 2011) – and the two neuropeptides – oxytocin (OXT) and arginine vasopressin (AVP) – which are also associated with our ordinary concept of empathy. Hence, these data have been taken to imply that we have come to discover such natural endowment. Thus, empathy has been considered a good candidate for reducing or eliminating ethics to its material and natural grounds. To oversimplify this line of thought – that, as such, has hardly been strongly endorsed by scholars –, one might claim that if all we need to know in order to act and judge morally refers to empathy – a claim I have shown we have independent reasons to be skeptical about – and if empathy is identical to the functioning of some areas of our brain or of OXT and AVP, then ethics can be reduced to the functioning of these areas and/or of these two neuropeptides.

The aim of this section is to challenge this perspective, even admitting, just for the sake of the argument, that one could claim ordinary empathy is all we need for moral action and for moral judgment. Once again, the goal is not denying any role to empathy in ethics, but rather to clarify that, in its ordinary use, it is not sufficient to understand our capacity to judge and act morally as a whole.

The perspective I want to challenge assumes two very specific and controversial concepts of both empathy and naturalism. On the one hand, empathy is conceived of as an umbrella concept (Preston and de Waal 2002; Shamay-Tsoory 2011; Rifkin 2009; Baron-Cohen 2011) encompassing abilities that I would claim are better understood outside the domain of empathy. For instance, Preston and de Waal believe helping behavior and guilt are part of the concept of empathy itself (as can be seen in Preston and de Waal's figure in [2002, 4]). On the contrary, helping behavior is usually considered a possible consequence of empathic engagement rather than being one and the same thing with the underlying and mostly unconscious mirroring of others' emotional states (see also § 5). Obviously, if one collapses this and other possible consequences of empathy onto its very concept and if one defines ethics as helping or cooperative behavior solely, then such a reduction becomes clearly feasible. However, ethics does not merely involve helping or cooperative behavior – there are duties of justice, that cannot be derived from helping or cooperating, and, some may claim, even self-regarding duties – and it seems more accurate to avoid overestimating empathy's power – as I have shown in § 2 and 3.

On the other hand, while the view according to which ethics can be reduced to the functioning of the areas and/or of the two neuropeptides connected with empathy is certainly a naturalistic one, naturalism does not necessarily imply reduction or elimination. Alternative versions of naturalism without reductionism and eliminativism are available – such as liberal naturalism which aims at setting ethics' possibility conditions instead of eliminating it (De Caro and Macarthur 2010). Even granting for the sake of the argument (against the evidence provided in § 2 and 3), that empathic engagement is necessary and sufficient for *any* occurrence of moral behavior or moral reasoning, and that underlying such engagement are the relevant neural and neuropeptidic activities, this does not necessarily imply eliminativism. Reductionists and eliminativists think we would be better off if we could get rid of the multiple levels of discourse we use. According to them, our ordinary way of talking about morality is basically metaphorical or even delusive, and we had better avoid it. And yet, neither reduction nor elimination follows directly from granting the abovementioned conditions (i.e. empathy is necessary and sufficient, and its occurrence correlates with the relevant neural and neuropeptidic activities), so the potential benefits and pitfalls of reduction or elimination can be assessed on their own. What consequences would the elimination of a level of analysis have on our moral practices? By getting rid of our ordinary moral discourse, we risk losing several of its important features (agreeing with Marr's conclusions about vision; see Marr 1982). It would, for instance, be extremely hard to talk about moral responsibility, free will, and moral agency and about the praiseworthiness and blameworthiness of an action and the fittingness or appropriateness of a moral judgment. While a reductionist might advocate she is neutral about whether agency and free will exist, eliminating the level of discourse in which these concepts are used would obtain the same results of an actual denial. Analogously, if we are interested uniquely in the physical basis of moral judgment and moral behavior, then it would be almost impossible to discuss whether a certain action or judgment was appropriate: we would have to restrict ourselves to the consideration of whether the judgment or action actually took place. Hence, reductionism would in practice eliminate any space for normative ethics, even if it claims to be neutral about it.

Let us take stock. What I have done up to now is to focus on the outcomes of an overestimation of empathy's scope and of the contribution it might make to morality. Hence, as mentioned earlier, the analysis I have conducted should provide sufficient reason to be prudent when it comes to evaluating both empathy's definition and its role in ethics. However tempting the idea of reducing ethics to empathy or, at least, of the latter being necessary and sufficient for the former might be, I hope to have shown that the risks and the faulty steps such an approach would have to face are too many to be ignored and that a more promising path should be found. In what follows I will put forth what I take to be a more promising interpretation of the connection between empathy and ethics starting from a different and more fine-grained definition of the former.

5. Empathy, Sympathy, and Morality

The aim of this section is to provide a positive account of the *actual* role empathy can play in moral behavior and in moral judgment, once one has accepted that our ordinary definition of empathy, as well as our commonsensical idea of its direct connection to ethics, is exaggerated.

Before describing how I take empathy to be contributing to the typical development of a moral conscience, it is necessary to define what falls within empathy, and what falls outside its scope. As mentioned earlier – in § 2 and 3 – our ordinary concept of empathy encompasses several different phenomena: emotional identification, perspective-taking, cognitive empathy, theory of mind, the ability to feel together with others, the ability to identify and name emotions, the capacity to understand what others feel, the ability to put oneself into the other' shoes, the intention to help others and to care for them and for their well-being. While some have distinguished between affective and cognitive empathy (e.g. Shamay-Tsoory, Aharon-Peretz, and Perry 2009), I would like to define empathy in its minimal and non-reducible features, all other abilities being things that can be built up on the basis of empathy but that are not within the scope of its core features. What one can find in newborns and in toddlers is a form of emotional identification or, even better, of emotional attunement[4] with others (Eisenberg and Strayer 1987; Meltzoff and Moore 1977, 1983; Pfeifer et al. 2008; Simner 1971), as suggested in the following passages:

> Empathy refers to a person's capacity to feel within or in another person's feelings (Langfeld 1967, 138), and most researchers now consider it "an emotional response that stems from another's emotional state or condition and that is congruent with the other's emotional state or situation." (Eisenberg and Strayer 1987, 5)

> whereas sympathy stems from the perspective of an observer who is conscious of another's feelings, empathy stems from that of a participant who vicariously merges with another's feelings. (Escalas and Stern 2003, 567).

By focusing uniquely on emotional attunement as the core feature of empathy (similarly, Prinz 2011b, 212) – namely, the one that can be found in all occurrences of empathic engagement both in newborns and in typical adults – one avoids the risks entailed by a too broad, simplistic, and ordinary understanding of it.

In adults, but not in newborns, this core feature is often accompanied by the ability to identify and name emotions – the contrary of the alexithymic trait responsible for the atypicality in the moral judgment of individuals with ASD. While to empathize one needs to *feel* something to some extent in line with (valence suffices) what the other is feeling, the ability to identify and name the emotions felt is usually there, but not necessarily. I can feel something in witnessing someone else's emotion and still be unable to say what I am actually feeling – either because of the novelty of the emotion or because I am focused on what I could or should do for that other person. Analogously, cognitive empathy, perspective-taking, and theory of mind are often strongly connected with empathy's core and yet none of them is necessary. I can empathize with someone without knowing anything about that person, without trying to mentalize her, or without putting myself into the other person's shoes. When facing a strongly expressed emotion, I do not need to resort to any other ability or process: the emotion seems to be directly transfused (Smith 1774, I.i.1.6; Hume [1739] 2000, III.iii.3.5 and III.iii.1.7; Debes 2016; Raphael 2007). This, however, does not mean that all of these other abilities are useless or irrelevant for our understanding and sharing of others' emotional states. It simply implies that mentalizing and putting oneself in someone else's shoes are instruments we use when things go less smoothly. When I do not understand someone's reaction, the emotion she is feeling, or the reason why she is in such state, then I can resort to projecting myself into the other (Smith 1774, I.i.1.2) or to impersonating that other person (Smith 1774, VII.iii.1.4). Besides this role in clarifying unclear situations or emotions, these mechanisms have also an extremely important role in the development of a moral conscience and of our moral abilities.

Before focusing on this, however, let me say a few more words about why the intention to help others and to care for them should not fall within the scope of empathy. Empathy can be a good starting point for either helping someone or for caring for that person; however, it is not necessary nor sufficient for helping or caring. Let me focus first on helping behaviors: empathy and helping can occur each without the other. On the one hand, I can empathize – i.e. I can feel to a certain extent what that person is feeling – without being motivated to help that person. And, on the other hand, I can help someone without feeling anything. I can feel sorry for someone's pain and still refrain from helping that person – think of the way in which we might sometimes feel sorry for a homeless person without helping her at all. On the contrary, I can help someone without feeling anything but simply because I know it is the right thing to do. Furthermore, as mentioned earlier, helping behavior can also be the consequence of amoral, egoistic, or even immoral drives: I can, for instance, help others because I expect them to reciprocate or because I want to be seen as a good person, to manipulate or deceive people. Hence, empathy and helping behavior are not conceptually connected. It is, however, true that from an evolutionary standpoint it might well be that the ability to feel someone else's pain is the most direct drive to helping that person, and still this does not make helping an instance of empathy. In fact, if that was the case, we would at least be able to find that one of the two concepts is either necessary or sufficient (or both) to the other one and, as I have shown, that is not so.

The connection between caring and empathy is slightly different since one could claim that empathy is necessary but not sufficient for caring. Indeed, the most typical example of caring in the interpersonal sphere usually refers to family members' relationship. In this context, it seems quite obvious to say that a fundamental feature of a family relationship is the ability to emotionally attune to each other and that, from this, caring can flourish. This perspective can account for the fact that in order to care empathy is not sufficient; some much more structured sentiments and the knowledge of someone's life plans, expectations, desires, and the like are also needed. And yet, it has difficulties in accounting for at least two things: that one could care for things that are not people (e.g. the environment); and that we do not know whether emotional attunement is actually necessary for caring also among persons. First, I can care for the environment without emotionally attuning to it or to the future generations who will suffer the consequences of us being disrespectful of it. I can behave in ways that make explicit my interest in promoting the conservation of the environment without this sharing mechanism. Hence, it seems reasonable to think that either we are talking about a different kind of caring or we should grant that empathy is not always necessary for caring in contexts that are not interpersonal – it might still be very relevant and most likely the most typical way of developing care in interpersonal relationships among typical individuals. Second, given a certain interpersonal relationship, one could wonder what comes first: Is it empathy or care? Are occurrences of emotional attunement that build up care or is care that makes emotional attunement more likely to take place? If the latter was the case, then one could not claim that empathy is necessary for caring, but rather that they are often correlated and that caring for someone increases the likeliness and intensity of empathy (in line with the evidence shown in § 2). Hence, the two are usually and typically connected, but that is not a sufficient reason to think either that one is necessary to the other or that caring is an aspect of empathy itself, for I can certainly empathize with people with whom I am not in a caring relationship – e.g. the crying stranger passing by in the street.

Having provided this minimal definition of what empathy is does not yet answer the question of its actual contribution to the development of a moral conscience. Once one has accepted that empathy is not sufficient for moral behavior and moral judgment, and that a characterization of its core elements like the one I put forth avoids most of the risks reviewed above, one can still wonder: how and to what extent can empathy contribute to morality?

The ability to empathize, to attune with others' emotional states, works as an enabling condition to develop sympathy, this being the ability to understand and judge others' emotions, behaviors, and character traits (in a Smithian perspective: see Smith 1774; see also Songhorian 2019). While empathy is amoral and can lead, as it has been shown, also to immoral behavior; sympathy is the result of a perspective-taking in which the spectator takes a normative standpoint – either social or moral depending on the spectator (Brown 2016, 238). As Darwall points out: 'sympathy [...] is felt as from the perspective of "one-caring"' (1998, 261). It is only at the level of sympathy, then, that judgments on the appropriateness of a behavior or of an emotion can be passed. Before that, our empathic engagement holds no normative standpoint on what happens. It is only when such a standpoint is reached that one can truly be taken to pass moral (or social) judgments. Likewise, it is only when the agent can reflect upon an action to be performed that such action can be said to be truly motivated by moral reasoning. Before that moment, my helping someone only on the basis of the feeling I felt for that person is compatible with many different explanations of my motives and intentions. It is only when one develops a moral conscience and evaluates the actions to be performed as an observer would do that the motivations are genuinely moral. This, clearly, does not mean that one cannot perform a good action with wrong motivations or, at least, with amoral motivations; but simply that it does not seem to be the best example of moral agency. The golden rule of moral agency should imply producing good consequences in the world for good reasons. These two elements might not always be in place, but our standard should be to look for both.

In this perspective, typical human beings are seen as endowed with some empathic abilities. In Smith's words:

> How selfish soever man may be supposed, there are evidently some principles in his nature, which interest him in the fortune of others, and render their happiness necessary to him, though he derives nothing from it except the pleasure of seeing it. (Smith 1774, I.i.1.1)

This typical endowment, however, does not grant *per se* that one is to become a morally good agent. Were it that way, we would not have to deal with cases such as that of *Schadenfreude*, sadism, ASD, or psychopathy, and again we would risk reducing normative ethics to its natural or typical grounds. Furthermore, empathy understood this way can hardly lead to morality since it is only capable of instinctively and immediately attuning to emotions that are strongly expressed and easily recognizable (mostly, basic emotions; see Ekman 1992a, 1992b; Ekman, Friesen, and Ellsworth 1972;

Ekman, Friesen, and Tomkins 1971). In order to share and understand more complex emotions and to be able to judge them, subjects need to move from the basic ability to attune to each other to acquiring mentalizing and perspective-taking capacities. The need of such further abilities does not deny the role of an affective engagement but renders it only one of the aspects – notably a very important one – needed to develop the capacity to judge and act morally. Growing up, individuals would learn to put themselves into the others' shoes in order to understand what they are going through and to judge the appropriateness of their behaviors. This is achieved by moving from empathy to sympathy, from a natural endowment to a normative criterion. Real spectators, in Smith's thought, project themselves into the other's situation and/or impersonate that other to understand and to pass judgment on her behavior or her emotional reactions to a given situation. In this process of projection and impersonation, empathy is crucial since spectators have to imaginatively attune with the other's emotions, and they achieve this goal through a process that is more cognitively charged and more conscious than the one that occurs when I feel bad because I see someone in despair. I decide to understand whether that person acted correctly, and I try to feel as she might have been feeling. I choose to do that, while I do not choose to empathize with the stranger on the street. While empathy involves no imagination in its basic sense, sympathy is always accompanied by imagination: it would be impossible without empathy, perspective-taking, impersonation, and projection.

The stage of real spectators' sympathy, while necessary for understanding how one can go from empathy to a moral conscience – again given one has a typical empathic endowment –, is not the end of the story. Indeed, in order to have a proper moral conscience, one has to develop one's impartial spectator at the same time from the experience had with real ones and abstracting from that. Without this further step – as Sir Gilbert Elliot privately wrote to Adam Smith (Raphael 2007, 36) –, one would be unable to distinguish morality from social conventions. Criticism of a given social practice would be impossible, as well as moral progress or reformation. While, under real spectators' gaze, agents are interested in being praised and in avoiding being blamed – with the hypocrisy and conformism this might entail – under the impartial spectator's one, they are interested only in being praiseworthy and in not being blameworthy (Smith 1774, III.2.1–2). Hence, not only the spectator is different, but the normative criterion differs as well. The impartial spectator represents the way humans can develop their moral character (Weinstein 2016, 352) starting from a certain natural endowment. A virtuous moral conscience is achieved when one 'really adopts [the sentiments of the impartial spectator],' when one 'almost identifies himself with […] that impartial spectator' (Smith 1774, III.3.25).

This section aimed at providing a positive account of a fine-grained definition of empathy and a more promising reconstruction of its contribution to ethics. Before concluding by showing how I think this reconstruction is more suited to answer the challenges seen above (§ 6), let me summarize what I take empathy to be actually doing. Empathy is an ability most individuals are endowed with. Those that have this ability can develop a moral conscience by following the evolution from empathy to the sympathy of the impartial spectator I have just described following Adam Smith. Hence, empathy is an enabling condition for such conscience to develop, but it is not necessary for *any* moral judgment or moral action. When a subject has to judge (or perform) a behavior she is familiar with, she might not need to actively attune affectively. And yet, *some* experience with affective attunement is needed for being able to develop our impartial spectator. Empathy is, thus, *necessary for the development* of the sympathetic and impartial spectator. However, once our moral conscience is in place, we do not need to empathize each and every time to pass moral judgment or to behave morally.[5]

Moreover, it might well be the case that having empathy makes the development of such moral conscience much easier. And yet, this model accounts for two things: *(a)* it does not imply that having empathy makes it necessary that one develops into a morally decent human being (various things can go wrong along the way); *(b)* it does not entail that if one has no empathy or has an empathy deficit then she could not be a morally decent human being. My claim is that, *given* typical empathy, a Smithian approach is the most promising, direct, and easy one to develop a moral conscience and to become morally good agents. And yet, I am not claiming that without empathy one could not reach a normative understanding of ethics by other means.

6. Concluding Remarks: Why *This* Account?

At this point one might share the diagnosis, but not the therapy. One might agree with the risks and problems I have identified for our ordinary understanding of empathy and of its role in ethics (§ 2-4) but find the solution I propose (§ 5) unconvincing. To this possible objection I might reply that my proposal accounts for all the risks and problems identified and that, to the best of my knowledge, I was unable to find further counterexamples or problems that it is not capable of solving. This, of course, is not sufficient to claim that there are no such problems or counterexamples, but it clearly moves the burden of proof to those who want to advocate for a different characterization of empathy or for a different interpretation of its role in ethics.

Let me conclude by showing how I think my proposal would solve the problems I started with. We have seen that empathy is biased (§ 2). And yet, this is not a problem for those who recognize that empathy is an *amoral* ability from which we can develop a moral character as well as an immoral one. In the account I advanced, it is not empathy *per se* that functions as the criterion to judge and act morally, that being properly only the sympathy of the impartial spectator, and, hence, the fact that our emotional reactions can be biased is not too problematic. In fact, to judge and act morally one has to add a certain level of impartiality that counteracts the biases that might be there at the basic and natural level. The *impartial* spectator cannot be biased and that is what counts in ethics. We have also seen that the relationship between empathy and ethics seems problematic when one considers *Schadenfreude*, sadism, ASD, and psychopathy (§ 3). In my account, *Schadenfreude* and sadism pose no particular problem, since we can grant these subjects have typical empathic abilities but have directed them towards rejoicing in others' pain rather than feeling bad about it. The disjunction of empathy and ethics that I have argued for makes it extremely easy to account for these behaviors. Slightly different is the story as far as ASD and psychopathy are concerned. High-functioning ASD subjects seem fully capable of moral agency and moral judgment. The prediction my account would make, should the empirical evidence point at some basic empathic difficulties – a thesis that seems more and more disconfirmed by recent data (Patil et al. 2016) –, would be that one can still reach an understanding of moral norms and be a proper moral agent even without empathy. As I have said, empathy would make the affective pathway toward the sympathetic engagement of the impartial spectator natural and easy, and yet it does not make the former necessary for *any* development of a moral conscience. If ASD subjects really had no empathy, it would still be possible for them to be moral. However, given the recent interpretations of ASD's issues in social cognition as referring to an imbalance in empathy or to the alexithymic trait often associated with autism, the data on this set of subjects are not the best one to account for the dissociation as one may conclude they do not, in fact, lack empathy. A better case might be that of psychopathy. Even though they usually engage in some form of immoral behavior, this is not necessary: being incapable of empathy does not necessarily 'doom one to manipulating or killing others' (Hoffman 2000, 36). Most of the times, psychopaths might be unable or unwilling to develop an impartial spectator, but again this is a deficit or an unwillingness that does not derive directly from empathy (or lack thereof) and that the framework proposed here can account for. Finally, we have seen that a too direct connection between empathy and ethics can easily lead to reductionism. A Smithian perspective, on the contrary, while being naturalistic in spirit, does not run this risk insofar as it does not derive the normative criterion from empathy itself. The desire to be praiseworthy and to avoid being blameworthy is not derivable from empathy. On the contrary, it is there in the first place together with empathy (or even without it).

For these reasons, I take the Smithian account proposed here as a good candidate to explain the extent to which empathy can contribute to ethics without running the risks intrinsic in an overestimation of its powers and in an overly optimistic view of a necessary and sufficient relationship between them. Empathy, in this account, is certainly not sufficient for ethics in general, and it might also not be necessary. And yet, *given* a typical endowment of empathy, its development into the sympathetic engagement of the impartial spectator seems a good candidate for explaining the affective and easy route to morality typical individuals mostly experience.

Notes

1. Clearly, there are many cases that are much more complicated than the one which considers comparable consequences on those we help. For instance, if by using the same resources I can only slightly ameliorate my relatives' well-being while I can radically change a stranger's life, would my preference still be justified (Singer 2009, 130-131)? Would it be permissible to spend 10 on a toy that would only make my kid slightly happier as opposed to paying for life-saving therapy for a distant stranger?
2. According to Smith, subjects with ASD cannot be characterized as having a deficit in empathy, but as having an excessive empathic engagement that, rather than being directed towards others, is interiorized in *personal distress*. Hence, these subjects are not apathic when facing others' emotions. On the contrary, they have an erroneous overreaction, their feeling is imbalanced, and they are unable to identify the subject of that emotional state, because of a difficulty in distinguishing between the emotional states that originate in the self and those that originate in others.
3. This conclusion might be rejected by refusing to focus only on the consequences when considering the morality of an action. In fact, if one considers intentions as crucial to the evaluation of a behavior, then one might claim that psychopaths' intentions are evil or uniquely conventional (as opposed to being properly moral). And that, for their intentions to be moral, empathy is in fact needed.
4. The concept of an emotional attunement rather than that of identification is to be preferred for two reasons. First, it allows for an imperfect isomorphism between the emotions felt by the two individuals involved: it is often the case that, in empathizing with someone's emotion, I do not feel the exact same emotion, but a slightly different one (often a less intense one) with the same valence (positive or negative). The concept of identification renders this typical fact of our empathizing experience more difficult to grasp immediately. Second, attunement is more neutral than identification also as far as the self-other distinction is involved. Saying that A identifies emotionally with B seems to have a stronger implicature on the direction of the process and on the fact that is A that projects or simulates B. On the contrary, emotional attunement seems to convey weaker stereotypes. Attunement can also be an interpersonal enterprise – we attune with each other –, whereas it seems obvious that only an individual can identify with someone else.
5. The account presented in this paper differs from Prinz's (Prinz 2011b, 213-221) because I grant empathy's role in enabling moral development in typical individuals, and because I am interested in underlying that, while I deny that empathy is necessary for moral judgment and moral

conduct, I do not mean to imply that it can never accompany and prompt them.

Disclosure statement

No potential conflict of interest was reported by the authors.

ORCID

Sarah Songhorian http://orcid.org/0000-0002-0847-5276

References

American Psychiatric Association (APA). 1980. *Diagnostic and Statistical Manual of Mental Disorders*. 3rd ed. Washington: American Psychiatric Association.
Baron-Cohen, S. 2011. *Zero Degrees of Empathy: A New Theory of Human Cruelty*. London: Penguin uk.
Batson, C. D. 2011. *Altruism in Humans*. Oxford: Oxford University Press.
Battaly, H. D. 2011. "Is Empathy a Virtue." In *Empathy: Philosophical and Psychological Perspectives*, edited by A. Coplan and P. Goldie, 277–301. New York: Oxford University Press.
Blair, R., C. Sellars, I. Strickland, F. Clark, A. Williams, M. Smith, and L. Jones. 1996. "Theory of Mind in the Psychopath." *Journal of Forensic Psychiatry* 7: 15–25. doi:10.1080/09585189608409914.
Bloom, P. 2014. "Against Empathy." *Boston Review. A Political and Literary Forum*, Accessed 11 September 2018. http://www.bostonreview.net/forum/paul-bloom-against-empathy
Bloom, P. 2017. *Against Empathy: The Case for Rational Compassion*. London: Penguin Random House.
Brown, V. 2016. "The Impartial Spectator and Moral Judgment." *Econ Journal Watch* 13 (2): 232–248.
Churchland, P. S. 2011. *Braintrust. What Neuroscience Tells Us about Morality*. Princeton: Princeton University Press.
Darwall, S. 1998. "Empathy, Sympathy, Care." *Philosophical Studies* 89: 261–282. doi:10.1023/A:1004289113917.
De Caro, M., and D. Macarthur. 2010. *Naturalism and Normativity*. New York: Columbia University Press.
de Waal, F. B. M. 2009. *The Age of Empathy: Nature's Lessons for a Kinder Society*. New York: Broadway Books.
Debes, R. 2016. "Adam Smith and the Sympathetic Imagination." In *Adam Smith: His Life, Thought, and Legacy*, edited by R. P. Hanley, 192–207. Princeton: Princeton University Press.
Decety, J., and J. M. Cowell. 2014. "Friends or Foes: Is Empathy Necessary for Moral Behavior?" *Perspectives on Psychological Science* 9 (4): 525–537. doi:10.1177/1745691614545130.
Eisenberg, N. 2000. "Emotion, Regulation, and Moral Development." *Annual Review of Psychology* 51: 665–697. doi:10.1146/annurev.psych.51.1.665.

Eisenberg, N., and R. A. Fabes. 1998. "Prosocial Development." In *Handbook of Child Psychology, Vol. 3: Social, Emotional, and Personality Development*, edited by N. Eisenberg, 701–778. 5th ed. New York: Wiley & Sons.

Eisenberg, N., R. A. Fabes, P. A. Miller, J. Fultz, R. Shell, R. M. Mathy, and R. R. Reno. 1989. "Relation of Sympathy and Personal Distress to Pro-Social Behavior: A Multimethod Study." *Journal of Personality and Social Psychology* 57 (1): 55–66. doi:10.1037/0022-3514.57.1.55.

Eisenberg, N., and J. Strayer. 1987. *Empathy and Its Development, Cambridge Studies in Social & Emotional Development*. Cambridge: Cambridge University Press.

Eisenberg, N., Q. Zhou, and S. Koller. 2001. "Brazilian Adolescents' Prosocial Moral Judgment and Behavior: Relations to Sympathy, Perspective Taking, Gender-Role Orientation, and Demographic Characteristics." *Child Development* 72 (2): 518–534. doi:10.1111/cdev.2001.72.issue-2.

Ekman, P. 1992a. "Are There Basic Emotions?" *Psychological Review* 99 (3): 550–553. doi:10.1037/0033-295X.99.3.550.

Ekman, P. 1992b. "An Argument for Basic Emotions." *Cognition and Emotion* 6 (3–4): 169–200. doi:10.1080/02699939208411068.

Ekman, P., W. Friesen, and P. Ellsworth. 1972. *Emotion in the Human Face: Guidelines for Research and an Integration of Findings*. New York: Pergamon Press.

Ekman, P., W. V. Friesen, and S. S. Tomkins. 1971. "Facial Affect Scoring Technique: A First Validity Study." *Semiotica* 3 (1): 37–58. doi:10.1515/semi.1971.3.1.37.

Escalas, J. E., and B. B. Stern. 2003. "Sympathy and Empathy: Emotional Responses to Advertising Dramas." *Journal of Consumer Research* 29 (4): 566–578. doi:10.1086/346251.

Fuchs, T. 2017. "Empathy, Group Identity, and the Mechanisms of Exclusion: An Investigation into the Limits of Empathy." *Topoi*. doi:10.1007/s11245-017-9499-z.

Gaertner, S. L., J. F. Dovidio, and G. Johnson. 1982. "Race of Victim, Nonresponsive Bystanders, and Helping Behavior." *The Journal of Social Psychology* 117: 69–77. doi:10.1080/00224545.1982.9713409.

Hare, R. D. 1999. *Without Conscience: The Disturbing World of the Psychopaths among Us*. New York: Guilford Press.

Hoffman, M. L. 2000. *Empathy and Moral Development: Implications for Caring and Justice*. New York: Cambridge University Press.

Hume, D. [1739] 2000. *A Treatise of Human Nature: Being an Attempt to Introduce the Experimental Method of Reasoning into Moral Subjects: A Critical Edition*, edited by D. F. Norton and M. J. Norton. New York: Oxford University Press.

Kauppinen, A. 2014. "Moral Sentimentalism." In *The Stanford Encyclopedia of Philosophy*, edited by E. N. Zalta, Accessed 11 September 2018. http://plato.stanford.edu/archives/spr2014/entries/moral-sentimentalism/

Kunstman, J. W., and E. A. Plant. 2008. "Racing to Help: Racial Bias in High Emergency Helping Situations." *Journal of Personality and Social Psychology* 95: 1499–1510. doi:10.1037/a0012822.

Lamm, C., J. Decety, and T. Singer. 2011. "Meta-Analytic Evidence for Common and Distinct Neural Networks Associated with Directly Experienced Pain and Empathy for Pain." *NeuroImage* 54 (3): 2492–2502. doi:10.1016/j.neuroimage.2010.10.014.

Langfeld, H. S. 1967. *The Aesthetic Attitude*. New York: Kennikat.

Marr, D. 1982. *Vision. A Computational Investigation into the Human Representation and Processing of Visual Information.* New York: Freeman.

Matthews, E. 2014. "Psychopathy and Moral Rationality." In *Being Amoral: Psychopathy and Moral Incapacity*, edited by T. Schramme, 71–89. Cambridge: MIT Press.

Meltzoff, A. N., and M. K. Moore. 1977. "Imitation of Facial and Manual Gestures by Human Neonates." *Science* 198 (4312): 75–78. doi:10.1126/science.198.4312.75.

Meltzoff, A. N., and M. K. Moore. 1983. "Newborn Infants Imitate Adult Facial Gestures." *Child Development* 54 (3): 702–709. doi:10.2307/1130058.

Nichols, S. 2004. *Sentimental Rules: On the Natural Foundations of Moral Judgment.* New York: Oxford University Press.

Oakley, B. A. 2011. *Cold-Blooded Kindness: Neuroquirks of a Codependent Killer, or Just Give Me a Shot at Loving You, Dear, and Other Reflections on Helping that Hurts.* Amherst: Prometheus Books.

Oxley, J. C. 2011. *The Moral Dimensions of Empathy: Limits and Applications in Ethical Theory and Practice.* New York: Palgrave Macmillan.

Patil, I., J. Melsbach, K. Henning-Fast, and G. Silani. 2016. "Divergent Roles of Autistic and Alexithymic Traits in Utilitarian Moral Judgments in Adults with Autism." *Scientific Reports* 6: 1–15. doi:10.1038/srep23637.

Pfeifer, J. H., M. Iacoboni, J. C. Mazziotta, and M. Dapretto. 2008. "Mirroring Others' Emotions Relates to Empathy and Interpersonal Competence in Children." *NeuroImage* 39 (4): 2076–2085. doi:10.1016/j.neuroimage.2007.10.032.

Pratto, F., and D. E. Glasford. 2008. "Ethnocentrism and the Value of a Human Life." *Journal of Personality and Social Psychology* 95: 1411–1428. doi:10.1037/a0012636.

Preston, S. D., and F. B. M. de Waal. 2002. "Empathy: Its Ultimate and Proximate Bases." *The Behavioral and Brain Sciences* 25 (1): 1–20; discussion 20–71. doi:10.1017/S0140525X02000018.

Prinz, J. 2011a. "Against Empathy." *Southern Journal of Philosophy* 49 (s1): 214–233. doi:10.1111/j.2041-6962.2011.00069.x.

Prinz, J. 2011b. "Is Empathy Necessary for Morality?" In *Empathy: Philosophical and Psychological Perspectives*, edited by A. Coplan and P. Goldie, 211–229. New York: Oxford University Press.

Raphael, D. D. 2007. *The Impartial Spectator: Adam Smith's Moral Philosophy.* Oxford: Oxford University Press.

Reevy, G., Y. M. Ozer, and Y. Ito. 2010. *Encyclopedia of Emotion.* Santa Barbara: ABC-CLIO.

Rifkin, J. 2009. *The Empathic Civilization: The Race to Global Consciousness in a World in Crisis.* Cambridge: Polity Press.

Saucer, D. A., C. T. Miller, and N. Doucet. 2005. "Differences in Helping Whites and Blacks: A Meta-Analysis." *Personality and Social Psychology Review* 9: 2–16. doi:10.1207/s15327957pspr0901_1.

Shamay-Tsoory, S. G. 2011. "The Neural Bases for Empathy." *The Neuroscientist: A Review Journal Bringing Neurobiology, Neurology and Psychiatry* 17 (1): 18–24. doi:10.1177/1073858410379268.

Shamay-Tsoory, S. G., J. Aharon-Peretz, and D. Perry. 2009. "Two Systems for Empathy: A Double Dissociation between Emotional and Cognitive Empathy in Inferior Frontal Gyrus versus Ventromedial Prefrontal Lesions." *Brain: A Journal of Neurology* 132 (3): 617–627. doi:10.1093/brain/awn334.

Simner, M. L. 1971. "Newborn's Response to the Cry of Another Infant." *Developmental Psychology* 5 (1): 136–150. doi:10.1037/h0031066.
Singer, P. 2009. *The Life You Can Save. How to Play Your Part in Ending World Poverty*. London: Picador.
Singer, T., B. Seymour, J. O'Doherty, H. Kaube, R. J. Dolan, and C. D. Frith. 2004. "Empathy for Pain Involves the Affective but Not Sensory Components of Pain." *Science* 303 (5661): 1157–1162. doi:10.1126/science.1093535.
Slote, M. 2007. *The Ethics of Care and Empathy*. London: Routledge.
Slote, M. 2010. *Moral Sentimentalism*. New York: Oxford University Press.
Slote, M. 2013. "On Virtue Ethics." *Frontiers of Philosophy in China* 8 (1): 22–30.
Smith, A. 1774. *The Theory of Moral Sentiments: An Essay Towards an Analysis of the Principles by Which Men Naturally Judge Concerning the Conduct and Character, First of Their Neighbours, and Afterwards of Themselves. The Fourth Edition*. London: Kincaid and Bell.
Smith, A. 2009. "The Empathy Imbalance Hypothesis of Autism: A Theoretical Approach to Cognitive and Emotional Empathy in Autistic Development." *The Psychological Record* 59: 489–510. doi:10.1007/BF03395675.
Songhorian, S. 2019. "Three Conceptions of Sympathy in Adam Smith." manuscript.
Takahashi, H., M. Kato, M. Matsuura, D. Mobbs, T. Suhara, and Y. Okubo. 2009. "When Your Gain Is My Pain and Your Pain Is My Gain: Neural Correlates of Envy and Schadenfreude." *Science* 323 (5916): 937–939. doi:10.1126/science.1165604.
Weinstein, J. R. 2016. "My Understanding of Adam Smith's Impartial Spectator." *Econ Journal Watch* 13 (2): 351–358.
Xu, X., X. Zuo, X. Wang, and S. Han. 2009. "Do You Feel My Pain? Racial Group Membership Modulates Empathic Neural Responses." *The Journal of Neuroscience: the Official Journal of the Society for Neuroscience* 29 (26): 8525–8529. doi:10.1523/JNEUROSCI.2418-09.2009.

The Empathetic Soldier

Kevin Cutright

ABSTRACT
Empathy's relation to the conduct of war is ambiguous. It is mentioned sporadically in international relations theory and, perhaps surprisingly, in official military doctrine. Yet empathy's role in the military profession remains obscure, partly because it sits uneasily in military culture. Many military professionals struggle with how it is to be integrated with other, more clearly martial, virtues. Add to this struggle the confusion over what empathy actually is, and it quickly becomes easier to dismiss it or keep it at the fringes of consideration. It is my intent to clarify the concept of empathy in light of recent scholarship, and then to show the relevance of empathy to the tactical and strategic demands of war. Empathy bolsters soldiers' understanding of human actors in the operational environment and it improves soldiers' overall intentions. These benefits derive from the nature of empathy as an understanding of another's experience, including emotions, beliefs, perspectives, or intentions, and the incorporation of this knowledge into further deliberation, especially important moral judgments.

Army leaders show empathy when they genuinely relate to another person's situation, motives, and feelings. Empathy does not necessarily mean sympathy for another, but identification that leads to a deeper understanding. Empathy allows the leader to anticipate what others are experiencing and to try to envision how decisions or actions affect them. Leaders with a strong tendency for empathy can apply it to understand Army civilians [employees], soldiers and their families, local populations, and enemy combatants. The ability to see something from another person's point of view, to identify with, and enter into another person's feelings and emotions, enables the Army leader to better interact with others.
- U.S. Army Leadership Manual

Empathy is mentioned sporadically in international relations theory and U.S. military doctrine, yet empathy's role in the military profession remains obscure, partly because it sits uneasily in military culture.[1] Many struggle with how it is to be integrated with other, more clearly martial, virtues, particularly in regards to empathy with enemies. Add to this struggle the confusion over what empathy actually is, and it quickly becomes easier to dismiss it or keep it at the fringes of consideration. It is my intent to clarify the concept of empathy in light of recent scholarship, and then to show the relevance of empathy to the tactical and strategic demands of war. Empathy bolsters soldiers' understanding of human actors in the operational environment and it improves soldiers' overall intentions.[2] These benefits derive from the nature of empathy as an understanding of another's experience, including emotions, perspectives, or intentions, and the incorporation of this knowledge into further deliberation, especially moral judgments.

The nature of empathy

For the term 'empathy' to warrant our attention, it must meaningfully refer to something. Scholars have applied the term to different phenomena, often in contradictory fashion, and popular usage commonly equates it to sympathy or compassion (Batson 2009; Matravers 2017). In a recent introduction to the subject, the authors conclude:

> Given this history of the term 'empathy,' and the multiple uses to which it has been put during its short life, it is not surprising that the contributors to this volume often differ in what they mean by the term. In our view, this does not in any way present a difficulty. We believe that it would not be a good idea, even if it were possible, to attempt to regiment the term into one single meaning. (Coplan and Goldie 2011, xxxi)

I find this unsatisfying and untrue. The variety of definitions *does* present a difficulty, it generates much confusion, and it probably contributes to empathy's dismissal instead of its thoughtful consideration. It is important to remain open to the possibility of different kinds of empathy, but the contradictory definitions undermine a meaningful conception of it. As these authors highlight, the term is relatively young, so perhaps conceptual confusion is to be expected. However, it should not be embraced as a fine state.

In this section, therefore, I aim to be ecumenical in considering various conceptions of empathy, but also committed to an essence such that the term remains meaningful. Straightaway, with only a brief explanation below, I will follow the lead of many scholars and distinguish empathy from sympathy (Darwall 1998; Coplan and Goldie 2011, x–xi; Gallagher 2012, 360–362; Zahavi 2014, 115–117; Matravers 2017, 115). I will reserve my ecumenical effort for the variety of theories that treat empathy as some kind of understanding of another and not as care for another. I will not be able to resolve the debates between even these remaining conceptions of empathy. Instead, I will offer only a working definition of empathy in light of the literature and my own intuitions and analysis. I settle for this provisional definition in order to persist with the overall project of empathy's role in the military profession. By the end of this section, I hope to have made the definition clear and reasonable, not utterly convincing.

Empathy vs. sympathy

Empathy is importantly different than sympathy. Empathy is understanding what another thinks or feels, but it is not care for another's well-being (Darwall 1998, 261–270). Zahavi (2014, 139) observes, citing Edmund Husserl: 'Whereas empathy is a form of understanding, sympathy involves care and concern.' The two concepts are related; in fact, empathy may prompt and aid sympathetic concern, and sympathy may prompt attempts at an empathetic understanding of another. Conflating the terms is probably more common because of David Hume's and Adam Smith's usage of 'sympathy' in their works on moral theory; the phenomena they describe, however, correspond to the epistemic role of what we now call empathy. As noted by Stephen Darwall (1998), Hume's conception (Hume [1739] 2009, 317–319) resembles the mirroring of another's emotions in lower-level empathy, while Smith's conception (1759, 9) resembles the imaginative perspective-taking in higher-level empathy (both lower- and higher-level empathy are terms that I introduce below). The term 'empathy' did not enter the English language until a century after Hume and Smith (Stueber 2006, 5–6), which makes it harder to fault them for the confusion.

Research reinforces the intuition that empathy leads to sympathy, but it also shows that it does not necessarily do so (Batson 1991; Darwall 1998, 272–273). It can, in fact, inhibit sympathy toward some individuals while promoting it for others, given the ease with which we empathize with fellow members of cultural or social groups and the difficulty we can have in empathizing with those outside of these groups. Thus, empathy can introduce a morally problematic partiality. This concern has fueled some to argue against empathy's presumed contribution to morality (such as Prinz 2011; Bloom 2016). It also highlights the difference between empathy and sympathy.

The lay of the land

There are four general schools of thought regarding how we come to an understanding of another, specifically, another's mental states. These theoretical clusters vary in their details about the understanding that is possible and in the methods through which we achieve it. The first school of thought claims that we theoretically infer another's mental states (known variously as 'theory-theory' or 'theory of mind'; see Apperly 2011). This mode of understanding is often differentiated from empathy, but at least some researchers equate the two (see, for example, Ickes 2003). The second school of thought defines empathy as imaginatively simulating another's mental states (known as 'simulation theory;' see Goldman 2006, Stueber 2006; Coplan 2011; Matravers 2017). The third school of thought treats empathy as a theoretically unmediated perception of another's mental states (what I will call 'direct perception theory;' see Stein, Husserl, Scheler, and Schutz, as summarized and extended by Zahavi [2014, 115-191]). Finally, the fourth school of thought explains empathy as comprehending another's mental states through narrative competency (what I will call 'narrative theory;' see Gallagher 2012; Hutto 2008). Some theorists offer hybrid theories that incorporate elements from different areas, while other accounts are more exclusive, ruling out other conceptions as different phenomena in the larger topic of social cognition. Sometimes, rival conceptions are treated as necessary precursors for empathy instead of actual instances of empathy. To set the stage for a working definition, I offer a brief summary of these four schools of thought and the general themes of lower-level empathy and higher-level empathy that one finds within them.

Theory-theory

Derek Matravers clarifies this curious phrase 'theory-theory' by saying 'it is the *theory* that we each have a *theory* as to how people work' (2017, 26). In navigating our social world, proponents claim that we each construct a folk psychological framework to interpret what others do and what they likely think or feel. This approach to empathy involves one's cognitive reasoning abilities to infer what another's mental states must be, given the other's circumstances, temperament, history, and other relevant knowledge. (Therefore, I also refer to this school of thought as 'theoretical inference.') In this account of empathy, another person's mental states are assumed to be inaccessible to oneself in any direct manner. All one can do is theoretically consider what it would be like for oneself to be in the other's situation. In discussing the empathy required of the psychotherapy professional, William Ickes notes that 'the therapist must be able to accurately infer, from one moment to the next, the content of the client's successive thoughts and feelings' (2003, 67).

Consider a basic case of empathy in which one person witnesses another person shut a car door and catch his fingers between the door and the car frame. The empathizer naturally winces in virtual pain despite nothing happening to her own finger. Furthermore, she knows that the actual pain is the other's and not her own. Under theory-theory, the empathizer infers that the other is in pain because of the premise that smashed fingers hurt, which has been previously established by her own relevantly similar experiences, or by observing how others have reacted in a painful manner to relevantly similar experiences. To empathize with this victim of the car door is to identify what mental states he is experiencing through observation and reasoning.

In addition to *what* another's instantaneous mental states are, empathy as theoretical inference can reveal more general or enduring mental states that answer (at least partially) *why* another behaves the way he does. With the car door victim, a further empathetic effort might draw the empathizer's attention to the victim's young son and the fact that the son cried out just as the victim was closing the car door. The empathizer surmises that the son's cry distracted the victim at exactly the wrong moment, such that he failed to move his fingers appropriately. The empathizer has seen other parents react immediately to a child's cry, and she applies this knowledge to the case at hand. In this manner, the empathizer has ascertained what mental states the victim is immediately experiencing and has gained at least a limited grasp of why.

Simulation theory

The development of simulation theory grew out of a concern that the theoretical complexity proposed by theory-theory is untenable in light of a closer look at actual empathetic moments. When someone winces in pain while witnessing fingers smashed in a car door, the instantaneous reaction and understanding seem to defy the methodical calculations offered by theory-theory. Even the realization of the victim's distraction due to the cry of his son is a part of the empathizer's more global and simultaneous perception of the victim's situation than an act of deliberate reflection. Some theory-theorists respond by saying this deliberation is honed and habituated in most humans to a level of instinctual speed, but simulation theorists maintain that something else must be going on to overcome the inaccessibility of another's mental states. While theoretical inference may corroborate empathetic efforts, simulation theorists argue that its role is secondary and cannot explain empathy itself (Stueber 2006, 21). In addition, simulation theorists criticize theory-theory for its poor fit with developmental psychology. Children exhibit an understanding of others' mental states in infancy, yet at that same age, they are incapable of the theoretical reasoning required by theory-theory (Decety and Meltzoff 2011).

Instead, proponents of simulation theory argue for a different conception of cognitive abilities to overcome the inaccessibility of another's mental states: that of simulating another's circumstances in one's own mind. Amy Coplan defines empathy as an 'imaginative process in which an observer simulates another person's situated psychological states while maintaining clear self-other differentiation' (Coplan 2011, 5). In simulating another's situation, the empathizer not only imagines being in the other's circumstances, but, importantly, imagines being *the other* in those circumstances. This 'other-oriented perspective-taking' achieves an empathetic understanding far more reliable than 'self-oriented perspective-taking' (Coplan, 9–15). It is this kind of imaginative effort that produces the empathizer's understanding of the car door victim's pain and his distraction by his son (an understanding of both *what* and *why*), not the overtly inferential effort of theory-theory. Furthermore, in imagining the other in his circumstances, the empathizer runs them through her own mental framework 'offline,' as compared to the full 'online' engagement with her own circumstances (Darwall 1998, 271). Thus, offline simulation is seen to overcome the challenge to theory-theory of overly deliberative reflection. It also connects with the intuition that empathy is not purely theoretical; it is less of a 'cold affair, [different than] the way we understand how an airplane flies. Empathy requires first of all emotional engagement' (de Waal 2009, 72). Mentally simulating another's circumstances more readily accounts for the holistic combination of affective and cognitive components in the other's experience.

Simulation theory may have received an empirical boost with recent neuroscientific discoveries. Beginning in the 1990s, scientists observed that certain neurons in the brain fired not only when a subject performed a certain action, but when the subject observed that same action in another (Fogassi and Gallese 2002, 14–19). There was 'mental mimicry' even when there was not 'behavioral mimicry' (Goldman 2011, 34). This mental mirroring led to the label of 'mirror' neurons, and specific types of mirror neurons have been associated with behavior, sounds, and emotions (Coplan and Goldie 2011, xxix–xxx). The research has radically changed theories concerning child development. A few decades ago, the consensus was that infants were 'asocial and egocentric,' becoming socially aware in later stages of development. Now, infants are believed to have certain basic social capacities from birth, such as imitation and intersubjective communication (Decety and Meltzoff 2011). In general, the mirror neuron system is seen to help unveil the plans or intentions of others, and thus, provide at least a limited means to overcome the inaccessibility of other minds.

Direct perception theory
Some philosophers, however, resist the above schools of thought out of a concern that they miss the other-centered character of empathy. Drawing on phenomenological accounts of empathy by Edith Stein, Edmund Husserl, Max Scheler, and Alfred Schutz, Dan Zahavi argues that theory-theory and simulation theory fall prey to an 'egocentric predicament,' since they artificially restrict the phenomenon of empathy to what we might attribute to others from our own experience (Zahavi 2014, 110). To achieve a theoretical inference about another, one must insert one's own experiences or mental states as premises to interpret the other's circumstances. Similarly, Zahavi is concerned with simulating another's situation because it draws on one's own experiential base. Neither conception, in his view, accounts for the basic fact of being able to directly perceive the mental states of others. When the empathizer witnesses the father's fingers

crunched in the car door, the pain is more immediately available to her than either theoretically inferring it or simulating it. 'I experience rather than imagine or infer my friend's distress' (Zahavi 2014, 126). Empathy is not a conjecture about another's mental states, as if they were 'unobservable, theoretical posits,' but a perception of mental states in one's experience of the other (Zahavi 2014, 154). Zahavi thinks that this error of projecting mental states onto the other in the more cognitively complex accounts undermines them as proper descriptions of empathy. Instead, Zahavi defines empathy as a 'perceptually based and theoretically unmediated experience of the other' (Zahavi 2014, 98).

The direct perception account does not assume an 'epistemological gap' between the input one receives by attending to another and the output of the other's mental states, as in theoretical inference and simulation (Zahavi 2014, 175). Theory-theory suggests that this gap is overcome through conscious deliberation; simulation theory suggests that it is overcome by sub-personal processes of offline simulation. The proposal of direct perception, however, is simply that this gap is not present. Empathy is the *theoretically unmediated* perception of another's mental states; we perceive another's pain, or anger, or joy, like we perceive a lemon (Zahavi 2014, 98, 178). It is the other's mental state 'itself that I am facing, there is nothing that gets in the way, and the state is experienced as actually present to me. This is precisely what distinguishes empathy from other, more indirect forms of social cognition' (Zahavi 2014, 180). Under the theory of direct perception, the inaccessibility of other minds is a false assumption.

More precisely, the assumption is greatly exaggerated. While Zahavi maintains that empathy uniquely reveals various 'surface attitudes' of an affective or cognitive nature, he does not think it provides 'an especially profound or deep kind of understanding. In order to obtain that, theoretical inferences and imaginative simulations might very well be needed' (Zahavi 2014, 142, 151). In other words, conceiving of empathy as direct perception restricts it to providing the *what* of another's experience, but not the *why* behind it. For Zahavi, the empathizer's wincing in pain at the car door victim's injury counts as empathy; the further realization that the son's cry distracted the victim does not.

Zahavi thinks the discovery of mirror neurons is important, but he remains wary of the claims made in light of it. Mirror neuron researchers often say that mirror neurons allow 'direct experiential understanding of others,' yet also speak of mirror neurons enabling an inner imitation through which the empathizer discerns the meaning of others' actions – the *why* instead of just the *what* (Zahavi 2014, 160). Zahavi finds a tension here, since only the former stance seems to respect the phenomenological point about the givenness of the other's experience. With imitation, the empathizer projects meaning instead of receiving it (or maintaining it as unknown). Furthermore, Zahavi warns that we must be precise with what mirror neurons actually provide. They may help 'decode another agent's motor intentions, [but] they cannot help us to determine his or her prior intentions' (Zahavi 2014, 159). It is overly ambitious to claim that mirror neurons reveal the meaning behind the behavior, even if they plausibly convey the person's particular mental states of the moment.

Narrative theory

Zahavi's projective error is an important challenge to theory-theory and simulation theory, but some think that Zahavi risks an error in the other direction by limiting empathy to only that which is directly perceived in face-to-face encounters. Shaun Gallagher, for example, offers a phenomenologically informed concept of 'direct social perception' that closely resembles Zahavi's theoretically unmediated perception (Gallagher 2015, 452). However, Gallagher maintains empathy as something more than this perceptual act, something that requires an understanding of 'the context of the other, where context means more than perceptual context and includes historical and cultural aspects' (Gallagher 2012, 377). When we empathize, Gallagher suggests that we aspire to the meaning behind the other's actions, not just the other's current mental states. Empathy is more of an achievement than it is a default, automatic, and largely subconscious perception: 'Yet, saying that I empathize with you, seems to suggest more than just understanding your mental state; it seems to mean more than simply perceiving that you are in pain...' (Gallagher 2012, 358).

Gallagher, therefore, crafts his definition of empathy with an emphasis on understanding the *why* instead of merely the *what*. He argues that our employment of narrative frameworks is the best explanation for how we empathetically understand others:

> [Narratives] give us a form or structure that we can use in understanding others. That is, we learn from narrative how to frame an understanding of others. We start to see others engaged in their actions, not simply in terms of the immediate and occurrent context. We start to see them as engaged in longer-term projects (plots) that add meaning to what they are doing. (Gallagher 2012, 371)

By defining empathy in terms of narrative competency, Gallagher thinks he can avoid the egocentric predicament that motivates Zahavi's critique of theory-theory and simulation theory. The empathizer is not restricted to her own experiences from which she projects certain mental states onto the other. Instead, the empathizer's familiarity with a variety of narratives frees her to genuinely receive the other's experience on its own terms. Gallagher says:

> If we take this other-directedness [of empathy] in a strong sense, then it is not just that empathy is oriented to the other in a way that allows me to reduce the other to my own experience; rather, it means that I am open to the experience

and the life of the other, in their context, as I can understand it, not in terms of my own narrow experience, but in terms that can be drawn from a diversity of narratives that inform my understanding. (Gallagher 2012, 372)

Also, grounding empathy in narrative competency helps to accommodate the empathetic moments we seem to have for others outside of face-to-face encounters. Whether faced with the stories of struggling communities in distant lands, or historical figures in a biography, or fictional characters in text, film, or other media, there is something right in saying that we come to understand, at least to some extent, what they think and feel. Empathy seems the appropriate term for these phenomena, in addition to the understanding prompted by face-to-face encounters.

If we return to the case of the car door victim, the narrative approach to empathy would categorize the empathizer's wincing in pain as a pre-empathetic moment of direct social perception. It may contribute to empathy, but the genuinely empathetic turn is in understanding the victim's commitment to the welfare of the young child given the father-son relationship, which helps to explain why the victim was distracted to the point of failing to move his fingers out of the way of the car door.

Lower-level and higher-level empathy

It has probably become apparent in these summaries that there is a distinction in the literature between lower-level and higher-level cognitive phenomena. Lower-level empathy is generally considered to be subconscious, automatic, and revealing 'surface' mental states of emotion and immediate intentions. Higher-level empathy is seen as conscious, voluntary, and revealing deeper or more enduring mental states, including broad intentions or the meaning behind the behavior (Coplan and Goldie 2011, xxxiii). The research on mirror neurons has arguably substantiated the notion of lower-level empathy, whereas its support for simulation theory (or other conceptions of higher-level empathy) remains controversial (Stueber 2006, 131–151; Matravers 2017, 52–61).

Zahavi's account of direct perception counts as lower-level empathy. Coplan's simulation theory and Gallagher's narrative approach count as higher-level empathy. When empathy is grounded in theory-theory (as in Ickes 2003), then this grounding would also count as higher-level empathy, in that it is conscious, voluntary, and aiming for the meaning behind the behavior. Zahavi restricts empathy to only the lower-level form; in his account, higher-level cognitive processes should be treated as other elements of social cognition, not as another form of empathy. Alternatively, Coplan argues the opposite: lower-level processes should not be considered empathy, but simply necessary for it (Coplan 2011, 5). Gallagher also maintains empathy as something more than an automatic and shallow understanding of another's momentary mental states.

Some accounts, however, recognize both levels as forms of empathy. Karsten Stueber distinguishes between basic and reenactive empathy; Alvin Goldman distinguishes between mirroring and reconstructive empathy (Stueber 2006; Goldman 2011). While not identical, their conceptions conform to the general distinction above between lower- and higher-level forms of empathy. Stueber's framework will suffice as an example of accommodating both.

Stueber's basic empathy is 'our theoretically unmediated quasi-perceptual ability to recognize other creatures directly as minded creatures and to recognize them implicitly as creatures that are fundamentally like us' (Stueber 2006, 20). This notion of basic empathy closely resembles Zahavi's direct perception. Both accounts give empathy a perceptual character, and both describe empathy as our means of identifying another as a sentient person rather than an inert object (Zahavi 2014, 118–125). Stueber's basic empathy also indicates another's immediate motor intentions and emotions, as facilitated by the mirror neuron system (Stueber 2006, 147).

Stueber's basic empathy, therefore, gives the empathizer a *that* – that someone is, say, angry. His reenactive empathy proceeds further to give the empathizer a *why* – why someone is angry. He defines reenactive empathy as 'using our cognitive and deliberative capacities in order to reenact or imitate in our own mind the thought processes of the other person..' (Stueber 2006, 21). Stueber's higher-level empathy is a simulative one similar to Coplan's above. Unlike Coplan, however, Stueber maintains the lower-level processes as a form of empathy. Both provide an understanding of another, and together, they provide a more complete picture of the other's experience.

Working definition

I want to suggest that the nature of empathy is grasping the felt characteristic of another person's experience (Smith 2015, 712). This felt characteristic is not restricted to feelings, but includes the feel of things beyond immediate feelings, such as desires, convictions, intentions, worries, commitments – nearly any part of another's mental life, including the feel of her cognitive life (at least, how it feels to have certain cognitive commitments or inclinations). If one's friend says, 'I just voted for the candidate whom I've been campaigning for over the last several weeks,' there are both cognitive and affective states associated with this experience. The friend's cognitive states of, say, believing her preferred candidate is the best one, or believing it is important to exercise one's right to vote, etc., exists concurrently with affective states of hoping the candidate follows through on her platform, or fretting about the candidate's chances of winning, or feeling confidence in the campaigning effort, or feeling relief that the campaigning is over, or, more importantly, a complex combination of these. Furthermore, these cognitive and affective states are mutually causative, meaning they may prompt or reinforce each other. Empathy is understanding, to some degree, how this overarching experience of voting (after campaigning) feels for one's friend, given a complex interplay of cognition and affect grounded in specific circumstances and context.

Empathy is not, therefore, just assigning a generic feeling of hope or nervousness to one's friend. As Scheler suggests, empathy is not 'simply a question of intellectually judging that somebody else is undergoing a certain experience; it is not the mere thought that this is the case…' (as cited by Zahavi 2014, 118). Empathy is specifically oriented on the other's experience in its phenomenality. In other words, empathy provides a limited understanding of what another experiences; not a description of that experience (which depends, among other things, on the empathizer's ability to verbalize it), but the phenomenal nature of it. As a working definition, then, I endorse Joel Smith's conception of empathy as an experiential understanding of *what* another feels or thinks, not just a propositional or theoretical understanding *that* the other feels or thinks a certain way (Smith 2015, 712–713). Accordingly, theory-theory cannot serve as an adequate conception of empathy, because it is, by definition, a propositional or theoretical approach to another's mental states.

Lower-level empathy complies with this definition of empathy as long as the felt characteristic that it produces is attributed to the other person. In some accounts of lower-level empathy, this condition is not met ('affective empathy' in Maibom 2014, 2–5; 'mirroring' in Goldman 2011, 33). For example, one lower-level process that is sometimes considered a kind of empathy is emotional contagion. In this process, one catches the emotion of another (or the shared emotion of a group) as one's own affective state, without recognizing it as another's. However, I will follow most empathy theorists in considering attribution necessary for empathy: the empathizer has 'some sort of intentional attitude directed toward the target by which the resonating state is linked to him' (Goldman 2011, 34; see also Stueber 2006, 20; Coplan 2011, 5; Gallagher 2012, 358; Zahavi 2014, 189; Matravers 2017, 76). In defining empathy as an understanding of another's experience, I am restricting it to those affective or cognitive states that one attributes to another, whether or not it is also a state that one shares.

Higher-level empathy can also meet this definition of empathy – the felt characteristic of another's an experience – despite the risk of projecting one's own thoughts and feelings onto the other. Zahavi's work captures the basic idea that empathy entails a receptive mode of taking in another's experience, but it does not account for the possibility of the receptive mode persisting through an imaginative or theoretical consideration of the other. It is possible to imagine and theorize about the other while respecting the givenness of the other's experience. One can maintain an attitude akin to Stephen Darwall's recognition respect, whose object 'is not excellence or merit; it is dignity or authority' (Darwall 2009, 122–123). The respect is in recognizing the other's experience as valid or legitimate in a minimal sense: it is an experience being had by a human. (Such respect does not entail agreeing with the other's perspectives, feelings, intentions, plans, or commitments, which would rise to the level of Darwall's appraisal respect.) Simulation and theoretical inference need not be strictly projective if the empathizer maintains Darwall's recognition respect and allows her pursuit of empathetic knowledge through imaginative effort to be informed and corrected by the input and authority of the other. Although Zahavi's definition of empathy as a theoretically unmediated perception of the other is a careful elucidation of considering another without preconceptions, we should also be open to the possibility of theoretically mediated efforts to attend to the other with a similar commitment.

In this regard, at least some imaginative efforts, like Coplan's other-oriented perspective-taking, can be done respectfully and do not necessarily involve the strict, one-way projection motivating Zahavi's concern, and can, therefore, contribute to empathetic understanding. The same can be said regarding Gallagher's narrative approach to empathy. The key is the respect with which the empathizer makes these attempts. Genuinely pursuing empathy is to 'quarantine our own preferences, values, and beliefs' in order to grasp those of another (Coplan 2011, 15), and there is nothing inherent to imaginative or theoretical efforts that rule this out. In fact, recent neuroscientific research indicates that different parts of the brain engage when taking on a self- vs. other-oriented perspective, providing some empirical basis for this possibility (Lamm, Batson, and Decety 2007).

Given that both lower-level and higher-level empathy are compatible with this working definition, I will include both. I share Zahavi's projective concern of higher-level processes, but I also share the intuition of Gallagher and others that empathy refers to an achievement that is something more than a shallow understanding of another's surface mental states. In line with Stein and Stueber, I propose that we should consider empathy as a perception-like faculty in which higher-level empathetic abilities build on lower-level empathetic input. Conceiving of lower-level empathetic processes as akin to sensory input is already present in the accounts of Zahavi, Stueber, Gallagher, and Coplan (though, to be precise, the latter two want to restrict the term 'empathy' to higher-level processes). Furthermore, the idea of empathy as the combination of raw sensory input plus higher cognitive processing helps to illustrate how they complement each other and how the empathetic endeavor can go wrong.

On the one hand, lower-level empathy unrefined by higher-level empathy can result in knowing less than what could be known. The empathizer would only perceive the other's immediate mental states with no appreciation for the *why* behind his behavior. It would be similar to the error of raw visual input with no higher cognitive processing – seeing color and shape but not piecing together the image to perceive *tree*. Admittedly, there may be some rudimentary interpretation built into lower-level empathy; Zahavi notes the philosophical work that establishes the sub-personal interpretation of context that occurs in visual perception (Zahavi 2014, 163–164). However, this does not do justice to the contributions that higher-level processes make in understanding the full meaning of another's experience.

Conversely, higher-level empathy unanchored by lower-level empathetic input can result in the error of projection that motivates Zahavi's critique of theory-theory and simulation theory. If not corrected by the perceptual act of lower-level empathy (as enabled, perhaps, by the mirror neuron system) the theoretical or imaginative work of higher-level empathy is free to draw conclusions about the other's mental states based solely on assumptions about the other, or based on the empathizer's own experiences, values, intentions, or prejudices. In Coplan's words, 'we don't just fail to understand others' subjective experiences; we often assume that we do understand them, which leads to a new set of problems' (Coplan 2011, 11–12). It would be similar to the error of cognitive processing overriding raw visual input, which, when taken to an extreme, is a moment of hallucination, 'a seemingly real perception of something not actually present' (Oxford English Dictionary). When higher cognitive effort at empathizing with another is not tethered by a receptive mode toward the other's actual experience, it risks turning into an overly theoretical, presumptuous, and self-deceiving exercise.

Taken as a cohesive whole, lower- and higher-level empathy each contribute to the achievement of understanding the other's experience in its synergy of cognitive states, affective states, and specific circumstances.

Empathy and soldiering

There is a crucial epistemic upshot to empathy. It offers what 'no third-person form of scientific understanding can: understanding of another person from the "inside"' (Coplan 2011, 18). Coplan and Zahavi call this inside view an 'experiential understanding' of another's lived experience (Coplan 2011, 17; Zahavi 2014, 151). Cultural anthropologists distinguish between an 'emic' and an 'etic' understanding, where 'emic' refers to the meanings and interpretations that determine behavior and 'etic' refers to only the observable behavior itself (Lavenda and Schultz 2007, 43). The physical sciences aim solely for an etic understanding of their inanimate subjects; there is no sense in a chemist seeking an emic understanding of molecules. The subject matter of physical science lends itself to explanation through causal relationships derived from observable behavior. When accurate, these explanations offer a great amount of certainty and predictive power. In the social sciences, on the other hand, practitioners seek a greater understanding of 'the meaning of actions,' the impetus behind decisions, which yields less certainty and predictability (Coplan and Goldie 2011, xv-xvi). Unlike the chemist, the psychologist and anthropologist study 'molecules with minds of their own' (Gaddis 2002, 111). Empathy is inherent to the practice of the social sciences insofar as they aim for this 'inside' knowledge instead of strict causal principles, which human nature persistently defies. As Stueber concludes, 'empathy must be regarded as of central epistemic importance and as the epistemic default mode in understanding other agents' (2006, 219).

This distinction between etic and emic understanding is similar to Eleonore Stump's difference between 'knowledge *that*' and 'knowledge *of*.' Stump draws a correspondence to left-brain and right-brain skills, respectively. The precision and analytic detail associated with the left hemisphere of the brain lend themselves to propositional knowledge *that*, while the breadth of focus and capacity for narrative associated with the right hemisphere is better for interpersonal knowledge *of* (Stump 2010, 23-25). The difference shows up in the contrast between 'knowing about Andrew' vs. simply 'knowing Andrew,' or 'what I know about Iraqis' vs. 'the Iraqis I know.' Stump argues that both types of knowledge are important and that neither is reducible to the other, though she notes that propositional knowledge is by far the most common in philosophical discourse. This predisposition becomes most pronounced when humans are involved: 'The deficit will perhaps be undetectable in work on modal logic or philosophy of mathematics, but in any issues where the interactions of persons make a difference it is more likely to be in evidence' (Stump 2010, 25).

Besides modal logic and philosophy of mathematics, this deficit is visible in the study and practice of war. Military professionals have often approached war as physical scientists, treating their subject as inert and requiring only a sufficient level of etic understanding to achieve victory. An extreme example is the work of Adam Heinrich Dietrich von Bulow, a Prussian military theorist who claimed to have reduced military strategy to a geometrical science involving the lines of operation between attacker and defender (Gat 2001, 81-96). A less extreme example, but one that nevertheless displays the same deficit, is the U.S. military's investment in cultural knowledge over the last 17 years.

Once the conventional conflict against the Iraqi army ended in the summer of 2003, military forces faced the more interpersonal and political challenge of establishing security and fostering a new regime in Iraq (paralleling the effort in Afghanistan). In the ensuing years, each branch of the U.S. military established cultural centers of expertise, mandated culture awareness training, increased incentives for fluency in foreign languages, and revised the curriculums of professional education to better address cultural matters (Abbe and Halpin 2009, 20–31). The most public and controversial effort involved hiring anthropologists and sociologists to embed with military units and provide cultural expertise (Jaschik 2015; Kassel 2015). However, this investment in propositional knowledge about the Iraqi and Afghan cultures provided only meager improvement in the ability to persuade, influence, and win the cooperation of the populace. Military personnel remained ill-prepared to take on persuasion in the wake of coercion, or more accurately, to weave the right mix of these into operational plans (and continues to face this struggle in Afghanistan).

Empathy is the key element that balances the military's customary predisposition for an etic understanding with the vital insights of an emic understanding. As Carl von Clausewitz (another Prussian military theorist) states, the 'essential difference is that war is not an exercise of the will directed at inanimate matter...continual striving after laws analogous to those appropriate to the realm of the inanimate matter was bound to lead to one mistake after another' (Clausewitz 1832, 149). An etic understanding of war is necessary since it involves inanimate elements like terrain, weather, and weapon ranges; but this understanding is insufficient by itself. Military personnel also require an emic understanding that accommodates the human element. Empathy helps to attain that emic understanding, to employ cultural knowledge not as simplistic rules of behavior, but as the foundation for grasping another person's unique sense-making.

Keeping killing in its place

Along with the epistemic benefit of an emic understanding of others, empathy carries a corresponding moral benefit. Soldiers with empathy are more capable of maintaining the act of killing as a necessary and regrettable task instead of treating it as their overarching *raison d'etre*. In the language of the just war tradition, empathy enables soldiers to maintain a right intention toward a just and lasting peace. Specifically, empathy aids soldiers in resisting the dehumanization of others, especially enemies. Empathy reveals the bare fact of an enemy's humanity, as well as elements of his experience, including values, desires, and intentions. These elements are useful for tactical decisions in fighting an enemy, but even more importantly, they improve judgments regarding a shared peace and undergird a right intention toward that peace.

There should always be an eye kept toward the end goal of peace, even by soldiers.[3] Their conduct affects the prospects for peace. While killing, injuring, incapacitating, threatening, and forcefully detaining others are inherent to combat actions, they must be done in light of the overarching purpose they are to serve. Furthermore, while soldiers may need to attenuate empathetic impulses to proficiently complete these combat actions, it should be a temporary interruption of one's empathetic faculty, not a denial of the enemy's humanity.

Maintaining the humanity of the enemy is commonly considered impossible; for many, it is a self-evident truth 'that men cannot kill an enemy understood to be honorable and like oneself' (Shay 1994, 103). Contrary to the argument that soldiers *must* dehumanize enemies to kill them, however, there are at least some moments when they *cannot* dehumanize enemies because of intimate encounters with them. Michael Walzer offers some of these instances, drawing on veterans' memoirs in which they describe the difficulty of firing their weapons at enemy soldiers 'who look funny, who are taking a bath, holding up their pants [as they run along a trench], reveling in the sun, [or] smoking a cigarette' (1977, 138–143). Richard Holmes observes that the 'concept of a hateful and inhuman enemy rarely survives contact with him as an individual' (1985, 368). These moments are, admittedly, only brief glimpses at the humanity of individuals, glimpses that are often buried under the propaganda of the war effort and the piercing emotions of struggle and loss inherent to war. However, simply stifling these empathetic moments leads to the dangers of dehumanization and embracing killing as one's overarching purpose. Right intention is lost. In reconciling the humanity of enemies with a duty to kill them, there must be an alternative to dehumanization, which merely tries to deny the former.[4]

Instead of dehumanizing enemies, I suggest a management of one's empathy that is similar to the management of one's senses. Just as one can attune one's ear to detect certain sounds over others, one can focus one's empathy in selective ways. This empathetic attunement already happens in various contexts, and there are immoral moments of it in which we get too selective. This partiality is particularly common in war, where the empathy with one's comrades can drown out the empathy with enemies or noncombatants. The case of justified killing in war, however, counts as a morally appropriate moment.

Outside of this concession for the justified killing act, empathy should not be suppressed in war. Indeed, it cannot be, at least with any finality, given the instinctive nature of lower-level empathy, the unavoidable empathetic moments that occur in war, and the introspection that follows combat for most every soldier. Soldiers are humans, and therefore, are hard-wired for empathy. Despite extensive military training, a human automaton is an impossible goal. It is also an immoral goal, since an automaton cannot maintain a disposition to a just and lasting peace, but must be equipped with merely a program of activity. It thus lacks the judgment needed to properly wield lethal force across the range of circumstances a soldier may face. Thirdly, an automaton is a tactically foolish goal: it cannot adapt to genuinely novel circumstances, since it is only equipped with a checklist, however elaborate.

Consider a recent example of pursuing a just and lasting peace in the heat of combat. Phil Klay offers an account of how acts that demonstrate the right intention can rival, and probably exceed, acts of tactical skill in contributing to the defense of the United States. He compares the actions of a U.S. Marine platoon leader in braving the dangers of combat in Iraq, killing (lawfully) numerous enemy combatants, with the actions of a Marine infantry squad and medical team in caring for those wounded in a firefight. The medical team proved unable to save the life of a dying Marine; however, immediately after this man's death, the enemy sniper who had shot him arrived at the base. Klay continues:

> That dead Marine's squadmates had engaged the sniper in a firefight, shot him a couple of times, patched him up, bandaged him and called for a casualty evacuation to save the life of the man who'd killed their friend.... And the medical staff members, still absorbing the blow of losing a Marine, got to work. They stabilized their enemy and pumped him full of American blood, donated from the "walking blood bank" of nearby Marines. The sniper lived. And then they put him on a helicopter to go to a hospital for follow-up care, and one of the Navy nurses was assigned to be his flight nurse. He told me later of the strangeness of sitting in the back of a helicopter, watching over his enemy lying peacefully unconscious, doped up on painkillers, while he kept checking the sniper's vitals.... That nurse, in the quiet, alone with that insurgent, with no one looking as he cared for his patient. That was an act of war. (Klay 2017)

Klay means an act of war in a strategic sense, one that helps to win the war of ideas rather than only the lethal clashes on the ground. The tactical skill and lethality of the Marine platoon leader above is more commonly associated with securing a nation, but the moral courage of these Marines in caring for the wounded insurgent contributes in vital ways, as well. As Klay comments later, the reputation of the U.S. in maintaining a right intention initially spared American and Iraqi soldiers (and noncombatants) from the dangers of combat, since Iraqi soldiers surrendered in great numbers in 2003, anticipating fair treatment. After the dehumanizing crimes against detainees at Abu Ghraib, however, and the subsequent swelling of the insurgency's ranks, the country's stained moral reputation 'had started killing American soldiers.' Avoiding dehumanization has its own contribution to make to a nation's security.

Concluding thoughts

Achieving empathy is harder than it may first appear, as Gallagher underscores in his work. We are swayed by our own emotional capacity and the phenomenality of our own experience. We easily and unconsciously presume that another's experience will mimic our own. We may even stubbornly resist the possibility of a different phenomenality than what we have correlated to the same kind of circumstances. Empathy, however, entails an appreciative understanding that recognizes another's experience as genuine even if not the same as ours. Being empathetic does not require agreeing with the other's perspective or adopting the other's perspective as our own, but it does require recognizing the other's authority regarding his own experience. We are not free to dismiss the other's experience as incomprehensible or impossible, because its possibility is instantiated in the other person and empathy reveals the person's experience to us.

There is, therefore, always a thread of solidarity between empathizer and the other in some kind of shared human nature or shared conditions for the possibility of experience. This shared human condition enables both a minimal degree of solidarity and a minimal degree of empathy, despite great socio-cultural differences. Beyond this foundational solidarity, however, the myriad differences with the other take over, and the correspondence of solidarity and empathy falls away. The *understanding of* another's experience becomes pointedly distinct from *identifying with* another's experience.

To empathize is to expose oneself to a kind of vulnerability. Seeking an empathetic understanding of another's experience means exposing oneself to its affective aspect. This aspect may be unfamiliar, unpleasant, uncomfortable, inconvenient, or painful. It can also be unnerving and possibly damaging in some way. In empathetically considering the immoral behavior of others, Stump writes,

> The mirror neuron system [underlying empathy] gives the viewer some no doubt limited sense of what it feels like to do such things and to want to do them. And feeling what it feels like to do and to want to do such things can be very troubling if the things in question are deeply revulsive to one's moral sensibilities, to one's own beliefs and desires. (Stump 2018, 160)

So it is understandable that we sometimes resist empathy. Indeed, avoiding the affective character of another's experience is sometimes commendable. In combat, for example, soldiers need to carefully manage 'emotional engagement' with the injuries and suffering of enemies, noncombatants, and comrades that might otherwise overwhelm their judgment with empathetic pain (de Waal 2009, 72). The soldiers remain obligated to recognizing the injuries and the suffering in a propositional sense, even if they rightly avoid an empathetic appreciation. Yet, these avoidances should remain temporary interruptions to their automatic lower-level empathy enabled by the mirror neuron system. As de Waal observes, the 'automaticity' of mirror neurons does not mean a lack of control: 'My breathing, for instance, is fully automated, yet I remain in charge' (2009, 79). Or, it is like the faculty of seeing or hearing, whose exercise is generally automatic, with only occasional exceptions to shade one's eyes and avoid looking directly at the sun or to wear earplugs and avoid exposure to harmful levels of sound. The soldier may need to interrupt empathy, but, like seeing or hearing, it ought to be temporary due to the relevant awareness that the faculty provides. Furthermore, the soldier has a concomitant need to process stifled emotions that are inextricably linked to war.[5]

These limited exceptions aside, empathy is good to achieve because it is an experiential understanding that reveals what another is experiencing and why (empathy's instrumental value), and because it expresses recognition respect (in this manner, empathy is an end in itself). Empathy reinforces the humanity of others, which is particularly vital for soldiers exposed to countervailing forces that threaten to dehumanize others.

Notes

1. For a sample of empathy in theories of international relations, see Laura Sjoberg, *Gendering Global Conflict: Toward a Feminist Theory of War* (New York: Columbia University Press, 2013), Matt Waldman, 'Strategic Empathy: the Afghanistan intervention shows why the U.S. must empathize with its enemies,' New America Foundation (April 2014); and Robert Scales, 'Clausewitz and World War IV,' *Armed Forces Journal* (July 2006). For empathy in U.S. military doctrine, see U.S. Army Field Manual 3-24 *Insurgencies and Countering Insurgencies* (2014); U.S. Army Field Manual 3-07.1 *Security Force Assistance* (2009); U.S. Army Doctrinal Publication 6-22 *Army Leadership* (2012); and U.S. Army Doctrinal Reference Publication 6-22 *Army Leadership* (2012). The epigraph is taken from this last reference (p. 3-3).
2. The term 'soldiers' sometimes refers to only junior enlisted members of an army, but I use it in its more general form to refer to members of any rank. In addition, many points regarding soldiers apply just as well to members of the Air Force, Navy, and Marines.
3. The degree and extent of this obligation varies with one's position and duties. Soldiers in the heat of combat should not be focused on what peace terms the opposing political leaders might accommodate. They should, however, remain attentive to the possibility of their enemy counterparts surrendering. The degree of obligation increases for those soldiers involved not in the heat of combat, but in the cooler endeavors of determining strategic objectives, planning the campaigns to secure those objectives, and assessing the war's progress.
4. The pacifist response is to deny the latter – there is never a duty to kill. While I part ways with the pacifist stance at a certain point, I share Brian Orend's concern that there can be an 'embarrassing arrogance' in just war literature regarding pacifism (2001, 435–436). We all ought to have a pacifist commitment to non-violent conflict resolution as a default. It is a *prima facie* commitment that even soldiers should maintain, understanding that their duties involve a judgment about circumstances that push past a threshold of this commitment. In counterinsurgencies, especially, with no clear front lines, this judgment is required of soldiers lower down the chain of command, despite it often being more difficult to make.
5. Stifling empathy, therefore, may lead to conditions like moral injury, a debilitating sense of guilt among veterans that is receiving increasing attention. For an introduction, see Jonathan Shay (1994); Nancy Sherman, *Afterwar: Healing the Moral Wounds of our Soldiers* (New York: Oxford University Press, 2015); and David Wood, *What Have We Done: The Moral Injury of Our Longest Wars* (New York: Little, Brown and Company, 2016).

Disclosure statement

No potential conflict of interest was reported by the author. Furthermore, the views expressed in this article are those of the author only and do not reflect the official views of any agency of the U.S. government.

References

Abbe, A., and S. M. Halpin. 2009. "The Cultural Imperative for Professional Military Education and Leader Development." *Parameters* 39: 20–31.
Apperly, I. 2011. *Mindreaders: The Cognitive Basis of 'Theory of Mind.'* New York: Psychology Press.
Batson, C. D. 1991. *The Altruism Question: Toward a Social-Psychological Answer.* Hillsdale, NJ: Erlbaum.
Batson, C. D. 2009. "These Things Called Empathy: Eight Related but Distinct Phenomena." In *The Social Neuroscience of Empathy*, edited by J. Decety and W. Ickes, 3–15. Cambridge, MA: MIT Press.
Bloom, P. 2016. *Against Empathy.* New York: HarperCollins.
Coplan, A., and P. Goldie. 2011. "Introduction." In *Empathy: Philosophical and Psychological Perspectives*, edited by A. Coplan and P. Goldie. New York: Oxford University Press, ix–xlvii.
Coplan, A. 2011. "Understanding Empathy: Its Features and Effects." In *Empathy: Philosophical and Psychological Perspectives*, edited by A. Coplan and P. Goldie, 3–18. New York: Oxford University Press.
Darwall, S. 1998. "Empathy, Sympathy, and Care." *Philosophical Studies* 89: 261–282. doi:10.1023/A:1004289113917.
Darwall, S. 2009. *The Second-Person Standpoint: Morality, Respect, and Accountability.* Cambridge, MA: Harvard University Press.
de Waal, F. 2009. *The Age of Empathy: Nature's Lessons for a Kinder Society.* New York: Three Rivers Press.
Decety, J., and A. Meltzoff. 2011. "Empathy, Imitation, and the Social Brain." In *Empathy: Philosophical and Psychological Perspectives*, edited by A. Coplan and P. Goldie, 58–81. New York: Oxford University Press.
Fogassi, L., and V. Gallese. 2002. "The Neural Correlates of Action Understanding in Non-Human Primates." In *Mirror Neurons and the Evolution of Brain and Language*, edited by V. Gallese and M. Stamenov, 13–35. Philadelphia: John Benjamins Publishing.
Gaddis, J. L. 2002. *The Landscape of History: How Historians Map the Past.* New York: Oxford University Press.
Gallagher, S. 2012. "Empathy, Simulation, and Narrative." *Science in Context* 25 (3): 355–381. doi:10.1017/S0269889712000117.
Gallagher, S. 2015. "The New Hybrids: Continuing Debates on Social Perception." *Consciousness and Cognition* 36: 452–465. doi:10.1016/j.concog.2015.04.002.
Gat, A. 2001. *A History of Military Thought: From the Enlightenment to the Cold War.* New York: Oxford University Press.
Goldman, A. 2006. *Simulating Minds: The Philosophy, Psychology, and Neuroscience of Mindreading.* Oxford: Oxford University Press.
Goldman, A. 2011. "Two Routes to Empathy." In *Empathy: Philosophical and Psychological Perspectives*, edited by A. Coplan and P. Goldie, 31–44. New York: Oxford University Press.

Holmes, R. 1985. *Acts of War: The Behavior of Men in Battle*. New York: Free Press.
Hume, D. [1739] 2009. *A Treatise of Human Nature*. Edited by L. A. Selby-Bigge. Revised by P.H Nidditch. Reprint. 2nd ed. New York: Oxford University Press.
Hutto, D. 2008. *Folk Psychological Narratives: The Socio-Cultural Basis of Understanding Reasons*. Cambridge, MA: MIT Press.
Ickes, W. 2003. *Everyday Mind Reading: Understanding What Other People Think and Feel*. Amherst, NY: Prometheus Books.
Jaschik, S. 2015. "Embedded Conflicts." *Inside Higher Ed*. 7 July 2015.
Kassel, W. 2015. "The Army Needs Anthropologists." *Foreign Policy*, 28 July 2015.
Klay, P. 2017. "What We're Fighting for." *New York Times*, 10 February 2017.
Lamm, C., C. D. Batson, and J. Decety. 2007. "The Neural Substrate of Human Empathy: Effects of Perspective Taking and Cognitive Appraisal." *Journal of Cognitive Neuroscience* 19 (1): 42–58. doi:10.1162/jocn.2007.19.1.42.
Lavenda, R. H., and E. A. Schultz. 2007. *Core Concepts in Cultural Anthropology*. 3rd ed. Boston: McGraw-Hill.
Maibom, H. 2014. "Introduction: (Almost) Everything You Ever Wanted to Know about Empathy." In *Empathy and Morality*, edited by H. Maibom, 1–40. Oxford: Oxford University Press.
Matravers, D. 2017. *Empathy*. Malden, MA: Polity Press.
Orend, B. 2001. "A Just War Critique of Realism and Pacifism." *Journal of Philosophical Research* XXVI: 435–477. doi:10.5840/jpr_2001_11.
Prinz, J. 2011. "Is Empathy Necessary for Morality?" In *Empathy: Philosophical and Psychological Perspectives*, edited by A. Coplan and P. Goldie, 211–229. New York: Oxford University Press.
Shay, J. 1994. *Achilles in Vietnam: Combat Trauma and the Undoing of Character*. New York: Scribner.
Smith, A. [1759] 2002. The Theory of Moral Sentiments, edited by K. Haakonssen. Cambridge: Cambridge University Press.
Smith, J. 2015. "What Is Empathy For?" *Synthese* 194: 709–722. doi:10.1007/s11229-015-0771-8.
Stueber, K. 2006. *Rediscovering Empathy: Agency, Folk Psychology, and the Human Sciences*. Cambridge, MA: MIT Press.
Stump, E. 2010. *Wandering in Darkness: Narrative and the Problem of Suffering*. Oxford: Oxford University Press.
Stump, E. 2018. *Atonement*. Oxford: Oxford University Press.
U.S. Army. 2009. *Field Manual 3-07.1: Security Force Assistance*. Fort Leavenworth: Combined Arms Doctrine Directorate.
U.S. Army. 2012a. *Army Doctrinal Publication 6-22: Army Leadership*. Fort Leavenworth: Combined Arms Doctrine Directorate.
U.S. Army. 2012b. *Army Doctrinal Reference Publication 6-22: Army Leadership*. Fort Leavenworth: Combined Arms Doctrine Directorate.
U.S. Army. 2014. *Field Manual 3-24: Insurgencies and Countering Insurgencies*. Fort Leavenworth: Combined Arms Doctrine Directorate.
von Clausewitz, C. [1832] 1976. *On War*. Tr. by Michael Howard and Peter Paret. Princeton, NJ: Princeton University Press.
Walzer, M. 1977. *Just and Unjust Wars: A Moral Argument with Historical Illustrations*. Philadelphia, PA: Basic Books.
Zahavi, D. 2014. *Self and Other: Exploring Subjectivity, Empathy, and Shame*. New York: Oxford University Press.

Sentimentalist Practical Reason and Self-Sacrifice

Michael Slote

> **ABSTRACT**
> For obvious reasons sentimentalists have been hesitant to offer accounts of moral reasons for action: the whole idea at least initially smacks of rationalist notions of morality. But the sentimentalist can seek to *reduce* practical to sentimentalist considerations and that is what the present paper attempts to do. Prudential reasons can be identified with the normal emotional/motivational responses people feel in situations that threaten them or offer them opportunities to attain what they need. And in the most basic cases altruistic/moral reasons involve the empathic transfer of one person's prudential reasons and emotions to another person or persons who can help them. Practical/moral reasons for self-sacrifice also depend on empathic transfer and can vary in strength with the strength of the transfer.

1.

In my opinion, self-sacrifice occupies the center of morality: I wouldn't be inclined to call someone a morally good or decent individual if they were totally unwilling ever to make any sacrifice of their own welfare for the sake of others. So in all consistency I hold that a full and adequate account of morality needs to be able to find a place for self-sacrifice. This is something I shall try to accomplish here, but rather than run through and criticize or borrow from more familiar accounts of the ethics of self-sacrifice, I am going to approach the issue from my own distinctive standpoint as a moral sentimentalist. I am going to try to show you how a sentimentalist can allow for reasons to sacrifice oneself, but I think I need to embed that account within a general sentimentalist framework for understanding practical reasons. And it is not obvious how a sentimentalist can really do such a thing. After all, sentimentalists think that moral virtue and moral claims about right and wrong, virtue and vice, are based in sentiment, not reason, and previous sentimentalists have been reluctant to connect, or have been at least ambivalent about connecting, morality with reasons for action.

For example, Hume in the *Treatise of Human Nature* claims that calm passions are often 'confounded' with reason (Book II, Part III, Section III), but almost immediately afterwards (Book II, Part III, Section VIII) he says that 'by *reason* we mean affections ... such as operate more calmly...'. Similarly, in Book III, Part I, Section I, Hume argues that there is no such thing as practical, as opposed to theoretical, reason; but he later goes on to claim that we can regard certain mild emotions or calm passions as instances of (practical) reason (Book III, Part III, Section I). So Hume is at the very least ambivalent about the possibility of practical reason(s), and I can think of no (theoretical) reason why a moral sentimentalist can't choose to be *either* an eliminativist *or* a reductionist about practical rationality/reasons. They can say there is no such thing, or, as sentimentalists, they can hold that practical reasons/rationality are in general understandable in emotional terms.

In the present essay, I am going to take the latter course and will then apply what I have said about practical rationality to the issue of self-sacrifice. In previous work, I have avoided saying that we have practical reasons to help others or sacrifice ourselves for others because I regarded the most serious work of moral philosophy as capable of being accomplished without committing oneself to such claims. In my book *Moral Sentimentalism* (Slote 2010), I used Saul Kripke's (1980) notion of reference fixing to argue that moral judgments can be based in empathy and yet be capable of being completely objective (and true), and I attempted to show that anyone who makes a moral judgment will automatically have motivation to act in accordance with that judgment. This gives one most of what rationalists have wanted from or believed present in morality and moral judgments – except for the issue of reasons for action. I never said (or denied) that the person who is motivated by moral considerations to help others has a reason to do so. But I am now going to show you how a sentimentalist can make sense of the idea of practical reason(s), and this general approach will then be applied to the issue of self-sacrifice. (I have elsewhere [Slote 2014] argued that recent efforts to revive psychological egoism and deny the possibility of genuine self-sacrifice involve various forms of conceptual confusion.) Overall, I believe it will add to the plausibility of moral sentimentalism if we can show, as against rationalist doubts, that it can give a broad and plausible philosophical account of reasons for action.

Hume's later remarks in the *Treatise* relating calm passions to reason seem to be a conciliatory effort, in relation to the rationalism he was familiar with, to make room for practical reasons or rationality. But Hume, who was the first person ever to discuss empathy in any kind of systematic way (of course, he lacked that term and used 'sympathy' instead), never related empathy to practical reason(s); and if we bring in empathy, I think we can offer a sentimentalist account of practical rationality/reason that is more nuanced and has more explanatory power than anything Hume's remarks about calm passions make available to us. I think both prudential reasons and altruistic (or moral) reasons emerge out of certain emotions and, at least in the latter case, via mechanisms of empathy, and if we can spell this out, we may be then be in a position to say something useful about the rational justification of self-sacrifice.

2.

I want to begin by talking about prudential reasons, the reasons we have to pursue (or not undercut) our own overall or future well-being or happiness; but then I hope later to connect what I have said about prudential reasons with the kinds of altruistic reasons that are so often thought to be characteristic of and necessary to the moral life. And I don't propose at this point to argue against other views of prudence so much as to frame, in sentimentalist terms, an intuitively plausible and theoretically useful conception of prudential reasons that can then also help us understand the altruistic reasons of morality. Let's begin with an example.

Imagine a man trapped in a burning house. There are no accessible windows and only one accessible door, but he finds that that door is stuck. The distress and fear he initially felt on realizing the house was on fire then turns into a kind of desperation. He continues pushing on the door to see if he can make it open before the fire engulfs him, but he also starts banging on the door in order to attract the attention of anyone outside who might be able to help him open it (it is too late for anyone to quickly put out the fire).

The man clearly has (a) reason, (a) prudential reason, to try to escape through that door, but I want to add that that reason has to do with the emotions he feels while trying to escape. It is rational from the standpoint of prudence for someone trying to escape a raging fire to feel distress, fear and alarm at his situation, and if he finds the only possible avenue of escape to be blocked, it is entirely understandable that his distress and fear should turn into a kind of desperation. But one can go further with and by means of this initial example. It is an essential part of his being practically or prudentially rational in this situation that he should feel the kind of distress and/or fear we are attributing to him. (We are not talking about someone who wants or is trying to commit suicide.) He isn't indifferent to what is happening to him, and neither does he merely *prefer* to open the door and save his own life – that is, he doesn't treat the issue of life and (painful) death as if it were like choosing which of his two favorite flavors of ice cream he preferred on a given occasion. Rather, his attitude toward living, freedom from pain/suffering, and good health involves *caring* about these things, and caring about something means thinking it is important – which in turn involves emotion or at least a disposition to feel negative emotion when what one considers important is threatened or at risk and also positive emotion when the threat or risk doesn't eventuate.

I want to say that a normal, e.g. non-suicidal, rational person has or is disposed to have emotions like fear and distress when their (long-term) welfare or happiness is threatened in certain significant ways and like relief and joy if and when the threat doesn't materialize or is evaded. In my view, their overall prudential rationality *consists* in their having or being disposed to have such situationally based emotions: in other words, consists in their *caring* about such things.[1] But what can one then say about the particular situational reasons such a prudent person has? They have reason or a reason to promote or preserve their own present and future welfare, but in particular circumstances that reason is informed by, well, information about what the circumstances require of one in order to further the goal of one's own well-being. So the man in the burning house has prudential reason in general to try to promote, to care about promoting, his own future welfare, and in the circumstances that means trying to escape through the one door that seems to allow for an escape from the fire that is burning all around him. He has reason to try to escape through that door, but I think we can also say that his eagerness or strong desire to escape through that door is the *locus* of that reason.

Reasons for action, reasons to do one thing rather than another, are commonly supposed (by philosophers) to have motivational force. If one recognizes that one has a reason to do something – and the man in the burning house may at some level think that he has reason to try to escape through the one door – then one is at least to some extent motivated to act accordingly. The man is afraid of the fire, fears for his life, and in the circumstances as he knows them, that makes him want to escape through the one accessible door. But he doesn't merely *prefer* to escape through that door. In the circumstances he cares a great deal about getting through that door, and the caring, of course, leads to distress and perhaps even desperation as the door continually fails to yield to his pushing. And those emotional reactions are expressions of his caring, of his eagerness or strongly felt desire to get through that door. But I want to say that it is the emotional caring itself that constitutes his reason to try to escape through the given door.

Now what I am calling the caring is not some generalized state or disposition that is exemplified in all sort of different circumstances. A woman can feel hope, for example, at many times of her life but the hopes she has as a newly-wed are not the same hopes the feels when she later gets divorced and hopes to be able to salvage something good out of the remainder of her life. Similarly, when the man of our example cares strongly, even desperately, about getting through that door, he has a strongly felt desire to get through that door, and that desire, that state of caring, is not identical with any earlier episode of desire or caring. But as a particular psychological state that exists only in the given circumstances, the man's state of caring or strongly felt desire can be construed, in sentimentalist terms, as (the locus of) his situationally specific reason to try to get out through the one door. But these conclusions rest, at least partly, on the earlier-mentioned thesis that prudential rationality requires and rests on the disposition to have various sorts of emotions in various kinds of circumstances. The sentimentalist can, therefore, understand prudential rationality and reasons (reductively, if you will) in terms of emotion or sentiment.

3.

I would like now to use what we have just been saying about prudential rationality and prudential reasons to give an account of altruistic reasons that, as with prudential reasons, sees them as grounded in or constituted by various sentiments. But in order to extend our sentimentalist account in this way, empathy has to be brought into our discussion. The picture of moral rationality we arrive at is going to be more complex – but also, I think, somewhat more philosophically interesting and rewarding – than what we have just been saying about prudential rationality because it will intersect with widely influential present-day rationalist views about our reasons for action in a way that redounds, I believe, to the disadvantage of the latter – and I believe nothing I have just said about prudential rationality/reasons cuts as sharply and as significantly against ideas that have great currency in Western moral philosophy. I want to begin our discussion by saying some general things about how empathy is supposed to work here.

The kind of empathy I am going to focus on is what has been variously called emotional, associative or receptive empathy. There is also such a thing as projective empathy, or simulation, which involves putting oneself into the shoes or the head of another person. But emotional/receptive empathy, as the name implies, involves taking in the feelings of others in a way that one is very often unaware of: hence all the talk of empathic contagion or even osmosis. Whatever else associative/emotional empathy involves, it also is or contains a psychological mechanism (often said to be underlain by the functioning of mirror neurons), and I want to say that that mechanism allows not only for the interpersonal transmission of emotions, but for the interpersonal transmission of reasons to the extent they are grounded in relevant emotions. Just as (other things being equal) empathy transmits emotions more strongly when the person on the receiving end is (physically or personally) closer to the person whose emotions are being transmitted, it more strongly transmits the reasons for action of someone who needs help if they are closer to the person on the receiving end, thus giving the latter *more or stronger* reason to act helpfully the more strongly the first person's reason is transmitted by empathy. Bradford Cokelet once said to me in passing that empathy as such might give us reasons, but what I want to say is a bit different and more specific. It is not that having empathy for someone's fears or anxieties is itself automatically or obviously a reason to help them avoid what they fear because the fears could, after all, be irrational. Rather, empathy *transmits reasons* from one person to another and does so by reflecting and registering the emotions that accompany and/or constitute situationally prudential rationality, the fears that it is rational for someone to have if, as per our previous example, they seem to be trapped in a burning house and the strong concern such a person will have to get out of that house through what seems to be the only possible exit. But let me now embed these inchoate ideas in something more structured and definite.

Most philosophies and philosophers have been willing to grant that being prudent on one's own behalf is a condition of rational desire, choice and action. And that is how common sense views the matter too. If someone doesn't care about or act to protect their future health (or freedom from severe pain), we think and most philosophers have thought that they count as practically irrational: they have strong practical reasons to desire and act differently. Of course, on a sheer desire-based view of rationality, there might be nothing irrational in all of this: after all the person who doesn't act to ensure their later health or freedom from pain presumably doesn't *care* about these things, doesn't desire things to be any different, and such theories also typically presuppose that such a person needn't be under any strictly cognitive misapprehensions. But I am just going to set desire-based theories aside during our further discussion. Most of them end up being qualified to include a condition of rational consideration of one's desires that makes them approach or even extensionally coincide with the kind of prudential theory of self-interested rationality I have been and am going to be working with, and in any event I am trying to be commonsensical here, and prudential theories seem to conform to our antecedent ordinary intuitions about practical reasons and rationality better than other sorts of approaches. (This point is explained further and somewhat qualified in footnote 1.) It seems practically and prudentially irrational not to be concerned with one's future health or freedom from pain even if, or perhaps especially if, one has no present desire for future health or freedom from pain.

What is really controversial, however, is the frequently-made assumption that morality or moral considerations as such give all of us practical reasons for desiring things to be a certain way and for choosing or acting accordingly. Now you may say that the idea that morality offers practical reasons really isn't controversial because almost all philosophers think it does. And indeed most Western ethicists – Aristotelians, Kantians and even many utilitarians – are rationalists about morality and think that morally relevant considerations and explicit (valid) moral conclusions are automatically reason-giving. But I such rationalism doesn't in fact fit our ordinary commonsense thinking about reasons and rationality. The rationalist has to say that a psychopath who doesn't care about anyone else has (some non-egoistic) reason nonetheless to help someone who they know needs their help and may also have to say that there is something practically irrational about such a person if they lack any motivation to help others. But ordinary folk don't think in this way about psychopaths. They tend to regard the psychopath who doesn't care about anyone other than themselves as cold-hearted or even heartless, and they certainly think of them as morally criticizable or deficient (their actions reflect a lack of concern for and even malice toward others). But ordinary folk don't usually think of or criticize such a person as irrational, and to ordinary ways of seeing things it seems quite a stretch to claim that the psychopath has a (strong) reason to help others that they don't recognize and are never motivated to act on, as strong a reason as those of us who care about others (who we don't personally know) have for helping them.

In what follows I shall mention a line of response to this point that is available to the ethical rationalist, but also indicate how that response doesn't completely answer the objection I have just made to ethical rationalism. However, for the moment, I just want to emphasize that ethical or moral rationalism is far from self-evident or even commonsensically intuitive. And as we shall see, there are theoretical/philosophical reasons for doubting ethical rationalism and for recognizing a previously unsuspected foundational role for the emotions within practical reason(s) as directed toward other people. I believe that that foundational role operates through or by means of empathy, so let me spell out why I think such a view of emotion's role makes better theoretical or philosophical sense of the phenomena of ethics than any rationalistic approach. And my argument will be strictly a priori, even though it will refer to the empirical phenomenon/concept of empathy.

Many people have said that empathy is an emotion, but we philosophers think we know better. We think that sympathy is an emotion, but that associative empathy is a *mechanism* whereby emotions like sympathy or fear or joy are transmitted 'osmotically' or 'contagiously' from one person to another. So the gist of what I am going to argue for now is that empathy is not only a mechanism for the transmission of emotions but also a mechanism for the transmission of reasons for action, where the transmission of the reasons of necessity and on a priori grounds operates *via the empathic transmission of emotions*.

Let me begin here by returning to the example of the man in the burning house and complicating it by bringing in the point of view of an observer who happens to be outside that house. As you are passing by a house one afternoon, you notice that it is on fire and that someone, trying desperately to escape the fire raging inside, is screamingly loudly and banging repeatedly on a stuck door that won't allow them to leave the house. So you go to help and pull on the door from the outside, and let's say that your combined strenuous efforts make the door come unstuck and that the person inside finally escapes through that door. We have previously assumed that the person inside the house has or had a pretty strong prudential reason to want to escape through that particular door. Perhaps there were no windows in that room, the person found himself there, and the fire was coming on fast. And, as I have mentioned, in such a situation the person facing such a fire will feel fear and some desperation if their most immediate means of escape seems blocked. That fear and perhaps even the desperation are in the circumstances rational from a practical point of view; they are what a rationally prudent person with a desire for self-preservation would or easily could feel in those circumstances. The person has reason to be afraid at the very least and to care strongly about getting through that one door.

Now the person outside (if I may switch from a second-person to a third-person reference) hears screams and violent banging from inside the house and recognizes the fear and desperation that are causing all that activity. They recognize the danger to the person inside and empathically register how the person inside is feeling about his situation, and they act on that basis. And I want to say that the reason the person inside the house has for trying to get out of that particular door is transmitted to the person outside through the latter's empathically feeling and identifying with what the other person feels, wants and cares about at that point. The fear and practical concern of the one are empathically conveyed to and felt by the other, and if the first has prudential reason to fear for his life and try to get through the door, then the latter has what we can call an empathic, moral or altruistic reason to help that person get through that door on the basis of the focused fear and concern that have been empathically conveyed to them.

But remember that this doesn't have to mean that empathy with someone automatically or always gives an empathizer reason to act on behalf of that other person or their desires. If someone's fear is irrational and bears no relation to actual prudence, if it is the fear of flying, for example, and is based on an irrational belief that flying is dangerous, then that fear may be conveyed empathically to an observer, but be validly discounted or qualified as a reason for helping them make a train reservation instead. The reason if any for helping them make such a reservation is not the danger of flying, but the fear itself as a state so unpleasant that one wouldn't want to prolong it for someone unnecessarily. And of course there will sometimes be reason not to help the person escape their fears but to want them to fly in a state of fear because if they don't, they are going to miss, say, their granddaughter's wedding.

So I am suggesting that it is only reasons, only emotions that make rational sense in prudential terms, that transmit rational force to those who empathically register the feelings of another. When I go along with the irrational fear of someone who wants to take a train instead of a plane, I am perhaps registering their present state of fear, but (according to the present view) that is not what gives me a non-prudential and moral or empathic reason to help them take the train, if I have it. What gives me such a reason, rather, is my registering of or sensitivity to the unpleasant feelings they will or would have *in the future* if they have or had to take a plane.

This (arguably *a priori*) philosophical picture of how reasons are transmitted and acquired roots such processes in epistemically-based emotion and so views (altruistic) practical reason as in important respects intrinsically involving emotion rather than as separate from, opposed to, or merely causally connected to emotion. And we have to now ask why we should accept such a theory when we already have available to us what looks like a much more straightforward rationalist/cognitivist approach to (altruistic) practical reasons that views them as transmitted to us through the non-emotional cognitive apprehension or recognition of other people's reasons. The origin of such an approach lies, I think, in Thomas Nagel's (1970) *The Possibility of Altruism*, though something like it can be found in the work of other recent ethical rationalists. Why should we bring in emotion when we already have this more familiar way of viewing things? I think we have to answer this question if the sentimentalist approach to reason transmission is to make any philosophical headway. But answer it I think we can, and our answer, by showing what the sentimentalist approach allows us to better explain, will give us good reason to accept our sentimentalist approach.

Nagel (1970) argues (roughly) that reasons transmit both across time within a given person and simultaneously between different individuals once they are correctly apprehended. Someone, for example, who says they recognize that they later will have a reason to do something, but who (in the absence of conflicting reasons) makes none of the known necessary preparations for doing that thing, shows himself not to have fully *apprehended* or *recognized* the future reason they claim to recognize or the reason they presently have to make preparations for later rational action. According to Nagel, they are cognitively dissociated from their future selves and in effect don't clearly see what will happen to them in the future as part of the same one life they are now leading. And similar points apply, for Nagel, to the recognition, apprehension or appreciation of reasons across persons. Someone who doesn't see the pain of another person as giving them some reason to help relieve that pain doesn't (on Nagel's view) fully acknowledge, apprehend or appreciate the reality of the other('s pain) or of the reason the other has for wanting to relieve their own pain.

Now I think there are some important aspects of the transmission of reasons for action that this rationalistic theory cannot account for, and this is something that Nagel himself actually seems to acknowledge at one point in his book. But before I get into this problematic aspect of this rationalist account and explain why the sentimentalist approach doesn't face similar problems, I would like to consider a more immediate objection that someone might make to Nagel's view.

The immediate objection is that it seems implausible to suppose, as Nagel's view must, that a psychopath doesn't really or fully grasp the reality of those whom they are motivationally indifferent or hostile to and the reality of what such people actually feel. Psychopathic or sociopathic con artists are notoriously capable of 'getting inside the heads' of their intended victims, so how can the rationalist say that they lack a reason or motivation to help rather than hurt such people only because they don't grasp the reality of what or whom they are meeting and/or dealing with? Nagel and other rationalists assume that the normal person who grasps the reality, say, of another person's pain will automatically have a reason to help that person that translates into their having at least some motivation to do so. And I have no desire to question that assumption. But, then, if the con artist doesn't have a reason or motivation of this kind and if that lack of reason and/or motivation reflects, as Nagel might claim, the con artist's failure to grasp or appreciate the reality, say, of the other person's pain, what makes the difference here? Why, to put things as John McDowell (1997) does, isn't the pain of the other salient for the con artist the way it is for the normal person?

Well, let me suggest that empathy may make the difference here between a psychopathic con artist and a normal or moral person. Psychopaths may be able to get into the heads of others, but, as I have already pointed out, this is or may be what in the literature of psychology is called projective empathy, and they characteristically lack the ability to empathically feel what others are feeling. That is, they lack the capacity for associative or receptive empathy and feel joy at the other's pain rather than feeling the other's pain. So if a psychopath fails to appreciate certain facts about another's suffering, fails to see those facts as salient in a way that would motivate them toward helping the other person, that may be precisely because they lack the capacity for a kind of empathy that involves sharing or sharing in others' feelings. But if one has to bring in the absence of empathy to explain the difference between what the normal person (cognitively) appreciates and has reason/motivation to do and what the psychopath or sociopath fails to (cognitively) appreciate and fails to have a reason/motivation to do, then one's account of reasons has to bring in a sentimentalist element that undercuts the strictly rationalistic character of what Nagel initially proposed. It can no longer separate the cognitive and the motivational from the emotional in the way rationalism essentially seeks to do. (This is not, again, to question the tight connection the rationalist seeks to draw between the full cognitive apprehension of certain facts and relevant motivation to act.)

In that case, the view we end up with when we press Nagel's rationalism in the above manner is very close to and may eventually force one toward the sentimentalist ideas about the transmission of reasons I outlined earlier. But now I want to mention some further considerations that favor the sentimental view of transmission over any kind of pure rationalism about such transmission *in regard to normal non-sociopathic personalities*. Nagel's view as it stands has a hard time dealing with the psychopath's lack of moral motivation or reasons, but it also cannot account for differences in the strength/force of the interpersonal transmission of reasons in various cases involving very normal people.

For example, we typically empathize more with family members than with strangers, and that means that the pain distress of family members empathically transmits itself to us more strongly than the pain distress of mere strangers does. Because of the way empathy operates on our relations with others, therefore, we tend to feel more sympathetic, altruistic concern for family members than for strangers who may have similar problems. *And there is reason to infer from this that we have more reason to be concerned with family members than with strangers we meet or people we only know about second hand.* That, at least, is what naturally follows out of our earlier view that traces interpersonally transmitted reasons to processes of empathy, and in itself such a view doesn't seem at all implausible. But a purely rationalist theory of reason transmission à la Nagel has no way of explaining such differences in the strength of the altruistic reasons we have. For all it says, the reason I have to relieve the evident pain of a family member is no stronger than the reason I have to relieve the evident pain of a stranger I have just met. So such a theory doesn't in itself tell us that when we have to choose between helping a suffering family member and helping a suffering stranger, we typically have more reason to help the family member, and this last assumption is something we certainly should want to be able to support and justify with a theory of practical reasons.[2]

At the very least, therefore, Nagel's rationalism seems radically incomplete as a theory of (altruistic) reasons and of reason transmission. It can explain the fact that reasons are transmitted, but not the difference we would tend to assume there is between the strength of the reason we have to help a family member and that of the reason we have to help a total stranger. And Nagel himself seems to recognize this problem: he allows that there may be reasons more specific or specialized than any he has dealt with that differentiate self and other and different classes of others, but claims that 'the acknowledgement of prima facie reasons to help others [in general] is a significant result' (1970, 127f). And he goes on to say (1970, 133) that his theory of the objective (i.e. agent-neutral or impartial) reasons everyone has to help everyone else doesn't explain why 'an individual is justified in paying more attention ... to the needs of those close to him than to the problems of humanity at large'.

So there are differences in the strengths of our reasons vis-à-vis others that Nagel's *The Possibility of Altruism* doesn't explain at all, much less explain in terms of his theory of how objective reasons are transmitted. But the view I outlined above does both of those things at the same time. It explains the difference in force or strength between our reasons to help family members or friends and our reasons to help others in terms of the difference in the force or strength with which, say, the distraught pain of a family member and the distraught pain of a stranger are empathically transmitted to us. And similar arguments can be applied to all the other areas where empathy underlies differences in our moral reactions (and judgments).

Thus when such a view of the central and foundational moral role of empathy is applied to the transmission of reasons for action, it can tell us plausible things about our altruistic/moral reasons that Nagel's account in *The Possibility of Altruism* doesn't tell us, and although Nagel (1986) later sought to say more about how and why we have, say, more reason to help family members than to help strangers (and about other sorts of moral distinctions we make in and about our lives), the resultant picture was much more impressionistic and less systematic, organized and explanatory than what one gets from tracing interpersonal reasons back to empathy and empathically transmitted feeling. I don't think any other ethical rationalist has done any better with this specific issue so on the whole our sentimentalist account of (the) reasons (that pertain to morality) has much to recommend it and is more useful, I think, for understanding the actual altruistic/moral reasons people have than anything that comes out of ethical rationalism. For it not only takes in our reasons to prefer family and a whole host of similar, familiar empathically-based moral reasons, but even explains the psychopath's failure to have *any reason* to help others.

I know that we would like to think we can give the psychopath or egoist a rational argument to show them that they have reason to behave better than they do, if only they could recognize what philosophy has to teach them. But I don't think psychopaths are going to respond motivationally to any of our philosophical arguments, and that may be in part because they simply lack any (non-egoistic) reason to care about or help others and because one simply cannot argue people into having reasons of this sort. As

I mentioned earlier, it is commonsensically plausible to suppose that psychopaths simply lack the reasons we think we have for helping others, and the difference here – and this too is a point of common sense – seems to lie in the fact that the psychopath is incapable of associative empathy with others, never feels what others feel, and for that (causal-explanatory) reason never really cares about anyone else. The sentimentalist (i. e. emotion-based) theory of reasons I have sketched can account for these plausible facts or assumptions much better than any form of ethical rationalism can, and so, in addition to the way the transmission of reasons works in ordinary people, the just-mentioned presumptive facts about psychopaths also support our sentimentalist theory of altruistic reasons. In other words, what we have said about the (differential) transmission of reasons between normal people supports our account, but so too does what it can say in intuitively plausible terms about psychopaths.

Alternatively, and reversing engines, we can say that our ability to account plausibly for the fact and *variable strength* of the 'normal' interpersonal transmission of reasons for action in empathic/sentimentalist terms also gives us a philosophical reason to believe that psychopaths altogether lack such altruistic reasons. It therefore gives us reason to strongly resist the general rationalist tendency to believe that *everyone* has reason to help others. Sentimentalism supports a more nuanced and less universalistic conception of altruistic reasons, once the sheer reality of psychopathy is taken into account, and that conception ties (certain aspects of) practical reason, emotion and empathy together much more tightly than the traditionally-understood dualism of reason and emotion would regard as possible or plausible. And within that tighter, conceptual relationship, it is emotion and empathy that have the foundational, grounding role.[3]

4.

However, before we conclude our general discussion of practical reasons, I think I should say just a bit more about the practical reasons of conscientiousness. Most of us take it that a situationally conscientious person, a person who is concerned to do what is morally required in a given situation, has some reason on that basis to actually do what is or what they take to be required of them. And I put things in this way because I don't want to assume that a psychopath is capable of having such reasons. Arguably, the psychopath is never morally conscientious and never feels guilt if they do what is considered wrong. And it is not even clear that they have the moral concepts that would allow them to speak meaningfully of what is right or wrong or morally required. I have offered (philosophical) reasons (in Slote 2010) for considering the psychopath to lack moral concepts precisely because they lack the capacity for emotional/associative empathy, but (again) I do not think we need to go into that particular issue here. The more interesting point, from the perspective of the present essay, concerns the reasons a conscientious non-psychopathic person has to do what they (let us assume correctly) take to be morally required of them. Do these represent a basically new kind of practical reason we have not yet considered?

But first a point about terminology. The reader may wonder why I am distinguishing reasons of conscience from altruistic reasons and I think I owe them at least a brief explanation. Altruism, as it is commonly understood, involves an intrinsic desire to help other people, and such desire is commonly regarded as involving an emotional connection to or involvement with others. But some rationalists, e.g. Kant, hold that the commitment to doing what is morally required of one doesn't entail that one have any feeling toward those whom a sense of duty impels one to help; and Kant never mentions empathy as in any way involved in moral conscientiousness. In any event, contemporary Kantians hold that altruistic reasons (e.g. reasons of or based in the 'natural virtue' of compassion) are quite different from reasons of conscience. But this difference is less plausible if one assumes a sentimentalist picture of what is involved in our moral concepts and thus in anyone's desire to do what is morally required of them. If (as I argued at length in 2010), moral concepts involve empathy, then altruistic reasons and reasons of conscience that involve thinking about moral right and wrong are not all that far apart. Indeed, and I hope you can see this without further argument, if moral concepts involve empathy, then reasons of conscientiousness cannot exist apart from altruistic reasons.

My argument (in 2010) claims that our capacity for making moral judgments depends on our having second-order empathy with the first-order empathy moral agents feel toward those they want to help. Such second-order empathy cannot exist in someone who lacks first-order empathy, and that means that when I feel it would be wrong for me to do something and have a reason of conscience not to do that thing, my having such a reason rests on my ability to have first-order reasons to help based on first-order empathy. So although I hold (Slote 2010) that there is something second-order about considerations of conscience, those considerations depend on the kind of first-order empathy with the feelings of others that I earlier argued is fundamental to our emotion-laden reasons to help others. Altruistic reasons and conscientious ones are more closely or deeply related than rationalism allows for.

So sentimentalism can offer an account of prudential, altruistic and conscientious reasons for action in contemporary terms and has very specific and marked advantages over ethical rationalism not only (as I have argued in Slote 2010) as an account of right and wrong and of moral semantics, but also within rationalism's home territory, as a general account of practical reason or rationality. What one might call practical sentimentalism seems to offer us the best way of understanding practical Reason/rationality.

5.

But now it is time to apply all of the above to the notion of self-sacrifice. Self-sacrifice can occur at the behest of conscience, but in many cases, indeed the most central ones for our moral imagination, self-sacrifice occurs because what we feel for another person and what they need motivationally overrides or preempts certain concerns of self-interest. What we have said above can give us a model of how this could occur. We said earlier that we tend to feel the suffering of another more strongly if they are someone we know and love rather than a total stranger, and empathy, of course, can help us explain this sort of phenomenon. But what was assumed in that discussion and is presupposed in every discussion of empathy I know of is that empathy tends to be more strongly aroused the *greater* the suffering or danger that is at issue; and this holds true whether the person arousing our empathy is someone close to us or is some distant person we only know *about*. This can give us a basic model of how to understand the possibility and reality of self-sacrifice.

To begin with, the quantity or size of suffering can make a difference even as between someone we know and love and someone we are merely acquainted with or only know about. For example, if I come home from work early in order to take my child out for an ice cream treat, my plans will probably change if I learn that my neighbor's house is in danger of being internally flooded as a result of a leak and I am in a position to help them out. My empathy with my neighbor's plight can empathically outweigh my child's likely disappointment at not being able to eat ice cream, and it is characteristic of the empathy of morally good or (as we sentimentalists and many people in general nowadays like to say) caring people that it can move one toward helping a mere acquaintance or relative stranger in great need of help in preference to providing some nice thing for someone one is more intimate with or generally cares more about.

Why shouldn't the same thing be possible with regard to a choice between helping or not hurting oneself and helping some stranger whose need at some moment is obviously greater than one's own? For example, in the case described earlier in which someone hears a person trapped in a house trying to escape via a certain door, it is possible that the person who hears the trapped person's attempts to escape is wearing a suit, a suit that will need cleaning if they go and help the trapped individual by pulling hard on the stuck door from the outside. But a good person, a caring person, won't pay heed to such self-interested considerations if the other person's need, what is at stake for the other person, is so much greater than any aversion one might have to having to pay for one's suit to be cleaned. A person trapped inside a burning house cares much more about escaping that they ever could about keeping a suit of theirs clean and neat, and even if empathy typically cannot make us care as much about another person's escaping as that person cares about his own escape, it can have enough force for us to overwhelm or obliterate any concern for our being inconvenienced by having to get a suit cleaned. We can through empathy feel someone's large or powerful reason to want to escape a burning house more strongly than we register our own smaller reason or concern to keep our suit neat and clean.

If someone is not like this, if they hesitate or more than hesitate to help a trapped person escape a fire because they don't want to get their suit dirty, then they are less caring as individuals than what we would expect most individuals to be like, and we can say that empathy operates less strongly in them than it arguably operates in good people. They are closer to a psychopath than most of us think we are, and they do not therefore share the altruistic reasons most of us have to help others in situations like the one of the man trapped in a burning house. This doesn't prevent us from condemning them morally, however. A good person's empathy operates in the stronger fashion, and if, as in the just-mentioned case, empathy doesn't operate in that fashion, then that shows the person in question not to be a caring individual. *Moral Sentimentalism* argued that actions that show us as lacking in empathy and/or caringness are morally wrong, so we can morally criticize the person who doesn't want to get their suit dirty, even while holding them to lack the altruistic reason or reasons most of us would have when faced with a man trapped in a burning building. (Similar criticism applies to those who refuse to help people of different race, religion, ethnicity or sexual orientation.)[4]

Only one more point then needs to be added. I have suggested that in most cases someone feels their own need more strongly than an empathic observer would, but does this have to be the case? It seems possible to me that a parent might feel a child's (present) need more strongly than the child herself does, and this opens up at least the possibility that a parent, friend or lover might sacrifice their own greater need to the lesser need of another person. All that would be necessary is that the parent or other would feel that lesser need more strongly than they feel their own greater self-interested need. Why couldn't empathy sometimes be so powerful as to make our concern for another stronger than what that person feels for herself or what we would feel if we were in their situation? I see no reason to rule out such possibilities, and if we don't then the way is clear for there to be cases of extreme self-sacrifice understandable in terms of extraordinary strengths of empathy. I cannot now prove to you that such cases exist, but in the light of what we have been arguing here, this possibility seems ripe for further moral-theoretic exploration.

Moreover, if such hyper-empathy *is* possible, it wouldn't necessarily follow that the person who felt another's distress more strongly than that other person would have reason or be rational to make some extraordinary sacrifice that was motivated by their extraordinary empathy. For one might question whether one person's reasons can be *magnified as reasons* through unusual empathic receptivity. This is another question whose further exploration is suggested by what we have been saying here. But in fact sentimentalists and rationalists (see Nagel 1986) alike need to be able to say more both about how or whether *enormous self-sacrifice* is possible and about how or whether such self-sacrifice can be rational if and when it occurs.

Notes

1. The issue of what to say about suicidal or depressed people who don't care about going on living or even, perhaps, about avoiding extreme pain, is a complex one. Where the impulse to suicide realistically reflects the facts of a given person's situation, there is probably no reason to describe them as irrational or imprudent; so perhaps we can say that where they aren't being realistic, their error or failing is more cognitive than practical. If they count as irrational and/or imprudent, it is because they don't or can't register or carefully enough learn the relevant facts. Similar points can be made about people who are depressed. The idea that putative instances of purely practical irrationality (*à la* Kant) are better conceived as defects of cognitive rationality is a major implication of Thomas Nagel's (1970) *The Possibility of Altruism* – though Nagel himself doesn't explicitly emphasize this point in the book itself. And in effect what I have just been saying about the suicidal and depressed represents a sentimentalist borrowing from what Nagel was saying on behalf of rationalism. The sentimentalist tends to see what are historically regarded as forms of pure practical irrationality as actually instancing some sort of cognitive defect (as well), and not just in the instances mentioned earlier in this footnote. For example and as we shall see later in this essay, the sentimentalist (or *this* sentimentalist) thinks it makes more sense to see the empathically deficient psychopath as cognitively out of touch with certain aspects of others than as failing to respond adequately to practical reasons they in fact possess. But such a view of things, as taken either by the rationalist or by the sentimentalist, runs up against the objection, initially launched by J. L. Mackie (1977) that it posits a kind of 'objective prescriptivity' in our relations with value matters, i.e. that it treats certain cognitive apprehensions of objective realities as intrinsically capable of also motivating us. Mackie thinks such a notion is 'queer', and people like Nagel and myself need to be able to answer this objection. I have given such an answer elsewhere (see Slote 2018; published in side-by-side English-language and Chinese-language versions). However, this is not the time or place to pursue this issue further.

2. Nor would it help Nagel here to point out that common-sense (rational) intuition tells us that we *ceteris paribus* have more reason to help family members than to help strangers or distant others. This still wouldn't explain *why* such a difference exists, and that is precisely what the appeal to empathic transmission allows us to explain.
3. We in the West have conceived of reason as separate or separable from emotion, and this has been thought not only about theoretical reason but about practical reason as well. The present essay gives us (theoretical) reason to doubt or deny that practical rationality is separable from emotion. Rather, as we have seen, it involves and is grounded in emotion. But then there is the other side of rationality, epistemic or theoretical rationality, and the question can naturally arise whether this important dimension or kind of rationality can be as conceptually separate from emotion as we have standardly and traditionally supposed. For reasons given elsewhere, I think the answer to this question has to be in the negative. All theoretical reasons and all theoretical reasoning are tied to belief, and I have argued at length in *A Sentimentalist Theory of the Mind* (Slote 2014) that belief, *all* belief, intrinsically involves emotional dispositions. If that is so, then both the main forms of rationality cannot be separated from and necessarily involve emotion(s). This totally undermines the received Western view that reason and emotion are separate and/or separable. (Confucian philosophy, by the way, doesn't make this assumption.) For the same (theoretical) reasons it also turns out that *there is no such thing as pure reason*. What I have just been telling you therefore adumbrates a critique of pure reason quite opposite to what Kant meant by the title of his most famous book.
4. Even when someone is unconscious or too ill to feel any relevant reason-constituting emotions, we can empathize with their (in many cases obvious) previous emotion-involving desires, fears and aspirations and have reason to help them on that basis.

Disclosure Statement

No potential conflict of interest was reported by the author.

References

Kripke, S. 1980. *Naming and Necessity*. Oxford: Blackwell.
Mackie, J. L. 1977. *Ethics: Inventing Right and Wrong*. Harmondsworth: Penguin.
McDowell, J. 1997. "Virtue and Reason." In *Virtue Ethics*, edited by R. Crisp and M. Slote. Oxford: Oxford University Press.
Nagel, T. 1970. *The Possibility of Altruism*. Oxford: Oxford University Press.
Nagel, T. 1986. *The View From Nowhere*. New York: Oxford University Press.
Slote, M. 2010. *Moral Sentimentalism*. New York: Oxford University Press.
Slote, M. 2014. *A Sentimentalist Theory of the Mind*. New York: Oxford University Press.
Slote, M. 2018. *The Philosophy of Yin and Yang*. Beijing: Commercial Press.

Pathophobia, Vices, and Illness

Ian James Kidd

ABSTRACT
I introduce the concept of pathophobia to capture the range of morally objectionable forms of treatment to which somatically ill persons are subjected. After distinguishing this concept from sanism and ableism, I argue that the moral wrongs of pathophobia are best analysed using a framework of vice ethics. To that end I describe five clusters of pathophobic vices and failings, illustrating each with examples from three influential illness narratives.

1. Introduction

An abiding theme of Audre Lorde's *Cancer Journals*, her reflections on her experiences as a woman of colour with breast cancer, is a 'fury at the outside world's viciousness, the stupid, brutal lack of consciousness or concern that passes for the way things are'. She castigates the 'arrogant blindness' of the healthy and privileged, the 'hurt' caused by the 'cold and silent eyes' of the women who shunned her, and other failures of empathy, understanding, and compassion (1997, 24, 25). Lorde also explores the intersectional character of such 'viciousness' – the ways that gendered and racialized discrimination combined with novel forms of prejudice against her ill body. But while the concepts of sexism and racism were available for the former, no such term existed for morally objectionable attitudes and behaviour targeted at somatic illness. Even today, some thirty years later, there exist the concepts of sanism and ableism, which refer to forms of discrimination against persons with mental illnesses and disabilities. But no concept currently exists to name discrimination specifically against those with chronic somatic illnesses.

The aim of this paper is to provide a concept to fill that gap – 'pathophobia', which gathers together the variety of morally objectionable attitudes, norms, and behaviours to which somatically ill persons are typically subjected. I sketch the concept and then argue that we can use it to articulate the moral wrongs of pathophobia by connecting it to the framework of *vice ethics*. I will describe five clusters of pathophobic vices and failings, illustrated with examples from three influential narratives of the social experience of illness: Havi Carel's *Illness*, which documents her diagnosis and early years with a life-limiting lung condition, and two breast cancer narratives, Kathlyn Conway's *Ordinary Life* and Barbara Ehrenreich's *Bright-Sided*, published in some countries as *Smile or Die*.

2. The Concept of Pathophobia

We need appropriately rich conceptual resources to identify, describe, and appraise forms of social oppression and to develop effective individual and collective ameliorative strategies. Pathophobia is intended to complement such existing concepts as racism, sexism, and homophobia. It tracks forms of socially scaffolded mistreatment which target those with somatic illnesses. (I, therefore, use the term differently from its current, idiomatic sense of 'a morbid fear of illness or of becoming ill', a fear that can, of course, motivate pathophobia in my technical sense).

A main source for detailed accounts of experiences of pathophobia are the testimonies and narratives offered by somatically ill persons and their carers, which are called 'pathographies', taking the form of autobiographies, diaries, letters, memoirs, and other forms of a creative product. For most of the twentieth century, people's writings about their illness tended to be didactic and paternalistic, offering advice and urging trust in doctors. But in the 1980s, a genre emerged that Anne Huntsaker Hawkins (1999, 6f) labels 'angry pathographies', documenting the callousness, coldness, and cruelty of doctors and healthcare systems. Into the 1990s, such critiques expanded to the wider social world and those instances of pathophobic 'viciousness' experienced across the many contexts of everyday life, with a main inspiration being Susan Sontag's analysis, in her classic essay 'Illness as Metaphor', of the oppressive character of the culturally entrenched 'mythology of cancer' (1978, 87).

Across these testimonies and narratives are detailed accounts and critically charged analyses of pathophobic phenomena, which are highly plural, shaped by three sets of factors. To start with, the forms taken by pathophobia will depend on the symptomology, effects and manifestations of an illness, and its cultural and symbolic associations. Sontag explores the moral, emotional, and symbolic meanings associated with different cancers: some appear 'ill-omened, abominable, repugnant', or as aesthetically 'obscene' or a moral 'disgrace' (1978, 9). Such associations and meanings are shaped by the typical effects of illnesses and their treatment modalities on a person's abilities and appearance. An illness may cause disfigurement, slurred speech, sweating, bodily convulsions, memory loss, and other changes that affect the specific forms taken by pathophobia. Illnesses will also have different social and medical statuses – recognised or accepted, 'contested' or 'stigmatised' – all of which alter the specific sorts of pathophobic attitudes and behaviours to which one may be subjected.

A second set of factors contributing to the plurality of forms of pathophobia are agential. An ill person is never just an *ill person*, since that will be one of their many intersecting social identities, so their sick bodies will also be gendered and racialized, and thoroughly embedded in specific socio-economic structures. Such identities affect both susceptibility to pathophobic mistreatment and the resources available to ill persons when attempting to cope with it, such as credibility, empathy, and trust. Lorde located the 'crisis' occasioned by breast cancer within a 'whole pattern' of gendered and racialized injustice with resonated with pathophobic prejudices to generate a ramifying structure of 'separation and powerlessness' (1997, 11, 13). A contemporary example is *Sick*, Porochista Khakpour's memoir of her experiences as a college-educated, Iranian immigrant, with a history of drug abuse, and Lyme disease, an illness whose status was openly contested by many of her doctors – all of which shaped the frequency, severity, and forms taken by the pathophobia she experienced (Khakpour 2018).

A final source of the plurality of pathophobia are features of wider cultural context. Ways of experiencing and responding to somatic illness are highly variable, depending on available and prevalent norms, ideals, practices, and stereotypes. Cultures supply scripts – some heroic and triumphalist, others accusative and shaming, often by invoking themes of personal failure and moral corruption (think of lung cancer and liver disease). Sontag said 'nothing is more punitive than to give a disease a meaning', which is why certain cultural conceptions of illness – such as the 'mythology of cancer' – ought to be made 'obsolete' (1978, 58, 88). Such cultural constructions of somatic illness will also affect the frequency and forms of pathophobia, especially when social norms and institutions tend to inscribe and enact morally objectionable attitudes towards and treatment of those with somatic illnesses.

There is a clear consensus within the pathographic literature on the morally awful character of pathophobia, across its many forms. Within the majority of the testimonial and narrative reports, there is an evaluatively charged rhetoric of anger, bitterness, and frustration, as in Lorde's talk of the 'fury', 'brutality', and 'stupidity' of the pathophobia that, for an ill person, 'passes for the way things are'. But knowing that pathophobia is wrong does not tell us the specific character of those wrongs, a problem complicated by the fact that pathographies employ a variety of moral languages – of injustice, violations of rights, and failures of autonomy, among others. Such pluralism generally suits the purposes of pathographers, whose main concerns are not in systematic moral theorising. Moral theory is not always useful, desirable, or necessary, and should therefore only be used carefully and sparingly. But developing a systematic framework, if done carefully and nondogmatically, can be useful – for instance, as a way of ensuring that certain deep, subtle features of pathophobia do not go unnoticed or misdescribed.

A respect for use of a plurality of moral vocabularies to describe pathophobia is consistent with the claim that certain of them can have distinctive advantages over others, relative to certain values or goals. In what follows, I propose that moral analysis of pathophobia is best served by a *vice-ethical* framework – a style of ethical theorising that focuses on the appraisal of moral conduct in terms of sets of failings or defects of character and, crucially, the social conditions that sustain and amplify them.

3. Pathophobia and Vices

Lorde's description of the 'viciousness' that infuses the everyday treatment of ill persons exploits the technical sense of vice as negative character traits or 'defects', in the sense of 'qualities that make us worse people' (Battaly 2015, 6). Some are broadly moral failings, such as cruelty or selfishness, while others are aesthetic, affective, or epistemic failings, such as snobbishness, coldness, or closed-mindedness, and there are many vices and many ways in which they can be grouped. Within recent Western character theory, the main focus has been on the virtues and such related positive notions as excellence, flourishing, and the good life. As a consequence, much less has been said about vices, failings, and corruption, and less work has been done applying those concepts to analyse specific social phenomena, such as pathophobia.

An exception is a recent work by Battaly 2015), who defends a pluralistic analysis of vice, according to which a trait can become vicious in two ways. An *effects-vice* is a trait that tends to create a preponderance of bad effects when exercised under typical or usual circumstances, where the bad effects can be defined in relation to any domain of value one likes. Cruelty, for instance, tends to create the bad moral effects of causing unnecessary and avoidable suffering to other people and creatures, such as physical harm or emotional distress – a clear example of a moral effects-vice. Dogmatism tends to obstruct one's ability to critically revise one's stock of beliefs in response to critical challenges or counter-evidence, making it an epistemic effects-vice. Such vices only need to *tend* to cause bad effects, since they might fail to do so in some circumstances and, relatedly, under conditions of oppression could sometimes create good effects – a possibility explored by feminist character theorists, such as Dillon (2012) and Tessman (2005).

A second type for a trait to become vicious is by expressing or manifesting bad values or motives, such as a desire to cause needless suffering to others, or an indifference to truth, which are morally and epistemically bad, respectively. Battaly calls these *motives-vices*, arguing that such traits reflect badly on one's character, quite independently of any effects they might create. A cruel person might never act on their dispositions to cause suffering out of calculated self-interest, but are still vicious in the sense of their possessing a negative character trait. Moreover, attributing a vice to an agent need not entail *blaming* them for its possession, since agents can acquire vicious traits due to the suboptimalities of their socialisation or due to corrupting environments (Battaly 2016).

The viciousness of a trait can, therefore, be located in its typical effects, or the motives and values it incorporates, or both of these. Certain traits are objectionable by virtue of their effects and motives, making these what Battally calls *hybrid vices*. More can be said about the structure and the components of character vices, and their relation to the virtues, but this is enough for present purposes.

I want to propose that moral analyses of pathophobia ought to be framed in the terms of vice ethics for two reasons: *narrative fidelity* and *descriptive richness*. It's vital that philosophical analyses of pathophobia are faithful to the lived experiences of those people who are subjected to it, for which the best source are pathographic testimonies and narratives (Kidd 2017a). Otherwise, the analysis is cut off from the concrete realities of pathophobia. When reading those pathographies, one consistently finds a vocabulary of vices, whether by way of explicit mention ('cruelty', 'selfishness') or through implicit descriptions ('they didn't care at all when I told them about my diagnosis').

A second reason to use a vice-ethical framework it that it enables rich descriptions of pathophobic actions and behaviour, since vice-terms are so-called 'thick' moral concepts – they combine evaluative and non-evaluative description ('cruel', for instance, has a degree of behavioural particularity and cultural specificity lacking from such 'thin' concepts as BAD or WRONG). Our concepts of vice typically include specifications of various associated forms of bodily comportment – cruel sneers, haughty tones of voice, smug facial expressions, and so on, all of which is exploited by pathographers. Indeed, the pathophobic vices are mainly to be sound in ordinary-everyday modes of behaviour comportment, rather than being confined to occasional dramatic instances of egregious moral failure.

Before going onto the pathophobic vices, two more technical comments are needed on the nature of vices, each of which is relevant to the philosophical study of pathophobia. First, the bearers of vices will primarily be individual agents, to some specific person whose actions and speech are vicious, such as a cruel doctor, thoughtless colleague, or cold-hearted stranger met on the street. But we also attribute vices to collective agents, such as dogmatic committees or unfriendly departments, and also to institutions, as when the United Nations Special Rapporteur on extreme poverty and human rights recently described the healthcare and social welfare system created over the last decade by the Conservative Government as 'cruel', since it now imposes needlessly prolonged, complex obstacles that make it difficult, if not impossible, for suffering persons to access the state support, without which their lives are substantially worsened. Attributions of vices to institutions, policies, and systems should be taken seriously within the project of analysing pathophobia, although my present focus is on agential pathophobia.

The second comment is that my analysis of pathophobia does not rely on the customary division of character traits into the categories of the ethical and the epistemic, which within Western character theory is attributed to Aristotle. We do not find a division of this sort in ancient Indian and classical Chinese character ethics, and there are two sorts of exceptions within the Western tradition: the indissolubly 'ethico-epistemic' virtues, such as truthfulness, and the occasional appearance of such additional classes as the civic and the spiritual virtues and vices. I think that the ethical-epistemic distinction does not help us to appreciate and organise the specific forms and interrelationships of the pathophobic vices and failings. To see why, let us look at them in detail.

4. The Clusters of Pathophobic Vices

I suggest that pathophobic attitudes, behaviour, and ways of thinking can be most usefully conceptualised, described, and analysed if we think about them in terms of *pathophobic vices*. Consultation of pathographic testimonies offers a huge range of candidates, of course, but also creates the problem of yielding a list that is too long and unwieldly to be useful for our practical and theoretical purposes. I keep a list of the vices mentioned in pathographies, which currently runs to about a hundred and twenty: the list is informative but unhelpful as a means of giving people easy, practical ways of thinking about pathophobia.

My strategy for cogently organising the variety of pathophobic vices into a workable system relies upon the neglected moral-theoretical practice of taxonomizing human failings into clusters organised around a generic type of salient feature. Earlier examples of this sort of exercise include the lists compiled by medieval Christian theologians of our sins and vices, or the Buddhist catalogues of our 'taints', 'cankers', and 'defilements'. I propose to classify the variety of pathophobic vices into five main clusters, construed as pragmatic artefacts to guide our practices of evaluation rather than delineations of some objective ordering. I think that some vices could fit into, or can straddle, different clusters, due to the conceptual and psychological continuities between certain traits. Moreover, the five clusters are not taken to be exhaustive: others can be proposed, as long as they show fidelity to the content of the pathographic testimonies. I suspect, for instance, that there is a cluster of 'vices of paternalism', such as condescension, dismissiveness, and pathocentric testimonial injustice, which all tend to subvert the social and epistemic agency of somatically ill persons (see Kidd and Carel 2017).

My procedure for taxonomizing the pathophobic vices is to describe the general type of failing characteristic of the cluster and then to sketch some illustrative examples of those vices using examples from the pathographies by Carel, Conway, and Ehrenreich. My modest aim is to establish the practical and theoretical utility of the vice-ethical framing of analyses of pathophobia. If that is not granted, there would be no point moving on to more complex issues about collective vices, blame and responsibility, and amelioration which presuppose that framing.

1. *Aversion cluster.*

The vices in this cluster involve failures to engage interpersonally with somatically ill persons in appropriate ways. Aversiveness might include flat refusals or expressions of reluctance to interact with them, or, when that cannot be avoided, adoption of behavioural styles that tend to diminish the quality and frequency of those interactions – staring and glaring at the visible signs of illness, for instance, or peremptory tones of voice, or monosyllabic answers to questions. Typical aversive vices, therefore, include aloofness, coldness, evasiveness, and rudeness, each of which can create a variety of bad effects – causing upset and distress, for instance, or depriving the ill person of the social and epistemic goods often acquirable only through interpersonal communication. Aversive vices can also manifest bad motives, such as an indifference to the social isolation of other people, an unwillingness to do the moral and emotional work that is often required when dealing with vulnerable persons, or what Carel calls an implacable indifference to those 'whose life trajectory is different' (2009, 48).

Pathographic testimonies frequently describe the embodied forms of the aversive vices and their objectionable effects and motives. Conway, for instance, describes the 'grimaces' of women who glare at her cancered body, which leaves her 'feeling grotesque', rather than 'seen and accepted' (2007, 136, 147). Carel describes the 'stares on the street' occasioned by her oxygen tank and nasal canula, and the blasts of 'awkwardness' that chill conversations with colleagues, alongside starker cases that teach her a grim lesson:

> '[It] is only a matter of time before another person – a drunk on the street or a rude teenager – who say something that will bring tears to my eyes, something that will make the true horror of my condition appear in broad daylight, my carefully constructed but fragile defences crumbling before it.' (2009, 48)

Such aversive pathophobia is complexly structured by roles and relationships and the social contexts pertinent to such experiences. Drunks and rude teenagers can be dismissed, given the marginal and incidental role they have in our life, but this is not true of those to whom one is more intimately related – friends and family, colleagues, healthcare practitioners, and others on whom one is more continuously and complexly dependent. Carel sadly describes the remorse and disappointment caused by 'those [friends] who never get in touch, or promise to but never do, of those who call or visit but never talk about the illness', offering that 'what is tragic about being ill is this silence' (2009, 54, 56).

These aversive traits assume the specific status of pathophobic vices because they tend to deprive chronically somatically ill persons of the practical, social, epistemic goods on which they are distinctively dependent. In life at large, even brief conversations can afford flickers of happiness, a sense of security, provide valuable information, and contribute to a sense of belonging in the world. Such small acts of recognition and affirmation as passing greetings can shape the character of one's day, while subjection to stares and glares can lend to the social world an oppressive character. Taken together, the effects of subjection to aversive pathophobic behaviour can range from anger and frustration to social isolation, diminished mental health, and the entrenchment of painful sense of estrangement from the world.

An interesting feature of the aversive vices is that they can be fed by morally good motives even when they have bad effects. Aversive pathophobia can result from contempt, indifference, and other objectionable feelings and motives, in ways that are obviously bad. But three other sorts of motives are more complicated. To start with, a lot of aversiveness is caused by negative aesthetic responses to illness, such as automatic responses of disgust or revulsion at the appearances, sounds, and odour of diseased bodies. Ehrenreich describes herself as 'transmogrified' by her cancer into a 'puking, trembling, swelling, surrendering significant parts, and oozing [thing]' (2009, 68). Many people report genuine difficulties when trying to exercise virtues of care and friendliness with the hesitancy, reluctance, and evident disgust that are their involuntary responses to the bodies of their patients – responses that range from 'squeamishness' and 'embarrassment' to 'panic and surprise' through to 'terror' and 'extreme discomfort' (Carel 2009, 57).

A second source of aversive pathophobia are the variations in people's interactive preferences and styles depending on the situation, the social context, and the particularities of their relationships to the person with whom they are engaging. Some ill people are happy to talk about their illnesses, for instance, while others are to do so only at certain times or in certain contexts. Some chronically ill people may have a default willingness to converse, that is unfortunately contingent on their constantly changing bodily capacities. Carel notes that a person with a limited lung capacity cannot easily afford the oxygen budget needed for many conversations and much socialising: the oxygen might not be flowing at the same rate as the wine and conversation, which can necessitate either silence or retreat (2009, ch. 4).

A third source of aversive pathophobic behaviour are the interactive difficulties that are often intrinsic to experiences of chronic somatic illness, which often significantly affect one's speech, memory, attention, stamina, energy, and mood. Conway recalls that during her cancer and its treatment, she had 'no sense of humour; nothing rolls off my back; I am no fun to be with' (2007, 200). The problem was that she could no longer participate in the norms and practices of typical forms of social intercourse, most of which are premised upon certain levels of bodily and psychological capacity. Think of the typical speed of conversation – about 120 to 160wpm for native Anglophone speakers – or the cognitive complexity of the phenomenon of circumstantial speech, where conversations drift away from, then return to, the original topic.

I suspect that many people who act aversively may have genuine, morally admirable desires to treat ill persons in properly respectful, sensitive ways. But without appropriate social norms and practices to guide their interactions, people freeze in a state of interactive uncertainty and come across as 'cold'. In these cases, aversive pathophobia would be a case of *backfiring virtue*, of having virtuous motives but vicious effects, owing to an absence of appropriate social guidance on the proper bodily performance of the virtues. The study of pathophobia can, therefore, reveal the existence of unusual forms of human vice.

2. Banality cluster.

The second cluster of pathophobic vices are interesting examples of traits that are usually minor moral failings that are elevated to major moral vices when exercised in the context of chronic illness. The vices of banality include glibness, superficiality, and triteness, which few of us would desire to possess even if equally few would regard them as substantive defects. I propose that what makes these traits into central pathophobic vices is that they all reflect failures to appreciate and honour the existential complexity of lived experiences of somatic illness. Condensed into those nine words is Carel's characterisation of being ill as a 'global disruption' of our 'habits, capacities, and actions', the structures of our experience, and the wider integrity and rhythms of 'the life-world' (2009, 8–9, 45). Such a fundamental alteration of our intermeshed orientation in the world which resonate a person's experience, agency, and understanding of themselves and the world. It is the fact and effects of failure to grasp the extent and the depth of these alterations which sets up a distinct set of vices of banality.

Pathophobic banality mainly shows itself in ways of thinking and talking about illness and especially in conversational exchanges with somatically ill persons, who often comment on the clichés, bland assurances, and trite pieces of wisdom endemic to many contemporary discourses about illness. Conway recalls things said to her during her cancer and treatment:

> Some people recount positive stories of survival. I hear about one woman who had breast cancer and cycles twenty miles a day throughout chemotherapy; another who looked gorgeous the entire time; a third who told no one of her diagnosis and acted as if her life were absolutely normal. Why are these stories not consoling me? (Conway 2007, 58)

Banality, in these cases, involved a lack of connection to Conway's own experiences. By failing to really connect with the particular course and structure of her needs, concerns, and preoccupations, remarks such as those cited as experienced as prosaic, predictable, and facile. Such lack of engagement is also a failure to evince any deep understanding of Conway's experiences, so vices of banality will include glibness, superficiality, triteness.

Such traits become vicious, when exercised in the context of chronic illness, for two related reasons. First, pathophobic banality has bad effects upon the ill persons, ranging from anger and frustration to a reinforced sense of alienation from others, consistent with an acute sense, reported by Carel, of lived experiences of chronic illness as an 'encounter between a body limited by illness and an environment oblivious to such bodies' (2009, 52–53). Second, banality often reflects a fundamental epistemic defect of many persons, namely, a failure to acquire a deeper insight or understanding of the complexities of lived experiences of chronic illnesses. Sometimes, the failure might reflect what Carel calls the 'obliviousness' of healthy persons, their 'inability ... to conceive of the lives of others' (2009, 46). Granted, such understanding can be very difficult to acquire, so banality of that sort is not *necessarily* or *automatically* blameworthy. In other cases, banality is rooted in more morally objectionable motives, feelings, and desires, as when Conway reports her suspicion that many people 'felt compelled to tell me these stories, I think, more for their benefit than mine – to quell the anxiety they felt' (2007, 3).

When appraising banality, one must remember that trite, superficial talk can serve to protect us from confronting the practical, emotional, and existential realities of chronic illness and can be useful for that reason, as many chronically ill persons and their carers well know. The viciousness arises when such banalities are not an occasional feature of discourse about illnesses – an act of pragmatic respite from the flow of overwhelming uncertainty, perhaps – but their continuous and defining feature. As a woman with a chronic illness put it to me:

> Above all else, I hate that *fucking* slogan – 'Whatever doesn't kill you can only make you stronger.' I see it *all the time* on T-shirts and on my Facebook feed and on those little planks of wood with inspirational messages that people hang in their kitchens. When people come out with that fucking slogan, they're ignoring everything that is specific to you as a person. They utter it, then leave you alone (personal communication, original emphasis)

The sense of safety that comes with remaining at the surface level is understandable, when one really confronts the complexity that lies in the depths of experiences of chronic illness, construed as a life-transforming experience. Since the vices of banality confine us to the surface of those experiences, it becomes increasingly impossible for people to appreciate, explore, and describe the inner complexity of what it is like to be chronically somatically ill.

A desire for such existentially deep reportage and discussion of experiences of chronic somatic illness is often accompanied, however, by an ambivalence on the part of many ill persons. Carel says she often desires the sorts of sincere, sustained conversations of this deep sort, but finds that her capacity to participate in them often varies synchronically and diachronically. Moreover, much depends on the particularities of her interlocutors and situation, all of which means, in practice, enormous uncertainty. One might prefer ritualised exchanges of banalities, or desire existentially deep exchanges, or, perhaps more likely, seek out some moderate position between those two poles:

> If they ask questions, I feel uncomfortable, as if they are prying. If they say nothing, I think they are selfish, self-centred, oblivious to my plight. If it is difficult to talk about illness, it is especially hard for ill people. But what I learned from my illness is that in times of hardship, grief, and loss, there is no need for original, illuminating phrases. There is nothing to say other than the most banal stuff: "I am sorry for your loss"; "This is so sad." (2009, 57)

Setting aside the complex variety of agential and structural sources of pathophobic banality, what is crucial from a vice-theoretic perspective is the character of a person's responses when realising the fact and extent of their banality. Understanding the phenomenological heterogeneity of experiences of chronic somatic illness across their situationally and culturally specific forms is hugely epistemically demanding (Carel 2016; Svenaeus 2000). But there are ways of trying to reduce the incidences and severity of pathophobic banality that do not require mandated crash courses in the phenomenology of illness, such as closer engagement with narrative accounts of illness, sustained challenges to entrenched discourses of banality, and other practices that might help one to avoid inadvertent banality.

3. *Callousness cluster.*

In a striking shift, the 'angry pathographies' of the 1980s focused on the common callousness of doctors, nurses, and healthcare systems, while the contemporary narratives by healthcare practitioners – such as Robert Klitzman's *When Doctors Become Patients* – report deep-seated worries that 'the system and practice of medical education may facilitate or even exacerbate callousness' (2007, 112). Pathophobic callousness, however, is not confined to healthcare and its agents, but stretches out into every domain of the social world of the somatically ill. I divide the vices in the callousness cluster into two sub-groups: the *vices of abuse* involve willingness or desire to exploit the vulnerabilities of ill persons, whether for pleasure or self-interest, and include cruelty and unkindness. Second, the *vices of abandonment* involve failures to experience and demonstrate care and concern for the vulnerable, such as negligence and selfishness, or what Lorde lamented as a 'stupid, brutal lack of consciousness and concern.'

The vices of callousness are opposed to compassion, gentleness, kindness, sympathy, and the human quality Carel judges to be in 'greatest shortage', namely empathy, the virtue or disposition whose absence 'hurts the most' (2009, 37). The systematic presence of patterns of abuse and abandonment, at the individual and collective levels, is a sad fact of human life, arising partly from our multiple and variably vulnerable bodies and identities, which build into our existence the permanent possibilities of 'morally dysfunctional or abusive interpersonal and social relationships and socio-political oppression or injustice' (MacKenzie, Rogers, and Dodds 2014, 9). The abuses and abandonments constitutive of pathophobic callousness are specific to the morally dysfunctional experiences, relationships, and socio-political situations of the somatically ill. To borrow the useful terminology of Jackie Leach Scully, experiences of somatic illness always have certain 'intrinsic vulnerabilities' – such as greater susceptibility to infection or fatigue – while subjection to pathophobia is a 'contingent vulnerability', the product of 'historical and contemporary relationships', which are shaped by 'patterns of social, cultural, and political responses' to oppressed groups (2014, 208, 209).

I want to focus on pathophobic callousness of healthcare practitioners and systems, rather than experiences in the wider social world, for two related reasons. First, shrugging off callousness is harder when it is perpetrated by people professionally charged with your health and treatment, whose conduct ought to evince what two virtue theorists call the 'allocentric virtues', traits aimed at 'intelligent caring about people', such as attentiveness and generosity (Gulliford and Roberts 2018). Such allocentric virtues are surely professional virtues for those engaged in healthcare practice, since their exercise is definitive of the morally and practically effective performance of their professional duties. Second, concern with callousness is central to narratives by doctors and by patients, to healthcare research and policy, and to wider sets of questions – ethical, legal, political, practical – about patient safety, medical training, and trust in healthcare systems.

Consider Conway's descriptions of her experiences of hospital care, immediately after her mastectomy, in a chapter poignantly titled, 'Loss':

> Not a single nurse ever attempts to talk to me. I feel tired, angry, almost frantic. It would be difficult to design a scenario more likely to make a vulnerable person feel out of control. I really need help and get no response. I am as much an object to the staff as is my pitcher of water or my adjustable bed; and even when they respond to my call, I am just another task, not a person in pain (2007, 80)

The callousness, here, involves failures to perceive and respond appropriately to her physical and emotional vulnerabilities following three major experiences – her breast cancer, major surgery, and the loss of her breast, all creating entangled feelings of pain, 'guilt', and 'shame' (2007, 93). The coldness, negligence, and indifference of the hospital staff continued until the day she was discharged:

> I'm going home, and aside from my surgeons, not one of the hospital staff has spoken to me about the mastectomy, the postoperative adjustment, or what to expect with the healing. No one has even asked me how I am doing. How little it would take to make me feel better (2007, 86)

The last remark underscores one of the most painful aspects of callous abandonment – the simplicity of small acts of attention and kindness contrast with their enormous moral effects, even if virtuously allopathic acts are often more demanding, practically and emotionally. Our admiration for those vocationally and professionally committed to caring for others reflects our sense of the demands and the importance of caring. The corollary is that we react more critically to acts of callousness by healthcare practitioners, who are professionally committed as well as morally obliged to exercise the allopathic virtues of intelligent caring.

Although narrative accounts of the callousness of healthcare practitioners sometimes aim to criticise the failings of specific individuals, many avoid attributions of blame and turn instead to the structural conditions – medical training, say, or workplace cultures – that may encourage or necessitate such failings. Confronted with pathophobic vices, one needs neither default to blaming, nor remain focused on individual-level explanations, since our character and conduct are deeply shaped by the contingencies of our formation and the suboptimalities of our environments. Consider Carel's account of an encounter with a sullen, emotionless nurse:

> What sort of training has made her able to stand there, saying nothing, offering no word of comfort or distraction? Does she do this every day, to all her patients? Does she feel anything but annoyance towards me? Is this exchange sanctioned by the National Health Service? Does she think of me as a person?' (2009, 47)

Confronted with pathophobically callous acts by healthcare practitioners, one should attend to the social and material conditions of their working environments. Those allocentric virtues usually incur significant exercise costs which cannot always be met by overworked nurses or doctors trying to do work that is practically exhausting, cognitively complex, and emotionally exhausting within an underfunded healthcare system dominated by a target-based culture. Considered in this wider context, concrete individual failings must be understood relative to wider professional and institutional structures – a claim that is obviously compatible with the claim that some callousness people are fundamentally inattentive and negligent.

I have focused on the vices of abandonment, mainly for the reason that they are the most commonly reported kinds of pathophobic callousness reported in the pathographic narratives and testimonies. But what of the morally severer failures that I labelled the vices of abuse? For descriptions of these, one has to turn to a different literature, the medicolegal and policy documents that record acts of sustained cruelty, exploitation, and violence meted out to aged and chronically ill people usually homed in medical and social care institutions. In the United Kingdom over the last decade, a series of high-profile cases of severe breaches of duties of care within National Health Service Trusts led to a 2018 policy review into cases of gross negligence. Named for its chair, Sir Norman Williams, the report found the investigation of cases of gross negligence was rare, while the prosecution was even rarer (Department of Health and Social Care 2018). A report in the same year by University College London and the Camden and Islington NHS Foundation Trust found evidence of abuse of elderly persons in 99% of care homes (Claudia et al. 2018). Here one sees patterns of abuse consistent with the worst forms of the vices of callousness that is being caused and exacerbated by structural changes to the UK healthcare system.

The study of the vices of callousness should, therefore, encompass the vices of abuse and of abandonment and take seriously both their individual and collective forms. I think this is true of all of the pathophobic vices, as explained in section two, but the existing empirical data indicates that agential callousness may be a secondary product of structural callousness – of a wider contingent structure of imperatives, constraints, and pressures that are tending to create healthcare systems that stifle the exercise of allopathic vices and instead establish conditions that increase the frequency of failures of empathy, compassion, and care (and how agents experience and respond to those conditions is, of course, shaped by their intersectionally complex social identities – a recent analysis of structural medical misogyny is Dusenberg 2017).

4. *Insensitivity cluster.*

The pathophobic vices often reflect broadly epistemic failings, as when Carel remarks on how many healthy persons are 'blissfully ignorant' of the fragility of their health which feeds a sort of 'obliviousness' – an inability to 'conceive of the lives of others' (2009, 32, 46). It is this obliviousness that particularly underlies the fourth cluster, the vices of insensitivity, the set of failures of awareness and responsiveness to the personal, intimate, distressing nature of the chronic somatic illness. Pathophobic insensitivity can manifest in all sorts of ways, from our speech to our facial expressions, attitudes, and actions (a neighbour of mine, shortly after being diagnosed with liver cancer, received a bottle of whisky as a birthday present bearing the message, 'Now you *have* to share it!')

Since vicious insensitivity takes many forms, I focus on insensitive forms of speech, specifically upon those that manifest the vices of *prurience* and *tactlessness*, which relate to our practices of questioning and the content and delivery of our speech, respectively. What characterises the pathophobically insensitive person is a tendency to talk in ways that cause anger, upset, and sadness (the effects-forms of the vice) and manifest failures of awareness of the sensitivities of ill persons or to attend properly to the content or timing of their words. The viciousness of insensitivity is clear in Conway's encounter with a friend – a nurse – who opines that illness must be harder for the elderly because they 'really know' they are 'going to die':

> Doesn't she know that I also feel that I'm dying? And I have young children. She rambles on, and I sense my rage building. I try to explain the sense of mortality I live with, but she tells me that I sound like her depressed mother. I'm stunned by her insensitivity and cut the lunch short to go home. (2007, 200)

Conway is 'stunned' due to her incredulity at what is being said, and an acute shock that it was being said by a friend – a trained nurse, no less – who, more than anyone else, ought to afford deep consideration and empathy.

Starting with the rather old-fashioned sounding vice of prurience, this used to refer to excessive curiosity about unwholesome topics, often of a sexual or erotic sort. I use the term more broadly to refer to a desire to acquire inappropriate sorts of epistemic goods, especially concerning the intimate or personal details of a person's life, such as their bodily health. In its pathophobic forms, this vice includes what is usually called 'morbid curiosity' about the effects of a person's illness on their body – an epistemic appetite for the graphic and gory details, the grisly and gruesome information that properly belong only to the person and healthcare staff. Such curiosity about ill bodies can be virtuously motivated, of course, if it reflects the fascination with the human body or a desire to better understand what a friend might be experiencing in their illness. Prurience, however, often has bad effects and reflects bad motives, which range from public embarrassment (when 'everyone knows') to angered indignity (at the violation of one's privacy) to acute emotional and psychological distress, of the sort described by Carel in her story of a 'Horrible Man' she met at a dinner party shortly after her wedding:

> "Oh wonderful!" says the man. "Are you going to have children?"

> My heart sinks. The question drops straight into my core and sits there, heavy. My mind goes blank. "No," I say, in a tone I hope sounds stern enough to ward off any further questions. But he presses on.
>
> "Why not?" he asks. I am beginning to panic, but am not sure how rude I can really be to this man, a friend of our friends. I want to scream at him "because I am dying of lung cancer, you idiot." I think how illegitimate this question has become for our generation, especially for couples in their mid-thirties, who are either having trouble conceiving or decided not to have children. I also think how personal, how damn personal, the question he is asking is.
>
> I want to hit him. I want to vanish from the table. A storm rushes through my mind.
>
> I say, "Because we can't." (2007, 45-46)

Unfortunately, despite Carel's manifest discomfort, the man 'presses on', 'relentless' in a way she describes as 'somewhere between sadism and sociopathy' (2009, 46). The viciousness here arises from both the intrusiveness of the questions, the 'relentless' insistence, and the man's insufficient attention to its effects. Indeed, later in the conversation, he comments explicitly on Carel's dismay (2009, 47).

A second vice of insensitivity is tactlessness, a failure to ensure the appropriateness of the timing, topic, and phrasing of one's utterances, statements, remarks, and other forms of speech with and about illness or somatically ill persons. In pathophobic cases, the failure is not a lack of articulacy, relevancy, or other Gricean norms, although those may play a role. Instead, the viciousness lies in the failure of attention and consideration about the effects of what one says and how and when one says it upon ill persons or those otherwise concerned deeply with illness (if, say, the audience includes the parents of a chronically ill child, for instance).

Carel offers a vivid instance of pathophobic tactlessness:

> Several times when I told people about my illness they asked, "So how long have you got?" The question always left me gasping for air, as if I've been punched in the stomach. After overcoming my horror at the casualness with which the question was asked, I wondered why they wanted to know (2009, 144)

Treating chronic somatic illness 'casually' is a failure to appreciate or acknowledge its severity by using modes of speech that register the urgent seriousness of the information. Tactfulness often involves careful circumspection and thoughtful phrasing rather than reliance on loosely idiomatic language whose casualness fails to cohere with the seriousness of the situation.

Carel proposes that much insensitive speech arises from a general thoughtlessness on the part of 'oblivious' healthy persons, who fail to anticipate in advance the insensitive nature of what they say until they hear themselves saying it:

> I remember telling an old friend about my illness and how much I deteriorated in the past year [...] When I told her I lost nearly 50 per cent of my lung capacity over a short period, she looked at me and said: "so if you lose about 50 per cent next year ..." It took me a long time to regain my composure that day. I never discussed my illness with her again (2009, 67-68)

The vices of prurience and tactlessness are just two of those in the insensitivity cluster, which encompasses a range of intermingled affective, epistemic, and ethical failings – indiscretion, impassivity, and thoughtlessness, for instance. Such vices evince a failure to recognise or know the actual or probable sensitivities of the somatically ill and lack of sense enough to act towards them in appropriately responsive, sensitive ways.

5. *Untruthfulness cluster.*

Susan Sontag starts her essay 'Illness as Metaphor' by declaring her a desire to find a 'truthful way of regarding illness' (1978, 3). Truthfulness devolves into a set of 'virtues of truth', defined by Bernard Williams as the 'qualities of people that are displayed in wanting to know the truth, in finding it out, and in telling it to other people' (2002, 7). Williams offers two – accuracy and sincerity – which must be augmented by the virtues of truth described by Lorde, which enable us to 'scrutinize not only the truth of what we speak, but the truth of that language by which we speak it' (1997, 31). Pathophobia can include failures to be truthful about the complexities and heterogeneity of experiences of somatic illness and, in particular, their various 'dark sides' – the anxieties, despair, frustration, loneliness, and sadness, of course, but also the fact that these often yield no positive personal goods and find no satisfying resolution.

The pathophobic vices of untruthfulness range from failures to desire, discover, or tell the truth about own or others' experiences of illness, or actively discouraging and interfering with such efforts on the part of others. I am not suggesting ill persons must blurt out each and every detail of their experiences, nor that they are obliged to act as 'witness [to] some of the realities of illness', as Arthur Frank describes the aim of pathography (2002, 5). Untruthfulness about illness arises when people do engage in pathography by providing their own testimonies or by engaging with those of others, whether through books, support groups, online fora, or during conversations. I, therefore, focus on vices of untruthfulness as they manifest in pathography, a striking case where pathophobic attitudes and behaviour are most visible among ill persons.

A powerful study of pathophobic untruthfulness is *Smile or Die*, a book by the medical writer and cultural critic, Barbara Ehrenreich, which explores the 'ideology of positive thinking' increasingly entrenched within American culture. Her central concept is that of 'bright-siding', a determined tendency either to deny or the 'dark sides' of aspects of human life – sickness and poverty, sat – or to insist that they are outweighed by the 'bright-sides', thereby glossing over their negative realities in conformity with a narrative of triumphal optimism that insists upon the 'triumph of attitude over circumstance' (2009, 150). Ehrenreich was inspired to write the book partly as a result of her own experiences with breast cancer, whose discourses were suffused with a monotone optimism which she elected to test, one day, with a post on a forum entitled 'Angry'. Her statements of angry at chemotherapy, insurance companies, and 'sappy pink ribbon cultures' were met with near-unanimous content and tone policing by the women on the forum:

> "Suzy" wrote to tell me, "I really dislike saying you have a bad attitude towards all of this, but you do, and it's not going to help you in the least." "Mary" was a bit more tolerant, writing, "Barb, at this time in your life, it's so important to put all your energies toward a peaceful, if not happy, existence. Cancer is a rotten thing to have happen and there are no answers for any of us as to why. But to live your life, whether you have one more year or 51, in anger and bitterness is such a waste [...] I hope you can find some peace."

This is the aggressive form of bright-siding that aims to confine and control illness discourses by active policing of their content and tone. Ehrenreich's truthful reports of the 'dark sides' of her cancer were interdicted, since they did not conform to the norms of optimism and triumph governing that discourse. The operative vices here include myopia and dogmatism, the related failures to admit certain pertinent dimensions of experiences of illness and defensively resist efforts to change the scope of the discourse.

The heterogeneity of experiences of illness means untruthfulness can take many forms, and many of these are usefully captured by the concept of 'bright-siding'. Sometimes, there is a denial of the 'dark sides' of illness, a refusal to admit the bitterness, frustration, and sadness incurred by, for instance, the friends who never call back or the permanent loss of one's hopes for a family or a career. Sometimes, the dark sides are acknowledged, but only if they can then be reclaimed within a narrative of triumphant reckoning with adversity. When the old friends stop calling, the initial sadness is soon replaced by the newer, better relationship one forms in the support group. After the diagnosis, one becomes resentful at the body that 'betrayed' – every tumour a 'traitor' – but then, after a while, one comes to feel more at home than ever within one's skin. In such cases, one sees the logic of 'bright-siding' – of 'battles' that end in victory, never in defeat, of journeys that are completed but never abandoned, of suffering that always transforms one morally for the better (there is a genre of pathographies that use the metaphor of cancer as a gift, one that 'gives' more than it 'takes', to the point of being 'the gift that keeps on giving').

Such cultures of 'bright-siding' encourage the vices of untruthfulness because they are hostile to truthful reportage of the complexity of experiences of somatic illness, especially the negative aspects and 'dark sides'. The content of pathographic testimonies is made to conform to the rigid dictates of optimism, heroism, and triumphalism, whether by omitting those dark sides or glossing over them, maybe by downplaying their awfulness and inflating or inventing their 'bright-sides'. The consequences are systematic failures of truthfulness about the variety of experiences of chronic illness, since to tell the truth about what it is like to be ill often means attending to the dark and the bright sides. Some experiences of illness are positive and deeply edifying and acknowledging this is a truth about illness worth telling (Brady 2018; Kidd 2012). But most experiences of illness as complexly textured and resist accurate, sincere description within the artificial strictures of 'bright-siding'. The vices of dogmatic optimism and myopia preclude the sorts of complexly discerning descriptions of most actual experiences of illness of the sort one needs for a properly truthful effort for what Sontag and Frank called a 'more truthful' attempt to 'bear witness' to living with illness.

A full analysis of the vices of untruthfulness is a complex task since they are motivated in so many ways and scaffolded by so many features of our societies. A natural fear of death, the difficulties of honesty, the understandable preference of publishers and readers for happy endings, the entrenchment of cultural and religious narratives that promise that suffering will be rewarded – to name just a few. It seems clear that truthfulness about illness requires us to acknowledge and confront the existentially disturbing realities of what it means to exist within forms of mortal existence whose fragility arises from our intrinsic embodied vulnerability and the contingent vulnerabilities arising from our dependence on a social world whose members and structures often respond to that fragile matrix of vulnerabilities with the variety of failings that constitute pathophobia. Truthfulness about our inherent embodied vulnerability and our awkward situation as perpetrators and subjects of pathophobia ought to be a main aim of any serious humanistic philosophical engagement with illness (see Ferry-Danini 2018; Kidd 2017b).

5. Conclusions

This paper introduces the concept of pathophobia to describe the range of objectionable sorts of treatment to which chronically somatically ill persons are typically subjected, whose wrongs can be analysed effectively using a vice-theoretical framework. I argued that we can usefully think in terms of five main clusters of pathophobic vices and failings, illustrating them with the testimonies offered by some influential illness narratives. Such vices can be objectionable due to their typical effects or their underlying motives and values, or they might be doubly vicious. It should be clear there is a lot of future work, too, which should include studies of structural pathophobia, investigation of specific vices and clusters, and the development of ameliorative strategies.

Acknowledgments

I am very grateful for insightful comments of two referees, Sophie Atkinson, Havi Carel, Craig French, Emma Jaura (who did invaluable research work on Conway's *Ordinary Life*), Matthew Ratcliffe, and to very collegial audiences at the Universities of Aberdeen, Sheffield, York and University College Dublin.

Disclosure statement

No potential conflict of interest was reported by the author.

Funding

I acknowledge the support of the UCD Centre for Ethics in Public Life and of Universitas21.

References

Battaly, H. 2015. *Virtues*. Cambridge: Polity.
Battaly, H. 2016. "Developing Virtue and Rehabilitating Vice: Worries about Self-Cultivation and Self-Reform." *Journal of Moral Education* 45 (2): 207–222. doi:10.1080/03057240.2016.1195732.
Brady, M. S. 2018. *Suffering and Virtue*. Oxford: Oxford University Press.
Carel, H. 2009. *Illness: The Cry of the Flesh*. 2nd ed. Stocksfield: Acumen.
Carel, H. 2016. *Phenomenology of Illness*. Oxford: Oxford University Press.
Claudia, C., L. Marston, J. Barber, D. Livingston, P. Rapaport, and P. Higgs. 2018. "Do Care Homes Deliver Person-Centred Care?" *PLoS ONE* 13 (3): e0193399.
Conway, K. 2007. *Ordinary Life: A Memoir of Illness*. Ann Arbor, MI: University of Michigan Press.
Department of Health and Social Care. 2018. *Gross Negligence Manslaughter in Healthcare: The Report of a Rapid Policy Review*. London: Department of Health and Social Care.
Dillon, R. S. 2012. "Critical Character Theory: Toward a Feminist Perspective on "Vice" (And "Virtue")." In *Out from the Shadows: Analytical Feminist Contributions to Traditional Philosophy*, edited by S. Crasnow and A. M. Superson, 83–114. Oxford: Oxford University Press.
Dusenberg, M. 2017. *Doing Harm: The Truth About How Bad Medicine and Lazy Science Leave Women Dismissed, Misdiagnosed, and Sick*. New York, NY: HarperOne/HarperCollins.
Ehrenreich, B. 2009. *Smile or Die: How Positive Thinking Fooled America and the World*. London: Granta.

Ferry-Danini, J. 2018. "A New Path for Humanistic Medicine." *Theoretical Medicine and Bioethics* 39 (1): 57–77. doi:10.1007/s11017-018-9433-4.
Frank, A. 2002. *At the Will of the Body: Reflections on Illness*. New York: Houghton Mifflin Harcourt.
Gulliford, L., and R. C. Roberts. 2018. "Exploring the "Unity" of the Virtues: The Case of an Allocentric Quintet." *Theory & Psychology* 28 (2): 208–222. doi:10.1177/0959354317751666.
Hawkins, A. H. 1999. *Reconstructing Illness: Studies in Pathography*. 2nd ed. West Layayette: Purdue University Press.
Khakpour, P. 2018. *Sick: A Memoir*. Edinburgh: Canongate.
Kidd, I. J. 2012. "Can Illness Be Edifying?" *Inquiry* 55 (5): 496–520. doi:10.1080/0020174X.2012.716203.
Kidd, I. J. 2017a. "Exemplars, Ethics, and Illness Narratives." *Theoretical Medicine and Bioethics* 38 (4): 323–334. doi:10.1007/s11017-017-9411-2.
Kidd, I. J. 2017b. "Phenomenology of Illness, Philosophy, and Life." *Studies in History and Philosophy of Biological and Biomedical Science* 62 (2): 56–60. doi:10.1016/j.shpsc.2017.02.005.
Kidd, I. J., and H. Carel. 2017. "Epistemic Injustice and Illness." *Journal of Applied Philosophy* 33: 172–190.
Klitzman, R. 2007. *When Doctors Become Patients*. Oxford: Oxford University Press, 2008.
Lorde, A. 1997. *The Cancer Journals*. San Francisco: Aunt Lute Books.
Mackenzie, C., W. Rogers, and S. Dodds, eds. 2014. *Vulnerability: New Essays in Ethics and Feminist Philosophy*. Oxford, UK: Oxford University Press.
Scully, J. L. 2014. "Disability and Vulnerability: On Bodies, Dependence, and Power." In *Vulnerability: New Essays in Ethics and Feminist Philosophy*, edited by C. Mackenzie, W. Rogers, and S. Dodds, 204–221. Oxford, UK: Oxford University Press.
Sontag, S. 1978. *Illness as Metaphor*. New York: Farrar, Straus & Giroux.
Svenaeus, F. 2000. *The Hermeneutics of Medicine and the Phenomenology of Health: Steps Towards a Philosophy of Medical Practice*. Dordrecht: Kluwer.
Tessman, L. 2005. *Burdened Virtues: Virtue Ethics for Liberatory Struggles*. Oxford: Oxford University Press.
Williams, B. 2002. *Truth and Truthfulness: An Essay in Genealogy*. Princeton: Princeton University Press.

Beyond Empathy: Vulnerability, Relationality and Dementia

Danielle Petherbridge

ABSTRACT
This paper brings together a phenomenological and vulnerability-theoretic approach to dementia. The paper challenges the view that subjects with dementia can simply be understood in terms of diminished cognitive capacities or that they have lost all vestiges of personhood or the capacity for meaningful interaction. Instead, drawing on vulnerability theory and the phenomenological work of Kristin Zeiler and Lisa Käll, an alternative view of persons with dementia is offered that is based on intersubjective and intercorporeal relations and accomplishments. A vulnerability approach to dementia is developed that not only provides the basis for empathetic responses to illnesses such as dementia but also points to the intersubjective constitution of subjects more generally. The argument developed is that the notion of vulnerability designates a form of openness to others and that such openness is a precondition for empathy.

Introduction

In his biography of Iris Murdoch's later years as an Alzheimer's sufferer, John Bayley writes of the way in which communication between them begins to dwindle and falter until it all but ceases. As he expresses it: 'Our mode of communication seems like underwater sonar, each bouncing pulsations off the other, and listening for an echo' (Bayley 1998, 59).[1] In his account of the onset of Murdoch's condition one sentence by Bayley is striking. He explains that one of the ways in which he tries to attend to Murdoch in the moments in which she struggles to find words or finish a sentence is to expose his own vulnerability, or as he puts it, to embark 'on a joky parody of helplessness, and [try] to make it mutual. Both of us at a loss for words' (Bayley 1998, 59).

What is particularly notable about Bayley's memoir is that he struggles not only with the loss of verbal communication with a woman whom he describes as once displaying a brilliant and creative mind but that he also assumes she has lost a sense of self or even her humanity. This is most tellingly revealed when in describing Murdoch, Bayley (1998, 60) claims:

> The Alzheimer face is neither tragic or comic, as a face can appear in other forms of dementia: that would suggest humanity and emotion in their most distorted guise. The Alzheimer face indicates only an absence: it is a mask in the most literal sense.

This is a common assumption about conditions of dementia such as Alzheimer's. Such perspectives often characterize dementia in the following terms: as a complete loss of self and personhood, a turning inwards, a disconnection from the world, loss of memory, an inability for meaningful interaction and loss of communication. The condition of dementia is therefore often described as a 'psychic' death before 'physical death' or as Bayley (1998, 217) puts it: 'like an insidious fog, barely noticeable until everything around has disappeared. After that it is no longer possible to believe that a world outside fog exists.'

In the consideration of dementia offered here, I wish to return to Bayley's subtle insight about mutual vulnerability with which this paper began, in order to offer an alternative view of dementia. More specifically, I offer an approach to dementia that draws on both phenomenological research and vulnerability theory to develop an intersubjective and intercorporeal perspective.

In order to assess what a phenomenological and vulnerability approach might offer, in the first part of the paper I explore problems associated with conventional approaches but also look at promising new directions in dementia research. In the second part, I discuss the phenomenological work of Kristin Zeiler (2014) and Lisa Käll (2017), who develop an alternative phenomenological approach to dementia. Both Zeiler and Käll argue that dementia should not be understood as a complete loss of self or identity, but rather that identity and personhood might instead be understood in terms of intersubjective or intercorporeal accomplishments, ones that continue throughout life but take different forms in older age. Finally, in the third part, I outline a vulnerability approach to dementia that I suggest compliments the work of Zeiler and Käll, and when brought together with an intercorporeal view, can provide a more empathetic response to such illnesses. The argument developed in the final section is that the notion of vulnerability designates a form of openness to others and that such openness is a precondition for empathy. A vulnerability approach has important affinities with phenomenological approaches to illness as well as pointing to the constitutive forms of interdependence that underlie empathetic forms of responsiveness.

1. Contemporary Discourses on Dementia

It is instructive to contrast medical and neuroscientific discourses about dementia with the accounts of carers and sufferers, such as the one outlined in Bayley's account of Murdoch discussed above. Although medical discourses, medical imaging and brain scans can highlight certain aspects of neurological degeneration, they cannot shed light on the 'human' and relational aspects of the issues arising with such illnesses. First-hand accounts and memoirs by sufferers and carers, as well as the work of therapists and 'social' researchers, engage more richly not only with issues of selfhood and personhood but also with the communicative, intercorporeal and intersubjective aspects of dementia.

Medical discourses on dementia tend to describe the condition in terms of neurodegeneration or in terms of any 'disorder where significant decline from one's previous level of cognition causes interference in occupational, domestic or social functioning' (Gale, Acar, and Daffner 2018). However, dementia often has multiple possible causes. It can be caused by diseases such as Alzheimer's or Parkinson's, by traumatic brain injury, psychological illness or chronic alcohol abuse, for example (Gale, Acar, and Daffner 2018). Strikingly, though, there is often very little consideration of the personal and relational aspects of the illness alongside the clinical description of dementia. More insidiously, the focus on clinical and cognitive dysfunction tends to set up a dichotomy between different classes of people, which is specifically intensified by common cultural assumptions about people of an older age, or rigid views about health and illness.

As Grenier, Lloyd, and Phillipson (2017) argue, popular views of old age and specifically of dementia often construct images of those who have 'failed' in old age. In other words, there tends to be a 'dichotomy between "healthy" "active aging"' and 'those who are frail and demented and thereby need care'. As they describe it, this distinction has sometimes been captured by the employment of terms such as 'the third age' (to refer to a successful aging lifestyle) and a 'fourth age' marked by a social position of decline, which is identified as 'unagentic' (Grenier, Lloyd, and Phillipson 2017, 318–319). Such distinctions and the fear and mystification surrounding dementia often form the basis not only of popular opinion but also of healthcare policy and fundraising campaigns. This kind of assumption is evident, for example, in an official UK Department of Health report from 2013 that states:

> We are facing one of the biggest health challenges ever, a challenge as big as fights against cancer, heart disease and HIV. Dementia steals lives. It also imposes a huge emotional and financial cost. It is time to fight back. (Grenier, Lloyd, and Phillipson 2017, 319)

Such descriptions of dementia tend to fuel a popular view that dementia is a dreaded disease and a 'horrific' end to later life, one that also causes a significant drain on resources and healthcare infrastructure rather than focusing on the personal and social aspects of the illness.

However, as Kitwood explains, although there is no doubt that the pattern of most people's behaviour changes with dementia, it is a matter of debate about how this might be interpreted. As he suggests, a person may lose full capacities, either because of neurological impairment or sometimes due to social-psychological factors or it may sometimes be attributable to the unsupportive responses of others. It is also noted, that people with dementia often express long-standing anxieties or psychological complexities that may not have been addressed in earlier years of their lives. In dementia, as the ability to deal with forms of anxiety is increasingly eroded, emotional and relational issues are often expressed in an exaggerated manner. For example, someone who has been extremely self-controlled throughout life may express episodes of rage, or use foul language and physical violence; or, someone who had managed to repress sexual drives throughout early years might express a heightened sexual drive and become sexually uninhibited (Kitwood 1997a, 13–22). It is unclear, however, that any of these symptoms should be regarded as a loss of self but might instead indicate a transformed self, one that changes over time.

Kitwood (1997a) argues that it is highly problematic to assume people with dementia are devoid of subjective experience or reduced to an egoic world that is so bizarre and disordered that they can no longer be addressed as persons or be engaged in meaningful forms of relationality. In fact, Kitwood makes a strong case for what he terms a 'bold and wholehearted venture into intersubjectivity' when engaging with dementia sufferers based on a notion of empathy. In Kitwood's (1997a,) terms:

> Empathy consists of an attempt to understand what a person may be going through, listening carefully to what they say, noticing what they do, and making sense of it all by drawing on our own experience; not feeling their emotions, but feeling the resonances of those emotions within ourselves.

He suggests that although we cannot directly enter another person's feeling or mental states, or their frame of reference, we can attempt to understand their emotions by empathetically engaging with the subject's pain and suffering. Kitwood's recourse to a notion of empathy is significant as empathy is often assumed to be the frame through which it is possible to relate to experiences of the other, even if we have not endured similar experiences or cannot enter others' mental states or feel their emotions. However, the argument developed here is that such empathetic forms of responsiveness must already assume an openness to the other that is more readily defined through a notion of constitutive vulnerability. As I discuss in the final section below, given experiences of illnesses such as dementia are often radically outside our modal space of experience (Ratcliffe 2012), a primary openness to others is a precondition for empathetic responsiveness. As discussed in the final section, a notion of vulnerability also provides an enriched account of the interdependence between persons with dementia and carers or family members that also accounts for the intersubjective and intercorporeal dimensions of personhood.

As both Agich (2003) and Kitwood (1997a, 1997b) suggest, it is the situated nature of individuals that helps to maintain a sense of self in dementia. Individuals need to be understood in relation to and in interaction with others, not reduced to internal egoic acts nor should it be assumed there is a loss of personhood based on the demise of internal cognitive abilities. Agich also problematizes the conventional view of selfhood in dementia that is often employed as a measure of 'failed aging'. Instead, Agich takes a relational view of the self, which emphasizes the socially embedded nature of selves and their connectedness to others. Like Kitwood, who highlights aspects such as attachment, comfort, inclusion and identity in dementia care, Agich emphasizes the importance of the need to consider the spatial, temporal, communicative and affective dimensions of care for older people rather than assessing them merely on the basis of a loss of certain capacities.

Moreover, this suggests that an individualistic idea of personhood or one based solely on individual cognitive capacities and memory is one that should be contested. Rather, the account of the subject outlined here is a relational one based on intersubjective and intercorporeal capacities, such that the self is understood in essential relations with others rather than in individualistic terms. The notion of selfhood explored in this paper is used interchangeably with the notion of personhood. In both cases, the conception employed is not based merely on cognitive and rational capacities such as memory, reflexivity and language. Instead the view offered here is a body-orientated and relational view of personhood or selfhood. It not only assumes that cognition is always already embodied but significantly that embodiment is central to personhood, and also highlights the ways in which selves or persons are constituted and affirmed through relation with others. Neither of these conditions alone is sufficient but taken together they offer a complex or thickly conceived account of personhood, one that continues and manifests in alternative ways throughout the life cycle.

It is with these insights in mind that I turn to a phenomenological analysis of dementia in section two below. I do so with a view not only of offering an alternative understanding of the continuation of selfhood in dementia but also to examine the importance of relationality in understanding personhood. Such an approach considers the ways in which the self is not only intersubjectively constituted but also examines the manner in which the changing self with dementia can express herself through embodied modalities. This suggests a more complex approach to the relationality of dementia that emphasizes not merely linguistic but specifically corporeal dimensions.

2. A Phenomenological Approach to Dementia: Intercorporeality and the Self

In a similar vein to Kitwood, Lisa Käll (2017) questions the problematic ways in which popular discourses about dementia are dominated by vivid imaginaries of a terrifying end to life that results in the 'dissolution or loss of self and identity' or considered 'as a mental death before physical death'. In contrast, Käll argues that 'the person afflicted with dementia still remains a person and retains vital aspects of selfhood' that can be maintained and fostered through interaction with others (Käll 2017, 359).

However, despite the advances in dementia research that are now questioning assumptions about the loss of the person or selfhood, Käll argues that more can be done to understand subjectivity and what it means to be a self in relation to others. Käll (2017, 359) suggests that often what is missing in contemporary research and what is sorely needed is a focus on what she terms the 'subjectivity of dementia'. She argues, however, that a turn to the focus on the 'subjectivity of dementia' should not be understood in a conventional sense of the isolated ego or simply in terms of (diminished) mental states but instead should be alert to: (1) a continually changing form of self throughout the life cycle; (2) alternative forms of self-expression that are communicated in embodied forms; (3) the embeddedness of the subject in intersubjective and intercorporeal social contexts and relational forms.

Käll draws primarily on the phenomenological work of Merleau-Ponty to emphasize the constitution and perpetual reconstitution of embodied subjectivity. She emphasizes the intercorporeal becoming of the subject and describes individual embodiment as a perceptual process of expression of subjectivity rather than understanding the subject in static terms. In this manner, she suggests that if we understand the subject in terms of changing modes of expression throughout the life cycle, we might more aptly describe embodied selves as 'in a state of continuous birth, *in statu nascendi*, endlessly achieved as relational and situated, but never brought to completion as fixed' (Käll 2017, 372).

Moreover, if we follow Merleau-Ponty, it is possible to argue that the embodied subject cannot be considered as an isolated being but is always already embedded in the social 'by which', he argues, 'we are in contact by the mere fact of existing' (Merleau-Ponty 1962, 421). In this sense, Merleau-Ponty emphasizes the embodied nature of subjectivity and the ways in which our embodied selves are constituted intersubjectively and intercorporeally from the background of a shared social world and with other human bodies who are always, already social beings. This intercorporeality creates a constitutive openness and vulnerability to others and means that subjects are *affected* by one another even on an elementary level but also that they potentially remain open to change (Diprose 2002, 55, 69; Petherbridge 2018, 71). As Merleau-Ponty explains in the *Phenomenology of Perception*, '... it is precisely my body which perceives the body of another, and discovers in that other body a miraculous prolongation of my own intentions, a familiar way of dealing with the world' (Merleau-Ponty 1962, 12). In this sense, as embodied subjects we exist beyond a level of individuation and can recognize others as embodied beings like ourselves with similar capacities for body-intentionality. Thus, although as Merleau-Ponty's work suggests we are 'body-subjects' we are also not trapped in 'our own world' nor subject to forms of complete closure or absolute sovereignty (Sullivan 2001, 70).

Building on Husserl's work, Merleau-Ponty offers a rich account of embodied relationality based on the notion of double-sensation, for example, the experience of one hand touching the other hand. If my right hand clasps my left hand, I experience a peculiar double-sensation. At one and the same time my right hand (the touching hand) is doing the feeling, it is feeling the surface of the left hand. Yet at the same time, my left hand feels like an object I am touching. However, it is not given to me just like any other object in the world (it is not like holding my pen and taking notes), instead I have a double feeling of not just touching an object but my other hand feels the touch at the same time (Merleau-Ponty 1968). The experience of double-sensation, of simultaneously being both subject and object, inside and outside, provides a model for understanding how it is that we perceive and experience other subjects. It is exactly the unique subject-object status of the body and the ability to experience double-sensation that also enables me to recognize and experience other embodied subjects. When my left hand touches my right or *vice versa*, I am experiencing myself in a manner that is indicative of both the way in which the other would experience me and that I can experience the other (Merleau-Ponty 1968; Käll 2017, 364–365).

This form of intercorporeality always involves an embodied openness to others. Such forms of embodied responsiveness indicate that in our interactions with others we open ourselves receptively to them rather than constituting the other in sameness, attempting to know the other at the level of abstract thought or apprehending their suffering only through the horizon of our own experience. The notion of 'intercorporeality' therefore points to the constitutive interconnection between bodies. It discloses the dynamic and contingent nature of embodiment, revealing not only embodied interrelatedness but the social, cultural and historical situatedness of the lived body. The importance of Merleau-Ponty's account is to indicate the constitutive nature of our corporeal interrelatedness and the porosity of the body, or rather the fluidity of bodily boundedness, as well as revealing the way in which our intercorporeality is also constitutive of subjectivity and our intersubjective world.

However, Merleau-Ponty also points to the ways in which our social interactions with others are also subject to forms of sedimentation that habitualize perception and bodily comportment, and impede our openness towards others. Forms of individual bodily comportment are both affected by, altered and limited by our bodily actions over time and through our interactions with others, and this is especially so later in life for people who suffer from dementia. What is often overlooked in dementia sufferers is that even when cognitive abilities diminish, or memory is challenged, subjects often still maintain a particular bodily style or express themselves in an embodied manner that indicates a constancy of selfhood. Subjects with dementia can often still move through the world or interact with others in particular ways given the habitualized forms of embodied knowledge that shape their own bodily style or mode of comportment.

However, as Kitwood notes, bodily forms of expression in dementia sufferers can often convey emotional suffering or a desperate need for interaction with others or an attempt at self-comfort when forms of relational engagement are extremely limited or withdrawn. Perrin describes the way in which

> [p]eople with very severe dementia show a range of bodily movements, such as rubbing parts of the body, pinching the face and hands, rocking to and fro, or crumpling and twisting items of clothing. These behaviors may be forms of self-stimulation: a last desperate bid to remain psychologically alive when the external environment has largely failed to provide them with security and occupation. (Perrin cited in Kitwood 1997a, 16)

In this respect, institutional models of aged care tend to be based on an assumed individualism and as Sherwin and Winsby (2010,) have noted are often based on 'task completion – such as dressing, bathing, feeding and documentation' rather than practices that foster relationality and subjective expression in alternative forms. In this sense, institutional aged care tends to be structured around attending to basic physical needs such as hygiene and feeding without being alert and attentive to social or subjective needs. A focus on medical needs, together with assumptions about a complete loss of selfhood, tend to result in very limited opportunities for self-expression or meaningful forms of relationality.

As a means of addressing such concerns Kristin Zeiler has developed a phenomenological approach to subjectivity in the case of dementia by emphasizing what might be termed relational and intercorporeal forms of subjectivity. Key to Zeiler's model is an analysis of what she terms joint activity in dementia care which gives rise to intercorporeal capabilities for dementia sufferers (Zeiler 2014). Her argument is that interaction between persons with dementia and family or carers through joint activities and intense face-to-face intercorporeality can give rise to intercorporeal capabilities and new forms of subjective expression. In this manner, through posture, touch, eye contact and movement she suggests that a 'shared space of dynamic intercorporeal engagement' is created and fostered (Zeiler 2014, 136). Zeiler argues that self–other joint activities enable individuals who cannot otherwise express themselves to do so in interactions with others that are often non-linguistic. Following Merleau-Ponty, the focus on intercorporeality shifts the emphasis from the individual and individual expressivity to the relation between subjects and forms of expression that are fostered in relation.

In her account, Zeiler makes some important distinctions between different conceptions of personhood, arguing that conventional conceptions of personhood such as the classic view offered by Locke '*often fail to acknowledge the role of embodiment in personhood*' (Zeiler 2014, 131, my emphasis). In this regard Zeiler makes distinctions between what she terms 'monadic cognition-orientated' conceptions of personhood in which personhood revolves solely around individual capacities such as cognition and memory, and 'mixed cognition-orientated' conceptions which are not only defined by individual capacities but also require a subject to be regarded as a person by others based on the capacities they possess. She contrasts the above-mentioned conceptions of personhood to two alternative views: one, a 'dyadic' view such that persons are understood in relation to others and to be considered persons must be recognized as such by others; two, a 'monadic body-orientated' conception whereby personhood is defined by pre-reflexive bodily capacities rather than merely cognitive ones but these are understood solely in individual terms (Zeiler 2014).

Zeiler argues that if we apply a 'monadic cognition-orientated' conception of personhood in dementia research and care, then there is little that staff in institutional care would be able to do to foster personhood. However, she asserts that there is much more scope both philosophically and in terms of forms of care if we adopt an embodied and intercorporeal conception. In this sense, she argues that although 'cognition is certainly important for personhood, it is unclear why capacities that involve cognition should be *necessary* for someone to qualify as a person' (Zeiler 2014, 134).[2] Zeiler demonstrates that even individuals who seem to have lost cognitive capacities and who cannot 'remember their name or past events still have a bodily know-how with regard to how to engage with others' (Zeiler 2014, 140, 134). Moreover, following a Merleau-Pontian line, Zeiler suggests that although dementia sufferers may not have verbal skills or be able to remember and recount past events linguistically, they still comport themselves with a particular bodily style, using particular gestures or bodily expressions that persist over time. Following Matthews, Zeiler argues that individuals therefore retain their individuality through their bodily style of being and that a person should be taken to be 'a unified being' not only if she can express herself through speech but also through gesture and bodily forms, or through interactions with others (Zeiler 2014, 135).

However, Zeiler makes the important claim that we should not consider a person to be a being who qualifies as such based *only* on certain bodily capacities. She suggests that extending beyond the cognitive account of personhood based on bodily capacities is a first crucial step. In a second step, she emphasizes that a body-orientated account of personhood should be conceived in relational terms rather than monadic ones. In this respect, she takes-up an insight from dyadic and mixed-cognition accounts, which argue that recognition of someone as a person by others is also a condition for personhood. On this score, Zeiler points to the recognition theory associated with Hegel and Honneth, that claims that personhood not only requires recognition by others but that subjects *only develop as persons in relations with others* (Zeiler 2014, 133). Her main point is to argue for both a relational conception of personhood but also to shift the emphasis away from accounts based solely on cognitive capacities to embodied ones. In this light, she argues for an account of personhood that is based on embodied capacities and intercorporeality as well as forms of embodied acknowledgement.

Zeiler (2014, 135) draws on recent dementia care and research that demonstrates the ways in which persons with dementia still retain capacities for singing and rhythmic movement despite a reduction in cognitive ability. Her specific analysis is based on a study of embodied and musical interactions between dementia therapist, Naomi Feil, and 87-year-old Gladys Wilson, who has been diagnosed with Alzheimer's disease and is described as virtually non-verbal.[3]

The analysis is based on a filmed interaction between Naomi Feil and Gladys Wilson. At the beginning, Gladys Wilson is seen sitting on her own in a wheelchair moving her hand and her legs repetitively in an apparent attempt at self-stimulation. In the next frame, we see Feil approaching Wilson and greeting her. Wilson clasps Feil's arm and pushes her down as if motioning her to sit. Feil bends and then sits down in order to attempt to be at eye-level with Wilson. Upon seeing a tear on Wilson's cheek, Feil gently touches Wilson's face as a means of communicating with her and

Wilson opens her eyes and looks at Feil. Feil asks Wilson whether she will let her in a little at which point Wilson begins rhythmically banging the arm of the chair with her hand. Feil begins to sing gospel songs that she knows have been especially meaningful to Wilson earlier in her life whilst gently stroking Wilson's arm. As Feil sings, Wilson moves her hand against the chair in rhythm to Feil's singing. As the interaction proceeds we see Wilson speed up the rhythmic movement of her hand against the chair and Feil tries to match the intensity of this movement with the rhythm of her singing. Finally, as Feil sings the lyrics to the song 'He's Got the Whole World in His Hands', Wilson audibly whispers the lines and sings along with Feil. She also opens her eyes fully and looks at Feil. In the last segment of the interaction after this intense joint-activity or mirroring, Wilson speaks with Feil and responds to her questions, indicating several levels of communication both embodied and verbal between them.

Zeiler argues that Feil and Wilson create a shared space in which each subject can express herself through a form of 'dynamic intercorporeal engagement'. She also highlights the way in which intercorporeality more generally should be understood as a form of 'basic openness to others' (Zeiler 2014, 136). This general openness to others is described as a form of 'primordial intercorporeality', which indicates that the subject is always constituted in relation to others (think for example of the way in which a child is constituted in relation to primary caregivers). This is contrasted to what Zeiler terms 'face-to-face joint activities' which she understands as forms of interaction in which 'self and other are intensively aware, connected and sensitive to each other' such as in the case of joint activity between Feil and Wilson (Zeiler 2014, 137). Her point here is that intense face-to-face intercorporeality in such forms of joint activity, enables capabilities to be fostered and developed that might not be possible outside of forms of interaction, especially for dementia sufferers. On this basis she argues that 'joint activity makes it possible for the participants in an activity to qualify as distinct yet thoroughly relational persons *because* it allows both of them to express themselves as unique-subjects-acting-together in a joint fashion' (Zeiler 2014, 138–139).[4] Moreover, her conception of intercorporeal capacities also allows for a conception of personhood that is maintained across time even when cognitive abilities are diminished. Wilson is able to express herself and her personhood through her embodied and musical interaction with Feil and this is something that can be maintained over time. Such capabilities for personhood are, however, not seen to be the property merely of one person but created through forms of interaction, and in this respect each person is able to do more through interaction with others than individually (Zeiler 2014, 138–139).

Although it would be a mistake to draw a distinct separation between cognitive and bodily intentionality more generally, the point being made here is more nuanced. The argument developed here is that when cognitive ability is diminished and subjects appear to be non-verbal, the capacity for bodily subjectivity can be maintained, or at least can be expressed through forms of embodied interaction with others. In this sense, it might be suggested that even where an explicit cognitive awareness of self or reflexive capacities are low, persons still maintain embodied habits and the capacity for forms of relationality that enable both the expression of self and forms of interaction with others. For example, even if a subject with dementia cannot remember a loved one's name, she can still share in bodily forms of interaction such as holding the loved one's hand or stroking her arm that are expressive of meaningful forms of relationality and the affirmation of self. In this respect, Zeiler points to the importance of 'intercorporeal memory' that signifies the ways in which self-other interactions are incorporated into the subject's lived body and how these embodied and intercorporeal 'memories' continue beyond cognitive impairment into later years of life.

Although Zeiler makes a distinction between what she terms 'primordial' and 'intense face-to-face intercorporeality', one of the important points I take from her analysis, in addition to her account of embodied and recognitive personhood, is that all forms of intercorporeality must first assume a primary form of openness to others that begins in infancy and continues throughout the life cycle. This is the focus of the discussion in the final section.

3. Vulnerability, Empathy and Dementia

In her analysis, Zeiler points to the importance of a primordial openness to the other that enables any kind of intercorporeality to first take place. Her analysis highlights the embodied nature of this basic openness to others and the world and the way in which subjects are constituted in and through relations with others. Another way we might describe the form of 'primordial intercorporeality' that Zeiler seeks to highlight is in terms of a notion of vulnerability. Moreover, I argue that the notion of intercorporeality that both Zeiler and Käll develop can be enriched when brought together with a theory of vulnerability that in turn also provides an alternative account of empathy.

The notion of vulnerability has been reconceptualized recently in the work of theorists such as Cora Diamond, Axel Honneth, Adriana Caverero, Judith Butler and Martha Fineman, as a constitutive and universal category. A vulnerability approach is based on notions of interdependence, reciprocity and intersubjectivity and as such offers an alternative to liberal conceptions of the individualistic and sovereign subject. Moreover, to speak of mutual vulnerability is to acknowledge forms of dependence and care that are prevalent throughout the life cycle. A notion of vulnerability highlights our corporeality and finitude, as well as the complexity of the human condition in terms of both positive and negative forms of relationality. The category of vulnerability has therefore also been employed as the basis for normative theories of intersubjectivity or interdependence, which might form the basis of an account of ethics, manifested, for example, in an ethics of care or based on a theory of recognition.

Here it is instructive to turn to Axel Honneth's account given the explicit manner in which he develops a notion of vulnerability based on a normative theory of mutual recognition. For Honneth, the fact of our vulnerability at birth requires forms of human relationality and care, or practical intersubjective responses that are also necessary throughout the life cycle. He highlights the ways in which primary vulnerability fosters the capacity for cultural development and social action through which humans shape their own nature, the natural environment and the social world more generally (Honneth and Joas 1988; Petherbridge 2016).[5] Human beings not only require basic care from the moment of birth but also rely on forms of social cooperation and basic forms of normative relationality to ensure their mutual well-being.

Moreover, Honneth also develops a strong intersubjective theory of subject-formation based on recognitive relations. In Honneth's (1995, 248) view there is a taken-for-granted assumption at the level of everyday life, 'that we implicitly owe our integrity to the receipt of approval or recognition from other persons'. According to this account, 'the integrity of human subjects, vulnerable as they are to injury through insult and disrespect, depends on their receiving approval and respect from others' (Honneth 1995, 248). For Honneth, human self-realization requires the basic ongoing affirmation of other subjects; it is only in this way, that the 'individual can unfold a practical identity' (Honneth 1995, 249). In this sense, recognition is understood to be necessary for the development of a positive relation-to-self, which requires forms of self-trust, self-respect and self-esteem that can only be achieved through affirming relations of recognition. In Honneth's view, not only breeches of physical integrity, but also abuses of psychological integrity, pose the 'risk of injury which can cause the identity of the entire person to collapse' (Honneth 1995, 249; Petherbridge 2016).

One of the benefits of Honneth's account is that he identifies the ways in which persons remain vulnerable to the ongoing need for recognition, not only in terms of embodied needs but also in terms of the affirmation of selfhood and subjectivity that is underpinned by a normative claim. For Honneth, then, constitutive vulnerability is understood through the lens of mutual recognition and this designates primary forms of relationality and normative forms of social interdependence (See Petherbridge 2016).

Embodied vulnerability is then a constitutive element that defines us as persons and it becomes a central category through which to examine the complexity of corporeal interdependence. However, it extends beyond the phenomenological account of intercorporeality by suggesting there is an ethical claim that is intrinsic to our vulnerable interdependence. In other words, it points not only to embodied capacities for expressiveness with others but also the ways in which these are intrinsically ethically inflected forms of interaction.

My own claim, however, is that vulnerability is best described as designating a general *openness towards the other*. Moreover, I suggest that the openness evoked by vulnerability is multidimensional: (1) it designates a form of corporeal openness that indicates the richness of embodied experience and intercorporeality at the same time as it evokes a propensity for suffering; (2) it refers to a psychological openness that affirms the individual through her relations to others and avoids monadic forms of closure; (3) it is a form of interdependence that evokes care for the subject in her needfulness but also means she is exposed to forms of power and abuses of vulnerability. In this sense, the notion of vulnerability designates our constitutive and needful openness to others that is prevalent from the moment of (and even prior to) birth and that indicates primary forms of psychological and embodied interdependence and relationality (Petherbridge 2016).

How then does a vulnerability approach enrich and inform an understanding of empathetic responsiveness to dementia?

Here I wish to turn to a brief discussion of the phenomenological account of empathy developed by Matthew Ratcliffe in the context of experiences of depression. This phenomenological account is instructive as it also shares affinities with the account of vulnerability I develop here in relation to dementia. It should be noted that the model of empathy that Ratcliffe prefers does not require the empathizer to replicate the empathee's experience but instead requires an acknowledgment of the differences between the experience of self and other, and the capacity to be able to appreciate a 'person's experience as *she experiences it*' (Ratcliffe 2014, 270).[6] As Ratcliffe describes it, then, according to this phenomenological view, empathy is a form of intentionality that should be understood as 'a distinctive kind of other-directed attitude' (Ratcliffe 2014, 271).

Ratcliffe's account is instructive not only in terms of understanding the structure of empathy in cases of depression but also in relation to illnesses such as dementia. Ratcliffe (2014) defines the kind of empathy required to relate to cases of depression as a kind of 'radical empathy' that he argues enables an appreciation of phenomenological difference, where certain experiences are outside our own general modal space of experience. He likens this to a kind of phenomenological reduction but one that can be enacted at an everyday level and that does not need to be viewed in highly reflexive or philosophical terms (see Ratcliffe 2014, 273; also 2012).

What is particularly significant about Ratcliffe's account of empathy is that he defines it as 'a perception-like exploration of experience, which progresses through a kind of interaction characterized by mutual connectedness and openness' (Ratcliffe 2014, 271). As he points out, our experiences generally take place in the context of a shared world or shared common ground that is taken for granted and against which it is possible to understand a certain range of experience (Ratcliffe 2014, 272). However, in the case of depression – and even more so in the case of dementia – this common ground is severely eroded or cannot be taken for granted and it can lead to 'an alteration in the structure of interpersonal experience' (Ratcliffe 2014, 274). Thus, in taking up Ratcliffe's account of empathy in relation to dementia, we could say that 'empathy consists of a kind of dynamic, quasi-perceptual exploration of another person's experience that involves relating to her in a distinctive kind of way' (Ratcliffe 2014, 275).

As Ratcliffe highlights such a form of empathy is fostered by 'patterns of action between people' and also involves a 'kind of mutual bodily receptivity' through which we relate to others in the realm of bodily feeling (Ratcliffe 2014, 275; see Gallagher 2001). In this respect, Ratcliffe suggests that we think of 'empathy' as a kind of 'mutual empathy', that is, 'as a progressively sophisticated experience of mutual understanding that develops through certain forms of interaction' (Ratcliffe 2014, 277).

However, in the case of dementia, it would be very difficult to apply Ratcliffe's account of mutual empathy, at least in a strongly defined manner. As discussed above, the kind of 'understanding' that arises out of joint action or interaction with persons with dementia is one of embodied understanding and not one that mutually occurs at a high level of reflexivity. What is revealing in Ratcliffe's account is that he explicitly suggests that '[t]he kind of care or concern that is needed for empathy [...] be [...] identified with the attentiveness and openness to the other person that is *partly constitutive* of such a process [of empathy]...'; or elsewhere he explains that empathy is an '"openness" to another person [that] is the starting point of a process that can develop to varying degrees' (Ratcliffe 2014, 277, 278).[7] Here Ratcliffe is suggesting that there is a constitutive element that is prior to and constitutive of empathetic responsiveness. Furthermore, he identifies this specifically as an openness and attentiveness to the other that is required for empathy. I suggest that the kind of constitutive openness to the other that Ratcliffe identifies is in fact a precondition for empathy – not merely part of the 'process' of empathy itself. My argument is that this primary openness is best understood as a constitutive condition of vulnerability that we all share, one that is first required for a person to even attempt to adopt the perspective of the other or to recognize the other's experience as one that is hers and distinct from one's own (Ratcliffe 2014, 277).

In the case of dementia this is particularly acute. First, because the experience of a person with dementia is radically different from a person who does not suffer from dementia, and second, because it is very difficult to speak of 'mutual empathy' as Ratcliffe defines it in the case of interactions between dementia sufferers and non-sufferers. In the case of dementia, I suggest that it is instead a mutual vulnerable condition that defines both persons in the relation and that enables them to respond to one another in affective and embodied forms of interaction. Although a person who does not have dementia may indeed respond empathetically to a person with dementia, the argument here is that he or she must first acknowledge a shared vulnerability and recognize the other's differently vulnerable state. In this sense, I agree with Ratcliffe that empathy first assumes a constitutive form of openness but argue that this is a shared condition that forms the background to any form of empathy, especially where, as in the case of dementia, this might be an asymmetrical relation and cannot be properly described as 'mutual empathy'. Thus, I suggest that what Ratcliffe refers to as 'openness' is best associated with a primary shared *condition* of vulnerability, and that this constitutive condition enables the *process* that Ratcliffe identifies as empathy. Moreover, in the case of dementia, mutual vulnerability is best explored through patterns of interaction that are achieved through the forms of intercorporeal action described by Zeiler and Käll that may lead to empathetic forms of responsiveness.

However, when conceptualizing a notion of vulnerability in the context of dementia, the claim that 'we are all vulnerable' should not be understood in a glib sense. A vulnerability approach to illnesses such as dementia enables a recognition of reciprocal vulnerabilities, not only in relation to those people diagnosed with dementia but also carers and family members. The vulnerability of carers and family members is also heightened in the context of dementia and in order to engage meaningfully and empathically with a subject of dementia, family members and carers often need to expose or acknowledge their own vulnerability. In this sense, therapists and social workers such as Naomi Feil, enable themselves to be vulnerable in relation with dementia sufferers, even if these are undoubtedly forms of relationality that are asymmetrical.[8] Acknowledging mutual vulnerability helps to create a space of mutual openness but also enables family members and carers to participate in interactions that enable alternative forms of expression and communication, such that both parties in the relation or interaction are transformed. In this respect, family members in particular are also interdependent in relation to subjects with dementia, and this creates its own vulnerabilities and the need to find alternative forms of relationality and expression. In this sense, as Stefan Merrill Block (2014) suggests, perhaps in relation to persons with dementia it is not a matter of trying to prove that some kind of coherent self remains until the bitter end, but rather to 'acknowledge the needs of a rapidly changing self'. On this note, he suggests that the way of relating to dementia sufferers is not to endlessly look for or to try to reconstruct the self as it was once known and feel endlessly disappointed but to find new ways of relating to a transformed self.

In this respect, a vulnerability approach shares many affinities with the phenomenological approaches offered by Zeiler, Käll and Ratcliffe. However, a vulnerability approach enables us to bring an account of interpersonal recognition together with the intercorporeal analysis and account of personhood that Zeiler and Käll argue is fostered through joint activity, and the empathetic forms of responsiveness that Ratcliffe describes. In this sense, the claim being made is that vulnerability extends beyond or behind empathy in the sense that it provides a primary form of openness and relationality upon which empathetic responsiveness is built. It could be suggested, then, that the condition of constitutive vulnerability as an openness to the other is in fact a precondition for empathy.

To return to John Bayley's musings about helplessness and the loss of communication in his relation with Iris Murdoch, we might suggest that the loss of words for which he yearns can be replaced by embodied forms of communication and intercorporeal forms of expressiveness (Bayley 1998, 59). Far from being 'a parody' of helplessness, acknowledging mutual vulnerability reveals an openness to the other in which the subject of dementia cannot only be recognized in her personhood but the ongoing interdependence of subjects can be avowed. In this sense, forms of vulnerability, relationality and intercorporeality are not something specific to those with dementia but are constitutive and formative for *all* persons. Such an approach stresses the fundamental importance of maintaining an openness to the other in the condition of mutual vulnerability that dementia evokes in order to enable empathetic forms of responsiveness.

Notes

1. John Bayley's memoir of his partner the philosopher Iris Murdoch is based on his experiences of her early on-set of Alzheimer's disease until just prior to her death in 1999.
2. As Zeiler (2014, 134) emphasizes, a narrow focus on cognition at the neglect of the interrelation between embodiment and cognition is out of step with current research not only in phenomenology but also cognitive neuroscience and developmental psychology, which recognize the embodied nature of cognition.
3. Zeiler's and Käll's analyses are based on a film entitled 'Gladys Wilson and Naomi Feil'. *There is a Bridge*. Memory Bridge. http://www.memorybridge.

org/documentary.php. Feil practices a form of what she terms 'validation therapy' which was developed as a way of relating to dementia sufferers with affirmation and empathy. In this context, validation includes forms of affirmation, respect and dignity that are communicated to the other through various mediums, as well as creating a space in which dementia sufferers can express themselves.
4. Zeiler and Käll both acknowledge that the relationality and interaction between Wilson and Feil is asymmetrical and that it is inevitably a power relation in which Feil is initiating the interaction (Käll 2017, 138–139).
5. See my previous work on vulnerability, especially D. Petherbridge, 'What's Critical About Vulnerability: Rethinking Interdependence, Recognition and Power', *Hypatia*, 31, 3 (Summer 2016). Some of the ideas explored in that essay are reinterpreted and discussed in an alternative manner here.
6. Ratcliffe offers an insightful account of empathy that builds on insights from Husserl and Stein but that differs from simulationalist accounts of empathy. The simulationist account builds in the requirement that understanding the experience of another person assumes having a similar experience, either by modelling or replicating another person's mental states thus enabling one to take up the other's perspective. In contrast the phenomenological account drawn from Husserl and Stein suggests that empathy involves a distinctive kind of intentionality and an other-directed attitude (Ratcliffe 2014, 269–271). In this sense, empathy has some perception-like features but is also unlike perception in the sense that the other's experience is 'given as belonging to the other' as such (Zahavi 2014, 134; 2010).
7. Ratcliffe (2014, 278) explicitly states that '[e]mpathy can thus be thought of in terms of participating in a kind of process and also in terms of openness to participation; 'openness' to another person is the starting point of a process that can develop to varying degrees'.
8. As noted above, such forms of relationality are also asymmetrical in the sense that therapists such as Feil, carers and family members often are the ones in a position to initiate such forms of interaction and can also chose to walk away from them, whereas dementia sufferers are not in a position to do so in the same manner.

Acknowledgments

This paper arose out of a workshop on 'Empathy, Illness and Vulnerability' held by the University College Dublin, Centre for Ethics in Public Life, in conjunction with Nottingham University and cosponsored by Universitas 21 in 2018. I wish to acknowledge the UCD Centre for Ethics in Public Life and to thank the participants of the workshop as well as the anonymous reviewers of the *International Journal of Philosophical Studies* for helpful comments on earlier drafts of this paper.

Disclosure Statement

No potential conflict of interest was reported by the author.

References

Agich, G. J. 2003. *Dependence and Autonomy in Old Age: An Ethical Framework for Long Term Care*. Cambridge: Cambridge University Press.

Bayley, J. 1998. *Iris: A Memoir of Iris Murdoch*. London: Duckworth Overlook.

Block, S. M. 2014. "A Place beyond Words: The Literature of Alzheimer's'." *The New Yorker*, August 20. https://www.newyorker.com/books/page-turner/place-beyond-words-literature-alzheimers

Diprose, R. 2002. *Corporeal Generosity: On Giving with Nietzsche, Merleau-Ponty, and Levinas*. Albany, NY: SUNY Press.

Gale, S., D. Acar, and K. Daffner. 2018. "Dementia." *The American Journal of Medicine* 131: 1161–1169. doi:10.1016/j.amjmed.2017.12.017.

Gallagher, S. 2001. "'The Practice of the Mind: Theory, Simulation, or Interaction?" *Journal of Consciousness Studies* 8 (5–7): 83–107.

Grenier, A., L. Lloyd, and C. Phillipson. 2017. "Precarity in Later Life: Rethinking Dementia as a 'Failed' Old Age." *Sociology of Health & Illness* 39 (2): 318–330. doi:10.1111/1467-9566.12476.

Honneth, A. 1995. "Integrity and Disrespect: Principles of a Conception of Morality Based on a Theory of Recognition." In *The Fragmented World of the Social: Essays in Social and Political Philosophy*, edited by C. W. Wright, 247–260. New York: SUNY Press.

Honneth, A., and H. Joas. 1988. *Social Action and Human Nature*. Translator R. Meyer. Cambridge: Cambridge University Press.

Käll, L. 2017. "Intercorporeal Expression and the Subjectivity of Dementia." In *Body/Self/Other: The Phenomenology of Social Encounters*, edited by L. Dolezal and D. Petherbridge, 359–385. Albany: SUNY Press.

Kitwood, T. 1997a. "The Experience of Dementia." *Aging & Mental Health* 1 (1): 13–22. doi:10.1080/13607869757344.

Kitwood, T. 1997b. *Dementia Reconsidered: The Person Comes First*. New York: Open University Press.

Merleau-Ponty, M. 1962. *Phenomenology of Perception*. Translator Colin Smith. London & New York: Routledge.

Merleau-Ponty, M. 1968. "The Intertwining – The Chiasm." In *The Visible and the Invisible*, edited by C. Lefort, translated by A. Lingus, 130–155. Evanston: Northwestern University Press.

Petherbridge, D. 2016. "What's Critical about Vulnerability: Rethinking Interdependence, Recognition and Power." *Hypatia* 31 (3): 589–604. Summer. doi:10.1111/hypa.12250.

Petherbridge, D. 2018. "How Do We Respond? Embodied Vulnerability and Forms of Responsiveness." In *New Feminist Perspectives on Embodiment*, edited by C. Fischer and L. Dolezal, 57–79. Basingstoke: Palgrave Macmillian. doi:10.1007/978-3-319-72353-2_4.

Ratcliffe, M. 2012. "Phenomenology as a Form of Empathy." *Inquiry* 55 (5): 473–495. doi:10.1080/0020174X.2012.716196.

Ratcliffe, M. 2014. "The Phenomenology of Depression and the Nature of Empathy." *Medicine, Health Care and Philosophy* 17: 269–280. doi:10.1007/s11019-013-9499-8.

Sherwin, S., and M. Winsby. 2010. "A Relational Perspective on Autonomy for Older Adults Residing in Nursing Homes." *Health Expectations* 14: 182–190. doi:10.1111/j.1369-7625-2010.00638.x.

Sullivan, S. 2001. *Living across and through Skins: Transactional Bodies, Pragmatism and Feminism*. Bloomington, IN: Indiana University Press.

Zahavi, D. 2010. "Empathy, Embodiment and Interpersonal Understanding: From Lipps to Schutz." *Inquiry* 53: 285–306. doi:10.1080/00201741003784663.

Zahavi, D. 2014. "Empathy and Other-Directed Intentionality." *Topoi* 33: 129–142. doi:10.1007/s11245-013-9197-4.

Zeiler, K. 2014. "'A Philosophical Defense of the Idea that We Can Hold Each Other in Personhood: Intercorporeal Personhood in Dementia Care'." *Medicine, Healthcare and Philosophy* 17: 131–141. doi:10.1007/s11019-013-9515-z.

Empathy, Respect, and Vulnerability

Elisa Magrì

ABSTRACT
This paper reconsiders Heather Battaly's argument that empathy is not a virtue. Like Battaly, I argue that empathy is a disposition that includes elements of virtue acquisition, but is not in itself a virtue in the Aristotelian sense. Unlike Battaly, however, I propose a distinction between care and respect. Drawing on Darwall's view of recognition respect as well as on phenomenologically inspired views of empathy, I argue that respect can be regarded as the moral feeling that is distinctive of empathy. In my view, the feeling of respect towards another's situated experience grants epistemic dignity, which is the recognition of the intrinsic significance of subjective experience. By way of conclusion, I suggest that the relation between empathy and respect can be relevant for an account of vulnerability that is not opposed to autonomy.

Introduction

Over the last decade, a large body of research has interrogated the relation between empathy and morality. Even though definitions of empathy are not congruous, empathy can *prima facie* be understood as a form of interpersonal and affective understanding. In this respect, some have argued that empathy is morally neutral (Prinz 2011), whereas others have linked empathy to care (Simmons 2014), altruism (Batson 2014), and moral deliberation (Svenaeus 2014). The problem as to whether empathy has moral relevance is all the more pressing if one looks at descriptions of empathy offered by clinicians and philosophers of psychiatry, which show that empathy can play a crucial role in helping patients to regain personal meaning (Halpern 2001; Ratcliffe 2015). Thus, it appears that an important aspect of empathy concerns its relation to moral motivation. If being empathetic implies attending and responding to another's situation, what type of motives drive empathy? If we assume that such motives have a moral quality, does it mean that empathy is a virtue?

With regard to this problem, I would like to go back to Heather Battaly's argument that empathy is not a virtue. This had led Simmons (2014) and Svenaeus (2014) to raise the concern that such a claim would deprive empathy of its moral relevance. In order to avoid this, Simmons (2014) has proposed to reconsider empathy as exclusive concern for the well-being of others, whereas Svenaeus (2014) has provided a very helpful comparison between empathy and *phronesis* that values empathy as an essential condition and source of moral knowledge. Interestingly, both Battaly and her critics move from the unquestioned assumption that the moral significance of empathy consists in caring for the other or for the good. By contrast, I wish to suggest that while empathy is not a virtue in the Aristotelian sense, its moral significance does not consist in the caring impulse. In this sense, I agree with Battaly that empathy may be a component of virtue acquisition, but it is not in itself a virtue (in the Aristotelian sense). Yet empathy can be morally relevant even when it is not driven by caring, as I intend to clarify in the second part of my paper by introducing the dimension of respect.

I will proceed by first examining Heather Battaly's argument concerning empathy and virtue, before tackling respect as the moral feeling at stake in empathy. In relation to this claim, I will draw a distinction between respect and care that is inspired by Stephen Darwall's account of recognition respect. Finally, I will consider why the relation between empathy and respect is relevant from a moral point of view in that it grants epistemic dignity, which is the recognition of the intrinsic significance of subjective experience, particularly of its affective and emotional background, which is captured by the phenomenological investigation of the horizon consciousness. In turn, I show that the relation between empathy and respect points to a further problematisation of empathy as a disposition to attend to another's distinctive horizon. Such a disposition is informed by a feeling of respect for the autonomy of another's subjective standpoint. This view bears important consequence for the appraisal of vulnerability, particularly when it comes to reconciling vulnerability with the concept of autonomy. I will sketch a solution to this problem in the last part of this article by offering a concrete example, that of OCD symptoms, where personal agency appears inhibited when in fact it is in need of further explication of its dispositional background. In my view, such explication is made possible by empathy when this is understood as an attitude that seeks to uncover the significance of another experience in light of their individual and affective background. As such, empathy can build up to other forms of moral behaviour, including care and love, and yet, while there can be empathy without care, there cannot be empathic dispositions without respect, which I consider the fundamental moral feeling that characterises empathy.

Reconsidering Battaly's Argument

My point of departure is Battaly's argument that empathy is not a virtue, as it must be either a skill or a capacity in the Aristotelian sense. Battaly proceeds by identifying four different views of empathy:

(1) Empathy as caring and/or sharing, and/or knowing
(2) Empathy as sharing by multiple means
(3) Empathy as sharing and knowing
(4) Empathy as knowing by multiple means

All four definitions of empathy revolve around broad definitions of caring, knowing, sharing or a combination of these. Battaly regards caring as a form of concern for the other's sake or for the truth, while she considers sharing a vicarious response, as in contagion, motor mimicry, or perspective-taking (i.e. perceiving a situation from an alternative point of view). Finally, she describes knowing as the ascription of a mental state to others regardless of whether the process underlying such an ascription is the result of cognitive grasp, inference, simulation or folk psychology. From this point of view, as Battaly points out, definition (1) is the vaguest, since it does not exactly specify what is required for caring, sharing and knowing. Examples of (1) are best friends and therapists, who often care about their friends/patients, and often share their emotions, and typically know about them too. However, there is no definite answer as to which of these combinations are necessary and/or sufficient. In some cases, there might be a prevalence of care, in others of knowing, etc.

By contrast, definitions (2), (3) and (4) consist of specific combinations of sharing and/or knowing. Definitions (2) and (3) assume that empathy must involve some shared mental states. However, sharing is necessary and sufficient in definition (2), whereas it is necessarily accompanied by knowing in definition (3), which arguably requires sharing the mental state of others and knowing or cognitively grasping their states without caring. Finally, definition (4) maintains that empathy is the ascription of a mental state to others as in mind-reading or folk psychology (Figure 1).

DEFINITIONS	CARING	SHARING	KNOWING
(1)	X	X	X
(2)		X	
(3)		X	X
(4)			X

Figure 1. Battaly's four definitions of empathy.

The second part of Battaly's argument consists in examining whether any of these definitions of empathy can be considered in terms of virtue. In doing so, she considers virtues in an Aristotelian sense as 'dispositions of appropriate action, emotion, perception, and motivation' which 'are not automatic, involuntary capacities; they are voluntary – we exert some control over their acquisition and operation' (Battaly 2011, 288). From this view, it follows that forms of sharing, such as motor mimicry, are involuntary capacities, hence they are not sufficient for virtues. Capacities are either innate or acquired in the standard course of development, but we lack control over their acquisition and operation. By contrast, Battaly argues, virtues require rational choice, hence deliberation.

According to Battaly, perspective-taking does not qualify as a virtue because, even though it is voluntary and we may have some control over it, an agent may forego opportunities to engage in imaginative perspective-taking. This is the case for those that Battaly calls 'empathic underachievers', who fail to perform imaginative position-taking to the best of their abilities for various reasons, for example because they fail 'to care about her clients or the truth' (Battaly 2011, 296). By the same token, Battaly (2011, 297) suggests that agents may fail to activate their relevant knowledge of folk psychology, because they lack 'sufficient concern for the truth, not because one fails to be good at mindreading via the theory theory'. Thus, there might be good perspective-takers, who are not however motivated by the good, therefore they are not practising any virtue. This is the case of 'skilled doctors, scientists, and generals – they may be motivated by appetites for wealth, fame or power, rather than by rational desires' (Battaly 2011, 299). From this, Battaly draws the conclusion that perspective-taking and mindreading are not virtues but abilities (Figure 2).

It appears that definitions (2), (3) and (4) do not suffice to make empathy a virtue, although they certainly include capacities and abilities that are necessary for the acquisition of virtue. Indeed, we cannot possess virtues without possessing some capacities, as the latter underlie all of our voluntary dispositions and abilities (Battaly 2011, 291). According to Battaly (2011, 301), if one wishes to pursue further the relation between empathy and virtue, then one should reconsider definition (1), developing

DEFINITIONS	VIRTUES	CAPACITIES	ABILITIES
(1)	?	?	?
(2)		X	
(3)		X	X
(4)			X

Figure 2. The relation between empathy and virtue in Battaly's argument.

a new theoretical concept which should include 'the dispositions to care about others and about the truth for their own sake'.

Despite the vagueness of the definitions employed by Battaly to distinguish between several types of empathy in social cognition and philosophy of mind, her overall argument is compelling in that it shows that empathy is a disposition that involves appropriate emotions, perception, motivation and understanding. Yet an important element of her argument deserves further attention and explication. Battaly's thesis that empathy is not a virtue essentially revolves around the implicit assumption that empathy has to be characterised as a form of rational choice that is driven by caring. While Battaly does not expand on care, it is evident from her argument that she regards caring (either for the sake of the other or for the truth) as the only form of moral motivation. As a result, abilities such as perspective-taking and knowing are easily ruled out as long as they do not constitute forms of deliberation or moral discernment.

However, the implicit assumption that empathy is a form of care is problematic in that it is not clear whether caring for the good entails caring for the welfare of the others, even when this conflicts with the others' outlooks and standpoints. For example, a good doctor does not fail to care for her patients' welfare when she examines whether her treatment will succeed in alleviating the patient's symptoms, and whether the cure is compatible with the patient's diet and clinical history. In this scenario, the doctor seeks to act for sake of her patient, which is compatible with a non-empathic behaviour. Indeed, the doctor may not take into account whether the cure she is proposing will affect the personal life of the patient or whether the treatment could be perceived by the patient as traumatic. Quite differently, the doctor might in addition consider if her cure will have an impact on the first-personal experience of the patient, and she will prepare the patient accordingly. In both cases, the doctor takes to heart the patient's welfare. Yet in the first case the doctor is exclusively disposed towards addressing the welfare of the patient, whereas in the second case the doctor relates to her patient's emotional and affective background. Thus, it appears that care is not only ambiguous with respect to what kind of good is at stake in different situations. It is also problematic when it comes to clarifying the specific directedness of empathy to another's affective and emotional situation, for the concern about the welfare of the patient may potentially hinder the understanding of the other's affective experience.

Furthermore, Battaly is not explicit about the relation between virtue and moral deliberation. In one sense, all the definitions of empathy she provides fail to show how empathy engages in moral deliberation about the means of achieving the good. However, it is questionable whether empathy would always need to engage in this type of deliberation. Indeed, in empathy we address another's situation without necessarily deliberating about the good, as in practical wisdom. The friend to whom I confide my personal struggles does not have to deliberate about the best means of helping me out in order to empathically related to my situation. In fact, he will manifest empathy by attending to my disposition in the present situation, and by further understanding how my experience might shape my affective and personal worldview. In another sense, however, it could be argued that empathy rests on the cultivation of moral feelings, hence deliberation is crucial for developing moral character as well as sensitivity to others' experiences. If this is the case, the problem consists in identifying the type of disposition at stake in empathy, and how such a disposition incorporates a specific form of sensitivity to others that might not necessarily develop into a caring impulse and yet involves responsibility. With regard to this, I suggest that the concept we need to look at is respect, which is the feeling that lends a normative character to the dignity to which every individual is intrinsically entitled. Empathy is indeed compatible with a disposition to respect others, which provides a fundamental ground for our relation to others.

It is important to notice that looking at empathy from this perspective is neither a commitment to moral neutrality, nor does it amount to depriving empathy of moral value. The question is rather whether empathy is driven by moral motivations other than caring, notwithstanding that empathy might as well be accompanied by other feelings and dispositions, including love, friendship and care. Yet these feelings are not necessary for empathy, for there can be empathy even when the caring impulse is not predominant. By contrast, introducing respect may help to better understand the form of disposition involved in empathy, as I shall now illustrate.

Empathy and Respect

Recall Stephen Darwall's (2010, 156) example of the difference between respect and care in his defence of recognition respect:

> Suppose that your daughter, aged twenty-something, has decided to take up something you consider bad for her, say, smoking cigarettes. Although she knows the health risks, smoking is nonetheless something she wants to do [...] You have her welfare at heart, and you correctly think that stopping would be better for her. Despite this, you think that it is her life to live and that it is not your place to try to get her to stop. Respect for her and her autonomy, that is, for her authority to lead her own life, leads you to restrain any benevolent impulses you might have in that direction.

According to Darwall, respect inspires a specific attitude towards others which is not informed by benevolence or care but rather by the recognition of the dignity or authority that each person has to make claims or demands of us. Darwall (1977) distinguishes between appraisal respect and recognition respect, arguing that the object of the former is merit or excellence, whereas the object of the latter is dignity. Appraisal respect appears when we hold someone in esteem for their character, merit and virtues. However, one's appraisal of a person may be higher than someone else's. Recognition respect, by contrast, involves no evaluation or appraisal of excellence, because it entails valuing someone intrinsically as a being with a dignity. Darwall appeals to the Kantian notion of dignity, which values rational nature as an end in itself, and demands mutual accountability. However, Kant does not distinguish between appraisal and recognition, and it is Darwall who has framed the problem of respect in terms of second-person normative authority. As he puts it: 'To be a person just is to have the competence and standing to address demands as persons to other persons, and to be addressed by them, within a community of mutually accountable equals' (Darwall 2006, 126).

Second-personal normativity amounts to reciprocal accountability. It means there cannot be any neutral or third-person point of view, for the authority that each individual demands of us equals the demands that we also make of others. As Darwall's example of the smoker suggests, respect for the autonomy of the other poses a question of responsibility. In demanding to be acknowledged, the daughter is simultaneously addressing her parents as being accountable for her claims, namely as standing to address her reasons. The relational model that takes place includes the awareness of belonging to a community of moral agents, where individuals are mutually accountable. Thus, respect cannot do without individuals who address each other within concrete situations and contexts.

As noted by Stern (2014, 322),

> although Darwall's picture departs from the Kantian picture of self-legislation in moving to legislation through and by others, nonetheless he manages to retain and capture a number of fundamental Kantian notions, particularly those of equal dignity and respect, in a way that contrasts with the more hierarchical divine command view, where God alone has the authority to legislate the moral law.

However, Stern has also objected that Darwall's view of second-person authority may fall prey to the difficulties of the Levinasian paradigm, according to which 'obligation is a matter of being "summoned" or "commanded" by the other, who thereby exercises authority in a manner that was once (and still may be) associated with the divine, but now becomes a second-personal relation between individuals' (Stern 2018). The problem of the moral imperative is a recurrent issue in Kant studies as well as in Kantian inspired philosophy, and Stern is certainly right in pointing out that obligation needs to rely on relationality rather than command.

However, when it comes to respect, an important difference needs to be drawn between the sheer obligation to respect others (without any settled inclination to do so) and the feeling that is inspired by the dignity of humanity as an end in itself. It is remarkable that for Kant respect is not an external command, but the feeling by means of which the representation of the imperative is practically effected (Kant 2015, 63), predisposing individuals to the cultivation of inclinations as well as to the formation of moral personality (Kant 1999, 52). To feel respect entails the capacity of respecting humanity in oneself just as much as in other beings. In doing so, 'we become less self-absorbed, we grow more attentive, perceptive of, and sensitive to the claims that others have on us' (Bagnoli 2003, 507). In this sense, respect is fundamentally relational, and it is not an exclusive prerogative of formed personality either, for it addresses the sphere of sensibility and affectivity.[1] The cultivation of respect and its relation to sensibility is not accounted for by Darwall, who nonetheless identifies personhood with 'the competence and standing' to addressing and being addressed by others in relations of mutual accountability. To have such a competence means that one needs to cultivate respect, for it does not come from without. In doing so, the agent comes to develop epistemic awareness of the value of respect as a form of mutual responsibility. Thus, respect does not manifest itself as a humanised form of divine command, because it is a feeling for which one needs to develop appropriate standing. Ultimately, respect amounts to cultivate sensitivity to what others are equally entitled, just as we are as well.

Furthermore, while the Levinasian summon is a call to infinite responsibility for the other (an obligation to make oneself present to the neediness of the other) (Levinas 1969, 244), Darwall's view of respect binds us to a mutual form of non-interference in others' lives. This, however, does not make respect a negative form of behaviour, whereby we just refrain from doing or acting for the sake of others for fear of imposing our authority onto them.[2] Respect is actually crucial for an ethics of care in order to discern and discriminate between appropriate forms of actions. To put it differently, respect represents the feeling that alerts us of the autonomy of the another's standpoint, even when this conflicts with our notion of the good. The crucial point is that, while respect informs care as well as of other forms of moral feeling and behaviour (e.g. caring, love, compassion), respect cannot be reduced to any of them in that it primarily provides a ground for acknowledging another autonomous standpoint. In this sense, I suggest that there is room for exploring respect as the moral feeling that characterises empathy once the former is no longer reduced to a secularised form of moral obligation. This is not to say that empathy and respect are the same phenomenon, but that empathy requires respect if it is a disposition that is directed to another's situated standpoint.[3]

To be sure, both empathy and respect originate in the mutual relationality of self and other, and they both involve an attitude towards individuals. However, while Darwall's view of respect binds us to normative relations of mutual accountability, the same does not hold for empathy. If I empathise with my friend's joy about the exam she successfully passed, my friend is not making a demand of me. It is important to notice that, while I do not owe empathy to my friend, my friend's experience appeals to the possibility that I can, in principle, respond to her situation.[4] Such possibility rests, for Darwall, on the exchange of reasons being made and claimed, but as I have noticed, respect presupposes a more fundamental disposition that is grounded on affectivity and sensitivity. Accordingly, empathy allows the decoupling of respect from mutual obligation, for respect is primarily enacted in interpersonal encounters when we seek to respond appropriately to others' affective and emotional states. In this sense, the relation between empathy and respect brings to light the dignity of subjective experience, namely the fact that another situated experience is worthy of attention and discernment for its own sake. Empathy binds the other in a relation of mutual addressing which has the potential to be actualised and taken up in more elaborated and conscious forms of acquaintance and relationality. While I can choose to not respond empathically to another's experience (as it is also the case in the second-personal relations described by Darwall), empathy presupposes the ability of responding to another's experience as worthy of attention and discernment.

It is precisely at this level that it is important to distinguish between recognition respect and appraisal respect. In one case (appraisal respect) empathy would depend on the appraisal of another's character, whereas in the other (recognition respect) empathy would address another's experience as worthy of attention in itself regardless of merit or character. In both scenarios, however, empathy needs to be understood within a concrete and situated relation. In relation to this problem, Drummond (2006) has argued in favour of appraisal respect within a phenomenological inspired view of empathy. On Drummond's account, the empathic experience of the other is the foundation for more complex experiences of them, such as sympathy and care. For example, attending to others' feelings, positions and bodily movements represents an empathetic encounter in that it allows us to recognise others as having bodily and emotional experiences, which affect us because of their characteristic and independent quality. While noticing my friend's sluggishness, I attend not just to her expression and movements but to the whole field of experience that her bodily appearance and character make available to me. Indeed, from a phenomenological point of view, empathy implies that we attend not just to features of perception but also to element of the affective world of the other subject.

In this regard, an important aspect of empathy is the capacity of discerning how another person is situated in her own affective and motivational context. To clarify this, it is helpful to recall the phenomenological concept of horizon. A horizon represents the backdrop that accompanies each experience, and it refers to the idea that experience can be explicated step by step, drawing on one's 'stock of sense' or reservoir of meaning (Husserl 1973, 31–39) A horizon is not objectifiable or determinable, and yet it works as a realm of possibilities that helps to situate another lived experience. In a sense, empathising with others implies the ability to be directed to another horizon, bringing to light and making sense of the affective quality of their experience. This means that empathy is not restricted to the perceptual grasp of another's expression, but it is best understood as a way to make sense of another's disposition towards her surrounding world. This is a process that occurs gradually, as it is always in need of further explication, for the specific quality of the other's situated experience solicits us to develop a more focused and attentive orientation. This is why empathy does not preclude but rather enables acquaintance and familiarity with others not just as embodied subjects but also as persons with their own character. Empathy consists in the process of further explicating another's nucleus of experience precisely as the centre of irradiation of a personal world, which has her autonomous form of position-taking. In this respect, phenomenologists like Husserl and Stein stressed that, while empathy brings to light the intersubjective nature of our experience, empathising with others also brings us to appreciate the alterity of the subjects we relate to. Empathy bridges the gap between self and other while disclosing, at the same time, the other's autonomous, yet interdependent, standpoint.

Following Stein (1964), empathising can be understood as an experience whereby perception is embedded with emotional understanding. In seeing my friend unable to concentrate, slow and distracted, I become attuned to a different situated experience than my own, one in which the usual sources of motivation that would matter for me are not at stake. In turn, this solicits me to further explicate my friend's experience by means of talking, asking questions, or sharing something together. This is why Stein stresses that empathy awakens what is sleeping in us, facilitating a stance of self-reflexion and self-knowledge. 'By empathy with differently composed personal structures we become clear on what we are not, what we are more or less than others. Thus, together with self-knowledge, we also have an important aid to self-evaluation' (Stein 1964, 106). For Stein, empathy is very close to a form of moral attention that discloses the salient elements of another's affective experience, and it can build up to other forms of moral experience, including sympathy and compassion. As Drummond (2006, 17) writes, 'sympathy and compassion are not necessary for the respectful encounter of another, but the underlying empathic structure is necessary since that is the condition for recognizing another free, conscious agency'. Such underlying empathic structure is not in itself devoid of moral character, and it is precisely at this level that Drummond introduces the dimension of respect: 'the recognition of the irreducibility of the other – a conscious, free being in her own right – creates the moral space in which we can locate respect' (Drummond 2006, 17). For Drummond, appraisal respect presupposes our empathic encounter with other persons as objects of moral perception. On his view, recognition respect is phenomenologically grounded in respect for meritorious persons: 'We do not – even in the encounter of the stranger – originally encounter persons as such, as merely possessing these capacities; we encounter only persons with particular characteristics and acting in particular ways on the basis of particular conceptions of the good' (Drummond 2006, 21).

Drummond's view rests on the idea that empathy is a way to relate to persons as having essential moral qualities. In this sense, empathy represents the affective and epistemological ground for appraising others' merits. By contrast, for Drummond (2006, 22), recognition respect can fail in those situations 'where particular manifestations of rational capacities are not empathically recognized as such, as, for example, when those speaking a foreign language or adopting different social practices are judged irrational and not worthy of respect'. For Drummond, recognition respect appears too abstract to do justice to actual encounters where the particularities of individual experiences call for a distinctive, cultivated form of moral attention, which for Drummond is provided by the appraisal of others' qualities. The problem with this view is that it equates individuality with personhood and character *tout court*, thereby downplaying the fact that empathy is primarily rooted in the disposition to apperceive others and to be affected by them at the level of sensitivity. While empathy can develop into an attitude that is directed to the other's character and personality (Stein 1964, 83 ff.), such a capacity rests on a basic form of sensitivity that is open to all forms of experiences regardless of their worth or character. This type of social sensitivity is embedded with the feeling of recognition respect that makes attending to another's experience an inclination to respond and to comprehend it. Within such a disposition, attention becomes a form of apprehension that facilitates more developed and conscious responses to others.

Attention is oriented to the salient features of another's world-horizon, in which I can partake by talking, asking questions, imagining their contexts and so forth. Waldenfels (2004) has famously argued that attention can be practised as a form of moral attentiveness, which makes the latter similar to an act of discernment. The notion of discernment goes back to Aristotle's concept of *sunesis* (Aristotle 2004, *Nic. Ethics*, VI, 1142b34–1143a18), which is often translated as the faculty of quick comprehension, although it is normally employed as a form of comprehension, where the emphasis is on the dialogical and communicative component of understanding (e.g. 'hearing or comprehending what someone says'). *Sunesis* is not the possession of practical wisdom but the capacity to acquire it. It is indeed very close to the phenomenological view of attention proposed by Waldenfels. Thanks to *sunesis*, we can grasp and discern the ethically relevant constituents of a situation, but we are not in the process of forming a choice; we do not prescribe and command an action, i.e. we do not deliberate in the full sense of the concept (Simon 2017).

Apprehending another's experience as the experience of a subject situated in her distinctive world-horizon and as capable of taking a position towards that very situation, is the standpoint of recognition respect. It is important to notice that recognition respect does not abstract individuals from their specific contexts and characters but recognises them as worthy of respect within reciprocal relations whereby their characters and choices are primarily valued as free and equal. Dignity and authority do not supervene on these encounters, rather they become actual in practical situations, when demands and claims are felt and apprehended at the level of affectivity and sensitivity. From this point of view, respect is an attitude of response that shares significant similarities with empathy. They are not driven by self-interest, in that they are concerned with the alterity of another's standpoint. They both aim to make another's experiential standpoint meaningful and worthy of attention. They are not primarily directed to the welfare of others, but rather to the explication of the particularity of another's experience in order to grant it dignity. They also involve the right, claim or authority that persons have to demand that they be allowed to have their own position-taking.

This provides an important normative claim for empathy, because it suggests that there can be empathy even in case of moral disagreement. The doctor who advises her patient not to smoke can still be empathic towards the patient's struggle to quit smoking. In empathising with her patient, the doctor is able to discern the impact that quitting smoking has on her patient in terms, for example, of the patient's habit of using smoke as a coping strategy. Such an empathic approach can foster an attitude of care as well, where the doctor suggests to the patient alternative ways of gradually quitting smoking. However, the empathic directedness of the doctor to the patient is primarily driven by an attitude of recognition respect for the patient's individuality. This is what I would like to call epistemic dignity, which is the dignity to which subjects are entitled to in virtue of the intrinsic salience and value of their affective experiences. Epistemic dignity is the recognition that individuals' affective experiences are worthy of attention and discernment in themselves, even when such experiences are characterised by irrational beliefs or do not inspire attitudes of care. As I shall illustrate in the following, introducing respect at the level of empathy would allow a reconsideration of the concept of vulnerability.

Epistemic Dignity and Vulnerability

Vulnerability has become a prominent concept in contemporary discussions of ethics as a condition that characterises human and non-human beings in virtue of their ontological individuation, but also, as Gilson (2018, 231) puts it, as 'a fundamental quality of openness, an openness to being affected and affect in turn'. For Gilson (2018), a comprehensive account of vulnerability is defined by four features: first, it is a shared fundamental condition. Second, it is a condition of potential, whereby to be vulnerable means to be open to an alterity that can only be determined in concrete circumstances. Third, vulnerability is differentially experienced by those who are differently situated, hence it is, fourth, ambivalent and ambiguous in both how it is experienced and its value. Accordingly, Gilson (2018, 231) argues that this characterisation of vulnerability 'is necessarily connected to relationality, the capacity to and necessity of being in relation with others. If vulnerability is of ethical and political import it is because it is the condition for relationality'.

The specific dimension of vulnerability I wish to draw attention to here is linked to what Gilson calls the radical difference and ambiguity of vulnerability. If vulnerability confronts us with a situated and yet ambivalent experience, and if interdependency starts with the recognition of the precariousness of our lives, what guarantees the acknowledgment of such intrinsic alterity as well as of its relational ground? It appears that vulnerability must entail the acknowledgement of the dignity of another's affective and situated experience in the first place. This means, however, that vulnerability can be potentially reconciled with a view of autonomy that is centred on the intrinsic significance of subjective experience. With regard to autonomy, however, Gilson tends to assimilate it to the notion of independence, arguing that such a concept cannot do justice to the complexity of vulnerability, which rather requires 'the ability to enter into formative relations' (Gilson 2018, 240), hence to partake in a range of relations that comprise flourishing. However, in my view, to reconcile vulnerability and autonomy does not mean to defend the concept of an invulnerable subject that is independent from others. Quite the contrary, the problem consists in examining whether vulnerability depends on the recognition that another experiential standpoint is meaningful and worthy of respect in itself. If this is the case, vulnerability calls for an attitude of empathy and respect that centres on the dignity to which individuals are entitled to for their own sake. This view can be fundamental to challenge forms of epistemic injustice characterised by misrepresentation and misrecognition of vulnerable experiences, for example, when individuals are stereotyped and misrecognised because of the apparent irrationality of their beliefs.

To illustrate this, I would like to examine a specific situation where individual agency seems inhibited, as in the OCD spectrum, which is normally described as a behavioural symptom whereby 'the individual feels driven to perform repetitive behaviours in response to an obsession or according to rules that must be applied rigidly' (DSM-5 2013, 80). OCD used to be classified as a form of anxiety, although it is currently listed in the DSM 5 as a 'neurodevelopmental disorder', including forms of behaviour as different as hoarding, skin picking and hair pulling. Standard definitions assume that OCD displays a vicious cycle between obsessionality (the occurrence of obsessive thoughts) and compulsivity (the urge to repeat a course of action despite repeated efforts not to do it). From this point of view, OCD represents a compelling case for philosophers, for it raises questions related to free will and responsibility.

To be sure, one of the well-established features of the phenomenology of OCD is a heightened sense of responsibility. Compulsive agents usually perceive themselves as facing a threat, which they do not have the power to avert, unless they engage in certain repetitive actions that can restore a sense of normality (e.g. if they do not check the lock again and again, they will be robbed; if they do not wash their hands over and over, they will get sick etc.). Another well-documented aspect is the sense of not getting the action 'just right' (e.g. not closing the door well enough), which is often considered a symptom of perfectionism or control. A well-known misconception about OCD is that it is just a form of ill-weakness, or that it involves a deficiency of choice in acting. In this regard, many philosophical accounts of OCD have drawn attention to the type of thoughts and patterns of thought that accompany obsessive-compulsive behaviour in an attempt to show that the lack of agency perceived by OCD patients is actually compatible with free will. In this regard, Szalai has provided an interesting argument, according to which:

> The agent takes this threat as a reason to act: she strives to eliminate the threat and, though that, the overwhelming thought itself. The agent is aware of acting for these reasons: if asked why she performed the compulsive act, she will reply something like 'So that my mother does not die' or 'Because those thoughts drive me crazy, I have to get rid of them'. (Szalai 2016, 52)

The problem with this view is that it fails to take into consideration that feeling of being unable to do otherwise that is distinctive of OCD patients. Szalai's hypothesis rests on the assumption that OCD patients are able to acknowledge the irrationality of their beliefs. This would indicate that patients are responsive to evidence, namely they are capable of gauging the likelihood of their perceived threats and adjust their beliefs accordingly. Szalai is certainly right in arguing that OCD patients are responsive and sensitive to reasons, but this does not mean there is a causal relation between the fact that they are in principle able to acknowledge the irrationality of their beliefs and their capacity to take actions against those very beliefs. Indeed, the missing element in Szalai's analysis is the threat perceived by the patient, which remains irrational despite its being defined as a reason to act. While Szalai's approach is helpful in uncovering the dimension of agency in the OCD spectrum, the motivational and dispositional aspects of OCD would deserve further attention. In this regard, a different approach to the problem can be found in von Gebsattel's phenomenological account of compulsive behaviour.

Von Gebsattel was a senior member of that circle of phenomenological psychopathologists that included Ludwig Binswanger, Eugène Minkowski, and Erwin Straus.[5] He got his doctorate in Philosophy with a dissertation on the irradiation of feelings under the supervision of Theodor Lipps, before receiving psychoanalytic training and earning a doctorate in medicine. While von Gebsattel's approach to psychotherapy is scientific in nature, he also maintained that the patient–doctor relationship requires a humanitarian foundation. In particular, he proposed a dialectical model that centres on the recognition that patient and doctor need to engage in a communicative partnership where they are both equal, despite the asymmetry of their roles ('a community of partners between irreplaceable persons', as in Welie 1995, 71).

Von Gebsattel's seminal paper dedicated to the world of the anankastic (namely, compulsive behaviour, from the Greek '*ananke*', meaning necessity) provides fundamental insights into the life-world of OCD patients. For a start, von Gebsattel does not consider emotional states as reasons to act, but as emotional spaces that can be described in terms of the salient features perceived by the patient within her world-horizon. In doing so, Von Gebsattel (1958, 176) draws attention to the fact that the compulsive 'suffers from a disturbance in the capacity to act, which is revealed especially as an impediment to beginning something new and completing something'. The crucial element concerns the difference between complete and incomplete actions. 'We see that an action can be completely executed, in the sense that it has served to implement a purpose, without being completed – or indeed, having occurred at all – in terms of its life-historical meaning' (Von Gebsattel 1958, 177).

The compulsive patient spends significant amounts of time washing her hands or checking the lock but fails to perceive that her course of action is complete despite having executed it accurately. The aspect highlighted by von Gebsattel can be recast in terms of the Aristotelian distinction between telic and atelic actions. Atelic actions do not have a terminal point: walking, playing an instrument, listening to music are all examples of activities that are actualised as soon as they begin. This is not true of telic actions, which can be described as events that occur at a specific time, e.g. eating an apple or washing hands. Compulsive symptoms can be understood in terms of a fundamental difficulty to deal with those actions that, despite being telic, are constitutive of atelic processes. While the non-compulsive person goes through her daily routine of going to the toilet, having breakfast and going out without experiencing these actions as repetitions, the anankastic person feels that she can never accomplish the sorts of actions she is engaging in because they occur within activities that are not complete. By repeating the same course of action, the compulsive individual conjures up a ritual in the effort to achieve a sense of completion that she cannot obtain from the mere execution of daily actions. She fixates on irrelevant parts or particulars of the sequence to the point that her actions become devoid of any goal: 'accuracy does not enter for the sake of attaining some purpose that matters, but has become an end in itself and has the characteristic features of the unmotivated, the reflexive, the formal, the sterile, and the rigid' (Von Gebsattel 1958, 180).

This suggests that, even when compulsive patients are able to self-ascribe their reasons to act and to take responsibility for their actions and beliefs, they are not yet addressing the processes and activities that threaten them, and that they perceive as unsafe and unstable. The rigidity experienced by compulsive patients is a symptom of a more fundamental lack of trust in the everyday world. As De Haan, Rietveld, and Denys (2013, 12) put it: 'The problem with patients with OCD is that they want to attain absolute certainty whereas the experience of certainty can never be absolute, but will always depend on basic trust'. It appears that the affective world of the compulsive exhibits the four aspects of vulnerability described by Gilson. Most notably, the affective horizon of the compulsive manifests an irreducible alterity, which is characterised by the difficulty to integrate everyday actions within a broader picture of one's own existence. This provides a different starting point for the understanding of OCD: before interrogating whether compulsive agents can take responsibility for their actions and whether they can divert a course of action by changing their beliefs, it is essential to ascertain why those very beliefs cannot be trusted by the patient in the first place, and how this phenomenon crucially affects their disposition to the world.

Von Gebsattel's approach provides a significant example of what it means to practise empathy in a way that is informed by respect for another's experiential and vulnerable standpoint. Establishing an empathetic relation to others means to be directed to another's situated experience as a nucleus of experience that is worthy of discernment even when it conflicts radically with our own worldview. By appreciating the alterity of the other's experience, we do not however refrain from comprehending it, but rather we respect the intrinsic quality of their affective dispositions. In empathising with others, one is primarily oriented to apperceive their world-directedness, thereby developing hermeneutic abilities that seek to explicate the others' affects and emotions. While such abilities develop over time, they are primarily inspired by an attitude of recognition respect. This means that empathy is not driven by any presumptions regarding the other's condition or their agency. On the contrary, by means of empathy, we seek to explicate another's affective horizon by engaging with them responsibly. Von Gebsattel's analysis of the compulsive sheds light on what it takes to apperceive the other's autonomous position-taking within their affective dimension, thereby contributing to a positive account of the relation between autonomy and vulnerability. His investigation shows that empathy provides the ground to reconcile the autonomy of the individual standpoint with the vulnerability that is intrinsic to affective experiences. This brings forth an attitude of response that involves attentiveness, sensitivity, and comprehension. Such a view appears particularly relevant when it comes to articulating the phenomenology of interdependency put forward by vulnerability, for it shows that epistemic dignity is paramount for any account of intersubjective relationality.

Conclusions

I have argued that the moral significance of empathy lies in the feeling of respect that makes another's experiential standpoint worthy of attention and discernment. While I agree with Battaly that empathy is not a virtue but a capacity that is fundamental for moral behaviour, I suggest that the moral motivation that characterises empathy is not the caring impulse, but respect. As such, empathy is a form of second-person relation that opens up the realm of interpersonal relatedness. Empathy originates in the appraisal of another's experience as worthy of attention in itself, whether or not I intend to act for the other's good. Accordingly, I suggested that Darwall's account of recognition respect is compatible with a phenomenological approach to empathy in that recognition respect can be considered as the feeling that ascribes epistemic dignity to another's experiential standpoint. In my view, empathy and respect share a common ground, for their both address another's experiential standpoint for its own sake while being rooted in the sphere of affectivity. Using Darwall's model of second-person authority, I have shown that empathy is not something that we owe to others regardless of the circumstances, but rather a dispositional dimension that holds others capable of engaging in the empathic response in concrete encounters. In this sense, I maintain that recognition respect, rather than appraisal respect, is fundamental for empathy to grow and further develop into more developed forms of moral behaviour.

Finally, I suggested that this view of empathy and respect provides a fertile terrain to reconcile vulnerability and autonomy. Most notably, my view is that vulnerability can be understood as a relational disposition that is, however, tied to the recognition that other affective experiences are worthy of attention and discernment in themselves, even when personal agency seems inhibited, as it appears *prima facie* in OCD symptoms. Drawing on von Gebsattel's analysis of OCD cases, I have shown in what sense empathy primarily consists in the disposition to uncover another's world-directedness as a meaningful and autonomous standpoint without any presumptions regarding the other's life, values or agency. In this sense, empathy provides a response to vulnerability that does not oppose or preclude the appraisal of autonomy. Admittedly, I have only sketched here a reconciliation of vulnerability and autonomy, which represents a direct consequence of the account of empathy and respect I defended. On my view, the relation between empathy and respect suggests that it is possible to vindicate the autonomy of subjective experience within the context of vulnerability without reducing the former to the quest for independency or the latter to a form of frailty and neediness.

Notes

1. For the relation between respect and inclinations, see also Crowther 1992. Clearly, this perspective posits significant issues I cannot here expand upon. For example, must individuals always be respected? For some, individuals forfeit respect by committing crimes such as murders and genocides. For others – myself included – murderers, rapists and torturers deserve condemnation and punishment, but they still ought to be treated with respect. It goes without saying that this problem is linked to pressing social and political issues related to the law and punishment I cannot address here. Another significant issue concerns what we mean by 'others' and whether the Kantian view of 'persons' is sufficient to account for non-human beings (for a discussion see Korsgaard 2004).
2. For a different view, see Kriegel 2017.
3. Interestingly, Darwall differentiates between empathy, sympathy and care, but he does not explore the relation between empathy and respect. One reason for that is that Darwall's view of empathy is quite broad, including a range of different experiences (contagion, simulation, projection, proto-sympathetic empathy), which make empathy's contribution to ethics less relevant than that of sympathy, which Darwall considers a primitive concern for oneself and for others. Ultimately, for Darwall, empathy involves sharing another's mental state from their standpoint, and it is compatible with several forms of simulation as well as with lack of concern (Darwall 1998).
4. A second-personal reason rests, as Darwall (2006, 8) has it, 'on the possibility of the reason's being addressed person-to-person'. Reasons addressed or presupposed are not agent-neutral and they would not exist without a - situated second-personal relation. Still, mutual accountability is a claim that allows discretionary authority. It follows that respect, like empathy, is a possibility whose enactment depends on the individual capacity to develop a stance to others' situation.
5. For a historical account, see Spiegelberg 1972.

Acknowledgments

The completion of this paper was supported by the Centre for Ethics in Public Life (CEPL) at UCD and the Irish Research Council. I wish to thank all the participants in the workshop 'Empathy, Vulnerability, and Illness', hosted by CEPL in November 2018, for a very constructive and stimulating conversation. Many thanks to Rowland Stout, Danielle Petherbridge and Ian Kidd for making that event possible in the first place, and to two anonymous referees for further comments on a previous draft of this article. I am also very thankful to Niall Keane for his corrections and helpful feedback.

Disclosure statement

No potential conflict of interest was reported by the author.

References

Aristotle. 2004. *Nicomachean Ethics*, edited by R.Crisp. Cambridge: Cambridge University Press.
Bagnoli, C. 2003. "Respect and Loving Attention." *Canadian Journal of Philosophy* 33 (4): 483–515. doi:10.1080/00455091.2003.10716552.
Batson, C. D. 2014. "Empathy-Induced Altruism and Morality." In *Empathy and Morality*, edited by H. L. Maibom, 161–191. Oxford: Oxford University Press.
Battaly, H. D. 2011. "Is Empathy a Virtue?" In *Empathy. Philosophical and Psychological Perspectives*, edited by A. Coplan and P. Goldie, 277–301. Oxford: Oxford University Press.
Crowther, P. 1992. "Authentic Moral Commitment – Kant's Phenomenology of Respect." *Filozofski Vestnik* 2/1992: 43–58.
Darwall, S. 1977. "Two Kinds of Respect." *Ethics* 88: 36–49. doi:10.1086/292054.
Darwall, S. 1998. "Empathy, Sympathy, Care." *Philosophical Studies: an International Journal for Philosophy in the Analytic Tradition* 89 (2/3): 261–282. doi:10.1023/A:1004289113917.
Darwall, S. 2006. *The Second-Person Standpoint. Morality, Respect and Accountability*. Cambridge-London: Harvard University Press.
Darwall, S. 2010. "Sentiment, Care, Respect." *Theory and Research in Education* 8 (2): 153–162.
De Haan, S., E. Rietveld, and D. Denys. 2013. "On the Nature of Obsessions and Compulsions. In Anxiety Disorders." In *Modern Trends in Pharmacopsychiatry*, edited by D. S. Baldwin and B. E. Leonard, 1–15. Vol. 29. Basel: Karger.
Drummond, J. J. 2006. "Respect as A Moral Emotion: A Phenomenological Approach." *Husserl Studies* 22: 1–27. doi:10.1007/s10743-006-9001-z.
DSM-5. 2013. *Diagnostic and Statistical Manual of Mental Disorders*. 5th ed. American Psychiatric Association. Washington-London: Publishig.
Gilson, E. C. 2018. "Beyond Bounded Selves and Places: The Relational Making of Vulnerability and Security." *Journal of the British Society for Phenomenology* 49 (3): 229–242. doi:10.1080/00071773.2018.1434972.
Halpern, J. 2001. *From Detached Concern to Empathy. Humanizing Medical Practice*. Oxford: Oxford University Press.

Husserl, E. 1973. *Experience and Judgment. Investigations in a Genealogy of Logic.* trans. James Churchill and Karl Ameriks edited by L. Landgrebe. London: Routledge & Kegan Paul.

Kant, I. 1999. *Religion within the Boundaries of Mere Reason*, edited by A. Wood and G. Di Giovanni. Cambridge: Cambridge University Press.

Kant, I. 2015. *Critique of Practical Reason.* trans. Mary Gregor. Cambridge: Cambridge University Press.

Korsgaard, C. M. (2004) "Fellow Creatures: Kantian Ethics and Our Duties to Animals." *The Tanner Lectures on Human Values Delivered at University of Michigan* 24: 77–110.

Kriegel, U. 2017. "Dignity and the Phenomenology of Recognition-Respect." In *Emotional Experience: Ethical and Social Significance*, edited by J. J. Drummond and S. Rinofner-Kreidl, 121–136. Lanham: Rowman & Littlefield.

Levinas, E. 1969. *Totality and Infinity. An Essay on Exteriority*, trans. A. Lingis. Pittsburgh: Duquesne University Press.

Prinz, J. J. 2011. "Is Empathy Necessary for Morality?" In *Empathy. Philosophical and Psychological Perspectives*, edited by A. Coplan and P. Goldie, 211–229. Oxford: Oxford University Press.

Ratcliffe, M. 2015. *Experiences of Depression. A Study in Phenomenology.* Oxford: Oxford University Press.

Simmons, A. 2014. "In Defense of the Moral Significance of Empathy." *Ethical Theory and Moral Practice* 17-1: 97–111. doi:10.1007/s10677-013-9417-4.

Simon, A. 2017. "*Sunesis* as Ethical Discernment in Aristotle." *Rhizomata* 5 (1): 79–90.

Spiegelberg, H. 1972. *Phenomenology in Psychology and Psychiatry. A Historical Introduction.* Evanston: Northwestern University Press.

Stein, E. 1964. *On the Problem of Empathy*, trans. W. Stein. Dorecht: Springer.

Stern, R. 2014. "Darwall on Second-Personal Ethics." *European Journal of Philosophy* 22 (2): 321–333. doi:10.1111/ejop.2014.22.issue-2.

Stern, R. 2018. "Levinas, Darwall, and Løgstrup on Second-Personal Ethics: Command or Responsibility." In *The Oxford Handbook of Levinas*, edited by M. L. Morgan. Oxford: Oxford University Press. doi:10.1093/oxfordhb/9780190455934.013.6.

Svenaeus, F. 2014. "Empathy as a Necessary Condition of *Phronesis*: A Line of Thought for Medical Ethics." *Medical Health Care and Philosophy* 17: 293–299. doi:10.1007/s11019-013-9487-z.

Szalai, J. 2016. "Agency and Mental States in Obsessive-Compulsive Disorder." *Philosophy, Psychiatry, & Psychology* 23-1: 47–59. doi:10.1353/ppp.2016.0001.

Von Gebsattel, V. E. 1958. "The World of the Compulsive." In *Existence: A New Dimension in Psychiatry and Psychology*, trans. S. Koppel & E. Angel, edited by R. May, E. Angel, and H. F. Ellenberger, 170–187. New York: Basic Books.

Waldenfels, B. 2004. *Phänomenologie der Aufmerksamkeit.* Frankfurt am Main: Suhrkamp.

Welie, J. V. 1995. "Viktor Emil Von Gebsattel on the Doctor-Patient Relationship." *Theoretical Medicine* 16: 41–72.

Empathy, Vulnerability and Anxiety

Rowland Stout

ABSTRACT
A concept of empathy as openness to the emotional perspective of another is developed in opposition to a concept of sympathy as agreement with the emotional perspective of another. Empathy involves knowledge of how things are emotionally for the other person, which is not the same thing as knowledge of the other person's emotions. Being open to another perspective requires the capacity to hold two perspectives in mind simultaneously – one that is one's own perspective and at the same time the adopted perspective. This is why empathy can be so challenging for someone suffering from some kinds of anxiety.

The English word 'empathy' as it figures in common usage and also in popular psychology has acquired a quite specific meaning; I suggest that it means *openness to the emotional perspective of another*. It is this idea that I want to explore here, working out what it amounts to and also why empathy, so understood, is sometimes so difficult to achieve.

The word was invented in 1909 as a philosophers' term of art to translate the phenomenologists' term 'Einfühlung'. Dan Zahavi (2014) has helpfully tried to articulate the idea they were after, tracing it through the work of Max Scheler, Edmund Husserl and Edith Stein. He describes it as a 'direct, experiential understanding of others.' (Zahavi 2014, 132) And to distinguish it as a kind of perception of the other as a subject rather than as an object, he writes: 'it is consequently important to emphasize that the other, rather than being given to me simply as a nucleus of experiences, is given as a centre of orientation, as a perspective on the world.' (Zahavi 2014, 139)

Zahavi's notion of empathy has no connotation of emotional sharing or understanding; instead empathy is regarded as a precondition for the sort of emotional response he describes as sympathy. 'Whereas empathy has to do with a basic perceptually-based understanding of others, sympathy adds an emotional response.' (Zahavi 2014, 115) But this is not the most useful way to mark a distinction between empathy and sympathy. Both empathy and sympathy may be considered in stripped down forms without any emotional content. A more interesting distinction is that between *being open* to someone else's perspective (whether emotional or not) and *agreeing* with someone else's perspective. Sympathy, like compassion, is feeling *with* someone. Empathy and Einfühlung are feeling *into* someone, in a sense that I will try to explain in this paper.[1]

Consider what someone might say at the end of a philosophical presentation: 'I have a lot of sympathy with your line of thought here.' Even though the assertion is invariably followed by the word 'but', it expresses at any rate partial *agreement* with the line of thought presented. A sympathetic audience is one that is disposed to agree with the speaker. In these cases there is no connotation of an emotional response. And when there is an emotional response we may still think of sympathy as agreement. I may say that I have some sympathy with the feeling of anger that my friend has concerning the treatment they have received. In doing so I am expressing (emotionally) partial agreement with them. And if I feel a wave of sympathy for the predicament and suffering of a group of migrants or refugees my emotional response is agreeing that their predicament is terrible and their suffering appalling.

Describing an emotional response as an agreement presumes some level of cognitivism about emotions, according to which an emotion is or involves an evaluation. Without this presumption it is difficult to see how sympathy is to be distinguished from emotional contagion. If I enter a room where everyone is gloomy I may become gloomy; but this is not the same as my having sympathy with them. When I sympathise with someone for being upset at being abandoned by their partner I am not upset at being abandoned by *my* partner; I am upset at *their* being abandoned by *their* partner. I am expressing an agreement with them that might have been expressed linguistically by saying: 'Yes I think you are right to be upset by that.' While agreeing with someone's emotional perspective may involve an emotional response, it is not the same thing as having the same emotions as them.

It is a peculiar feature of modern times that sympathy has acquired a bad name in some quarters. It is associated with a kind of supercilious and emotionally distanced attitude. Brené Brown, who is an academic social worker and influential self-help writer says: 'Empathy fuels connection. Sympathy drives disconnection.' (Brown 2013) This dismissive treatment of sympathy may be partly due to the fact that expressions of sympathy are very often formulaic and disingenuous. It is easy to write to someone saying that they have our deepest sympathy for their loss. If that always really were deep sympathy, sympathy would not amount to very much.

But there may be a deeper reason for thinking of sympathy as a limited emotional response to someone's distress. Because sympathy requires agreement it is limited by the degree to which one can agree. However sympathetic you genuinely are you have your own life and emotional point of view. So your agreement with someone else's emotional distress, unless you are very close to them indeed, is likely to be never more than partial. Moved by someone's distress you may be inclined to agree with it and to feel distressed yourself about their predicament. That is a sympathetic response. But from your point of view the world may not be as appalling as it is from the other person's. Your sympathy is limited by the degree to which you can agree with them and your agreement is bound to be only partial. As I will now argue, empathy is not limited in this respect.

I have already started using another questionable buzzword – *perspective*. I have proposed that having sympathy with someone involves agreeing with their (emotional) perspective to whatever extent is possible. It involves one's own perspective being or becoming close to that of the other person. And I claim that having empathy on the other hand requires having openness to another perspective without having to agree with it. Now I need to propose a way to understand what a perspective is.

I suggest that a perspective is a way of seeing things, describing things, thinking about things or feeling about things. A perspective is a *way* and ways are abstract things. They are what you specify when you answer how-questions like: 'How do you see this? How do you think about this? How do you feel about this?' Answering these questions by saying 'In this way,' is equivalent to saying 'From this perspective.' At one extreme we might think of Frege's modes of presentation as local perspectives or parts of perspectives on individual things. At the other, an entire ethical system is a perspective on how to live. If we describe a cup as being behind a pen we are employing a spatial perspective. If we see a dress as blue we are employing a visual colour perspective. If we think that vegemite tastes foul we are employing a taste perspective. If we think that the thing to do is to turn around and run away we are employing a practical perspective. If we describe someone as an awful person we are employing an evaluative perspective. And if we think that this is very scary we are employing an emotional perspective.

Now the central idea of this paper is that whereas sympathy is agreeing with another's emotional perspective, empathy is merely being open to it. And I will argue that being open to a perspective involves, in a sense to be explored later, being *vulnerable* to it. In the first instance we might think of openness as sensitivity. Being open to a perspective is being sensitive to it. Being sensitive to a perspective, which I have defined as a way of acting, thinking and feeling, does not require actually having that perspective and acting, thinking and feeling in that way. Instead being sensitive to a perspective is being disposed to act, think and feel in a way that is roughly isomorphic to that other way of acting, thinking and feeling.

Such sensitivity is manifested in interactive behaviour. For example, you may be sensitive to the way your partner is moving in a dance without repeating the very same dance moves. Perhaps when they move their left foot forward you move your right foot back and so on. Playful behaviour often involves this sort of sensitive interaction. In emotional interaction I may respond to things going well for you by congratulating you and respond to things going badly by commiserating with you. I am not repeating or simulating your way of responding to these situations as they are represented in your perspective, but I am responding to your situation in a way that is sensitive to your perspective. This is a basic form of openness to the perspective of another.

In humans such sensitivity may be *rational* sensitivity. Instead of merely behaving, thinking and feeling in a way that corresponds in some way to the way the other person is behaving, thinking and feeling I may behave in a way that makes sense or is rational given the way the other person is behaving, thinking and feeling. This does not need to involve rational deliberation. What it involves at the least is that my reason for behaving, thinking or feeling in the way I do is that things are such and such a way from the perspective of the other person. How things are for them gives reasons to me.

John Hyman has defended an account of knowledge as rational sensitivity. He claims that to know that p is to be able to act for the reason that p.[2] It follows from this conception of knowledge that when my openness to another's perspective involves rational sensitivity this means that I *know* their perspective, which means in turn that I know how things are for that person.

In treating empathy this way I am taking it to be an achievement of some sort. But our notion of empathizing is subject to a standard process/product ambiguity. I may be said to be empathizing with someone when I am merely in the process of achieving the sort of sensitivity characteristic of successful empathy. So even if I am not yet adopting someone's perspective in my interaction with them I may count as empathizing if I am listening to them and asking open questions with a view to achieving empathy.

Knowing how things are for someone is knowing what their world is from that perspective. As was made clear in the Zahavi quotation earlier, this is not the same as knowing what their state of mind is. Knowing how things are for you means I do know some aspects of your state of mind, but by no means all. And knowing your state of mind certainly isn't sufficient for the understanding that goes with empathy. Contrast: 'I can see how angry you are,' with 'I can see how aggravating that is.' If someone pleads for some empathy to be shown to them they are asking for someone to show them some understanding. They are not asking for someone to show them knowledge of what state of mind they are in; in fact that's probably the last thing they want. The sort of understanding that seems to be involved in empathy is knowing *how* they feel and *how* things are for them, not knowing *what* they feel. Of course, knowing what they feel will come about at the same time.

Someone born blind might know that someone is seeing something blue, but they cannot apply that visual perspective themselves to understand that person's world. Knowing what it is like to be someone with a certain perspective involves having the capacity to apply that perspective and to know what their world is like from that perspective. This is the moral of Nagel's (1974) 'What is it like to be a bat?' In empathy you are not looking into someone's mind; you are looking outwards towards their world, but from their perspective.[3]

So it is misguided to treat empathy, e.g. as philosophers like Karsten Stueber (2006) do, as a way of knowing what someone else's state of mind is – what is unfortunately termed 'mindreading'. I might say for example that I only realized what you must feel about some situation when I let myself empathize with you and saw how aggravating the situation really was. But it would be absurd to say that I only realized that you were angry when I empathized with you. What I realized was how it *felt* to be in that situation and that, rather than being a fact about your state of mind, is a fact about the situation – a fact that may only be graspable from a certain perspective that requires some degree of empathy if it is to be adopted.

The sort of openness and sensitivity that constitutes our ordinary conception of empathy is a particular kind of sensitivity manifested in a certain kind of communicative activity. In particular, in empathizing with someone you are accepting their perspective, and, in so doing, making them feel validated. But you don't actually have this perspective or act in the way recommended by it. What this communicative encounter provides is a way of being with someone emotionally; it is part of sharing life with other people – allowing their emotional lives a place in your life.[4] If you are empathizing with someone who is angry or frightened you don't have to become angry or frightened yourself – indeed that would somehow defeat the point of the empathic interaction. But instead you might say how aggravating or frightening the situation is. Your body language too acknowledges that perspective in ways that signal acceptance of it. You feel like communicating how frightening the situation is in the case of fear by cradling or protecting perhaps, and in the case of anger you feel like communicating some outrage through physical expressive means as well as through linguistic means of expression.

It is worth stressing that these are real feelings that you have in empathizing. But they are not exactly the same as the feelings of the person you are empathizing with. Feeling like expressing outrage on someone else's behalf is not quite the same as feeling like simply expressing outrage.

Feeling like expressing how frightening this situation is from the other person's perspective is not the same as feeling like simply expressing how frightening this situation is. Feeling for someone or 'into' someone are their own kinds of feelings, related to but not identical to the feelings of the person you are empathizing with. We would describe you as being *moved* in the empathic encounter, but we might have no standard emotional term for precisely what you were moved to feel.

To illustrate the difference between sympathy and empathy consider these two responses to someone who is sad about their situation. Sympathizing with them I feel sad about their situation too, although of course that does not mean I feel sad about my situation. (If I react by feeling sad about my own situation that is emotional contagion, which is a different thing altogether.) Empathizing with them I feel from their perspective their sadness. This does not mean I actually feel sad at all; I don't have to feel sad about their situation or my situation or even sad that they feel sad in their situation. Feeling sad-from-their-perspective involves feeling like interacting with them in a way that acknowledges how things are sad from their perspective. This might involve tears, but if it does, these will be tears that come from crying with someone not from crying about someone. Contrast this with my response to a child who is incredibly brave in a very sad situation and refusing to feel sad at all. If I burst into tears in response to an encounter with this child I am neither sympathizing nor empathizing. I am neither agreeing with their feeling nor feeling with them from their perspective. My feeling is my own – perhaps it is something like a feeling of poignancy. In the same way when I am moved by a picture of a dead child washed up on the beach my feeling is not one of empathy; there is no one there to empathize with.

In these empathic interactions you may be described as expressing the perspective of another person. You are acting, talking and feeling from within that perspective. You may be said to be adopting their perspective for the sake of the communicative encounter. This is clearly a sort of imaginative skill, but it does not have to be understood as requiring an act of simulation. It is merely a way of being rationally sensitive to their perspective in the context of an encounter that calls for acceptance or validation. Amy Coplan defines empathy as 'a complex imaginative process in which an observer simulates another person's situated psychological states while maintaining clear self-other differentiation.' (2011, 5) But I see no reason why adopting someone's perspective requires such a complex imaginative process.

Consider a simple example involving adopting a spatial perspective. Suppose I ask my dinner partner sitting opposite me at a table where the salt is and they tell me that it is behind the pepper. They have adopted my spatial perspective for the sake of that piece of communication. The salt is not behind the pepper from their perspective; it is in front of it. But this piece of sensitivity to my perspective requires no act of simulation. There is a sense in which they have put themselves in my shoes in making the assertion from my perspective about where the salt is. But they don't have to try to think what I think or imagine having the experiences I am having as a way of doing this. Even though they have put themselves in my shoes in telling me where the salt is they don't have to put themselves in my shoes first as a way of telling me this. In virtue of having the sort of sensitivity to my perspective that is realized in telling me where the salt is we can say that they have put themselves in my shoes. If it is the same with adopting someone's emotional perspective, then empathy does not depend on some prior imaginative capacity.[5]

As I have set it up, it looks as though empathy is limited to actual encounters with people. But can't we also empathize with characters in books or people being interviewed on television – people with whom we have no interaction? I think it is not difficult to extend the model to these cases. The thoughts and feelings we have in these cases are appropriate for a sort of validating communicative encounter even when no communication is possible. We may still feel like expressing outrage or protective support for example; and to this extent we are adopting the emotional perspective of the other person and empathizing with them.

Adopting a perspective is not the same as having the perspective. While you adopt another perspective your own perspective is still your own perspective. This means that empathy as a form of emotional engagement is less limited than sympathy. Sympathy is limited by the degree to which you can agree with someone, whereas empathy is not. But in some ways it also means that empathy is harder than sympathy. In empathy you have to be sensitive to two perspectives simultaneously – the one you have and the one you are adopting. As I have argued, sympathising with someone is agreeing with their perspective; this is *recentering yourself*. Empathising, on the other hand, is adopting a perspective that is not your own; this is *decentering yourself*. And this is a balancing act that, as we will see, may be quite challenging.

Your own perspective governs your overall attitudes and actions, but the particular communicative encounter you are having allows you to put these aside for the sake of that encounter and express in speech and action the attitudes from the adopted perspective. For this to be possible the encounter must be compartmentalised from the rest of your life. It must be a zone of behaviour where your own attitudes – the ones you have from your own perspective – do not need to be expressed. Otherwise the expression of attitudes from the other person's perspective would not be possible and, even if possible, certainly not effective. Adopting a perspective is not merely a matter of imitating the behaviour of someone who would be adopting that perspective; it is a matter of thinking, feeling and acting from that perspective. So if you are thinking that the other person is being irritating or stupid you are not actually adopting their perspective.

We can now start to see why empathy might be difficult. And this is not just that empathizing may sometimes be boring or unpleasant – requiring more patience than one currently has. While empathizing with someone one is simultaneously sensitive to two different perspectives. This sensitivity is manifested in different ways for the two perspectives, and manifested at different times. But if you are emotionally aroused it is hard to stop your own perspective from being expressed, even temporarily, for the sake of the encounter. For example if you are angry with someone it is difficult at the same time to adopt their perspective; your own feelings press in. Also, if their perspective is threatening to you – for example they are angry with you and you are not inclined to apologize – adopting it may involve an impossible juggling act between the two perspectives. Compartmentalisation in such cases becomes impossible.

It might be thought to be possible to adopt a perspective without being affected by it at all. Consider the serial killer, Harold Shipman, whose elderly patients reported him as an empathic doctor who understood what they were going through, before he murdered them. Or consider a sexual predator who gains the trust of someone by adopting their perspective and expressing their point of view in conversation with them only in order to seduce them. But it is not clear that in either case they are really adopting the other person's perspective rather than just giving a good imitation. After all, really to adopt the perspective of the other you have to feel like expressing their perspective. And this feeling is lacking in these two cases.

Being really open to someone else's perspective usually involves something like vulnerability. That is because your own perspective may come under challenge. The exception to this is when there is no conflict between the two perspectives, either because they are so close or because they do not intersect in the issues they make recommendations about. The vulnerability, when it does occur, is a consequence of the ways our own perspectives are formed and altered. Perspectives change in response to dialectical encounters. Once I see how it is possible to think or feel in another way about things my own way of thinking and feeling is in a dialectical encounter with this other way. In this dialectical encounter I somehow hold two perspectives simultaneously, albeit one is accepted and the other merely adopted. And I am forced into a Hegelian moment of self-consciousness, where I have a perspective on my own perspective and can think about what is the perspective for me to have.

So, inasmuch as I have this capacity for change, my own perspective is threatened by my adopting someone else's. And if my perspective somehow captures who I am then a threat to my perspective is a threat to me – a challenge to my identity. So the understanding of another person's perspective that is constitutive of empathy may lead to a kind of vulnerability. Of course I might be very sure that my own perspective will survive any challenge to it from an adopted perspective. And then, even though I am actually made vulnerable by adopting someone else's perspective I won't feel vulnerable. I am like the lion tamer who puts her head in the lion's mouth knowing it won't get bitten off. She has made herself vulnerable to the lion, but being confident that no harm will come to her, does not feel vulnerable. If you trust yourself to survive any challenge to your identity from adopting some other perspective then you may find empathy easier.

You may also find empathy easier if you don't care if your perspective is forced to change as part of a dialectical encounter. You may not have that much invested in the way you see your world and be quite happy to see things differently. But most people do rely on the robustness of their ways of looking at things to protect them from all sorts of psychological threats. Their perspective embodies defences of various sorts. They are frightened of change. And this suggests a relationship between anxiety and difficulty with empathizing. Whatever the cause of such anxiety it is clearly a barrier to empathy. Unlike the self-confident person, who is like the lion tamer with their head in the lion's mouth, the anxious person may not trust themselves to adopt another perspective and will then avoid making themselves vulnerable by empathizing with people who are coming from somewhere very different to themselves.

The psychological evidence for such a connection is difficult to read, however. This is partly because empirical psychologists often work with scales for measuring the capacity for empathy that may not be very sensitive to the distinctions I have been trying to draw in this paper.[6] But it is also because many studies aim to treat the capacity for empathy rather than the ease with which empathy may be engaged in. A very anxious person may have developed a heightened capacity to empathize with other people due perhaps to an excessive concern with what they think of them or perhaps due to a more acute need to be included in the other person's emotional life. But, despite having this capacity, they may suffer from a psychological barrier to empathizing with people when they fear that the other perspective will threaten them. This may account for the contradictory descriptions in the literature of the relationship between empathy and Emotionally Unstable (Borderline) Personality Disorder – a condition associated with a certain sort of anxiety. On the one hand the condition is associated with a heightened capacity for empathy – an acute sensitivity to the feelings of others. On the other hand the condition is marked by a lack of empathy – reduced concern for the feelings of others. This is reflected in the DSM-5 criteria for the condition, which includes under the category 'empathy' for Borderline Personality Disorder: 'Compromised ability to recognize the feelings and needs of others associated with interpersonal hypersensitivity (i.e., prone to feel slighted or insulted); perceptions of others selectively biased toward negative attributes or vulnerabilities.'

I want to finish by proposing one final way in which empathy may make one vulnerable, and be associated with anxiety. In this case the vulnerability is not a psychological matter but a metaphysical one, like Heidegger's Angst or Sartre's anguish. Acknowledgement of another world than one's own reveals the lack of necessity of one's own world. In someone else's perspective I exist only as a contingent thing that might not be there at all. I am not there as a necessary being – as I am in my own perspective. So empathizing with another makes me vulnerable to my own mortality.

Now, of course, this is only going to worry me if my contingency worries me. Far from it being a wound to see myself as fundamentally contingent it might be taken to be a great blessing. By being able to empathize with others and adopt perspectives which are not my own I realize that the world does not end with my death. My contingency within the world is equivalent to the world's capacity to survive my extinction. If I cannot adopt perspectives other than my own then I cannot but see my own death and the end of my own perspective as the end of everything. By learning to empathize I may defeat this fear of death.[7]

Notes

1. The distinction I am after here is not always respected in common usage; 'sympathy' and 'empathy' are often used interchangeably. But assuming that the distinction can at least sometimes be found in common usage my claim is that it is philosophically very interesting to elaborate it.
2. Hyman 2015, 162 ff. See also Stout 2006, chapter 9.
3. John Campbell (Campbell and Cassam 2016, chapter, 2) makes the same point in developing a relational account of perception.
4. It seems very natural to think that the disposition towards empathizing with others is an aspect of Aristotelian virtue. Paul Bloom's (2017) polemic against empathy, showing how empathy can lead one astray morally, really just shows that empathy by itself is not enough for virtue, but does not show that it is no part of virtue.
5. See Steven Hayes' (Hayes, Barnes-Holmes, and Roche 2001) work on 'Relational Frame Theory' for a psychological model in which the capacity to behave in a perspective-taking way precedes a strictly imaginative capacity.
6. See Davis (1983), Jolliffe and Farrington (2006) and Carré et al. (2013) for the development of these measures for empathy. They tend to bundle together a lot of different factors including such things as emotional contagion, which are no part of empathy as I have been treating the concept.
7. Thanks to Meline Papazian and Daniel Vanello for helpful comments and to the UCD Centre for Ethics in Public Life and to Universitats21 for supporting the project.

Disclosure statement

No potential conflict of interest was reported by the author.

References

Bloom, P. 2017. *Against Empathy: The Case for Rational Compassion*. London: Random House.

Brown, B. 2013, "Brené Brown on Empathy", *RSA Shorts video*. https://www.thersa.org/discover/videos/rsa-shorts/2013/12/Brene-Brown-on-Empathy

Campbell, J., and Q. Cassam. 2016. *Berkeley's Puzzle*. Oxford: Oxford University Press.

Carré, A., N. Stefaniak, F. D'Ambrosio, L. Bensalah, and C. Besche-Richard. 2013. "The Basic Empathy Scale in Adults (BES-A): Factor Structure of a Revised Form." *Psychological Assessment* 25 (3): 679–691. doi:10.1037/a0032297.

Coplan, A. 2011. "Understanding Empathy." In *Empathy: Philosophical and Psychological Perspectives*, edited by A. Coplan and P. Goldie, 3–18, Oxford: Oxford University Press.

Davis, M. 1983. "Measuring Individual Differences in Empathy: Evidence for a Multidimensional Approach." *Journal of Personality and Social Psychology* 44: 113–126.

Hayes, S., D. Barnes-Holmes, and B. Roche, eds.. 2001. *Relational Frame Theory: A Post-Skinnerian Account of Human Language and Cognition*. New York: Plenum Press.

Hyman, J. 2015. *Action, Knowledge and Will*. Oxford: Oxford University Press.

Jolliffe, D., and D. Farrington. 2006. "Development and Validation of the Basic Empathy Scale." *Journal of Adolescence* 29: 589–611.

Nagel, T. 1974. "What Is It like to Be a Bat?" *Philosophical Review* 83 (4): 435–450.

Stout, R. 2006. *The Inner Life of a Rational Agent*. Edinburgh: Edinburgh University Press.

Stueber, K. 2006. *Rediscovering Empathy*. Cambridge MA: MIT Press.

Zahavi, D. 2014. *Self and Other*. Oxford: Oxford University Press.

Index

Figures are shown in italics, and footnotes are indicated by "n" and the note number after the page number e.g., 100n77 refers to note number 77 on page 100.

abandonment 20–21, 22, 27, 194, 195, 196
abilities 71, 72, 155, 184, 227, *227*, 228, 240; cognitive 70, 71, 127, 147, 148, 208, 211, 214; empathic 4, 126, 133, 135, 136, 138; moral 126, 133; non-empathic 130, 132
ableism 183
abstract language 61
abuse 5, 24, 31, 185, 194, 196, 206, 216, 217
affection 7, 15, 18, 30, 75n21, 82, 85, 96, 100n77
affective empathy 106, 109, 150, 154
affective experiences 11, 228, 233, 235, 240, 241
affective state 42, 47, 48–49, 118, 153, 154, 156
Against Empathy: The Case for Rational Compassion 114
agency 11, 97n9, 189, 191; moral 126, 127–128, 131, 135, 138; and respect and vulnerability 225, 233, 237, 238, 240, 241
alexithymia 128, 133, 138
allocentric virtues 194, 195–196
alter-ego 83–84
alterity 89, 93, 233, 235, 236, 239–240
altruism 6, 10, 47, 107, 126, 129, 178, 224
altruistic reasons, of morality 167, 169, 175, 177, 178, 180
Alzheimer's 204, 205, 206, 213, 220n1
American Psychiatric Association 126, 127, 237, 252
amorality 51, 126, 133–134, 135, 137
analogising apperception 86, 87, 88, 90
analogising apprehension 87, 92
anxiety 11, 192, 207, 237, 244, 252, 253
apperception 86, 87, 88, 89, 90, 98n42, 98n44

appraisal respect 155, 229–230, 232, 234, 240
apprehension 87, 91, 92, 98n44, 173, 175, 234
appresentation 86–87, 88, 92, 93
ascription, of a mental state 226
ASD (autism spectrum disorder) 4, 32
associative empathy 10, 169, 171, 174, 177–178
attachment 6, 7, 15, 18, 30, 36n34, 208
attention 191, 195, 198, 233, 234, 235
attitudes 6, 7, 9, 30, 150, 183, 197, 235, 250; and naturalized theories of meaning 61, 62, 67–68, 70, 71, 75n16; pathophobic 185, 188, 199; propositional 66, 68–69, 74–75n14
atypical empathy 126, 127
autism 4, 6, 32, 128, 138
autonomy 10, 11, 15, 30, 31, 185; and respect and vulnerability 224, 225, 229, 230, 231, 236, 240, 241
aversion cluster, of pathophobic vices 189–191

backfiring virtue 191
banality cluster, of pathophobic vices 191–193
Baron-Cohen, Simon 4, 42, 124, 127, 128, 130
Batson, C. Daniel 34n7, 44, 46–47, 107, 112, 113
Battaly, Heather 11, 124, 186, 187, 224, 225, 226–229, *226*, *227*
Bayley, John 204–205, 220
behavioural theory 7, 59, 60, 61, 63–66, 70
behaviourism 59, 60, 68, 69, 70, 74n13

behaviouristic theory of meaning 7, 59, 60, 61, 63–66, 70
beliefs 6, 7, 9, 116, 186; and naturalized theories of meaning 67, 68, 69, 73–74n8, 74–75n14; and respect and vulnerability 235, 236, 237–238, 239; and soldiering 144, 155, 161
belonging 30, 91–92, 190, 230
benevolence 6, 16, 229
biases 5–6, 9, 17, 51, 252; and ethics 123, 124, 125, 126, 137–138
bio-social theory of meaning 61–63
Block, Stefan Merrill 220
Bloom, Paul 114–115, 119, 121n2
bodily capacities 190–191, 212, 213
bodily comportment 187, 211
bodily objectivity 72, 89
bodily style 211, 213
bodily subjectivity 215
body language 44, 248
Borderline Personality Disorder 252
'bright-siding' 199–200, 201

callousness cluster, of pathophobic vices 193–196
Carel, Havi 189, 190–191, 192, 193, 194, 196–197, 197–199
caring 2, 9, 46, 160, 194, 195; and ethics 133, 134, 135; and respect and vulnerability 225, 226, *226*, 228, 229, 240; and sentimentalism 167–168, 168–169, 179–180
categorical observation 84
Center of Medicare and Medicaid Services (CMS) 52
child development 63, 71, 72, 75n15, 75n20, 149, 227
chronic illness 191, 192–193, 201
classical empathy paradigm 117, 118–119
close relationships 27–28, 30, 31–32, 36n37
CMS (Center of Medicare and Medicaid Services) 52
co-constitution 8, 86, 96
cognitive abilities 70, 71, 127, 147, 148, 208, 211, 214
cognitive apprehension 173, 175
cognitive empathy 2–3, 6, 9, 112, 132, 133
cognitive neuroscience 220n2
cognitivism 245
compassion 2, 6, 10, 145, 178, 233, 245; and Husserl's forgotten question 97n10, 101n78; and neuroscience 103, 106, 111, 114, 115, 119; and pathophobia 183, 194, 196; and relational empathy 53, 55n9, 55n11

competence 51, 230, 231
compulsive behaviour 237, 238–239, 240
conceptual clarity 8, 104
conceptual divergence 120
conceptual diversity 8, 103–104, 107
conceptual problem 104, 105–111, 112–113, 119, 120
conceptualization: of empathy 3, 7, 19, 48, 49, 53–54, 124; and neuroscience 103, 104, 105, 113, 114, 115, 118, 119
conduct 61, 62, 186, 194, 195
conscience 178, 179; moral 132, 133, 134, 135, 136, 137, 138
conscientiousness 177, 178
conscious communication 61
consciousness 225; embodied 80, 81, 85, 97n21, 99n46; and Husserl's forgotten question 84, 86, 87, 88, 90, 92, 94, *95*, 97n19, 98n28, 98n42, 99n46, 99n51; lack of 183, 194; and naturalized theories of meaning 60, 61, 62, 65; self- 99n56, 251
consensus, in research 3, 7, 8, 41, 119
constituted and constituting subjectivity 93–94
constitutive value, empathy as 27–32
construct validity 108–109, 113, 121n1
convergence 8, 42, 86, 104
Conway, Kathlyn 184, 189, 191, 192, 194–195, 197
Coplan, Amy 3, 55n10, 106, 107, 249; and soldiering 145, 148–149, 152, 155, 156
courage, moral 160
credibility 10, 185

Darwall, Stephen 135, 146, 154–155; and respect and vulnerability 224, 225, 229–230, 231, 232, 240, 241n3, 241n4
Dasein 93
Days of Abandonment, The (Lea, Olga) 20–21, 22–23, 24, 25–27, 29–30, 32
decentering yourself 250
decision-making, moral 17, 32
defeasibility 7, 15, 17, 18, 32, 33
definitions of empathy 2, 3, 4, 5, 145–146, 151, 153–156; and ethics 126, 128, 129, 131, 132; and neuroscience 106, 107, 111–112, 112–113, 116, 118; and relational empathy 41, 47, 48–49, 49–50, 51; and respect and vulnerability 226, *226*, 227–228, *227*
dehumanization 158, 159, 160, 162
deliberation 144, 145, 148, 150, 227, 228, 247; moral 17, 224, 228–229
dementia 6, 10, 11, 204–221
dependence 201, 215–216

depression 217, 218
descriptive/normative dichotomy, overcoming the 70–72
descriptive richness 187
desires 5, 6, 69, 134, 170, 172, 182n4, 227; and pathophobia 191, 192, 193; and soldiering 153, 158, 161
development: child 63, 71, 72, 75n15, 75n20, 149, 227; moral 5, 6, 133, 134, 137, 138, 139–140n5
Dewey, John 59–60, 61, 63, 65, 70, 72–73n2
diadic mimesis 71
Diagnostic and Statistical Manual of Mental Disorders (DSM) 126, 127, 237, 252 251, 252
direct perception 9, 147, 149–151, 152, 153
discernment 11, 228, 232, 234–235, 239, 240, 241
dispositions 63–64, 74n10, 159, 167–168, 169, 187, 194, 253n4; and respect and vulnerability 224, 225, 227, 228, 229, 231, 232, 233, 234, 239, 240–241
double-sensation 210
DSM (*Diagnostic and Statistical Manual of Mental Disorders*) 126, 127, 237, 252
dynamic intercorporeal engagement 10–11, 212

Ehrenreich, Barbara 189, 190, 199–200
Einfühlung 1, 43, 44, 45, 54n4, 54n5, 105, 244, 245
Eisenberg, Nancy 111, 112
eliminativism 131, 166
embodied consciousness 80, 81, 85, 97n21, 99n46
embodied relationality 210
embodied subjectivity 209–210, 215
embodiment 208, 209, 211, 212, 220n2
emic understanding 156–157, 158
emotional attitude 61, 62, 72–73n2
emotional attunement 9, 35n13, 132, 134, 139n4
emotional contagion 2, 4–5, 34n8, 116, 119, 154, 245, 249, 253n6
emotional empathy 10, 169, 171, 174, 177–178
emotional identification 73–74n8, 132
emotional perspective 5, 11, 12, 25–26, 244, 245, 246, 250
emotional sharing 2, 244
emotional states 9, 10, 113, 116, 118, 232, 238; and ethics 127, 128, 130, 132, 133, 135, 139n2
emotional understanding 233
emotional world 11

empathetic attunement 159
empathetic engagement 6
empathetic responsiveness 204, 205, 208, 217, 218, 220
empathetic soldier 9, 144–162
empathic abilities 4, 126, 133, 135, 136, 138
empathic caring 2
empathic contagion 169
empathic dispositions 225
empathic distress 2–3, 97n10
empathic engagement 125, 130, 131, 132, 135, 139n2
empathic experiences 5, 48, 50, 51, 117, 232
empathic identification 7, 59
empathic perception 2–3
empathic processes 8, 103, 104, 112, 119
empathic receptivity 181
empathic transmission 171, 182n2
empathic understanding 2–3, 34n8, 74–75n14
empathy: affective 106, 109, 150, 154; associative 10, 169, 171, 174, 177–178; atypical 126, 127; cognitive 2–3, 6, 9, 112, 132, 133; emotional 10, 169, 171, 174, 177–178; in vivo 116; failed 22, 23, 24, 26; first-order 178; high-level 69, 71, 72; higher-level 146, 147, 152–153, 154–155, 156; hyper- 181; limits of 124–126; low-level 9, 69, 71; lower-level 146, 152–153, 154, 155–156, 159, 161; mutual 11, 218, 219; perceptual 68–69; projective 169, 174; proto-sympathetic 241n3; receptive 10, 169, 171, 174, 177–178; reenactive 153; relational 1, 7, 41–55; relational value of 1, 6–7, 15–36; second-order 178; Standard Account of 18, 21
empathy concepts 104, 106, 107, 108, 111
'empathy in vivo' 116
empathy-altruism hypothesis 47, 107
empathy-for-pain paradigm 117, 118–119
empirical research 2, 3–4, 19, 31–32, 104, 113, 120, 123
engagement: empathetic 6; empathic 125, 130, 131, 132, 135, 139n2; intercorporeal 212, 214; sympathetic 9, 138, 139
enormous self-sacrifice 181
epistemic access 88
epistemic awareness 231
epistemic dignity 11, 224, 225, 235, 236–240
epistemic injustice 23, 35n19, 236
epistemic verification 95
epistemological behaviourism 59, 60, 70

epistemological gap 150
epistemology 234
Epistemology Naturalized 64
epoché 83, 84, 85, 88–89, 98n28
ethical rationalism 171, 176, 177, 178–179
ethics: contribution of empathy to 123–140; vice 10, 183, 184, 187; virtue 10
'etic' understanding 156–157, 158
experiences: affective 11, 228, 233, 235, 240, 241; empathic 5, 48, 50, 51, 117, 232; of illness 183, 191, 192, 193, 194, 195, 199, 200, 201; intentional 80, 81, 82; lived 10, 43, 47, 187, 191, 192; moral 51, 233; pleasant 15, 18, 29; pure 42, 54n3; subjective 10, 11, 207, 224, 225, 232, 236, 241; unpleasant 161, 172–173, 251
Experience and Nature 59, 63
experimental research 113
extrinsic qualities, of empathy 24–25, 27, 30, 35n20
extrinsic value, of empathy 7, 15, 18, 25, 26, 27, 29

face-to-face intercorporeality 212, 214, 215
failed empathy 22, 23, 24, 26
feeling for 112, 231, 249; and relational empathy 7, 41, 42, 46–47, 49, 50, 51, 53, 55n9
feeling into 245; and relational empathy 7, 41, 42–44, 45, 46, 47, 49, 50, 51, 53, 54n4, 54–55n7, 55n9
feeling with 74n10, 80, 101n78, 245, 249; and relational empathy 7, 41, 42, 43, 44–46, 47, 49, 50, 51, 53, 54–55n7, 55n9
feminist theory 80, 81
'finding empathy' 8, 103–121
first-order empathy 178
fMRI (functional magnetic resonance imaging) 115–116, 117, 118
forgotten question, of Husserl *see* Husserl, Edmund
functional magnetic resonance imaging (fMRI) 115–116, 117, 118

Gebsattel, Viktor Emil von 238, 239
gestural attitudes 67, 71
gestural communication 61, 66, 67, 70
gestural interaction 61
gestures 7, 59, 60, 61, 62, 63, 66, 67, 70, 72, 72–73n2, 73n3, 213
goodwill, of the other 29, 30
guilt 47, 130, 162n5, 177, 195

happiness 3, 116, 135, 167, 168, 190
harmony 15, 18, 25, 29, 86

HCAHPS (Hospital Consumer Assessment of Healthcare Providers and Systems) 52
healthcare system 7, 41, 53, 184, 193–194, 196
Heidegger, Martin 93, 100n64, 253
helping behaviours 9, 22, 47, 130, 133–134, 135, 224, 229; and sentimentalism 171, 172–173, 174, 175, 177, 179
helplessness 30, 204, 220
Herder, Johann Gottfried 43, 45, 54n4
higher cognitive abilities 70, 71
high-level empathy 69, 71, 72
higher-level empathy 146, 147, 152–153, 154–155, 156
Honneth, Axel 213, 215, 216
Hospital Consumer Assessment of Healthcare Providers and Systems (HCAHPS) 52
human consciousness *see* consciousness
humanity 9, 74n12, 158, 159, 162, 176, 205, 231
Hume, David 1–2, 50, 67, 74n10, 99n46, 123, 133, 146, 166–167
Husserl, Edmund 8, 146, 147, 149, 221n6, 233, 244; forgotten question of 80–101, 96n7, 97n21, 98n28, 98n41, 98n42, 98n44, 99n46, 99n57, 100n60, 100n72
hyper-empathy 181

illness 10, 183–202
imagination 3, 4, 34n8, 84, 110, 118, 136; moral 179; and naturalized theories of meaning 74n10, 74–75n14; and relational empathy 48, 49, 50–51
imitation 45, 69, 71, 73n3, 75n17, 149, 150–151, 251; *see also* mimesis; mimicry
immoral behaviour 6, 127, 128, 129, 135, 138, 161
impartial spectator 9, 16, 135, 136, 137, 138, 139
impartiality 15, 17, 18, 126, 138
impersonation 136
individuality 54n4, 213, 234, 235
injury 150, 206, 216; moral 162n5
insensitivity cluster, of pathophobic vices 196–199
intelligent caring 194, 195
intense face-to-face intercorporeality 212, 214, 215
intentional experience 80, 81, 82
intentionality 84, 85, 210, 214–215, 217, 221n6
intentions 5, 6, 7, 8, 9, 87, 100n72, 116, 135, 139n3, 210; and naturalized theories of meaning 67, 70, 71, 73–74n8;

and soldiering 144, 145, 149, 151, 152, 153, 155, 156, 158
intercorporeal engagement 212, 214
intercorporeal relations 204
intercorporeality 10–11, 100n58, 209–215, 217, 220
interdependence 205, 208, 215, 216–217, 220
interdisciplinarity 8, 104, 105, 106–107, 120
international relations theory 144–145, 162n1
interpersonal relatedness 11, 240
interpersonal relations 7, 21, 43, 53, 71, 134
intersubjection 94
intersubjective relationality 240
intersubjectivity 3, 10–11, 71, 207, 215, 216; and Husserl's forgotten question 85, 86, 89, 93, 94, 100n64
intimacy 28, 29
intrinsic alterity 236
intrinsic qualities, of empathy 24–25, 27, 30, 35n20, 239
intrinsic value, of empathy 25, 26
intrinsic vulnerabilities 194, 201, 240

James, William 42, 54n3
joint activity 212, 214, 220
judgment 22, 136, 159, 161, 162n4; moral *see* moral judgment
just war 158, 162n4
justification 25, 26, 27, 36n28, 86, 94, 125, 167

Käll, Lisa 204, 205, 209, 210, 215, 219, 220, 221n4
Kant, Immanuel 86, 171, 178, 230, 231, 241n1
killing 129, 138, 158–160
kindness 10, 194, 195
Kohut, Heinz 45
knowing 133, 155–156, 157, 226, *226*, 228, 247, 248; and Husserl's forgotten question 8, 81, 82, 88, 95, 96, 100n60

language 7, 59–61, 63–66, 67; abstract 61; moral 51, 185; of psychology 108; symbolic 61, 63, 66
language attitudes 71
language learning 64, 66, 69
Levinas, Emmanuel 230, 231
limitations 9, 123, 124, 126
limits of empathy 124–126
linguistic naturalism 69
Lipps, Theodor 44, 45, 46, 238
lived experiences 10, 43, 47, 187, 191, 192

Logical Investigations 87, 90, 96, 98n44
Lorde, Audre 183, 185, 186, 194, 199
low-level empathy 9, 69, 71
lower-level empathy 146, 152–153, 154, 155–156, 159, 161
Lux, Vanessa 108, 110

manipulation 5, 24, 110, 117
Matravers, Derek 3, 49, 147
Mead, G.H. 7, 45, 59, 60, 61–63, 65, 66–70, 71, 72–73n2, 73n3, 73n4, 73n7, 74n11
meaning, theories of 59–76
measures, neuroscientific 8, 103–121
mental states 44, 63, 107, 109, 226, 241n3; and dementia 207, 209, 221n6; and relational value of empathy 18–19, 21, 25; and soldiering 146–147, 148, 149–150, 151, 152, 154, 155–156
mentalizing 54–55n7, 116, 132, 133, 136, 146, 227, 248
Merleau-Ponty, Maurice 85, 209–210, 211, 212, 213
methodologies 53, 68, 85, 110, 117
military doctrine 144–145
mimesis 71, 72, 75n16; *see also* imitation; mimicry
mimicry 45, 53, 69, 74–75n14, 149, 226, 227; *see also* imitation; mimesis
mindreading 54–55n7, 116, 132, 133, 136, 146, 227, 248
mirror neurons 4, 46, 169; and Husserl's forgotten question 80, 81, 91, 94–95, 97n9; and naturalized theories of meaning 55n9, 67, 68, 69; and soldiering 149, 150–151, 152, 153, 156, 161
mirroring 8, 46, 81, 96, 98n41, 130, 214; and naturalized theories of meaning 55n9, 69, 70, 74–75n14; and soldiering 146, 149, 153, 154
moral abilities 126, 133
moral agency 126, 127–128, 131, 135, 138
moral attention 233, 234
moral behaviour 6, 9, 11, 16, 34n5, 225, 240; and ethics 123, 124, 125, 128, 129–130, 131, 132, 134–135
moral competence 51
moral conduct 186
moral conscience 132, 133, 134, 135, 136, 137, 138
moral conscientiousness 178
moral courage 160
moral decision-making 17, 32
moral deliberation 17, 224, 228–229
moral development 5, 6, 133, 134, 137, 138, 139–140n5

moral disagreement 235
moral experience 51, 233
moral feeling 11, 224, 225, 229, 231
moral imagination 179
moral injury 162n5
moral judgment 5, 6, 7, 9, 12n2, 51, 144, 145, 166, 178; and ethics 123, 128, 129, 130, 131, 132, 133, 134–135, 137, 138, 139–140n5
moral justification 125
moral language 51, 185
moral motivation 5, 6, 11, 15–16, 166, 175, 224, 228, 229, 240
moral neutrality 229
moral objectivity 9
moral principles 17, 32
moral qualities 224, 234
moral rationalism 171, 176, 177, 178–179
moral relevance 18, 224, 225
moral sensibility 5
Moral Sentimentalism (book) 9, 166, 180
moral sentimentalism (concept) 9, 50, 123, 166
moral value 51, 229
moral virtue 6, 11, 124, 165
moral vocabularies 186
motivation: altruistic 47; to help others 171, 174–175; moral 5, 6, 11, 15–16, 166, 175, 224, 228, 229, 240
mutual empathy 11, 218, 219
mutual recognition 61, 216
mutual vulnerable condition 219
mutual vulnerability 11, 205, 215–216, 219, 220

Nagel, Thomas 10, 173–174, 175–176, 181, 181n1, 182n2, 248
narrative competency 147, 151–152
narrative fidelity 187
narrative theory 9, 147, 151–152, 155
naturalism 59, 60, 61, 66, 68, 69, 70, 130, 131, 138
naturalized theories of meaning 7, 59–76
negative feeling 31, 81
negative relationality 216
neuropeptides 130, 131
neurophenomenology 7, 67, 99n57
neuroscience 8, 71, 81, 91, 95, 99n57, 103–121, 220n2
non-empathic abilities 130, 132
non-reductionist naturalism 59, 60, 70

objectivity: bodily 72, 89; moral 9; of the object 86
obliviousness 192, 196–197

'observation sentences' 64, 65, 68
'observationality' 64
obsessive compulsive disorder (OCD) 11, 225, 237–238, 239, 241
'occasion sentences' 64–65
OCD (obsessive compulsive disorder) 11, 225, 237–238, 239, 241
old age 206
onlooker 83–84, 97n21; *see also* Other, the
ontogeny 61, 66, 70
openness towards the other 11, 236, 244, 246, 247, 248; and dementia 204, 205, 207–208, 210, 211, 214, 215, 217, 218–219, 220, 221n7
operationalized definitions 108–109
osmosis 169
Other, the 4, 5, 8, 11, 132, 133, 172, 174; dementia 204, 207, 210, 215, 217, 218–219, 220; Husserl's forgotten question 80, 81, 85–86, 87, 88, 89, 90–91, 92, 93–94, 95–96, 97n21; naturalized theories of meaning 60, 62, 63, 65, 66, 67, 71, 73n4, 73n7, 73–74n8; openness to another 244, 246, 247, 249, 250, 251, 252; relational empathy 44, 45, 48, 49; relational value of empathy 21, 23, 25, 29, 30; respect and vulnerability 225, 230, 231, 232, 234; soldiering 147, 148–149, 149, 150, 151–152, 154–155, 156, 157, 161
otherness 89, 93, 233, 235, 236, 239–240

pain 22, 23, 50, 51, 81, 195, 207; and ethics 127, 128, 133, 134, 138; and neuroscience 115–116, 117–118, 119; and sentimentalism 167–168, 170, 173–174, 175, 176, 181n1; and soldiering 147, 148, 149, 150, 151, 152, 161
pairing 88–89, 90, 91, 92, 95, 100n58
partiality 9, 15, 16, 18, 32, 146, 159
pathological altruism 126
pathophobia 10, 183–202
pathophobic attitudes 185, 188, 199
pathophobic banality 191–193
pathophobic callousness 193–196
pathophobic insensitivity 196–199
pathophobic untruthfulness 199–201
pathophobic vices 10, 183, 184, 187, 188–201
pathos 42, 54n2
Peirce, Charles Sanders 96
perception: direct 9, 147, 149–151, 152, 153; empathic 2–3; unmediated 147, 150, 151, 153, 155
perceptual empathy 68–69

personal distress 4–5, 113, 139n2
personality disorders 4, 6, 252
personhood 10–11, 231, 234; and dementia 204, 205, 206, 208–209, 212, 213, 214, 215, 220
perspective-taking 9, 44, 69, 103, 146, 148–149, 155, 226, 227, 253n5; and ethics 128, 129, 132, 133, 135, 136
phenomenological reduction 82, 83, 84, 87, 88, 89, 91–92, 92–93, 94, 98n28, 217–218
phenomenology 1, 2, 80, 85, 99n51, 193, 220n2, 237, 240; transcendental 84, 93
philosophy of existence 80, 81
philosophy of mind 2, 68, 81, 228
philosophy of science 104–105
phronesis 225
phylogeny 66
pleasant experiences 15, 18, 29
pluralism 5, 103, 104–105, 185, 186; and relational empathy 41–47, 49–50, 51, 54, 54n1
positive feeling 81
positive relationality 216
Possibility of Altruism, The 10, 173, 176, 181n1
practical rationality 166–167, 182n3
practical reason, sentimentalist 1, 9, 165–182
pre-linguistic cognition and communication 7, 59, 62, 69
pre-reflexive mechanisms 7
Preston, Stephanie 49–50, 112, 114, 116, 130
primordial intercorporeality 214, 215
Prinz, Jesse 5, 50–51, 139–140n5
privacy 28, 197
projection 43, 46, 53, 68–69, 93, 136, 155, 156, 241n3
projective empathy 169, 174
propositional attitudes 66, 68–69, 74–75n14
propositional language 62, 63, 64, 66, 70
prosocial attitude 5
proto-sympathetic empathy 241n3
proximity 125, 126
prudence 124, 167, 172
prudential rationality 168, 169, 170
prudential reasons, of morality 165, 167, 168, 169, 172
prurience 197, 199
psychological states 4, 74–75n14, 148, 169, 249
psychopathic personality disorder 6
psychopathy 9, 126, 128, 135, 138, 177

psychophysical unity 84, 85, 88, 89, 92, 98n28, 98n41
psychophysiological measurement 110
pure experience 42, 54n3
pure subjectivity 84
Pursuit of Truth 64

qualities: of empathy 22, 24–25, 27, 30, 35n20, 120, 239; moral 224, 234
questionnaires 110, 113, 117
Quine, W.V.O. 7, 59–60, 63–66, 68, 69, 70, 71, 72

radical translation 66, 68, 69, 72
Ratcliffe, Matthew 217–219, 220, 221n6, 221n7
rational sensitivity 247
rationalism 10, 165, 166, 169, 173, 174, 175, 181n1; moral 171, 176, 177, 178–179
reasons for action 9–10, 165, 166, 168, 169–170, 171, 174, 176, 177, 178–179
recentering yourself 250
receptive empathy 10, 169, 171, 174, 177–178
'reciprocal creation' 8, 86, 96
reciprocity 215
recognition, mutual 61, 216
recognition respect 154–155, 162; and vulnerability 224, 225, 229–230, 232, 234, 235, 240
recognitive relations 216
reductionism 123, 124, 129–132, 138, 166
reenactive empathy 153
reference fixing 166
reflection 42–43, 45, 81, 82, 83, 101n78, 148, 149
relational empathy 1, 7, 41–55
relational models theory 19, 35n21
relational significance 17
relational value, of empathy 1, 6–7, 15–36
relationality 10–11, 230, 231–232, 236, 240; and dementia 204, 207, 208–209, 210, 211, 216, 219–220, 221n4, 221n8
relations: intercorporeal 204; interpersonal 7, 21, 43, 53, 71, 134; recognitive 216
relationship goods 28–29, 30, 31, 36n32
relevance: of empathy 9, 15, 18, 144, 145; moral 18, 224, 225
repetitive behaviour 11, 237
research communities 8, 106–107, 120
research traditions 118, 119, 120

respect: appraisal 155, 229–230, 232, 234, 240; recognition 154–155, 162, 224, 225, 229–230, 232, 234, 235, 240

sadism 9, 126–127, 135, 138, 198
sanism 183
Sartre, Jean-Paul 94, 253
Schadenfreude 126, 127, 135, 138
scientific communication 105
second-order empathy 178
self 82–83, 93, 139n2, 139n4, 208–215, 220
self-consciousness 99n56, 251
self-esteem 7, 15, 18, 26, 29, 32, 216
selfhood 10–11, 206, 208–209, 211, 216
self-interest 5, 129, 170, 179–180, 187, 194
self-report 110
self-sacrifice 1, 9, 165–182
self-trust 7, 15, 18, 26, 27, 29, 216
sensibilities 5, 161, 231
sensitivity 173, 229, 231, 232, 234, 235, 240; and openness to another 246, 247, 248, 249–250, 251, 252
sensory states 116
sensory stimuli 60, 62, 64, 65
sentimentalism 165–182; moral 9, 50, 123, 166
sharing 2, 4–5, 11, 25, 47, 81, 133, 134, 174, 244; and respect and vulnerability 226, 226, 227, 233, 241n3
similarity 125, 126
simulation 68, 71, 150, 155, 169, 226, 241n3, 249–250
simulation theory 9, 68, 69; and soldiering 147, 148–149, 150, 151, 152, 156
Singer, Tania 49, 115–119
Slote, Michael 50–51
Smith, Adam 1–2, 35n15, 74n10, 123, 133, 135, 136, 137
social cognition 3, 128, 138, 147, 150, 152, 228
social conduct 61
social factors 10
social interaction 7, 32, 61, 63, 68, 72, 211
social neuroscience 4, 104, 105, 109, 115–119
social norms 29, 185, 191
social psychology 19, 31–32, 35n15, 45, 118, 119, 120; conceptual problem in 108–113
sociopathy 174–175, 198
soldiering 144–162
solipsism 85–86
somatic illness 10, 183–202
Sontag, Susan 184, 185, 199, 201

spectator, impartial 9, 16, 135, 136, 137, 138, 139
stability, in research 8, 103, 104, 112, 119
Standard Account, of empathy 18, 21
subjective experience 10, 11, 207, 224, 225, 232, 236, 241
subjectivity 85, 96, 211, 216; constituted and constituting 93–94; of dementia 209, 212; embodied 209–210, 215; pure 84; transcendental 84, 85, 86, 87, 88, 89, 93, 95, 95
suffering 33, 34n10, 81, 112, 125, 127, 161, 244, 245; and dementia 207, 210, 211, 217; and pathophobia 186–187, 188, 200, 201; and relational empathy 47, 48, 51; and sentimentalism 167–168, 174, 175, 179
sunesis 234–235
symbolic language 61, 63, 66
sympathetic engagement 9, 138, 139
sympathetic identification 66, 67

tactlessness 197, 198, 199
taxonomizing 111–112, 188, 189
taxonomy, of empathy concepts 10, 111–112
theoretical inference 147, 148, 149, 150, 155
theory of emotion 61, 72n2
theory of gestural conversation 67
theory of meaning: behaviouristic 7, 59, 60, 61, 63–66, 70; bio-social 61–63
theory of mind 54–55n7, 116, 132, 133, 136, 146, 227, 248
Theory of moral sentiments 67
'theory-theory' 9, 68, 147–148, 149, 150, 151, 152, 154, 156
Theunissen, Michael 91, 93, 96
thoughts 3, 4–5, 6, 20, 34n10, 147, 154, 237, 250; and relational empathy 42, 43, 44, 46
Titchener, Edward 43, 105
transcendence 83, 84, 87, 89, 93, 96, 97n19, 99n46
transcendental phenomenology 84, 93
transcendental principle of justification 8, 42, 86, 104
transcendental subjectivity 84, 85, 86, 87, 88, 89, 93, 95, 95
transcendentality 85
transmission of reasons for action 9–10, 169, 171, 174, 175, 176, 177
Treatise of Human Nature 67, 166
triadic mimesis 72

trust 6, 7, 10, 11, 216, 239, 251, 252; and pathophobia 184, 185, 194; and relational value of empathy 15, 18, 26, 27, 28, 29, 30

unconscious communication 61–62
unmediated perception 147, 150, 151, 153, 155
unpleasant experiences 161, 172–173, 251
untruthfulness cluster, of pathophobic vices 199–201
US healthcare system 7, 41, 53, 184, 193–194, 196

value: of empathy 1, 6–7, 15–36; moral 51, 229
vice ethics 10, 183, 184, 187
vices 10, 183, 186–202
viciousness 183, 184, 186–187, 191, 192, 197, 198
Vignemont, Frederique de 3, 48, 49, 118
virtue: backfiring 191; of compassion 178; empathy as 194, 224–225, 227, *227*, 228–229, 240, 253n4; moral 6, 11, 124, 165
virtue acquisition 224, 225
virtue ethics 10
virtues 6, 11, 124, 144, 145, 165, 178, 253n4; and pathophobia 186, 187, 188, 190, 191, 194, 195–196, 199; and respect and vulnerability 224–225, 226, 227–228, *227*, 228–229, 230, 240
Vischer, Friedrich Theodor 43–44
Vischer, Robert 44, 54n5
vocabularies 186, 187
vocal gestures 61, 62, 63, 75n21
vulnerability 1, 2, 6, 10, 161, 194, 201; and anxiety 244, 252, 253; and dementia 204, 205, 207, 208, 215–220; mutual 11, 205, 215–216, 219, 220; and openness to another 251, 252, 253; and respect 224, 225, 235, 236, 239, 240–241
vulnerability theory 204, 205

Waal, Frans de 49–50, 112, 114, 130
war 6, 9, 144–162
well-being 15, 16, 28, 53, 132, 146, 167, 168, 216, 225
Wispé, Lauren 109–110, 113
world-horizon 234, 235, 238

Zahavi, Dan 4, 5, 100n60, 100n64, 106, 244, 247; and soldiering 146, 147, 149–151, 152, 155, 156
Zeiler, Kristin 204, 205, 212–213, 214, 215, 219, 220, 220n2, 221n4